MANSFIELD COLLEGE, OXFORD

Frontispiece: Mansfield College today. (Photo: Chris Honeywell)

Mansfield College, Oxford

*Its Origin, History, and
Significance*

ELAINE KAYE

OXFORD UNIVERSITY PRESS

1996

Oxford University Press, Walton Street, Oxford OX2 6DP
Oxford New York
Athens Auckland Bangkok Bombay
Calcutta Cape Town Dar es Salaam Delhi
Florence Hong Kong Istanbul Karachi
Kuala Lumpur Madras Madrid Melbourne
Mexico City Nairobi Paris Singapore
Taipei Tokyo Toronto
and associated companies in
Berlin Ibadan

Oxford is a trade mark of Oxford University Press

Published in the United States
by Oxford University Press Inc., New York

British Library Cataloguing in Publication Data
Data available

Library of Congress Cataloging in Publication Data
Kaye, Elaine.
Mansfield College, Oxford : its origin, history, and significance
/ Elaine Kaye.
Includes bibliographical references and index.
1. Mansfield College (University of Oxford) I. Title.
LF741.M35K39 1996 378.42′574—dc20 95–38759
ISBN 0–19–920180–3

1 3 5 7 9 10 8 6 4 2

Typeset by Graphicraft Typesetters Ltd, Hong Kong
Printed in Great Britain
on acid-free paper by
Biddles Ltd
Guildford & King's Lynn

Acknowledgements

My first debt is to Mansfield College itself, whose history has been so rewarding to explore. I wish to thank the present Principal, Dennis Trevelyan, and all the Fellows, Lecturers, and other members of staff of the College, for their help and co-operation, and for extending to me the hospitality of the college over a period of four years. In particular I wish to acknowledge the help of the late Michael Mahony, and of the Librarian, Alma Jenner, who has helped to make my task so enjoyable.

Clyde Binfield has been a fount of information and encouragement, and has shared in the enthusiasm of the writing of this history. Geoffrey Nuttall, incomparable scholar, has been unstinting in his constructive criticism and help.

I am greatly indebted to Mark Johnson for the work he has done on the early history of the College, published in *The Dissolution of Dissent 1850–1918* (New York, 1987).

I also wish to thank the following: the Librarian and staff of Dr Williams's Library, London, the Registrar of the University of Oxford and his staff (for permission to consult and quote from files in the University Offices), the Keeper of the University Archives and the University Archivist (for permission to consult and quote from the University Archives), the Warden and Fellows, and the Librarian, of Merton College (for permission to consult the College Archives), the Librarian of the Angus Library, Regent's Park College, Dafydd Ap-Thomas, Geoffrey Beck, Tony Berezny, Carolyn Brock, Charles Brock, Walter Buckingham, Richard Buckley, V. M. (Mollie) Caird, John Creaser, Mark Curthoys, Ewart Dean, the late F. W. Dillistone, Duncan Forbes, the late Lord Franks, Michael Freeden, Michael Freeman, John Geyer, David Goodall, Timothy Gorringe (for providing access to the Minute Book of the Oxford Society of Historical Theology), John Gray, Nigel Hall, Brian Harrison, Walter Hartwell, Rachel Heaton (for permission to quote from unpublished letters of C. H. Dodd),

Acknowledgements

Linda Higgins, Roger Highfield, Peter Hinchliff, Geoffrey Hooper, Janet Howarth, the late John Huxtable, Scott Ickert, Daniel Jenkins, R. Tudur Jones, Peter Jupp, Gill Kirk, Arthur Kirkby, Philip Lee-Woolf, Denys Leighton, Anthony Lemon, Robin McGarry, Iain McIver, Alison McLachlan, Gladys Marsh, the late John Marsh, Nathaniel Micklem, Paul Morgan, Donald Norwood, Anthony Ogus, Elizabeth Radburn, John Reynolds, Dorothy Rhodes, Margaret Routley, Eric Shave, Noel Shepherd, Simon Skinner, Adele Smith, Donald Sykes, Richard Symonds, Anthony Tucker, Clare Wenham, John Whale, Mary Whale, Alec Whitehouse, Elaine Williams, Jan Womer, and Justine Wyatt.

I also wish to thank the Congregational Memorial Hall Trust (1978) Limited for their generous grant towards the cost of publication.

Finally, I should like to thank my sister Rosalind Kaye for help with proof-reading.

E.K.

June 1995

vi

Contents

Contents

List of Illustrations

Abbreviations

CQ	*Congregational Quarterly*
CR	*Contemporary Review*
CYB	*Congregational Year Book*
DNB	*Dictionary of National Biography* (2nd edn. 1908–9)
JURCHS	*Journal of the United Reformed Church History Society*
MCA	Mansfield College Archive
MCM	*Mansfield College Magazine*

Prelude

Our fathers loved these classic groves, the memories that hallowed, the fellowship that endeared, the studies that consecrated ancient hall and cloistered college; they went out sadly and with many a backward look, as men who loved not Oxford less, but conscience more.[1]

THOSE who came to Oxford to found Mansfield College in 1886 felt themselves to be the spiritual descendants of the clergy who were ejected from the Church of England in 1662. They believed that they were coming home to take up the 'broken thread' of their academic history, and in so doing to enrich the thought and learning of the University from which they had been for so long excluded.

The religious controversies of the sixteenth century had found a particular focus, in England, in the universities of Oxford and Cambridge. There the clergy were educated and the study of theology was predominant; its colleges and halls were religious foundations. It was in Oxford that John Wyclif had first challenged the authority of the Church. It was in Oxford that the Cambridge-educated Cranmer, Ridley, and Latimer were tried for heresy and burnt at the stake during the Catholic reign of Mary. By the end of the sixteenth century, despite the fact that Oxford was more conservative in religious ideas than Cambridge, there was a strong Puritan presence.[2]

Oxford played a major role in the controversies of the seventeenth century. The city formed the Royalist headquarters during most of the Civil War. When it fell to the Parliamentarians, Laudian clergy were banished, and Puritans took their place. At Christ Church

---

[1] A. M. Fairbairn, the first Principal, at the opening of Mansfield College buildings in Oxford, Oct. 1889. See *Mansfield College, Oxford: Its Origin and Opening* (London, 1890), 126.

[2] See Jennifer Loach, 'Reformation Controversies', in J. McConica (ed.), *The History of the University of Oxford*, iii: *The Collegiate University* (Oxford, 1986), and M. H. Curtis, *Oxford and Cambridge in Transition* (Oxford, 1959), chs. vii and viii.

John Owen,[3] who had been one of the Independent representatives at the Westminster Assembly of 1643, was not only Dean but also Vice-Chancellor; as one of the great theologians of Independency, Owen was a chief architect of the Savoy Declaration of 1658, and the thinker to whom Mansfield theologians of the 1930s and 1940s turned when they sought the roots and theological foundations of English Reformed Churchmanship.

In 1662, after more than a century of increasingly bitter religious and political conflict, a church settlement brought a measure of stability, if not what could truly be called peace, to English society. The attempts at comprehension during the first months of Charles II's reign had failed, and the Act of Uniformity (1662) restored the Church of England, with a revised Book of Common Prayer. The restored Church was not acceptable to most of those with strong Puritan sympathies.

All clergy were required to make a declaration of assent to every-thing contained in that book, including the Thirty-Nine Articles, be-fore St Bartholomew's Day (24 August); in addition, together with all teachers, they were to subscribe to a Declaration abjuring the Solemn League and Covenant with the Scots of 1643, and rejecting resistance to the Monarchy. If they had been ordained by their fellow presbyters during the Interregnum, they were to seek re-ordination by a bishop. The Corporation Act of 1661 had already restricted the government of corporate towns to those prepared to swear the Oath of Supremacy and take the Sacrament according to the practice of the Church of England. The so-called Clarendon Code which followed tightened further the restrictions on nonconforming clergy and schoolmasters.[4]

By St Bartholomew's Day, over 2,000 clergy[5] had been ejected from the Church of England for refusing to take the Oath of Uniformity. Of these, the majority were Presbyterians; 194, or approximately 9 per cent, were Independents; and a smaller group were Baptists.[6]

---

[3] For Owen, see *DNB* xlii. 424–8; Christopher Hill, 'John Owen (1616–83): "Cromwell's Archbishop"', in *The Experience of Defeat* (London, 1984); and P. Toon, *God's Statesman: The Life and Work of John Owen* (Exeter, 1971).

[4] In particular, the Conventicle Act of 1664 made all religious assemblies of five or more persons over 16 years of age illegal; and the Five Mile Act of 1665 forbade preachers and teachers who refused to take the required oaths to come within 5 miles of a corporate town, or of the parish where they had taught or preached.

[5] A. G. Matthews in *Calamy Revised* (Oxford, 1934) reckons that the exact figure for England was 1,909. To this number should be added 120 in Wales. See Michael Watts, *The Dissenters: From the Reformation to the French Revolution* (Oxford, 1978), 219.

[6] Watts, *The Dissenters*, 219.

Socio-economically, on average, the Presbyterians were the most pros-perous, the Quakers and Baptists least so, with the Independents in between.[7] Together, these three groups constituted what later became known as 'Old Dissent'.[8] Within Old Dissent itself, there can be dis-cerned two distinct strands of churchmanship: those who still yearned for a comprehensive, Reformed Church of England, in the tradition of Richard Baxter, and others who saw an absolute distinction between Church and State and emphasized the 'gathered' nature of the Church.

Dissenters, clergy and laity, were not only excluded from the Church of England, but from England's two universities (which required their students to subscribe to the doctrines of the Estab-lished Church—at Oxford for matriculation, and at Cambridge for graduation), and by the Test Acts of 1673 and 1678 from the right to hold civil, military, and crown offices.[9] Dissent, or Nonconformity, was now in effect institutionalized within English society. These Dissenting ministers and their followers had always set great store on learning. Most of those ejected had themselves been educated at Oxford or Cambridge, and some had been Fellows or Tutors.[10] It was a matter of deep concern after 1662 that the succeeding generation of ministers should receive an appropriate, scholarly, education.

Many of the ejected ministers therefore took pupils into their own homes and educated them privately. After the Toleration Act of 1689 had given Nonconformists freedom of worship, it was no longer necessary for them to conduct their affairs in secret. There is evid-ence for the existence of about twenty such private centres of learn-ing by that date; gradually they became known as 'Academies'.[11]

In time these informal academies developed into more formal-ized educational institutions. Some of them were founded or sup-ported by outside societies, such as the Congregational Fund Board,[12] the King's Head Society,[13] or the Coward Trust.[14] In the eighteenth

---

[7] Ibid. 346–66.

[8] This was to distinguish them from those who left the Church of England in the late 18th and early 19th cents. as part of the Methodist movement.

[9] These restrictions applied also of course to Roman Catholics and to Jews (offi-cially re-admitted to England in the 1650s).

[10] I. Parker, *Dissenting Academies in England* (Cambridge, 1914), app. i.

[11] See H. McLachlan, *English Education under the Test Acts: Being the History of the Nonconformist Academies 1662–1820* (Manchester, 1931).

[12] Founded in London in 1695.

[13] Formed in 1730 to encourage evangelical religion; it took the name from its place of meeting in London.

[14] Founded in 1738 by the will of William Coward, a London merchant.

century, at a time when the ancient universities were going through a lax period,[15] the Dissenting Academies were offering, for lower fees, an education which, at its best, was the most liberal and modern available in England. Unlike the English universities, which still used Latin, the Academies offered an education in English, and some of them included science in the curriculum. As R. Tudur Jones puts it: 'With their interest in science, their generally high standards of intellectual discipline, their numerous contacts with Scottish and Continental universities and their broad curriculum, the academies preserved the traditions of English higher education at a time when their ancient custodians were neglecting them.'[16]

While there had been little difference in practice between Presbyterians and Independents in the first half-century after the Restoration, there was a growing division during the eighteenth century between the liberal, intellectual tradition of the Presbyterians and the more orthodox tradition of the Independents or Congregationalists. Most of the Presbyterians moved towards Unitarianism, while the majority of Congregationalists, who preserved much of the intellectual tradition, remained orthodox and gradually became the largest and strongest of the Dissenting churches.[17]

The Evangelical Revival brought new members, new energy, and an increase in prosperity to Congregational churches. The 15,000 members of English Congregational churches of 1750 increased to 127,000 by 1838 (to which one can add 43,000 in Wales).[18] This was a much greater proportionate increase than that of the population at large. But it brought into the Congregational churches many who had little understanding of the Congregational tradition. Along with the emphasis on conversion experience and emotional fervour there often developed a suspicion of intellectualism. At the same time there was pressure for tests of orthodoxy among ministers, and the Academies tended to become narrower in curriculum.

[15] See e.g. L. S. Sutherland, 'The Curriculum', in L. S. Sutherland and L. G. Mitchell (eds.), *The History of the University of Oxford;* v: *The Eighteenth Century* (Oxford, 1986).

[16] R. Tudur Jones, *Congregationalism in England 1662–1962* (London, 1962), 143.

[17] For a discussion of Presbyterianism in the 18th cent. and its relation to Congregationalism, see Alan P. F. Sell, 'Presbyterianism in Eighteenth Century England: The Doctrinal Dimension', *JURCHS* 4/6 (May 1990), 352–86, and 'A Little Friendly Light: The Candour of Bourn, Taylor and Towgood', *JURCHS* 4/9 (Dec. 1991), 517–40, and 4/10 (May 1992), 580–613. See also Bernard Manning, 'Congregationalism in the Eighteenth Century', in *Essays in Orthodox Dissent* (London, 1939).

[18] See R. Currie, A. Gilbert, and L. Horsley, *Churches and Churchgoers: Patterns of Church Growth in the British Isles since 1700* (Oxford, 1977), 147–8, 151–2.

There was as yet no central organization in Congregationalism (the Congregational Union of England and Wales was not founded until 1831) to set standards of ministerial training, and there was no actual requirement that ministers should undertake any academic training at all.[19] Many, however, kept alive the tradition of a learned ministry, and it was from that tradition that Mansfield College originated.

---

[19] Even in 1864, Henry Allon told the Congregational Union Assembly that during the previous ten years, for every 28 college students who had entered the Congregational ministry, 25 entered without any college training. See *CYB 1865*.

I

Beginnings: Spring Hill College, Birmingham

MANSFIELD College owes its existence in the first place to the wealth and generosity of two families, both originally Anglican, but later Dissenters by conviction: heirs of the Evangelical Revival. Sometime shortly before March 1826, George Mansfield, of Spring Hill, Birmingham, consulted the Revd Timothy East,[1] minister of the Congregational Ebenezer Chapel, Steelhouse Lane, Birmingham, which George Mansfield attended, about the ultimate disposition of his wealth and property. He and his two sisters, with whom he lived, had no children. 'I have not, in my former course of life, done anything with it to glorify God. Tell me how I may now employ it for his honour,' he is alleged to have told Mr East.[2] It was Timothy East who then suggested founding a college for training men for the Congregational ministry.

Timothy East, whose parents were both members of the Society of Friends, had himself been trained at Gosport Academy under Dr David Bogue,[3] a graduate of Edinburgh University, one of the founders of the London Missionary Society and co-author of the monumental *History of the Dissenters* (4 vols., London, 1808–12). He would have been aware that of the ten Congregational colleges then in existence, none was in the Midlands.[4] He was also concerned about the need to raise the educational standard of Congregational ministers. Hence his suggestion to George Mansfield that he should leave his inheritance for the foundation of a college to train ministers. When

---

[1] For Timothy East (1783–1871) see *CYB 1872*, 315–17.
[2] See *Memorials of the Founders of Spring Hill College* (Birmingham, 1854), 2.
[3] For David Bogue (1750–1825) see *DNB* ii. 764–75.
[4] The colleges were: Homerton (1730), Wymondley (1790), Western (1752), Cheshunt (1768), Highbury (1826, successor to Hoxton), Newport Pagnell (1783), Idle/Airedale (1794), Rotherham (1795), Hackney (1803), and Blackburn (1816). Since these colleges often began informally, and moved from place to place, there is not unanimous agreement on the dates of foundation.

George Mansfield consulted his two sisters, they were enthusiastic about the proposal.

The Mansfield family, originally Anglican, came from Derby. According to an indenture of 10 March 1826[5] George Mansfield and his two sisters were 'the children of William Mansfield late of Derby in the County of Derby, Gentleman Deceased'.[6] According to the *Memorials* George Mansfield was born in 1764, Sarah in 1767, and Elizabeth in 1772. The family owned property in Leicestershire as well as Derby. The father is said to have been 'a strict Churchman who disapproved of his children's interest in the Dissenting churches'.[7] Little is known of George's life before he went to live with his sisters in Birmingham in 1824, except that after his father's death in 1795 he lived in Leicestershire on estates inherited from his father. 'It has been supposed, with some probability, that in early life he was too much addicted to such worldly pleasures as a country life affords to a gentleman of good landed property.'[8] The two sisters also spent time in Leicestershire, where they began to forsake the Anglican Church for both the Wesleyans and the General Baptists. When they returned to Derby, they forsook the Arminians also and identified themselves with the Calvinist Independents, with whom they were much involved in evangelical work not only in their own town, but also further afield.

In 1800 they spent three months in the nearby town of Tutbury assisting a friend, Mrs Greasley, in evangelical work. There they met Charles Glover, a Birmingham builder who was visiting some apprentices boarded out in Tutbury, in his capacity as a Guardian of the Poor. Charles Glover had been a widower for the past four years, and his friendship with Sarah Mansfield continued through correspondence and culminated three years later in their marriage in Tutbury Parish Church.[9] Not only the new Mrs Glover, but also her sister and her mother, now moved to Spring Hill, Birmingham, the

---

[5] MCA.

[6] A William Mansfield married Mary Storer in St Peter's Church, Derby on 4 Aug. 1754, and was described as a 'carrier'. And a person of the same name, though this time referred to as a 'currier', died aged 76 on 30 Mar. 1795—which, according to *Memorials of the Founders of Spring Hill College*, was the year of the death of George Mansfield's father. Although absolute evidence for this is elusive, it does seem reasonable to assume that George and Mary (née Storer) Mansfield were the parents of George Storer Mansfield and his two sisters. See *Derbyshire Parish Registers*, vi (London, 1909), and *Derby Mercury*, 2 Apr. 1795.

[7] *Memorials of the Founders of Spring Hill College*, 13.   [8] Ibid. 1.

[9] A. G. Matthews, *The Congregational Churches of Staffordshire* (London, 1924), 184.

estate which Charles Glover had bought and improved some years earlier.

It was not only a wealthy but also a devout household. Charles Glover, who was an Anglican until late in life, adapted the old laundry of the house as a small chapel, to which he invited neighbours and friends from St Mary's Chapel on Sunday evenings. The two sisters immediately involved themselves in evangelical work, especially in a Sunday School in their own home. Of the sisters a Birmingham minister (John Angell James) wrote: 'Mrs Glover and Miss Mansfield presented a striking contrast to each other: the latter, meek, gentle, sensitive and retiring; the former ardent, energetic, and almost restless in the cause of benevolence; the one the personification of the *active* virtues of Christianity; the other of its *passive* graces.'[10] They found their spiritual home in Livery Street Chapel, a recent secession from the Congregational church in Carrs Lane. The Livery Street site was never intended as a permanent arrangement, and in 1816 the foundation stone of a new building in Steelhouse Lane was laid; Charles Glover supervised much of the construction. In 1818, the new church, renamed Ebenezer Chapel, was opened, with the Revd Timothy East as its minister. The following year, Charles Glover, who had occasionally attended the Chapel with his wife and sister-in-law, became 'a Dissenter from conviction'.[11] He died two years later, in 1821, leaving the estate to his widow.

In 1826, acting on Timothy East's proposal, a Trust Deed for the proposed new College was drawn up and signed on 9 March; the Trustees were leading ministers and laymen of the Birmingham area. The Spring Hill estate was now vested in twenty Trustees (including Timothy East) for the purposes of 'a College or place of classical and religious instruction for young men devoted to the Christian ministry, among that denomination of Protestant Dissenters called Independents',[12] which was to be called Spring Hill College. According to the Deed, the Mansfield/Glover family was to continue to live on the estate but to pay rents to the Trustees. At least four-fifths of this rent was to be retained for the future college; one-fifth, or a smaller proportion, might be used to support the Birmingham Evangelical Association for the Propagation of the Gospel.

George Storer Mansfield died in November 1837. His sisters, who

---

[10] *Memorials of the Founders of Spring Hill College*, Introd. by J. A. James, p. x.
[11] Ibid. 7.
[12] *Abstract of the Trusts Contained in the Spring Hill College Deed*, MCA.

wished to see the College open, surrendered the lease of their house to the Trustees and moved to a small house nearby.[13] Of the three members of the Mansfield family, it was Sarah Glover above all who had provided the dynamic faith and resolve which led to the founding of the College.[14] She took a great interest in the new college, and she and her sister regularly entertained the students to tea on Saturday afternoons. In addition, they gave a generous donation to the College's endowment, which was added to other donations collected by Timothy East during the following months.

Timothy East and his fellow Trustees must have set to work immediately, for by the time the College opened in October 1838 they had not only raised a considerable sum, but they had appointed a Committee of Management of local ministers and laymen, drawn up a syllabus of study, and appointed examiners and two tutors (a third was soon to be invited). The ministerial committee members together with the tutors were to constitute a Board of Education, which was to meet monthly to consider admissions and matters concerning the curriculum, while lay members, together with a few of the Birmingham ministers, were to form a finance subcommittee. Visitors and examiners from other parts of the country were to act as assessors.

The concern for orthodoxy was such that each Trustee, committee member, tutor, and student was to

> ... profess and declare by writing under his hand that he believes in the unity of the Godhead, the divinity of Christ, the atonement made by his death for sin, the divinity and personality of the Holy Spirit, the necessity of the Spirit's influence for the illumination of the understanding and the renovation of the heart, and the plenary inspiration of the Holy Scriptures.[15]

In addition, students and tutors were to declare themselves 'Paedobaptist Dissenters'.

The opening ceremonies were held on 2–3 October 1838, with eleven students already enrolled. Two distinguished Congregational

---

[13] Elizabeth Mansfield died in 1847, her sister in 1853.

[14] Sarah Glover's role was later recognized by the erection of a memorial obelisk in Spring Hill ground, later removed to Oxford, bearing the legend, 'Dux femina facti'. The obelisk disappeared when the College embarked on a new building project in the 1950s.

[15] Quoted in *Report of the Committee of Management of Spring Hill College Birmingham for the Year 1838–39* (Birmingham, 1839), 5–6.

ministers were invited to preach: John Pye Smith,[16] Principal of Homerton College, London, regarded as one of the finest Congregational teachers, on 'The Piety and Learning Requisite to the Christian Ministry', and his former pupil Thomas Raffles,[17] minister of Great George Street Church, Liverpool, on 'The Duty of Christian Churches in Reference to Ministerial Education'. As the theological teacher of two of the three tutors of the new College, John Pye Smith may be regarded as one of the founding fathers of the Spring Hill/Mansfield tradition.

Dr Raffles, who had close connections with Blackburn Academy, which was about to move to Manchester, touched on a subject which was to be of crucial importance to both Spring Hill and its successor, Mansfield College. Munificent though the original endowment was, it was not sufficient to maintain the College on the scale and to the standard that its keenest supporters desired. More money had to be raised and the obvious contributors were the Congregational churches, especially in the Midlands. It fell to the College's Committee of Management (a group additional to the Trustees) to raise the extra money, and it proved hard to maintain this momentum. Timothy East, the first Chairman,[18] gave up much of his own pastoral work in order to travel all over the country seeking financial support; and he was soon joined in this enterprise by John Angell James, the famous minister of Carrs Lane Church in the centre of Birmingham, who was the first Chairman of Spring Hill's Board of Education.[19] By 1839 there were already 110 subscribers, mainly but not exclusively from the Midlands area; this number grew substantially during the following years. In 1844, the Committee of Management had to utter a strong plea for a recognition of the worth of spending money on colleges:

[16] For John Pye Smith (1774–1851) see J. Medway, *Memoirs of the Life and Writings of John Pye Smith DD LL D* (London, 1853) and *DNB* xviii. 494–5.

[17] For Thomas Raffles (1788–1851) see T. S. Raffles, *Memoirs of the Life and Ministry of Thomas Raffles DD LL D* (London, 1864) and *DNB* xvi. 603–4. He was one of the College's five examiners.

[18] He was Chairman of the Committee of Management from 1838 until 1843, when he left Birmingham because of 'matters strictly of a private nature' (evidently relating to finance) (*CYB 1872*, 316).

[19] John Angell James (1785–1859), like Timothy East, was a former student of Dr Bogue's Academy at Gosport, though at a later date. He was one of the prime movers in the foundation of the Congregational Union in 1831, and Chairman in 1838. He was Chairman of Spring Hill's Board of Education 1838–59. His book *The Anxious Inquirer* (London, 1834) sold almost half a million copies. See *CYB 1860*, 192–3.

[Your Committee] fear that the great majority of Congregationalists, however alive to the subject the body may appear to be comparatively, are even yet far too little impressed with the immense importance of their collegiate institutions. When Julian determined to extirpate Christianity from the empire, his most strenuous efforts were directed against its literature. The enormities of fanaticism which, in Luther's days, brought such disgrace upon the Reformation, and threatened almost to undermine it, commenced among simple-minded men, who had been persuaded to renounce an educated ministry. But in all periods of the church, with few exceptions, the great instruments of spiritual reformation have been men of learning—well-instructed men, who have added the resources of education to native talents and cultivated piety.[20]

Throughout its history, this was the ideal of Spring Hill.

The Committee's words were addressed to a constituency which was growing in numbers, prosperity, and confidence. Most of the old restrictions on Nonconformists had been abolished—the Conventicle and Five Mile Acts in 1812, the Test and Corporation Acts in 1828. In 1834 a Bill which would have allowed the admission of Nonconformists to the degrees of Oxford and Cambridge had been defeated in the House of Lords but was certain to be re-introduced. The founding of the *Congregational Magazine* in 1818 and of the Congregational Union in 1831 had encouraged a higher profile for Congregationalists in British society. Those who now entered Spring Hill were preparing for ministry in an increasingly confident denomination.

In the tradition of Dissenting Academies, Spring Hill was to offer a residential course both of general and of theological education, for it was anticipated that the students would initially be men of limited education; even in the later years most had received no university education before admittance. The course was therefore to be a six-year one in order to achieve a sufficient standard. The initiatory course was to include classical and Hebrew philology, English language and literature, mental philosophy (logic and ethics), and mathematics. When students had reached a satisfactory standard in these areas of study, they were to proceed to the theological course (though in some cases students might attend both courses simultaneously). The theological course included biblical languages and

[20] *Report of the Committee of Management of Spring Hill College Birmingham for the Year 1843–44* (Birmingham, 1844), 11.

exegesis; 'synthetical' theology, including 'Christian Evidences' (chiefly using the works of Paley), and 'Ecclesiastical Theology'—'a summary and comparison, with each other and the Holy Scripture, of the principal doctrinal systems developed in the controversial writings of the Fathers, Heresiarchs, and Schoolmen, or embodied in ecclesiastical confessions and creeds'; church history; and Christian ministry, including pastoral and liturgical studies and 'Church Government and Discipline'.[21]

This demanding programme was to be shared between just three tutors. It was not yet customary to use the term 'Principal', but the Resident Tutor, Thomas Barker, was regarded as the senior member of staff. His two colleagues were Francis Watts and Henry Rogers. Barker and Watts were thorough, conscientious, and upright, but uninspired and unimaginative as teachers. Henry Rogers was of another order—an exciting and stimulating teacher with a spark of brilliance.

Thomas Barker[22] had received his education first at Christ's Hospital, and then at Homerton College (under Dr Pye Smith). After sixteen years in the pastoral ministry he came to Spring Hill, where for the rest of his life he served as Resident Tutor in Biblical and Classical Philology. His intellectual passion, which was not shared by all his students, was for Hebrew. R. W. Dale, who entered Spring Hill in 1847, recorded that 'it was his custom to require the students to begin their Hebrew grammar on the second or third day after they entered the College; and work at the Hebrew Bible went on every week to the end of six years.'[23] To the sixth-year men he also taught Syriac. In addition to Old Testament studies, he was required to teach the New Testament and classical philology. His New Testament work apparently did not excite him to the extent that Hebrew did, especially in his later years. A. J. Griffith, who entered Spring Hill College in 1866, wrote that his friend John Hunter 'never took kindly, if at all, to the minute and punctilious method of exegesis which grim old Professor Barker used to try to drill into us through the medium of Dr C. J. Elliot's commentaries on some of Paul's

---

[21] See 'General Outline of the Plan of Education' in the appendix to the *Report of the Committee of Management of Spring Hill College Birmingham 1839–40*, 71–2. See also the Examination Papers, ibid., app. 1–70.

[22] Thomas Barker (1798–1870). See *CYB 1871*, 302–4.

[23] R. W. Dale, 'The History of Spring Hill College', in *Mansfield College, Oxford: Its Origin and Opening* (London, 1890), 7–8.

Epistles'.[24] He was regarded as 'a stickler for law and order' who found it difficult to maintain 'genial relations with his students'—conscientious but out of touch with young men.[25] But R. W. Dale's son tells us that when his students 'saw through the manner and found the man, they loved and trusted him with their whole heart'.[26] The longest-serving member of the original staff, he continued teaching until his death in 1870 at the age of 71.

Francis Watts,[27] another former student both of Dr Bogue at Gosport and of Dr Pye Smith at Homerton, was engaged as tutor in 'theology, church history and pastoral science'. Some years earlier he had met Thomas Barker, when they both worked as ministers in Hertfordshire. Just before arriving at Spring Hill, he had spent some time studying in Halle under F. A. G. Tholuck (no doubt at Dr Pye Smith's suggestion; John Pye Smith learned German in middle life in order to keep abreast of new theological ideas), and his fluent German enabled him to introduce students to some of the new ideas being developed in Germany. His exegetical work was always thorough. R. W. Dale described it thus: 'It was painstaking almost to a fault. He heaped up his German authorities for every possible interpretation of a doubtful passage until some of his students began to wonder whether it was possible to believe that the passage had any definite meaning at all.'[28] He failed to hold the real interest of his students, let alone to excite them, and it was said that the less industrious students took advantage of his essential kindliness and were able to divert him from their own shortcomings by seemingly innocent questions, not only in class, but even in examinations. His tedious method of lecturing led to student protest, and the class was in 'a most unorderly condition', which provoked him to appeal in turn to the Board of Education for 'a code of laws' for the class.[29] This was probably a contributory cause of his resignation in 1858. In later years he was travelling secretary to the newly founded Congregational Institute in Nottingham. This work brought him in touch with John Crossley, and led to his being invited to act as minister at Somerleyton; there he died in 1873 at the age of 72.

[24] L. S. Hunter, *John Hunter DD* (London, 1922), 26.
[25] T. W. Pinn, 'Reminiscences', in F. J. Powicke, *David Worthington Simon* (London, 1912), 139.
[26] A. W. W. Dale, *The Life of R. W. Dale of Birmingham* (London, 1899), 13.
[27] Francis Watts (1801–73). See *CYB 1874*, 361–2.
[28] Dale, 'The History of Spring Hill College', 13.
[29] Spring Hill JCR Minute Book 1840–86, entry for autumn 1855, MCA.

The outstanding tutor was Henry Rogers,[30] who, as a schoolboy in Hertfordshire, had been known to both his fellow tutors. Unlike Barker and Watts, he was never ordained. He came to Spring Hill after serving for some time as Classics Tutor at Highbury College (where earlier he had been a student), and then for six years as Professor of English Language at the new University College London. He was a regular writer for the *Edinburgh Review* (and indeed was twice offered the editorship) and for the *British Quarterly Review*, and his contacts with men such as Macaulay, Stephen, and Whately gave him a wider outlook than his colleagues. At Spring Hill he was required to cover a wide range of subjects, as tutor in English language and literature, mathematics, and mental philosophy. Dale remembered him as having 'a quick wit, a graceful fancy, an alert memory, and a great delight in vigorous discussion'.[31] He was the one tutor at Spring Hill who was able to fire his students with intellectual excitement. They flocked to his voluntary philosophy class, and studied Aristotle, Plato, Bacon, and Descartes with him. These thinkers, together with Burke, Butler, and Pascal, were, as it were, his friends. He allowed, if not encouraged, his students to debate the great issues of Christian belief, the difficulties they presented as well as their grounds in reason, and keen and lively debate was a feature of his classes. His teaching bore fruit in the number of his students who won the Gold Medal for Philosophy in the London University MA examinations.[32]

He was the author of several books, of which the most popular was *The Eclipse of Faith* (London, 1852), cast in the form of a dialogue with an atheist. When the book appeared, 'those of his students who had been at his afternoon readings for the previous two years, discovered that the imaginary conversations in that book bore distinct traces of the very real and ardent debates in which they had tried their strength against their tutor'.[33] He engaged seriously with the theology of both Tractarians and agnostics (exemplified in particular in the writings of John Henry Newman, and of his brother Francis Newman) and published some of his articles on these themes

---

[30] For Henry Rogers (1806–77) see Alan Sell, 'Henry Rogers and *The Eclipse of Faith*', *JURCHS* 2/5 (May 1980); and *CYB 1878*, 347–9.

[31] R. W. Dale, 'The History of Spring Hill College', 9.

[32] For example, in each of the three years 1852–4 a Spring Hill student won the Gold Medal. See Dale, *Life of R. W. Dale*, 82.

[33] Quoted ibid. 43.

in *Essays on Some Theological Controversies of the Time* (London, 1874). The anonymous obituarist in the *British Quarterly Review* wrote that 'there can be no doubt that Dr J. H. Newman, of the Oratory of St Philip, had a larger degree of Mr Rogers' respect than his brother, the deistic champion'.[34]

The students came under the influence of their tutors, and of each other. But there were other influences too, outside the walls of the College. Pre-eminently there were the Nonconformist preachers of Birmingham: John Angell James at Carrs Lane ('some amount of attendance there was exacted by college custom, if not by rule'[35]), R. A. Vaughan[36] at Ebenezer Chapel, Steelhouse Lane, and George Dawson at the Church of the Saviour, an independent church founded by a rump from the Baptist Mount Zion Chapel. George Dawson was the great charismatic figure: 'His lovely voice, his pellucid English, his utter naturalness, his scathing satire, his robust and uncompromising conscience, his scorn of ecclesiastical narrowness and hardness, his emphasis on the universal "grace" of Jesus Christ, his profoundly reverent spirit, especially as revealed in his wonderful prayers, were irresistible to many.'[37] Many came under his spell. Birmingham was politically exciting too in the mid-nineteenth century, and both the Chartist agitation and the revolutions in Europe brought many national and international figures to speak in Birmingham Town Hall, which lay within walking distance of Spring Hill.[38]

At first all the students were preparing for the Congregational ministry. But in 1845 there came a proposal that a few students who were not destined for the ministry should be admitted (chiefly in order to increase the revenues). This was entirely compatible with the earlier tradition of Dissenting Academies. Francis Watts had read a paper advocating such a policy at a meeting of representatives of the Congregational Colleges of England and Wales 7–8 January 1845. The issue was debated fully by the Committee of Management in 1848, and reported in the *Annual Report* for 1847–8. Some hesitation was based on the failure of earlier such experiments. Finally, however, the Committee's opinion was:

[34] *British Quarterly Review*, 67 (Jan. 1878), 201. [35] Dale, *Life of R. W. Dale*, 50.
[36] Robert Alfred Vaughan (1823–57), son of Robert Vaughan, President of Lancashire Independent College.
[37] Powicke, *David Worthington Simon*, 87. Dawson was minister of the Church of the Saviour from 1847 until 1876. See also R. W. Dale, 'George Dawson: Politician, Lecturer, and Preacher', *Nineteenth Century*, 2 (1877), 44–61.
[38] Dale, *Life of R. W. Dale*, 46.

that supposing the Ministerial Students to be always a majority, and the minority of Lay Students to be admitted only on the condition of a blameless moral character, and subjected after their entrance to the ordinary rules of the Institution, it is in the highest degree incredible that the religious character of the Theological Students can be injured by the association; that, on the contrary, it is much more probable that they will impart spiritual good to their lay-brethren than that they will derive any moral injury from them.[39]

It was further pointed out that Nonconformist families could not easily find higher education for their sons 'except at a great cost of money, or the still more formidable cost of great moral dangers and temptations'.[40] The plan was finally adopted in 1849, and two lay students were enrolled for the following session.

By this time, Spring Hill College had become affiliated to the new University of London, which had no religious tests, and did not confine its examinations or degrees to those resident in London. The University of London had been established in 1836 in order to comprehend both the claims of University College, which was avowedly secular, and those of King's College, which was Anglican; it was given power 'to perform all the functions of the Examiners of the Senate House of Cambridge',[41] and was granted a Royal Charter. Its chief functions were to examine candidates and to confer degrees. Application for affiliation to the new university was discussed and decided upon during Spring Hill's second year, and it received the Queen's warrant to submit students for the London degrees BA, MA, LL B, and LL D in 1840;[42] from then on, the majority of students appear to have prepared for these degrees in general arts subjects or in law. This meant that the standard of work done in the College received a further external validation (there were already Congregational outside examiners), and many of the students distinguished themselves. A table published in the *Congregational Year Book* for 1851 showed that the students at Spring Hill College had gained

[39] *Report of the Committee of Management of Spring Hill College Birmingham for the Year 1847–48* (Birmingham, 1848), 16.

[40] Ibid.

[41] Quoted in S. J. Curtis, *History of Education in Great Britain* (London, 1953), 409.

[42] *Report of the Committee of Management of Spring Hill College Birmingham for the Year 1840–41* (Birmingham, 1841).

more London University degrees than any other Congregational college (though Coward and Highbury Colleges had done almost as well).[43] Thus, within thirteen years Spring Hill had established its reputation as one of the leading Congregational colleges for ministerial training. The disadvantage was that the work for these degrees tended to take precedence over theological work.

For almost twenty years, the College proceeded without any great changes. The tutors and the Chairman of the Board of Education remained in office, and the course of study was little altered, though the changing world outside cannot have failed to influence students. The first hints of change for the College however had come during its second year of life, when the need for a new, purpose-built college was first expressed. The existing house was too small, especially as the number of students increased, and, apart from lecture rooms, the dining hall, and rooms for the Resident Tutor, could only accommodate six students. A row of six cottages was then built on the other side of the road to accommodate another twenty-four students. This tended to cause a division in the community outside formal teaching time. The College Annual Reports were careful not to stress the unsatisfactoriness of the building until the new one was opened, but then referred to this first building as 'ill adapted to its object, insalubrious in its site, excessively incommodious, with neither outward beauty nor internal convenience to recommend it'.[44] As Birmingham had begun to spread outwards along the Dudley Road, the College had found itself set between ironworks on one side and chemical works on the other, which hardly added to its attractiveness.

As early as 1840, 20 acres of ground on Moseley Common, three or four miles from the city centre, were purchased as a site for the College. Mrs Glover and Miss Mansfield had generously donated a further £2,000 towards a new building fund, and six donations of £500 each and many smaller ones were received. A vigorous fund-raising campaign in the Midlands over the next few years produced most of the money required (£11,000), and in 1854 work on a new building finally began. In 1857, at last, a splendid new building, with an imposing tower, was opened (pl. 1). This was to be the home of the College for the next thirty years.

---

[43] *CYB 1851*, 249.

[44] *Report of the Committee of Management of Spring Hill College Birmingham for the Year 1856–57* (Birmingham, 1857).

1. Spring Hill College, Moseley, Birmingham

The architect of the new building was Joseph James, architect also of several Congregational churches.[45] The *Congregational Year Book* for 1858 contained a description of the exterior thus:

The style is that of the early part of the fifteenth century, the details inclining more to the decorated period than to the perpendicular. The building forms three sides of a quadrangle, the main front being to the south. Glancing in the first place at the exterior, we find that in the centre of the south front is a battlemented tower, 78 feet in height, flanked by a bell turret carried 14 feet higher. In this tower is the principal entrance to the building. The doorway is exceedingly beautiful, the carving with which the face of the arch is enriched being a clever combination of many of the best examples, all wrought out with scrupulous care. One of the bands bears the inscription, 'The fear of the Lord is the beginning of wisdom': and on either side are shields inscribed, 'On earth peace, good-will to men,' and 'Glory to God in the highest'. Above the main entrance rise in succession three large bay windows, for the lighting respectively of the council-room, museum, and laboratory. The tracery of these windows is of a very elaborate character. A buttress to the right of the doorway struck us as being decidedly original in its beauty. To the west of the tower is the library, on the exterior of which a large amount of ornament has been lavished. It is lighted by four very large moulded windows of stained glass, supplied by the Messrs. Chance, of Spon Lane. Over the tracery of these is a rich pierced parapet, surmounted by four elegantly carved pinnacles. Immediately beyond the library, and forming the west angle, is the warden's house, flanked by an octagon turret, on the summit of which is a water-tank for the use of the establishment. To the east of the tower is the dining hall, with lecture-rooms over it, and beyond these, the matron's residence. The wings are in keeping with the main front, though not so rich in decoration. They are two-storeyed, and have transomed windows. At the end of each wing is a turret, intended to carry a bell.[46]

---

[45] These included Chapel in the Field, Norwich, Square Chapel, Halifax, Cemetery Road, Sheffield, Regent Street, Barnsley, and Dronfield. Joseph James was chosen to design the new building as the result of a competition. See *Builder* 11 (1853), 55–6 and 72, and 12 (1854), 260, 513, and 598.

[46] *CYB 1858*, 263.

The library was evidently the most elaborately decorated room inside, with carved chimney-pieces at each end surmounted by the head and shoulders of Dr Joseph Fletcher[47] at one end and Dr John Pye Smith at the other—'who may, we suppose, be regarded as the "representative men" of Nonconforming collegiate life'.[48] Each wing included accommodation for thirty-six students: studies on the first floor, with dormitories above. There was no chapel, for the students were still expected to attend a local Congregational church.

The writer boldly claimed that the building was 'the best of its class which the neighbourhood of Birmingham possesses', and commented on its excellent position: 'It may be somewhat bleak in winter, but it is dry and healthy, and in summer it must be a charming spot, commanding a fine and extensive view, and occupying a situation on the south side of Birmingham, very similar to that which Oscott College occupies on the north.'[49] The Committee could well feel proud of the College's new home.[50]

The College was hardly settled in Moseley before the resignation of both Henry Rogers and Francis Watts was announced. In 1858 Henry Rogers accepted an invitation to become President and Theological Tutor at Lancashire Independent College, while Francis Watts decided to find work in a climate more suited to his wife's health. The settled triumvirate was now broken up, and for the next ten years the College had to suffer frequent changes of tutor, while Thomas Barker provided a steady if dull continuity. R. W. Dale, now minister at Carrs Lane Church, helped with the teaching for a while; another former student, Henry Goward, acted as Assistant Tutor, and Dr Richard Alliott came from Cheshunt College to teach theology and philosophy until his death in 1863, after which George Bubier,[51] another former student of Dr Pye Smith's, took over this teaching. He had been minister of Downing Street Chapel (later Emmanuel Congregational Church), Cambridge for five years, before spending ten years at Hope Street Chapel, Salford, during which time he shared in the work of the Lancashire Independent College. He was a defender of Samuel Davidson in 1857.[52] The JCR Minute

[47] Joseph Fletcher (1784–1843) was the Principal of Blackburn Academy 1816–23. See *DNB* vii. 315.

[48] *CYB 1858*, 264.   [49] Ibid. 263.

[50] This building, largely unaltered, now forms part of Moseley School.

[51] For George Bubier (1823–69) see *CYB 1870*, 279–81.

[52] Samuel Davidson (1806–98) was Professor of Biblical Literature and Ecclesiastical History at Lancashire Independent College from 1843 until 1857. He resigned after pro-

Book reveals Bubier to have been a sympathetic and genial tutor, and his sudden early death in 1869 was a great loss. Perhaps the most important change of all in these years was the election of Dale as Chairman of the Board of Education in 1860 in succession to John Angell James, for Dale was to play a crucial role in the College's move to Oxford twenty-six years later.

It is not surprising that the discipline slackened. The Annual Report for 1863–4 refers briefly to 'some grave cases of irregularity' but does not elaborate. On the other hand the JCR Minute Book is a little more expansive: 'On Wednesday Dec 10th 1862 Mr Barker after morning prayers made a communication to the students informing them that he had discovered that there existed in the House "a fearful amount of crime, immorality, vice and profanity" and that the Committee were about forthwith to proceed to the Investigation of the case.'[53] The following day, five students were summoned and specifically charged with 'Irreverence at Evening Prayers, Habits of Loose Conversation, and commencing a system of Insubordination in the House'. The result of the investigation was the expulsion of three students after a 'trial' both in the College and in the City. After a great outcry, and complaints of 'a lack of pastoral oversight', the students were eventually reinstated.

In 1869 the College entered on an important new phase of its life with the appointment of David Worthington Simon[54] as Theological Tutor, and in effect, Principal. Simon brought a new influence into the College, for he had lived in Germany for much of the fifteen years preceding his arrival in Birmingham. The son of a Congregational minister, he had trained for the ministry at Lancashire College under Robert Vaughan, Robert Halley, and the allegedly 'unorthodox' Samuel Davidson. He did not find these lecturers stimulating, though he enjoyed talking to Davidson about books, biblical theology, and Germany. Davidson had connections at Halle, and arranged for Simon to continue his studies there. Simon had two very short ministries in England, then spent some time in Manchester translating German theological works (notably five volumes of Isaak Dorner's *History of the Development of the Doctrine of the Person of*

---

tests among the College Committee against his articles on 'The Text of the Old Testament Considered' in the 10th edn. of T. H. Horne's *Introduction to the Critical Study and Knowledge of the Sacred Scriptures* (London, 1856).

[53] Spring Hill JCR Minute Book 1840–86, 39, MCA.

[54] See Powicke, *David Worthington Simon*.

Christ[55]), before moving back to Germany. He earned a doctorate from the University of Tübingen for a thesis on 'The Dissenting Sects of Russia', and then served as the representative of the British and Foreign Bible Society in Berlin. Here his theological 'hero', Isaak Dorner,[56] became also his friend.

Though not of the stature of Dale or Fairbairn, Simon was the finest theologian who taught on the permanent staff of Spring Hill. Now, for the first time, Spring Hill had a true systematic theologian on its staff. He was a thinker, adventurous sometimes, and, after having experienced much regurgitated, repetitious teaching in his own college days,[57] was determined to stimulate his students to think for themselves. The fact that he was sometimes regarded as 'dangerous', and that 'Simon's men' were often looked upon with some suspicion, shows that he may have succeeded.[58] In his letter of acceptance, he wrote: 'I have been bold enough to think that my experiences in Germany—that land of the profoundest intellectual struggles—would stand me in good stead.'[59]

Simon's two colleagues were to be John Massie and George Deane. Massie, a layman who had graduated in Classics at Cambridge after the abolition of some of the religious tests, was to teach New Testament, classics, and patristics.[60] Deane,[61] a former student at Cheshunt, who had a particular interest in science, and who had taken a D.Sc. at London University in 1869, was to take responsibility for mathematics, natural science, and Old Testament. He wrote in his letter of acceptance that in coming to Spring Hill 'I sacrifice a much more lucrative scientific position which is within my reach.'[62] His thinking about the relation between Christianity and science was expressed in a sermon preached during the British Association

[55] Published Edinburgh 1861–9. Simon's co-translator was W. L. Alexander.

[56] Isaak August Dorner (1809–84), Lutheran theologian, Professor of Theology at Tübingen 1853–62, and at Berlin 1862–84.

[57] See Dr John Brown, 'Reminiscences', quoted in Powicke, *David Worthington Simon*, 33.

[58] See J. C. G. Binfield, 'Chapels in Crisis: Men and Issues in Victorian Eastern England', *Transactions of the Congregational Historical Society*, 20/8 (Oct. 1968), 237–54.

[59] Quoted in the Minute Book of the Spring Hill College Committee of Management and Mansfield College Council 1866–1916, entry for 15 June 1869, MCA.

[60] John Massie (1842–1925), the son of the Revd Robert Massie, was one of the early Nonconformist students at St John's College, Cambridge, where he took the Classical Tripos. He was never ordained. See *MCM* 12/9 (Dec. 1925), 219–25.

[61] For George Deane (*c*.1838–91) see *CYB 1892*, 169.

[62] Quoted in the Minute Book of Spring Hill College Committee of Management and Mansfield College Council 1866–1916, entry for 6 Sept. 1869, MCA.

Conference taking place in Bristol in 1875: 'The fires of science may purge away some theologic dross; but only that the truth shall shine forth in its golden glory.'[63]

Changes in the curriculum brought a new ethos. Simon made theology *interesting*. The earlier theological tutors had relied heavily on Paley's *A View of Evidences of Christianity* (1794) and *Natural Theology* (1802) as irrefutable grounds for religious belief. Simon changed this. He used the work of his German mentors, especially Dorner, to help the students to develop for themselves an adequate Christian response to some of the new intellectual challenges of the later nineteenth century. One of the outside examiners of the theological papers wrote:

> I have wished it had been my privilege to have such teaching and guidance in preparation for the battle of thought and faith, on which all true men sooner or later must enter. The value of a Theological course, in which the truth is so deeply and thoughtfully grounded, can scarcely be estimated—specially in a time like the present, when we are threatened on all sides by what will prove to be, as I believe, the most exhaustive and destructive scepticism the Christian Faith and the Christian Church have ever had to confront.[64]

Simon took critical thinking seriously, recognized the challenge of science, and knew that the Church had to abandon some of its old formulations in order to interpret Christianity to a new age. Inevitably this was controversial, for explorations on the frontiers of theology and religion touch deep feelings, and the line between 'heresy' and 'orthodoxy' is not always as clear as some would wish.

The 'Rivulet Controversy' within Congregationalism in the mid-1850s had revealed the unease about responding to recent German theological work. While the *Eclectic* and the *Nonconformist* welcomed Thomas Toke Lynch's *Hymns for Heart and Voice: The Rivulet* (London, 1855), another journal, the *Morning Advertiser*, declared that it 'might have been written by a Deist' and that it was 'pervaded

---

[63] G. Deane, *The Relations of Christianity and Science* (London, 1875), 15.

[64] *Report of the Committee of Management of Spring Hill College Birmingham for the Year 1871–72* (Birmingham, 1872), 17. See also Dale A. Johnson, 'The End of the Evidences: A Study in Nonconformist Theological Transition', *JURCHS* 2/3 (Apr. 1979), 62–72, in which he charts the change at Spring Hill from reliance on works like Paley's *Evidences* to the study and discussion of contemporary theological writing.

throughout by the Rationalist theology of Germany'.[65] The ensuing heated controversy revealed a deep suspicion, not always informed, of German theology.[66]

It was unease about orthodoxy, and implicitly about the lack of scholarly theologians, both at Spring Hill and in the wider setting of English Congregationalism, which contributed to the crisis which took Spring Hill College to Oxford.

[65] Quoted in A. Peel, *These Hundred Years: A History of the Congregational Union of England and Wales 1831–1931* (London, 1931), 222.

[66] See R. Tudur Jones, *Congregationalism in England 1662–1962* (London, 1962), 249–53.

II

The 1870s: The Debate about Theology, Education, and Ministry

IN 1869, the year in which Simon became Principal of Spring Hill, the Chairman of the Congregational Union was the Chairman of the College's Board of Education, R. W. Dale.[1] At the Union's Autumn Assembly in Wolverhampton, Dale presided over the session at which the following resolution was carried:

> That this Assembly regards with great satisfaction the continued efforts made in Parliament to secure the nationalisation of the Universities of Oxford and Cambridge by the removal of those religious tests which, practically, limit the use of them to one party in the state.
>
> Designed as these seats of learning originally were, and as they unquestionably should be, for the use of the entire nation, this Assembly can accept no change as final which shall allow any section of the community to remain excluded on account of its religious belief from either of the universities, or any of their colleges, or from any of their emoluments, offices, or advantages. It rejects as injurious and unreasonable the idea that such an extension of their privileges would make university life less religious than it is; but, on the contrary, it doubts not that the removal of religious tests, by unfettering conscience, would strengthen and quicken it, and would thus promote, not only religion, but also that mutual respect which class legislation so unjustly destroys.[2]

Two years later, in 1871, almost all religious tests at Oxford and Cambridge were finally abolished; a Nonconformist presence in the ancient universities was now a possibility. This was the culmination

---

[1] Robert William Dale (1829–95) was a student at Spring Hill College 1847–53, and minister of Carrs Lane Church, Birmingham from 1853 until his death in 1895 (co-pastor with John Angell James from 1853 until 1859). See A. W. W. Dale, *The Life of R. W. Dale of Birmingham* (London, 1899) and *DNB* xxii. 529–31.

[2] *CYB 1870*, 91–2.

of a long political campaign, within and without the universities themselves, supported by University Liberals and Nonconformist leaders, but blocked for several decades by conservative Anglicans.[3] In 1854 the Oxford University Act had abolished religious tests for admission to the BA degree, and two years later a similar change took place in Cambridge. The 1871 Act abolished all University religious tests for degrees other than Divinity degrees, and for all University posts except where a clerical qualification was specifically attached.[4] After a further Act in 1877, and the appointment of University Commissioners to draw up new statutes, clerical Fellowships for other than college chaplains gradually disappeared.[5] Oxford and Cambridge were now open to Roman Catholics, freethinkers, Jews, and Nonconformists; for the first time since the Reformation, the two ancient universities could make some claim to be considered national universities.[6] Anglicans now established separate colleges, in or near Oxford, for their ordinands: Cuddesdon College (1854), St Stephen's House (1876), and Wycliffe Hall (1877).

Nevertheless Anglicanism continued to predominate in the religious life of Oxford—every college chapel held regular Church of England services, for example, from which non-Anglicans had to seek exemption—and the influence of the Oxford Movement was still strong in 'Puseyite circles'.[7] This caused much heart-searching among both the Nonconformist and the Roman Catholic communities. Was it right to send young, relatively immature men to a milieu so different from that in which they had been brought up?

[3] See W. R. Ward, *Victorian Oxford* (London, 1965), ch. xi for a full account of the struggle.

[4] An Act to Alter the Law Respecting Religious Tests in the Universities of Oxford, Cambridge and Durham, and in the Halls and Colleges of those Universities. However, the Act applied only to colleges then in existence. In 1875 A. I. Tillyard, supported by the Liberation Society, unsuccessfully challenged the right of Hertford College (incorporated in 1874) to restrict a Fellowship to 'Protestant Episcopalians'. See *Nonconformist*, 4 July 1877.

[5] In Balliol, for example, in 1861 9 of 12 Fellows were ordained, but only 1 in 1881; in Merton, in 1860 11 out of 29 were ordained, but only 5 in 1880. See W. G. Addison, 'Academic Reform at Balliol 1854–82', *Church Quarterly Review*, 153 (1952), 89–98. Academic teaching and research was now becoming a profession. See A. J. Engel, *From Clergyman to Oxford Don*, (Oxford, 1983).

[6] For a discussion of Nonconformist attitudes to Oxford and Cambridge in the 19th cent., see D. W. Bebbington, 'The Dissenting Idea of a University: Oxford and Cambridge, in Nonconformist Thought in the Nineteenth Century', Hulsean Prize Essay, University of Cambridge, 1973.

[7] Edward Bouverie Pusey, Regius Professor of Hebrew and Canon of Christ Church, was the last of the Tractarian leaders in Oxford, and survived until 1882.

Would they not soon succumb to the prevailing Anglican atmo-sphere?[8] Or worse, would they adopt the more fashionable agnostic attitudes? There had already been suggestions earlier in the century that Dissenters should establish separate halls at Oxford and Cam-bridge;[9] but that would have made it more difficult to criticize Anglican exclusiveness within other colleges.

There was a growing conviction among Congregationalists that theology was being neglected among them; that something was amiss with the education and training of their ministers; and that their principle of an 'educated ministry' now required that their ministers should, without abandoning Dissenting principles, enter the mainstream of English cultural and intellectual life. The devel-opment of local grammar schools, and the foundation of Noncon-formist schools such as Mill Hill (1818), Caterham (1811), Silcoates (1831), Taunton (1847), and Tettenhall (1863), now enabled the sons (and in some cases daughters[10]) of moderately affluent Congrega-tional families to gain places at universities. Their ministers could not afford to ignore these new educational opportunities, nor to lag behind their congregations in intellectual attainment.

Much of the debate about ministerial training took place in the Assemblies of the Congregational Union. At that same Autumn As-sembly of 1869 at which the Congregational Union had resolved to support the abolition of religious tests, and over which R. W. Dale had presided, Neville Goodman, a Congregational layman and Cam-bridge graduate,[11] had addressed the gathering on the subject 'How We May Best Avail Ourselves of the Universities of Oxford and Cambridge for the Education of our Ministers'.[12] He looked forward to a time when the ancient universities would no longer be con-fined to the sons of the so-called 'better classes', but would become 'gold fields where thirty or forty thousand of the sons of the nation,

---

[8] For the debate among Roman Catholics, see A. Stacpoole, 'The Return of the Roman Catholics to Oxford', *New Blackfriars*, 67 (May 1986), 221–32; and V. A. McClelland, *English Roman Catholics and Higher Education 1830–1903* (Oxford, 1973). Newman's plan to open an Oratory in Oxford 1864–5, and thereby encourage Roman Catholic students to study in Oxford, was forbidden by the English Roman Catholic bishops. Not until 1896 was the Roman Catholic Clarke Hall, later Campion Hall, opened in Oxford.

[9] See e.g. R. Vaughan in *British Quarterly Review*, 13 (1851), 167.

[10] Milton Mount College, for the daughters of Congregational ministers, opened in 1873 in Gravesend.

[11] Neville Goodman was a Scholar of Peterhouse, and Senior in the Natural Sciences Tripos 1865.

[12] See *CYB 1870*, 95–105.

without respect of class, or sect, or condition . . . will find the results and the rewards of their labours'.[13] That Congregational students should go to Oxford and Cambridge he felt all would agree; the question at issue was 'at what moment we ought to go up and possess the land'.[14] He listed three advantages of study at an ancient university: a stimulus to high attainment generated by the atmosphere and associations of the place, 'a definiteness of thought, and a precision of language', which were the marks of a scholar, and, 'last and least', a certain social status. The disadvantages he described as cost, the risks of diversion, and 'the danger of defection', but saw these as outweighed by the benefits, and as things which could be overcome. While admitting that 'defection' to Anglicanism might happen, he offered the view that if larger numbers of Dissenters were to reach the ancient universities, influence could work in more than one direction; 'the influx of dissenting students would be a very valuable element in building up that moral sentiment, and exciting that religious fervour, which must eventually be substituted for that hollow system which relies upon proctorial acuteness and enforced prayers.'[15] Nonconformists could contribute to and enhance the religious life of a university. Yet he did not favour any separate Dissenting college; it would, he felt, fail to command respect, either from potential students and staff, or from the rest of the university.

In 1873, two years after the abolition of religious tests at Oxford and Cambridge, Eustace Conder, one of the best-known Congregational ministers of his day, and one of Spring Hill's most distinguished old students, was elected Chairman of the Congregational Union.[16] For his address to the Assembly of the Union in October 1873 he chose as his subject 'The Decay of Theology'. In it, he lamented the decline of systematic theology, which would prove 'an immense loss' unless it could be replaced by 'nobler, truer, sounder systems'. 'Is it not true that whatever place Systematic Theology may maintain in the studies of our pastors, it has been for many years in steady course of disappearance from our pulpits; and that the number has been continually increasing among our hearers who account this disappearance a blessed riddance?'[17] The old orthodoxy, the strict Calvinism of men like John Angell James, which

---

[13] Ibid. 95.   [14] Ibid. 96.   [15] Ibid. 103.
[16] For Eustace Rogers Conder (1820–92) see *CYB 1893*, 214–17.
[17] *CYB 1874*, 68.

held that only 'the Elect' were destined for eternal life, had been rejected by the men of Conder's generation, and theology had been lifted onto 'a broader foundation of direct appeal to Scripture and experience'. The old theology was 'not overthrown by argument,' but 'burst asunder by the expansive force of love'.[18] There was a new emphasis on the Person of Christ. Conder traced these new developments to the influence of men such as Coleridge, Carlyle, and Maurice, and to the development of science. But he asked where the constructive theologians of the 'new theology' were to be found: 'We have iconoclasts in plenty, but where are our architects? Good and solid work is being done in Bible interpretation, which will remain to the honour of our generation; but where are the theologians at whose feet teachers of others will sit thirty years hence?'[19] The theology of the future 'will be the fruit of deeper study of God's truth' and so would surpass the 'grand, but metaphysical, overweening, hard featured if not hard hearted systems of the past'.[20] He sounded a warning note and asked his hearers to accept the challenge. This alleged neglect of constructive theology within Congregationalism was brought into sharp focus in 1877 at the 'Leicester Conference', whose story has been told fully by Mark Johnson.[21] The Autumnal Assembly of the Congregational Union of that year was to be held at Leicester, and, as an adjunct to the main conference, a group of ministers of the 'broader' outlook planned a special meeting, at which they intended to air their own theological explorations with like-minded colleagues. It was advertised in the religious press as 'a public conference of those who feel that agreement in theological opinion can no longer be held to be essential to religious communion'.[22] The central influence on most of the men behind this meeting was James Baldwin Brown,[23] who in turn had been deeply influenced by F. D. Maurice (while indebted most

---

[18] Ibid. 72.   [19] Ibid. 76.   [20] Ibid. 80.

[21] Mark Johnson, *The Dissolution of Dissent 1850–1918* (New York, 1987). I am greatly indebted to Mark Johnson's book, which explores in great detail the tensions within English Congregationalism towards the end of the 19th cent., and their effect on Mansfield College.

See also Mark Hopkins, 'Baptists, Congregationalists and Theological Change: Some Later Nineteenth Century Leaders and Controversies' (Oxford D.Phil. thesis, 1988).

[22] Quoted ibid. 76.

[23] For James Baldwin Brown (1820–84) see Elizabeth Baldwin Brown, *In Memoriam James Baldwin Brown* (London, 1884); *CYB 1885*, 181–4; and J. C. G. Binfield, *So Down to Prayers* (London, 1977).

of all to A. J. Scott[24]); though by the time Maurice's teaching had filtered down to some of the 'Leicester' men, it had lost much of its real content.

The meeting in Wycliffe Chapel was not a part of the official programme, though it had every appearance of being so, and it was not welcomed by the official organizers. The Chapel had been booked by the organizers without previous reference to the Union officials. Two papers were read: James Allanson Picton[25] spoke on 'Some Relations of Theology to Religion', and Thomas Gasquoine[26] on 'Freedom of Theological Thought and the Spiritual Life'. Picton 'was the biggest mistake the promoters of the conference made. He had the reputation of being the most unorthodox minister within the pale of the Congregational Union.'[27] His basic point was that religious feeling, rather than theological creed, was what bound Christians together. The meeting attracted not only supporters of the enterprise but critics too—amongst them the Principal of Spring Hill College, D. W. Simon, a former fellow student of both Picton and Gasquoine at Lancashire College. Simon spoke against the tenor of the papers, and further developed his response in an article in the *British Quarterly Review* in January 1878.[28] But because he was known to encourage his students to think things out for themselves, he did not entirely escape the suspicion that all was not well with theology at Spring Hill.

The conference immediately raised a furore within the Congregational Union and in the Congregational press (especially the *English Independent* and the *Christian World*). Subsequent calls for resolutions and affirmations of orthodox, Evangelical faith foreshadowed the response to later theological controversies. After much debate and heart-searching, the next meeting of the Assembly, in May 1878, discussed a formal Resolution, drawn up by a special subcommittee, affirming that, in view of the fact that 'the primary object of the Congregational Union, is, according to the terms of its own constitution, to uphold and extend Evangelical religion',

[24] Alexander John Scott (1805–66) was a Church of Scotland minister who became the first Principal of Owens College, Manchester 1851–7.

[25] James Allanson Picton (1832–1910) was a serving Congregational minister from 1856 until 1876, subsequently Liberal MP for Leicester 1884–94.

[26] Thomas Gasquoine (1833–1913). See *CYB 1914* for an outline of his career.

[27] Johnson, *The Dissolution of Dissent*, 78.

[28] *British Quarterly Review*, 68 (Jan. 1878), 153–73 (an unsigned article).

the assembly appeals to the history of the Congregational churches generally, as evidence that Congregationalists have always regarded the acceptance of the facts and doctrines of the evangelical faith revealed in the Holy Scriptures of the Old and New Testaments as an essential condition of religious communion in Congregational churches; and that among these have always been included the Incarnation, the Atoning Sacrifice of the Lord Jesus Christ, His Resurrection, His Ascension and Mediatorial Reign, and the work of the Holy Spirit in the renewal of men.[29]

Among those who spoke in the two-day debate in favour of the Resolution was R. W. Dale. Eventually the Resolution was passed by 1,000 votes to 20.

The disturbance aroused by that meeting in Leicester was out of all proportion to the actual amount of dangerous free-thinking amongst Congregational ministers. But it touched an already existing feeling of unease. If college-trained ministers *could* express such views, what was going on in the colleges? And what of those who continued to enter the ministry without college training? In the absence of episcopal authority, whose responsibility was it to guard and guide the expression of the faith once delivered to the saints?

Already moves had been afoot to bring about some co-operation and rationalization among the colleges. As early as 1845 a conference of delegates from the Congregational theological colleges was held at the Congregational Library in London, at which Francis Watts and John Angell James had represented Spring Hill.[30] In the early 1870s, concern about the colleges came to the fore in denominational debates. At the Autumn Assembly of the Congregational Union in 1871 Henry Allon, former student and now *éminence grise* of Cheshunt College, and minister of Union Chapel, Islington, read a paper to a sectional meeting on 'The Amalgamation of the Colleges'.[31] He reminded his hearers first of the Congregational tradition of 'an educated and cultured ministry':

---

[29] *Nonconformist*, 9 May 1878, 470.

[30] *Minutes of the Proceedings of a Conference of Delegates from the Committee of Various Theological Colleges Connected with the Independent Churches of England and Wales* (London, 1845), 7–8 Jan. 1845. Printed as an appendix to the bound volume of *Spring Hill College Reports 1839–54*, MCA.

[31] *CYB 1872*, 102–15.

The names of some of the most illustrious Biblical scholars and theologians of English Protestantism are to be found among early Nonconformist ministers. And when the Act of Uniformity made the education of a Nonconformist minister an illicit thing, no solicitude of both pastors and Churches was greater than to provide a succession of learned and godly men. Private and surreptitious academies sprung up in various places, some of them migratory, that they might elude the vigilance of their persecutors. In these the alumni spent many years of laborious study before they were permitted to take upon themselves the holy office of glorious peril which their learned fathers of the secession handed down to them.[32]

Those candidates for the ministry who were already well educated were able to follow this tradition. But many, perhaps most, were not. 'The real problem is how to deal with those who, when they become candidates for the ministry, possess only such rudimentary knowledge as the village school and self culture of an apprenticeship have supplied.'[33] Such a person could not be transformed into a scholar within four or five years. 'Few things can be more inimical than for ministers to be palpably inferior in general culture to any important class of their auditors.'[34]

This, Allon stressed to his hearers—a point which was to be reiterated in the coming years—was a matter of concern to every church, and to all the churches together. It was the responsibility of the churches as a whole to ensure that the resources for the training of future ministers should be used as efficiently as possible. This manifestly was not yet the case. Two or three professors in each college shared the teaching of all subjects, and so were unable ever to become real scholars. To meet this problem, Allon made four proposals: the arts and theology curricula should be clearly separated in all colleges; graduation in arts should be required before admission to a theological course (rather than the two being studied concurrently); money should be raised from the churches in support of theological education; and college education should be rationalized by some amalgamations—Allon's 'dream' was not of a Nonconformist presence in the existing universities, but of two Nonconformist universities, one in London and one in Manchester.

[32] Ibid. 104.   [33] Ibid. 113.   [34] Ibid. 106.

In 1872 the Council of New College, London, whose chairman was the redoubtable Dr Thomas Binney,[35] made an approach to Spring Hill with a view to some kind of association.[36] Spring Hill's response was to draw up a plan according to which Spring Hill would offer the first four years of the course, and New College the last two.[37] It then transpired that the New College Council expected Spring Hill to move to London, whereas Spring Hill had no such intention, and the plan foundered amid ruffled feelings.[38] A few months later another plan was discussed, this time an association with Lancashire Independent College. But that too came to nothing.

Simon was well aware of the problems in the existing arrangement; of the dangers inherent in encouraging theological exploration among those who had only slender foundations on which to build; and of giving one man (himself at Spring Hill) the whole responsibility for teaching theology and philosophy. This danger was later exemplified in the controversy surrounding one of his former students, J. T. Stannard, about whom Simon was frequently troubled. Stannard attracted great publicity in Huddersfield, where he was minister of Ramsden Street Chapel, and beyond, for his unorthodox views. The fact that he was one of 'Simon's men' did not go unnoticed. Ultimately he was ejected from his pastoral charge amid a blaze of publicity, and became minister of Milton Congregational Chapel, Huddersfield.[39]

Those who were in the best position to judge believed that Simon was orthodox in his faith, but that his method of teaching allowed students to construct edifices of faith without proper foundations. Guinness Rogers wrote of him on 14 October 1883, in response to a request for a testimonial from Edinburgh:

> I believe him thoroughly evangelical. Dale has the highest opinion of him. If I have any doubt it is not as to his own doctrine, but as to his mode of dealing with men. He has gone through serious sifting himself and has come right. This makes him take

[35] Thomas Binney (1798–1874) had retired from his outstanding forty-year ministry at the King's Weigh House in 1869.

[36] See Minute Book of the Spring Hill Committee of Management and Mansfield College Council 1866–1916, entries for 3 May and 17 June 1872, MCA.

[37] Ibid. 13 Sept. 1872.   [38] Ibid. 10 Dec. 1872.

[39] See J. T. Stannard, *The Divine Humanity* (Glasgow, 1892); *CYB 1890*, 187; and Binfield, *So Down to Prayers*, 158, 159, 197, 198.

not only hopeful but optimistic views of others; and his expression of this tendency has got him into trouble.[40]

However, a greater influence than Simon on some of the students was F. D. Maurice, who died in April 1872. F. J. Powicke, one of Simon's students at Spring Hill (1872–7), wrote much later in life that although Simon found Maurice an insufficiently systematic thinker and did not encourage his students to read him, nevertheless

> a Mauriceian cult grew up, and probably did more to shape our theology than the lectures of the principal . . .
>
> I may be wrong, but I incline to say that a majority of our younger ministers in 1877 bore the Mauriceian stamp, if under that description may be included what they drew from Thomas Erskine, McLeod Campbell, A. J. Scott, and George MacDonald.[41]

He attested to the great influence of James Baldwin Brown, a friend of Maurice, over them all, and claimed his as 'the real victory' after Leicester.[42] From Maurice, Powicke claimed to have learned to treat the Bible as 'a book of life' rather than as 'an infallible book of texts'; to resist the attraction of Unitarianism (for Maurice had fought his way 'step by step' to belief in the Trinity, and therefore his approach was from the side of experience, as distinct from Simon's metaphysical approach); and a belief in the possibility of salvation for the whole human race. It was not Maurice's thought as such, but his thought undigested and lazily appropriated, which caused the trouble.

Simon's own unease had led him to suggest to the College Committee of Management as early as 1875, well before the Leicester Conference, that some link might be made with Oxford or Cambridge.[43] On 7 April 1876 the following resolution was passed by the Committee: 'That in the judgment of the Committee steps should be taken to secure the advantages offered by Oxford University for the students of Spring Hill College, and that a Subcommittee be

---

[40] Quoted F. J. Powicke, *David Worthington Simon* (London, 1912), 140.

[41] F. J. Powicke, 'Frederick Denison Maurice: A Personal Reminiscence', *CQ* 8 (1930), 171, 172. For Maurice's influence on Congregationalists of the period, see also A. Mackennal, *Sketches in the Evolution of English Congregationalism* (London, 1901), 195–206. Mackennal was a student at Hackney College 1854–7. Towards the end of his life, he was Chairman of Mansfield College Council, from 1892 until 1904.

[42] Powicke, 'Frederick Denison Maurice', 172.

[43] Powicke, *David Worthington Simon*, 108.

appointed to consider how this object may be secured with the least alteration in the present arrangements of the College.'[44] It was moved by the Revd G. B. Johnson,[45] minister at Edgbaston Congregational Church and alumnus of Coward College, and seconded by Simon.

A month later, on 5 May, the subcommittee, which included Simon, R. W. Dale, Alexander Mackennal, John Massie, and George Deane, brought a series of recommendations. The main proposal was that intending students for the ministry who were able to pass the Matriculation Examination for Unattached Students at Oxford[46] should be able, at the discretion of the Board, to graduate in an arts subject at Oxford. They would spend the eight weeks of each University term in Oxford, and the remaining four weeks of the Spring Hill term in Birmingham, in the special study of Hebrew, and in further preparation for the Oxford degree. The Spring Hill tutors would exercise a general supervision of their work through personal visits and correspondence during the Oxford term, and through personal tutoring at Spring Hill. Students who were not sufficiently well qualified would continue to take the whole course in Birmingham. The College would award exhibitions to the Oxford students, and also pay University dues and tutorial fees.

These proposals generated a lengthy discussion, but the Committee did not reach agreement. In the end they found a way out by resolving 'That inasmuch as the year for which this Committee holds office will soon expire, in the judgment of the Committee, it is undesirable to continue the consideration of the Report.'[47] Nevertheless, at the Annual Meeting of the College in June 1877 the Chairman (J. A. Cooper) proposed not only an amalgamation of some Congregational colleges, but the removal of 'such a College as Spring Hill' to Oxford or Cambridge, to be used as a theological hall. 'They had fought the battle of University tests to little purpose if they did not crown their successful efforts by giving their students the opportunity

---

[44] Minute Book of the Spring Hill College Committee of Management and Mansfield College Council 1866–1916, entry for 7 Apr. 1876, MCA.

[45] George Burlingham Johnson (1819–1902). Immediately before coming to Edgbaston in 1858 he had deputized for Thomas Binney (by whom he was much influenced) at the King's Weigh House while Binney was in Australia. His obituarist in the *CYB 1903*, 184 described him as 'broad-minded, large-hearted, of charming manners and elegant speech', but also 'as robust a champion of truth and liberty as God ever made'.

[46] A system inaugurated in 1868, intended for those who could not afford the expense of membership of and residence in a college.

[47] Minute Book of the Spring Hill College Committee of Management and Mansfield College Council 1866–1916, entry for 5 May 1876, MCA.

of enjoying advantages from which unrighteous laws so long excluded them.' This proposal was opposed at this stage by R. W. Dale:

> no one who was acquainted with the inner life of Oxford and Cambridge could be ignorant of the fact that those educational arrangements were regarded with the deepest dissatisfaction by a large number of most eminent members of both universities, and to assume that they would secure the kind of education the supporters of Spring Hill College desired for their students, even in arts, at Oxford and Cambridge, was to labour under a very false, and what was likely to be a very pernicious, impression.[48]

The opposition of Dale, and the removal of G. B. Johnson to Torquay because of poor health, meant that the proposal then lapsed.

It was only months after this that the Congregational Union met for its Autumn Assembly in Leicester, and that the controversial 'Leicester Conference' took place. The meeting of 16 October at Wycliffe Chapel overshadowed everything else in the press reporting. But on the very next day, in the same building, at a sectional meeting (an official part of the Congregational Union meetings), the Revd Thomas Robinson read a paper on 'Desirable Reforms in our College System'.[49] He repeated Henry Allon's point that the existing system was wasteful: 'Our system is so contrived as to obtain the minimum of results for the maximum outlay.'[50]

> When you understand this vicious system, you cease to wonder that original research is almost an unknown term in our colleges, or that so few first-rate contributions to theological literature ever proceed from them. . . .
>
> Now, who is to blame for this state of things? Why ourselves, of course. Our professors, many of whom are men of great intellectual power, could take their place among the guides and leaders of thought in England, but we will not let them. We make them hewers of wood and drawers of water instead. I, for one, protest against this dishonour done to the choicest minds that God has given us.[51]

He repeated the suggestion that the arts and theology curricula should be separated, and pointed out that an arts course could be provided

---

[48] *Nonconformist*, 27 June 1877, 654. [49] *CYB 1878*, 121–6.
[50] Ibid. 121. [51] Ibid. 122.

much more cheaply by Owens College, Manchester[52] or by a Scottish university. Not only would it be more economic, it would be more valuable socially and intellectually for the students, who would experience 'the full forces of the whole main current of national thought'. As it was, they only met 'a little community of men who are all of one way of thinking, all looking forward to the same kind of work, and all taking a disproportionate interest in the gossip and tittle-tattle of the Congregational Churches'.[53] The colleges, meanwhile, should be prepared to discuss some form of amalgamation.

Simon and Henry Allon, among others, contributed to the ensuing discussion. The result was the formation of a College Reform Committee, with thirty college representatives and fifteen representatives of the Congregational Union, which met intermittently over the next seven years. Its most constructive achievement was the establishment of the so-called Senatus Academicus, a body of representatives of nine Nonconformist theological colleges, who, together with a number of outside examiners, conducted theological examinations for their students.[54] The Chairman, Henry Spicer, was a layman, a member of Allon's church in Islington.

The following year Spicer presented a paper on 'The Reform of the College System' to another sectional meeting. In his mind at least, the decline of theology in the Congregational churches and the state of the colleges were linked: 'Evangelicalism, the spiritual food and mental stimulus of our fathers, appears to be degenerating into a mystic sensationalism, with which, at any rate, the intellect has little to do.'[55] He suggested that a confederation of Congregational colleges should organize 'high-class theological examinations', and might eventually seek a royal charter to confer degrees. This was in line with Henry Allon's earlier suggestion of two Nonconformist universities.

A year later, the Chairman of the Congregational Union, Samuel Newth, Principal of New College, London, chose as the title of his Chairman's address in October 1880 'The Church and the College';[56] echoing the concern about the standard of education in the colleges, he nevertheless sought to defend their teachers, who worked so hard, and who, he pleaded, deserved help, not criticism. His own

---

[52] Owens College, the forerunner of the Victoria University of Manchester, was founded in 1851.

[53] *CYB 1878*, 124.   [54] See *CYB 1880*, 455–6 for the syllabus of its examinations.

[55] *CYB 1880*, 115.   [56] *CYB 1881*, 102–21.

suggestion was for three colleges of 150–200 students each, in London, Manchester, and Bristol.

In October 1881 the College Reform Committee presented its report. Its recommendations were in line with earlier ones. Arts and theology should be separated; students should take their arts courses in universities or university colleges; and the Congregational colleges should concentrate on theology. The Congregational Union was urged to promote two Boards of Education, one for the north of England and one for the south, in order to carry out these suggestions. The last suggestion was the one to be implemented first. The authority to implement the other suggestions had to be left to individual colleges and churches, which meant in practice that only a very resolute individual would be able to turn these proposals into a reality.

When these Boards were constituted, Spring Hill was given a choice, and decided to align itself with the Southern Board. R. W. Dale and Simon were among the Spring Hill representatives. These Boards achieved little. The reason lay primarily in the nature of Congregationalism. Each college was supported and financed by a particular group of constituents, local churches and wealthy individuals who felt a loyalty to a specific institution. The Congregational Union had no power actually to coerce the colleges into some national system, and local feeling and prejudice prevented the establishment of any rational and efficient system of ministerial training.

The crux of this issue, which found its focus in the debate about the colleges, was the whole position of Nonconformity within British life. Should it continue as a separate culture and churchmanship, existing alongside Anglicanism and Roman Catholicism, or should it enter what was regarded as the mainstream of cultural and religious life, to which it was now free to contribute its distinctive ideas, and from which it had much to gain.[57] Was there a grain of truth in Matthew Arnold's view that while Nonconformists were 'walking staunchly by the best light they have' there was a want of 'sweetness and light'?[58] And what was the right relationship between religion and education?[59]

According to A. M. Fairbairn, Mansfield's founding Principal, the first person to suggest the founding of a Nonconformist *college* (a somewhat different concept from that of a non-residential theological

---

[57] *CYB 1882*, 34–40.
[58] M. Arnold, *Culture and Anarchy* (1869), ed. R. H. Super (Ann Arbor, 1965), 236.
[59] See Bebbington, 'The Dissenting Idea of a University', 53 for a discussion of this.

hall, which Mansfield became) after the repeal of the University Tests Act at Oxford was Gladstone, in the course of discussions with Nonconformists on education in 1871 or 1872. 'He himself informed me of the matter, and he recalled it to the late Dr Allon at the time Mansfield was opened. And Allon confirmed his version,' wrote Fairbairn to Alexander Mackennal in 1894.[60] This was further confirmed by Sir Arthur Haworth, who recollected that Gladstone had asked his father (Abraham Haworth), 'Why don't you Nonconformists set up a college in Oxford?'[61]

Gladstone had begun meeting a group of Nonconformist, mainly Congregational, ministers at Newman Hall's home in Hampstead in the 1860s. On 25 January 1866, for example, he met a group of Dissenting ministes there; 'the teeth and claws not very terrible,' he noted in his diary.[62] For long he was reluctant to abolish University tests—'I cannot draw a distinction in principle between the exclusiveness of the University and the exclusiveness of the Established Church; and I believe the day to be distant when England will consent to separate them,' he wrote to Newman Hall on 18 June 1865.[63] Nevertheless it was Gladstone's Government which abolished the religious tests in 1871. He had become convinced that both justice and the ultimate well-being of the Anglican Church (since it would remove a significant cause of hostility) demanded this. In addition, his party's power depended to a considerable extent on Nonconformist support.[64]

The exact date of Gladstone's suggestion has not been identified, though it could well have been on the occasion of a Nonconformist deputation, whose secretary was J. Carvell Williams, to press for the abolition of University tests, early in 1870;[65] or a later one, led by T. B. Potter, on 17 May 1871.[66] The subject may have come up again in

---

[60] Quoted in W. B. Selbie, *The Life of Andrew Martin Fairbairn* (London, 1914), 165–6.

[61] *MCM* 12/4 (July 1928).

[62] *Gladstone's Diaries*, vi, ed. H. C. G. Matthew (Oxford, 1978), 413.

[63] See Newman Hall, *Autobiography* (London, 1898), 267. See also G. I. T. Machin, 'Gladstone and Nonconformity in the 1860s: The Formation of an Alliance', *Historical Journal*, 17/2 (1974).

[64] The veneration in which Nonconformists came to hold Gladstone is demonstrated by the letters which his wife and son received from all kinds of Nonconformist societies after his death. See Glynne-Gladstone MS 1055, Clwyd Record Office, Hawarden.

[65] Liberation Society, Minute 427, 11 Feb. 1870. See W. H. Mackintosh, *Disestablishment and Liberation: The Movement for the Separation of the Anglican Church from State Control* (London, 1972), 264.

[66] *Gladstone's Diaries*, vii, ed. H. C. G. Matthew (Oxford, 1982), 496.

1875 (16 February), when Gladstone spent the evening with a group of Nonconformist ministers, including R. W. Dale, at Newman Hall's house.[67] While Gladstone's concept of a separate college for Nonconformists was not in accord with the concern of most Nonconformists for equality and the end of any form of Anglican exclusiveness, his encouragement added impetus to the movement.

During the 1870s and early 1880s the idea was intermittently suggested and debated among Congregationalists, especially in the columns of the *Nonconformist and Independent*. Some were afraid that Oxford (or Cambridge) would spoil men from 'simple homes and simple surroundings' and make them unfit to minister in 'the more modest environment' of Congregational churches, and would turn them into 'superior persons'.[68]

This debate and the anxiety which was being expressed inevitably influenced Spring Hill. Simon was now even more convinced that Congregationalists should take advantage of the opportunity to study at Oxford or Cambridge, and by 1883 he had come to favour theological as well as arts education being centred in one of the ancient universities. On 13 August 1883 he addressed a meeting of influential Congregationalists at the Reform Club, Liverpool on 'The University Training of Congregational Ministers'. The organizers were 'Messrs Atkin and Hargreaves of Rock Ferry', personal friends of Simon, and supporters of his proposal. Among the audience were Sir James Allanson Picton, a prominent Liverpool architect, father of James Allanson Picton who spoke at the Leicester Conference, and Sir Edward Russell,[69] editor of the Liverpool *Daily Post*. Not present, but said to be in sympathy with the proposal, were William Crosfield and W. S. Caine.[70] Later the address was printed in pamphlet form for wider distribution.[71] He proposed the entire preparation of a certain number of the best ministerial candidates in a college at

---

[67] Hall, *Autobiography*, 271–2. [68] A. Spicer in *MCM* 8/1 (Mar. 1912), 6.

[69] Edward Richard Russell (1834–1920) was Liberal MP for Glasgow, Bridgeton 1885–7, created Baron Russell 1919.

[70] Powicke, *David Worthington Simon*, 109. William Crosfield (1838–1909) was a department chairman of Liverpool Mortgage Insurance Company, and Liberal MP for Lincoln 1892–5. He later served on the College Building Committee, and gave a generous subscription. William Sproston Caine (1842–1903) was at the time Liberal MP for Scarborough; he was Civil Lord of the Admiralty in Gladstone's administration 1884–5. Fairbairn recounted that, more than a year earlier than this, Mr Caine had invited James Bryce to address a meeting on the same theme. See Selbie, *Life of Andrew Martin Fairbairn*, 167.

[71] No extant copy has been discovered. But it is described in some detail in Powicke, *David Worthington Simon*, 109–15.

Oxford or Cambridge, and a six-year course. 'I think that in the majority of cases a certain general culture, a widening of the mental horizon, a deprovincialisation could not but result, which it is hopeless to expect at present.'[72] Such a college would free its graduates from a feeling of inferiority—'a sense which sometimes begets a very disagreeable form of self-assertion'[73]—and provide the kind of general stimulus and broad experience which he himself had enjoyed in Germany. 'Would not the thought of becoming an Oxford or Cambridge student be likely to fire the holy ambition of a higher order of men who now think comparatively little, or even slightingly, of our own Colleges?'[74] Such a college would also, he believed, prove a rallying point—in the form of Sunday services and occasional lectures—for Nonconformists at the University. In answer to the charge that such a college might encourage sectarianism, he believed this not to be the case with a non-residential institution, rather 'there would ensue a diminishing of sectarianism through a lessening of the ignorance which prevails as to our principles and methods'.[75] Having failed to convince the Spring Hill Committee to respond to this challenge, he urged some other person or group of people to do so instead. The meeting endorsed Simon's proposal 'with scarcely a note of dissent'.

Two months later, Simon met his old college friend J. B. Paton,[76] one of the great statesmen of nineteenth-century Congregationalism, Principal of the Nottingham Congregational Institute (a college offering a shorter course than the normal), just before the Congregational meetings in Sheffield, and persuaded him to transform the general recommendations of his paper on 'College Reform' into a specific proposal to establish a Divinity Hall at Oxford or Cambridge. Paton therefore addressed a sectional meeting on 10 October, and proposed the establishment of two or three theological lecturerships at Oxford or Cambridge, in order to provide advanced theological teaching to Nonconformist graduates (though the lectures would be open to all). There followed a heated discussion. Paton argued that many of the existing Nonconformist students at Oxford and Cambridge, representing 'the flower of English Nonconformity', would be attracted to further study at a Nonconformist Divinity

---

[72] Quoted ibid. III.   [73] Ibid. III.   [74] Quoted ibid. II2.   [75] Ibid. II3.

[76] Paton was a former Spring Hill student. See J. L. Paton, *John Brown Paton* (London, 1914). After retirement, J. B. Paton gave half his books to Mansfield College library—the John Brown Paton Collection—and half to Westminster College, Cambridge.

Hall, and all Nonconformist students would benefit from its presence. Others, including R. F. Horton's father T. G. Horton (who a decade earlier had been so insistent that his own son should go to Oxford or Cambridge), opposed the idea, believing that the Free Churches would find it difficult to work together.[77] There was no positive outcome, and Simon felt frustrated again. He was perhaps not fully aware of the developments already taking place in Oxford.

On 8 November 1883, the Secretary told the Spring Hill Committee of Management that he had learned that Principal Simon had received an invitation to become Principal of the Theological Hall of the Scottish Congregational churches at Edinburgh, which he intended to accept. Simon was urged to remain in Birmingham, but he was not to be deflected. On 5 December his letter of resignation was read out. His concluding words were: 'May I . . . venture to express the hope that my removal will become the occasion of some new movement that shall result in the College realizing more completely than ever before the intention of its founders to provide the most efficient possible training for candidates for the Congregational ministry.'[78] Three years later, his wish was granted, though at the time he did not receive the credit due to him for his part in the creation of Mansfield College. It was ironic that it was within a month of that meeting on 5 December at which his letter of resignation was read out that R. W. Dale suggested that Spring Hill should move to Oxford or Cambridge.

The initiative now passed to Dale, Chairman of the College Board of Education since 1859, the most illustrious Spring Hill old student, and one of the outstanding Congregationalists of the nineteenth century. He had come to realize the advantages of a move to one of the ancient universities especially in the light of the growing numbers of Nonconformist students at Oxford and Cambridge. The knowledge that within English Congregationalism there was now a theological college teacher of sufficient calibre to direct a Nonconformist college in Oxford—Andrew Martin Fairbairn, Principal of Airedale College, Bradford—may have influenced him. Now that there was a vacancy for a principal, Fairbairn's participation in the scheme was made possible. Dale set about moving Spring Hill to Oxford.

[77] See the report of the meeting in the *Nonconformist and Independent*, 25 Oct. 1883, 971.
[78] Minute Book of the Spring Hill College Committee of Management and Mansfield College Council 1866–1916, entry for 5 Dec. 1883, MCA.

III

The Move to Oxford

The greatest work done for and by Independency since 1662.[1]

ALREADY in Oxford pressure was growing for a stronger Nonconformist presence there. For many, the argument was based on principles of justice and equality; for others the argument also included an appeal to what Nonconformists could contribute, not only for the sake of Nonconformity, but also for the strengthening of a more liberal approach to theology.

Sometime during the decade before the move to Oxford, probably about the year 1880, R. W. Dale (pl. 2) received a letter from T. H. Green, Fellow of Balliol College, later Whyte's Professor of Moral Philosophy at Oxford.[2] They had first met in the 1860s, when Green was engaged as an Assistant Commissioner to the Schools Enquiry Commission to make a special report on King Edward's School, Birmingham, of which Dale was a Governor; and for four years, 1878–82, they were fellow Governors of King Edward's.[3] Green was one of the greatest influences on the ablest young undergraduates in Oxford, a man whom Dale greatly admired as one who combined original speculation with 'a practical life of great sagacity and of great vigour'.[4] The first layman to become a Fellow of Balliol, he regarded religion as 'the middle term between political philosophy and social action'[5] and practised all three. He was an outstanding tutor, influencing his pupils as spiritual adviser as well as intellectual

---

[1] A. M. Fairbairn to R. W. Dale, 18 Dec. 1883. Quoted in W. B. Selbie, *The Life of Andrew Martin Fairbairn* (London, 1914), 169.

[2] For Green, see Melvin Richter, *The Politics of Conscience: T. H. Green and his Age* (London, 1964), and G. L. Thomas, *The Moral Philosophy of T. H. Green* (Oxford, 1987).

[3] See the report of a speech by R. W. Dale at a public meeting in Oxford Town Hall to consider ways in which Green might best be commemorated in *Oxford Chronicle and Berks and Bucks Gazette*, 20 May 1882.

[4] Ibid.

[5] P. B. Hinchliff, *Benjamin Jowett and the Christian Religion* (Oxford, 1987), 164.

2. Robert William Dale

guide, and occasionally preaching in the college chapel. He did not wholly adhere to any religious communion; earlier in his life he had, according to James Bryce, considered the Unitarian ministry,[6] and it was not unknown for him to worship in a Nonconformist chapel. He was in as good a position as any to know of the needs and concerns of the young undergraduates of Nonconformist as well as Anglican background. His letter therefore carried weight with Dale, who, according to his son, was strongly moved by it. It included these words:

> The opening of the national universities to Nonconformists has been, in my judgment, an injury rather than a help to Nonconformity. You are sending up here, year after year, the sons of some of your best and wealthiest families; they are often altogether uninfluenced by the services of the Church which they find here, and they not only drift away from Nonconformity—they drift away and lose all faith; and you are bound, as soon as you have secured the opening of the universities for your sons, to follow them when you send them here, in order to defend and maintain their religious life and faith.[7]

This letter subsequently became famous, though it was not made public until after the opening of the College. A Nonconformist presence in Oxford was now presented as an obligation and a duty, not only as a beneficial idea.

Green was not the only Oxford don who was ready to welcome a Nonconformist college. Whereas in the middle of the nineteenth century the High Church Anglicans had dominated Oxford's religious life, the liberal Anglicans now had a growing influence. Benjamin Jowett, Master of Balliol since 1870, Vice-Chancellor 1882–6, and a leading representative of the liberal school of theology, had long supported a more open approach to theology and the admission of Nonconformists to degrees. He wanted 'a university and a college in which religion and rational enquiry did not conflict'.[8] His liberal views did not find favour in all quarters, but there is no doubt that he was one of the most influential figures of late nineteenth-century Oxford. He added strength to Green's appeal to Dale,[9] and later gave

---

[6] James Bryce, *Studies in Contemporary Biography* (London, 1903), 92.
[7] Quoted in A. W. W. Dale, *The Life of R. W. Dale of Birmingham* (London, 1899), 10. The letter itself was presumably destroyed along with Dale's other papers.
[8] Hinchliff *Benjamin Jowett*, 3.   [9] Selbie *Life of Andrew Martin Fairbairn*, 163.

both practical and public support to the new college. Not only Jowett, but Edwin Hatch,[10] Vice-Principal of St Mary Hall (the last of the medieval academic halls), and Reader in Ecclesiastical History from 1884 until his premature death in 1889, and William Sanday,[11] Dean Ireland's Professor of the Exegesis of Holy Scripture from 1882, were ready to welcome Mansfield. Hatch's Bampton Lectures of 1880 (published in 1881 as *The Organisation of the Early Christian Churches*) were hailed by Nonconformists as 'the one modern attack upon sacerdotalism which the sacerdotalists have not dared to answer'.[12] At Merton, the liberal Warden Brodrick had for long been sympathetic to the Nonconformists' right to education on equal terms with Anglicans, on the grounds of justice and for the sake of education.[13]

Dale was now stirred to action. He himself had received his general as well as his theological education at Spring Hill College at the end of the 1840s, and had been stimulated by the teaching of Henry Rogers. With the intellectual equipment acquired at Spring Hill, limited though it may have been in some ways, he had risen to be one of the two finest Congregational theologians of the century (the other being Andrew Martin Fairbairn) and a model for Congregational ministers for generations to come. He valued theological learning: 'one of the conditions of real power and permanence on the part of any great Christian community was, that it should have in it a fair number of men of great theological learning.'[14] His greatest theological work was *The Atonement*,[15] an interpretation of the work of Christ which 'so incorporated the fundamental or governing thought of the new liberal theology as to modify, without surrendering, the old Evangelical doctrines'.[16] His most influential book within

---

[10] In an article in *Methodist Times* (11 June 1885), Hatch had welcomed the possibility of a Nonconformist presence in Oxford; Oxford could offer 'culture' to Nonconformists, while Nonconformists could offer the best alternative to High Anglicanism. The University itself could prove a unifying influence for both groups. For Hatch (1835–89) see *DNB* ix. 149–50 and S. C. Hatch (ed.), *Memorials of Edwin Hatch MA* (London, 1890).

[11] William Sanday (1843–1920). See *DNB 1912–21*, 482–4. From 1895 to 1920 he was Lady Margaret Professor of Divinity at Christ Church.

[12] Hugh Price Hughes in *Methodist Times*, 11 June 1885, 369.

[13] George Charles Brodrick (1831–1903) was Warden of Merton from 1881 until 1903. See *DNB Second Supplement 1901–11*, 230–1. In 1866 he had been one of the main speakers at a public meeting in the Free Trade Hall in Manchester in support of the abolition of University religious tests.

[14] Report of Dale's address at the Annual Meeting of Spring Hill College, *Nonconformist and Independent*, 28 Sept. 1882.

[15] R. W. Dale, *The Atonement* (London, 1875).

[16] A. M. Fairbairn in Dale, *Life of R. W. Dale*, 707.

the denomination was his *Manual of Congregational Principles*.[17] The reputation he had acquired as the minister of Carrs Lane Church, Birmingham, as civic leader in the city, as a leader within the Congregational denomination, and on the national political stage, ensured that his advocacy of the scheme would win respect and support.

His younger brother Thomas had been able to take advantage of the university reform of the 1850s by reading Mathematics at Trinity College, Cambridge, where he was third wrangler in 1862. At Cambridge, he became a 'Churchman', and therefore, when he was elected to a Fellowship at Trinity College, he was able to make the necessary subscription to the Articles of the Church of England.[18] He devoted the rest of his short life to college teaching and administration. The two brothers remained close, and R. W. Dale was deeply shaken when Thomas died suddenly, aged 43, in 1883. This connection with Cambridge may have facilitated Dale's visit there 'to ascertain what amount of sympathy a Congregational College—should one be established—could reckon among the more liberal theologians of the place'.[19] But it seems he received little encouragement, and did not pursue the idea.

Over the next few years, Dale made four great contributions to the establishment of Mansfield; he took responsibility for the difficult and tedious negotiations with the Charity Commission and with the Spring Hill Trustees; he secured the co-operation and support of the Congregational Union; he raised much of the necessary money; and he ensured that the leadership of the new College would be placed in the hands of Andrew Martin Fairbairn.

In Oxford there was a growing number of Nonconformist staff and students who provided a nucleus of support for a Congregational college for training ministers. Amongst the early Congregational undergraduates in Oxford were two who were to achieve eminence in the future: Nathaniel Micklem,[20] a future lawyer whose son was to become the third Principal of Mansfield, and Robert Forman Horton,[21] later to become the much loved minister of Lyndhurst

---

[17] R. W. Dale, *Manual of Congregational Principles* (London, 1884).

[18] Dale, *Life of R. W. Dale*, 519.

[19] Ibid. 496. No date given, but presumably between 1880 and 1884.

[20] Nathaniel Micklem (1853–1954) was called to the Bar in 1881. He served as Liberal MP for Watford 1906–10. He was a QC during Queen Victoria's reign, and survived to be QC again under Queen Elizabeth II.

[21] For Horton see R. F. Horton, *An Autobiography* (London, 1917) and A. Peel and J. A. R. Marriott, *Robert Forman Horton* (London, 1937).

Road Congregational Church in Hampstead, London. Both came up to New College, Oxford in 1874, and formed what was to prove a lifelong friendship. The fact that each in successive years was elected President of the Oxford Union indicates both their own ability and their acceptance, as Nonconformists, into 'élite' student society. Neither succumbed to the dangers which T. H. Green had described.

It was Horton, already intent on a future career in the ministry, who was particularly to prepare the way for Mansfield. The son of a Congregational minister, he had spent five years at Tettenhall College, a recently founded Nonconformist school at Wolverhampton, followed by two more years at Shrewsbury, the public school which his father believed could best prepare him for the university course at Oxford or Cambridge which he hoped his son would follow. T. G. Horton, the father, had spent some time at Edinburgh University but otherwise received no formal ministerial training. On hearing of his son's decision to enter the ministry, he wrote (1 December 1892):

> I think it most important that many of our ministers in the future should be educated at those ancient seats of learning. The Puritans shone there once, and why not again? . . . As for our Denominational Colleges, there is not one of them fit for you to enter. The professors are of an inferior order, and very few of the students even approach mediocrity.[22]

R. F. Horton, therefore, charted a course for Nonconformity in Oxford. He had a glittering undergraduate career: President of the Union, President of the New College Essay Society, where 'I enjoyed on the whole the happiest hours I spent in Oxford',[23] college oarsman, and winner of the best First of his year in Greats. After his death, Nathaniel Micklem wrote of his friend's 'wonderful vitality and charm' as an undergraduate, his brilliance as a talker, and his 'nimble wit'.[24] Alongside this brilliance in work and play, Horton was quietly preparing for his future work in the ministry. He visited the poor in the slum areas of Oxford, took a class in the Ragged School in St Ebbe's every Sunday, and regularly attended college chapel services as well as services at George Street Congregational Church.

---

[22] Quoted in Peel and Marriott, *Robert Forman Horton*, 56.
[23] Quoted ibid. 76.   [24] Quoted ibid. 70.

He found the strongest influence in Oxford to be militant agnosticism:

> The time when I entered the University was one of great spiritual upheaval and consequent unrest. Positivism had attracted some of the most brilliant men of the past generation: Congreve, Beasley, Frederic Harrison; and though the religion of Comte . . . had certainly not gained a footing in Oxford, its negative principle, its relegation of theology to the first and lowest of the three stages of human progress, had produced an impression that no one could hold the Christian faith and be abreast of the time. . . . if any scholar of Balliol or a University prize man was a Christian, and contemplated taking orders, he was regarded as a freak.[25]

But in the circles in which Christianity was still accepted, High Anglicanism, in the wake of the Oxford Movement, was still strong:

> The religious life of Oxford at that time was to be found in Puseyite circles. Pusey[26] was still living, a venerated and saintly figure. Canon King[27] followed him at Christ Church as the friend and spiritual guide of a certain section of undergraduates. The Evangelical party maintained a genuine but feeble life. . . . and to be quite candid, the evangelical atmosphere in the university was stifling and unattractive.[28]

From Pusey, whose lectures he attended, he got 'such help as his antiquated and prejudiced scholarship was able to give'.[29]

In 1879 Horton was elected to a probationary Fellowship and Tutorship in Ancient and Modern History at New College. For the next five years, his time was divided between Hampstead and Oxford. In Hampstead he began preaching in the 'little iron church' which was soon to experience metamorphosis into the large Gothic structure in Lyndhurst Road, home of the congregation to which Horton gave the rest of his life. In Oxford he fulfilled his teaching duties, continued to visit in the poorer areas, and took on the role of guide and adviser to Nonconformist undergraduates. It was in

---

[25] Horton, *Autobiography*, 31.

[26] Edward Bouverie Pusey (1800–82), Tractarian leader, was Regius Professor of Hebrew from 1828 until his death in 1882. See *DNB* xvi. 496–504.

[27] Edward King (1829–1910), another Tractarian, and a saintly figure, was Regius Professor of Pastoral Theology 1873–85 before becoming Bishop of Lincoln.

[28] Horton, *Autobiography*, 34–35.   [29] Ibid. 56.

this last role that he helped to prepare the way for Mansfield. And it was this which kept him in Oxford for so long.

In two letters to the *Nonconformist and Independent* (10 March and 7 April 1881) he expressed concern at the number of Nonconformist students who were 'going over' to the Established Church, and asked, 'Can Oxford show a single instance of a Churchman joining the ranks of the Free Churches, as a result of the introduction of those who profess Free Church principles?';[30] 'that fresh and vigorous Nonconformity which was admitted into the ancient citadel by the removal of Religious Tests' was being emasculated.[31] Oxford was tolerant and Nonconformists lacked conviction, so that 'the sepulchral splendour of an established religion is the most convenient veil under which their practical but unconfessed infidelity may escape the eyes of the curious'.[32] There was an urgent practical need for a free society of Nonconformist students which would study Nonconformist principles and provide 'a rallying place' for Nonconformist freshmen.

A leader in the *Nonconformist and Independent* two months later contrasted the conditions of Nonconformity in Cambridge with its position in Oxford:

> Compare our sanctuary at Oxford with the noble building which has been reared at Cambridge,[33] and in which special services are, from time to time, conducted by our most eminent ministers, and a very simple and prosaic reason will be found why, on the whole, the condition of Nonconformity at Cambridge is so flourishing, while at Oxford it is so poor.[34]

The 'sanctuary at Oxford' was George Street Congregational Church, in the centre of the city, founded in 1832 as a secession from New Road Chapel. It was not a particularly strong church, either financially or numerically. When its minister, David Martin, resigned because of ill health in 1879, a few members realized that this was an opportunity to strengthen the Nonconformist presence

---

[30] *Nonconformist and Independent*, 10 Mar. 1881, 217.

[31] Ibid. 7 Apr. 1881, 310.   [32] Ibid.

[33] Emmanuel Church, Cambridge moved to a site in Trumpington Street in 1874. See B. L. Manning, *This Latter House: Emmanuel Church, Cambridge 1874–1924* (Cambridge, 1924).

[34] *Nonconformist and Independent*, 19 May 1881, 471.

in Oxford by inviting a preacher of some eminence, and they were able to attract the support of the University Towns Committee (a committee of the Congregational Union, established in 1881, whose main work was in Cambridge[35]), and even the possibility of financial help.[36] Horton was an obvious candidate, but he turned down an invitation because he already felt committed to Hampstead.[37] Dale Johnson has charted the unsuccessful negotiations and missed opportunities of the church in the 1880s which prevented it from ever exercising the kind of community-cum-university ministry that was established at Emmanuel Church, Cambridge.[38]

Horton, not dismayed but rather emboldened by the lack of response to his letter to the *Nonconformist and Independent* early in 1881, founded a Nonconformists' Union which met with the approval of the new Vice-Chancellor, Benjamin Jowett, in 1882.[39] Fortunately the Minute Book of this Union survives among the Mansfield College Archives.

Seventeen men (we may suppose that women members were not considered), out of a possible 100 Nonconformist undergraduates,[40] gathered in Horton's rooms in New College for the inaugural meeting on 10 May 1881. Horton told the meeting

> that Nonconformity neither got much good, nor did much good in Oxford, and that when men who were Nonconformists went down, they made no better show, because they had been brought up in one form of faith and had come up to be confronted by another very different one, and so they went right into the extreme High

[35] See *Congregational Year Books 1881–4* for the reports of this committee, and A. Peel, *These Hundred Years: A History of the Congregational Union of England and Wales 1831–1931* (London, 1931), 313. Its chief achievement was to arrange some 'Special Sermons' by distinguished preachers at Emmanuel Congregational Church, Cambridge.

[36] George Street Congregational Church Minute Book I, entry for 27 July 1880, Oxfordshire Record Office.

[37] Ibid. 25 Mar. and 1 Apr. 1881.

[38] Dale A. Johnson, 'Pastoral Vacancy and Rising Expectations: The George Street Church, Oxford 1879–86', *JURCHS* 3/4 (Oct. 1984), 131–8. The church was closed in 1933, and the building was then pulled down to make way for a cinema. For Emmanuel Church, Cambridge see Manning, *This Latter House*.

[39] Peel and Marriott, *Robert Forman Horton*, 105.

[40] Although Peel and Marriott assessed the number as 200, the estimate of 100 made by James Bryce in the *Nonconformist and Independent* (19 Apr. 1883) is more likely to be accurate. According to Selbie, the number of graduates and undergraduates who were 'avowed Nonconformists' was 'less then 50'. See Selbie, *Life of Andrew Martin Fairbairn*, 174.

Churchism reaction or else they presented a pitiful spectacle of a chronic suspension of judgment on most vital matters.[41]

They resolved to meet again to draw up a list of objects of their Union and to elect a committee. They declared their desire to help Nonconformist undergraduates who might feel isolated, to learn more about the principles of English Nonconformity, to strengthen their faith, and 'to present to members of the established church the true meaning and aim of Nonconformity'.[42] In addition, a Greek Testament class was to meet regularly on Sundays. Horton was elected chairman, and a committee representing Methodists and Baptists as well as 'Independents' was elected; the Independent members, apart from Horton, were J. P. Legge, Queen's, and Joseph King, Trinity.[43]

At first, there was considerable discussion about the Union's attitude to Disestablishment and the priority to be given to it. In June 1881 Horton urged that 'the aggressive and negative aspects of Nonconformity should not be too prominently put forward but that the positive aims and action of Nonconformists should be insisted upon'.[44] And in the following February, in his inaugural presidential address, James Bryce claimed that Nonconformity 'was not a purely negative principle but embodied the truth of the need of having a free unconstrained spiritual life. . . . The function then of the Union should be to bring men together and make them know and discuss subjects connected with this principle from both the philosophical and historical side.'[45]

This Union met regularly until the opening of the new Mansfield College building. No one could have complained that Horton himself lacked conviction. His address to the Nonconformists' Union on 26 November 1882 castigated the fashionable intellectual 'suspended judgment'; instead he urged his hearers to search for 'certitude' (a sense of certainty). Oxford showed two routes: Newman's way through an external authority, or the alternative way directly through doing God's will as revealed through Christ—'the life and death and

---

[41] Oxford University Nonconformists' Union (OUNU) Minute Book 2, MCA.

[42] Ibid. 4.

[43] Joseph King (1860–1943) was a student at Trinity College, Oxford. He later attended Airedale College, but did not enter the ministry. He was called to the Bar, and served as Liberal MP for North Somerset 1910–18. For some years he was a member of Horton's congregation in Hampstead, and then a member of Haslemere Congregational Church.

[44] OUNU Minute Book 7.   [45] Ibid. 14–15.

resurrection of Christ transacted in your own person'.[46] The latter route he had 'proved and found not wanting'; and this, he claimed, was what Newman would ultimately have found within the Church. It was a powerful address, and even today, the conviction throbs through the pages of the printed sermon.[47]

The Union had influential support. James Bryce, who combined a political career in London (MP for Tower Hamlets at the time) with the Regius Chair of Civil Law in Oxford, and whose own background was Presbyterian, accepted the Presidency and attended several meetings;[48] the Vice-Presidents were Professor T. H. Green, whose premature death early in 1882 meant that he never actually attended, and James Legge,[49] first Oxford Professor of Chinese, and also one of the first Nonconformist Fellows of an Oxford college (Corpus Christi), who had been a missionary with the London Missionary Society in China. W. H. Fremantle, liberal Anglican Chaplain of Balliol, attended and spoke on more than one occasion.

On 20 April 1883 W. B. Selbie, then an undergraduate at Brasenose College, later to become the second Principal of Mansfield, was elected secretary. Three weeks later, on 12 May, A. M. Fairbairn delivered a lecture to the Union on 'The Study of Theology and the Training for the Ministry'. In the discussion which followed, the suggestion was made that a Free Church Theological Hall might be established in Oxford, an idea favoured not only by Nonconformists.[50] After the lecture, 'a distinguished member of the University' (his identity is unknown, but we can assume that he was an Anglican) wrote or spoke to Fairbairn in the following terms:

> There are two points of view, quite other than the denominational from which I would like you to regard this matter. There is only one view of religion here—the High Church view; men must accept it, or they find nothing religious. Many men cannot or will not accept it; and are driven in order to escape from it to deny religion. Such a view of religion as you present—as was presented

---

[46] R. F. Horton, *The Courage of Conviction: An Address Delivered before the Oxford University Nonconformists' Union, 26 November 1882* (Oxford, 1882), 12.

[47] Ibid.

[48] James Bryce (1838–1922), later Viscount Bryce. See *DNB 1922–30*, 127–35. As a Scottish Presbyterian, he had successfully claimed exemption from signing acceptance of the Thirty-Nine Articles when offered a scholarship at Trinity College in 1857.

[49] James Legge (1815–97). See H. E. Legge, *James Legge* (London, 1905).

[50] See Selbie, *Life of Andrew Martin Fairbairn*, 164.

last night—would save these men, or many of them. Some of the finest intellects that come to Oxford are being lost to Christianity for the want of another than the High Church Theology. That other Theology you men of the Free Churches alone can give; you can give it here only by creation of a Theological School that will affect the Universitites; and it is a duty you clearly owe to the nation and to our common religion to give it.[51]

Fairbairn's lecture and the subsequent discussion formed the substance of two articles which appeared in the *British Quarterly Review* in April 1884 by Fairbairn and Bryce.[52] Fairbairn contrasted the situations in England and Scotland. In Scotland, the universities were national institutions, open to all. Professors were held in high esteem, and every village community included graduates; 'this academic spirit had right royal influence.' In England, on the other hand, many communities, such as Bradford where Fairbairn then lived, had been little touched by the ancient universities. Now, however, there was a change—these universities 'are the very foci of all the energies that work for change': 'The fight for the freedom of the Universities was a fight against the tyranny of the Church, but for the authority of Religion; and it is the duty of those who prevailed to see that the end of the tyranny does not also become the death of the authority.' It was the *duty* of the Free Churches to settle in Oxford and Cambridge. 'We are the historical representatives of independence and freedom in religion for the sake of religion.'[53] He advocated the establishment of a Theological Hall whose students would take their first degrees in the older colleges; and whose pulpit would be open to the Nonconformist preachers excluded from college and university pulpits. James Bryce supported this proposal, claiming that it would benefit not only Nonconformity, but the University as well. On the one hand, the future Dissenting ministers would benefit from the teaching of liberal Anglicans such as S. R.

---

[51] Quoted in handwritten circular from Alexander Hannay, Memorial Hall 1884. Book of Building Fund Circulars, MCA.

[52] *British Quarterly Review*, 79 (Apr. 1884), 373–98. Bryce's article was based on a lecture delivered at a meeting convened by W. S. Caine more than a year earlier. See Selbie, *Life of Andrew Martin Fairbairn*, 167. Bryce had also suggested the founding of a Nonconformist college at Oxford or Cambridge during his speech at the ceremony for the laying of the foundation stone of Lyndhurst Road Congregational Church in April 1883, reported in the *Nonconformist and Independent*, 19 Apr. 1883.

[53] Ibid. 380.

Driver[54] and William Sanday, and from the broader cultural environment; on the other, the teaching of Free Church theologians free from 'religious tests' would bear witness to 'the truth that Christianity can and must stand by her own strength'.[55]

Fairbairn visited Oxford again in November 1883 at the behest of the Congregational Union. The *Congregational Year Book* for 1883 had reported that a 'memorial' had been received, 'signed by Fellows, Graduates and Undergraduates of the Universities of Oxford and Cambridge, asking the Union to make arrangements, if possible, for the delivery of lectures by eminent Nonconformists to those towns on such themes as their experience may suggest'.[56] If this request came through the Oxford University Nonconformists' Union, the Minute Book does not record it. The Cambridge plan came to nothing, but three lectures were delivered in the new Examination Schools in Oxford in November 1883: Fairbairn spoke on 'Free Churches and the Ideal of Religion', the Revd Richard Glover, a Baptist, on 'The Place of Faith in Religion', and Dr Eustace Conder on 'The Function of the Christian Ministry'. The Report on the Oxford lectures of 1884 spoke of the importance of a more permanent Nonconformist presence with the University. Though the actual attendance was apparently disappointing, the organizing committee had been encouraged 'by the discovery that not a few men of eminence connected with the universities, though not themselves Nonconformists, looking not to the interests of Nonconformity, but to the interests of the universities as seats of learning, and to the present condition of religious faith in England, are prepared to welcome the teachers of the truth as we hold it'.[57]

By this time Fairbairn and Dale were in communication. On 18 December 1883 (just after Simon had announced his resignation from Spring Hill) Fairbairn wrote to Dale a long letter about the proposed Oxford college, which deserves to be quoted in some detail:

> I am glad to have your letter and to hear what great matters have been before our Spring Hill friends.
>
> The scheme is a two fold one: a Theological School and—pray don't smile at the too large terms—a University Pulpit or Chapel.

---

[54] Samuel Rolles Driver (1846–1914), Regius Professor of Hebrew at Christ Church 1883–1914. *DNB 1912–21*, 162–3.
[55] *British Quarterly Review 79*, 398. [56] *CYB 1883*, 7–8.
[57] *CYB 1885*, 5. See also a letter from W. R. D. Adkins (later Sir Ryland Adkins), Balliol College, in *Nonconformist and Independent*, 6 Dec. 1883.

A. The School. This should not be a Hall or Residential College, but strictly a School, a place devoted to instruction in special subjects. It would not seek to withdraw undergraduates from the older colleges, or keep them from sharing and feeling to the utmost the common life of the university, or undertake any responsibility in connection with literary or degree work: but would be simply a Theological School or College. The men received need not be required to be only Oxford or Cambridge men: they might come from other universities, or our own colleges, the one thing needful being that they be qualified to begin the study of theology as preparatory to the work of the Ministry. This relates, of course, simply to men on the foundation, as it were, but the scheme ought to be elastic enough not only to permit, but to invite the presence of men who either wish to know special departments in Theology, or to make it (the College) their field of academic and moral discipline without being committed to our Ministry.

The number of Professors or Tutors should be not less than four, with the New Testament, the Old Testament, Systematic Divinity, and Church History as their subjects. If it be found possible to have a larger staff, so much the better: room in any case ought to be reserved for occasional Lecturers or readers.

Considering the traditions and customs of Oxford, it would be well to have a fellowship or two carrying tutorial duties, and thus securing the services for a year or two of the more distinguished students who might be put in training for similar posts elsewhere.

B. The Pulpit or Chapel. If a Hall is built the Chapel ought to be made a special feature of it. In any case a Pulpit ought to be instituted, and services maintained, with the view of reaching and influencing members of the university. This Pulpit ought to be so worked as to introduce our foremost men to the mind and spirit of the place. The immediate charge of the Pulpit may be vested in the Senate or Head of the school, the Professors being also Preachers: but opportunity should be afforded for the appearance of selected Preachers, men who should be able by their fresher thought and directer speech to quicken the undergraduate mind. The Pulpit seems to me a matter of prime importance: without it the School would not make its presence sufficiently felt in the university, or serve one of its greatest ends, reach and affect those young men who need to be saved to the Free Churches, while not intended for the Ministry.

But all this implies a School equipped in the most efficient way. And what you say as to endowments seems to me to show how it is possible. Your resources should be made the endowment fund, and the Union challenged to put down a suitable building free of debt. Were the matter well stated, I believe it could be accomplished, and were it, I am sure it would be the greatest work done for and by Independency since 1662.[58]

For Fairbairn and his supporters, it would mean the renewal, in Oxford, of those principles for which Nonconformists had been excluded from Oxford for two centuries.

Five days before Fairbairn wrote that letter, Nonconformity in Oxford suffered a setback; on 13 December Horton left Oxford for good. His decision to leave Oxford for Hampstead and the Congregational ministry at the end of that year had already been made.[59] But his departure was marred by what he felt to be a rejection by the University. Jowett and J. R. Magrath,[60] anxious to strengthen the Nonconformist presence in Oxford, nominated him as an examiner in the Pass Examinations on 'The Rudiments of Faith and Religion', an examination which tested knowledge of parts of the Old and New Testaments and the Thirty-Nine Articles (for which Nonconformists could substitute a Pauline Epistle). Although Horton's nomination was approved on 6 December by a majority of 53 to 44 of Congregation, the body of resident dons, the vote was then challenged and taken to Convocation, in which all Oxford MAs could vote, a week later; on 13 December Convocation overturned Congregation's decision by a majority of 576 to 155. The idea of a Nonconformist examining Anglicans in their knowledge of the Thirty-Nine Articles was more than some of those outside Oxford could take. Though it was not a personal vote against Horton he took it as such, and the wound inflicted remained with him. Years later, he wrote in his autobiography: 'no power known to man can alter the feeling which pervades the Established Church, especially in its stronghold, Oxford, that to differ from the Church and to seek Christian life and service outside its borders is not only schism or heresy, but a disqualification for mingling with polite society, if not

---

[58] Quoted in Selbie, *Life of Andrew Martin Fairbairn*, 167–9.

[59] It was at about this time that he became famous for his remark, 'I will wear no clothes to distinguish me from my fellow Christians.' Others added a comma after the fifth word.

[60] Provost of Queen's 1878–1930, Vice-Chancellor 1894–8.

for taking part in the life of the State'.[61] Though Horton had been the chief inspiration of the Nonconformists' Union, the meetings continued without him, the subjects ranging from social questions, church reform, missions, and the progress of Christianity to the Nonconformist attitude to creeds.

Dale's proposal that Spring Hill should move to either Oxford or Cambridge was first put to a subcommittee of the Spring Hill Management Committee, a subcommittee appointed in December 1883 to consider the future of the College when Simon's decision to leave was reported as final. With this suggestion before it, the Management Committee meeting on 10 January 1884 resolved: 'That a Sub-Committee be appointed for considering the expediency of making Spring Hill College a Theological Hall and removing it to Oxford.'

The actual formal decision to move to Oxford was made by the College's Committee of Management at a special meeting on 22 May 1884, after hearing the report of the subcommittee. Twelve voted in favour, five against, and one was neutral. It was agreed that the new Hall would be non-resident; that the new buildings would be funded by contributions raised from 'friends of the scheme', not from any existing funds; that the level of scholarships should be raised to enable students to take their 'literary courses' as well as their theological courses at Oxford; and that 'a Special Committee of representative Congregationalists be appointed by the Trustees and Committee to assist the Committee in constructing a scheme to give [the proposals] effect'.[62] The next step was to persuade the Spring Hill Trustees of the wisdom of this proposal, and then to negotiate the necessary alterations to the Trust Deed with the Charity Commissioners.

The next few months were spent working out the implications in more detail. In August a deputation from the Trustees and Management Committee met with a representative of the Charity Commissioners, who directed them to prepare two statements, one presenting the grounds on which changes to the Trust Deed were asked for (by the majority), and the other stating the grounds on which a minority had objections to them.

Dale's statement (dated 24 October) on behalf of the majority was prefaced by an analysis of the two main developments which had made such a move to Oxford a necessary course: the opening of the

---

[61] Horton, *Autobiography*, 59.

[62] Minute Book of Spring Hill College Committee of Management and Mansfield Council 1866–1916, entry for 22 May 1884. MCA.

ancient universities to Nonconformists, and the reorganization of grammar schools, where the ambitious sons of many Congregational families were receiving an education which prepared them for entry to Oxford and Cambridge. A college such as Spring Hill would hardly attract such men. 'A very considerable number of young men belonging to the lower middle classes—which form a large proportion of every Congregational Church—now receive an education which would have been altogether beyond their reach in 1826, and by means of Exhibitions many of them find their way to Oxford and Cambridge.' He then sought to demonstrate that the original intentions of the founders would still be maintained, though modified to meet changing circumstances. The original deed had allowed for the support of 'all or any of the Colleges or Seminaries belonging to Paedobaptist Protestant Dissenters in England'; and it was not stipulated that such a college should provide an 'initiatory' as well as a theological course. It had also required the assent of Trustees, members of Committee, and professors to a series of theological definitions, while students were allowed to declare their belief in their own words, and the Board of Education was left to determine whether it satisfied the requirements of the Deed. But Dale pointed out that at least two of the theological professors had been allowed to state their belief in their own words. He therefore suggested the same flexibility for all signatories, as well as 'a slight verbal change in the creed itself'.[63]

The minority view (undated, but presumably also October), presented by the Committee Chairman, J. A. Cooper, was that the College should remain in Birmingham (though the minority agreed with the majority that the College should in future be non-residential, with its teaching confined to theology). They preferred a link with the new Mason's College in Birmingham (founded in 1880); they pointed to the clauses in the Trust Deed which laid down that the College should not be more than 5 miles from Birmingham, that Trustees should live within 30 miles, and that some Trustees should be members of Ebenezer Chapel; and doubted the wisdom of surrendering 'the healthy influence of the life of a large town' in favour of the rarefied atmosphere of Oxford.[64]

On 3 December the Charity Commissioners replied that they were

[63] See Minute Book of Spring Hill College Committee of Management and Mansfield Council 1866–1916, entry for 16 Dec. 1884, which includes Dale's statement.

[64] Ibid., for Cooper's letter.

59

prepared in principle to support the wish of the majority.[65] Dale
wrote to his wife on 6 December that he was encouraged by an
interview with one of the Commissioners that morning, adding, 'It
is a great business; one of the greatest that I have ever had a hand
in, and it means much anxious work for the next two years.'[66]

These negotiations with the Charity Commissioners were reported
to the Committee of Management at its meeting on 16 December.
The decision to move was now accepted by the whole committee
without rancour, and six months later the subscribers too gave their
approval. Meanwhile, on 17 February 1885, it was agreed that the
name of the College should be changed to Mansfield College in
honour of its founders. The Annual Report 1885–6 noted:

> Fitly is the new College called by the name of the large-hearted
> family in whose Christian loyalty and zeal it had its origin; and,
> as it will be a training-school for a truly Protestant and Evangelical
> Ministry, it is a co-incidence of more than passing interest that it
> also bears the name of that particular district in the great Father-
> land of Germany, in which was nurtured the young life of MARTIN
> LUTHER.[67]

Finally, in September 1885 the difficulty over the declaration of
faith was resolved in a compromise measure; Trustees and professors
alone were to make the following affirmation, in their own words
if they wished:

> That he believes in the Unity of the Godhead, Father, Son and
> Holy Spirit: in the Divinity of Christ, in the atonement from sin
> made by His Death; and in man's need of the Spirit to re-
> enlighten his mind and renew his heart; that he believes the Holy
> Scriptures to contain a revelation of God's grace to man and the
> rule of man's faith and duty to God; and that he accepts and
> approves the practice of Infant Baptism. He shall also declare that
> he is a Dissenter from the Established Church.[68]

Others were not required to subscribe in this way. 'With this concession the advocates of freedom had to be content.'[69] It was now

---

[65] Ibid., for the reply of the Charity Commissioners.
[66] Quoted ibid. 500. [67] *Spring Hill College Annual Report 1885–86*, 17.
[68] Minute Book of the Spring Hill College Committee of Management and Mansfield
College Council 1866–1916, 445, MCA. 'Plenary inspiration' in the earlier form was here
replaced by 'a revelation of God's grace'.
[69] Dale, *Life of R. W. Dale*, 498.

agreed by the Charity Commissioners that the Spring Hill Endowment could be used for the support of a college in Oxford, provided that none of it was put towards the cost of the new building.

Reports of this compromise found little favour in the Cambridge Nonconformist Union (founded 1883 in succession to the Cambridge University Society for Religious Equality, after the virtual abolition of clerical Fellowships), where news of the negotiations over the declaration of faith in the Trust Deed had prompted a resolution against the founding of any Nonconformist college at either Oxford or Cambridge; such a declaration seemed to the Cambridge society to be a reversion to sectarian education. Fairbairn had a rough ride when he visited Cambridge in May 1886 and tried to explain the aims and purpose of Mansfield.[70] But one of the leaders of that opposition, John (later Sir John) McClure, later 'fell under the spell' of Fairbairn, and frequently preached in Mansfield Chapel.[71]

On 14 March 1885 Dale had written to Alexander Mackennal,[72] minister of Bowdon Downs Congregational Church, near Manchester, who later succeeded Dale as Chairman of the Mansfield College Council: 'Fairbairn is invited to be Principal and Professor of Dogma. I think he will accept: indeed I would never have gone so far with the scheme unless I had had the strongest reason for believing that he would.'[73]

The formal invitation to Fairbairn to become Principal was sent in March 1885. Wishing to be certain that the invitation was to Oxford and nowhere else, and that the changes in the Trust Deed were fully approved by the Charity Commission, he delayed acceptance until the negotiations were completed in September. The Spring Hill Committee of Management heard of his letter of acceptance on 15 October.

Andrew Martin Fairbairn ensured that Mansfield College was respected from the beginning of its life in Oxford. He had already made his mark as Chairman of the Congregational Union in 1883, and had established an impressive reputation as Principal of Airedale College for the training of Congregational ministers in Bradford

---

[70] See the *Nonconformist and Independent*, 11 June 1885, and Selbie, *Life of Andrew Martin Fairbairn*, 194–7.

[71] *MCM* 12/2 (June 1922), 29.

[72] Alexander Mackennal (1835–1905). See Dugald Macfadyen, *Alexander Mackennal* (London, 1905).

[73] Quoted Dale, *Life of R. W. Dale*, 501.

since 1877. He was one of a considerable company of scholars educated in Scotland who have enriched the life of Mansfield.

Fairbairn was born in Inverkeithing, Fife in November 1838, almost exactly one month after the opening of Spring Hill College. His father, a miller, and his mother were members of the United Secession Church, the Church which was soon to unite with the Relief Synod to form the United Presbyterian Church. From his mother 'there came everything that ever went to make any man of me that is'.[74] The family moved to Edinburgh when he was 6, but their poverty compelled the young Fairbairn to leave school when he was 9 and to work as an errand boy. His mother encouraged him to read, and for the next ten years, during the time when his more privileged contemporaries were receiving secondary education, he was doing hard practical work in shops, or in a flour mill, during the day, and studying in the evenings.

It was not long before the young Fairbairn began that theological pilgrimage which was to lead him eventually to English Congregationalism. He left the Secession Church of his parents and joined the Evangelical Union, founded by James Morison in 1843. Morison had moved from the Calvinism of his United Secession minister father, through moderate Calvinism, to a belief in Universal Atonement. For preaching this doctrine, he and three other ministers were excommunicated from the Secession Church in 1841; Morison's congregation in Kilmarnock left with him. In 1843, he and twelve others formed the Evangelical Union, and were then joined by some ministers and ministers-in-training of the Scottish Congregational Union (formed 1812) who had also rejected the narrow view of the Atonement. The new denomination grew quite rapidly, so that by 1875 there were eighty-two Evangelical Union churches. It was under the influence of the Evangelical Union Church in Leith, where the Revd Joseph Boyle was minister, that Fairbairn decided at the age of 18 to prepare for the ministry.

Thus when Fairbairn entered the Evangelical Union Academy in Glasgow (where Morison himself taught) in 1857 at the age of 19, he was already coming under the influence of Congregational thought, and the transition to English Congregationalism later in his life seems not to have presented any difficulty to him. The fact that the Evangelical Union merged with the Congregational Union of

---

[74] Quoted Selbie, *Life of Andrew Martin Fairbairn*, 309.

Scotland in 1894 indicates that there were no serious theological differences.[75]

The Evangelical Union Academy held its classes during August and September, enabling the students to attend University classes during term. Thus Fairbairn combined study at the Academy with attendance at classes at Edinburgh University. He found Morison 'an unsparing critic', 'exact and laborious as a scholar'; and, looking back in later life, he reflected that 'the narrow circle within which he moved and to which he had been shut up, did not tend to broaden his mind'.[76] The University, on the other hand, offered a wider, philosophical perspective.

Formally qualified three years later, he became minister of a church in Bathgate, a country town between Edinburgh and Glasgow. Here he worked prodigiously hard, rising every day at 5.30 a.m. and spending long hours in his study. But his reading brought him to a crisis; he found he could no longer accept the theology in which he had been trained, confessing to a friend that 'he had not an inch of ground beneath his feet'. In desperation he temporarily gave up his pastorate and left for Germany in 1865.

> Well do I remember the day when, feeling cheerless, forsaken of God, unpitied and unblest of men, I left the manse to take my way to Germany, never expecting to return. Life seemed a ruin; all its plans had been thrown down; and in the desolation one's best and only hope was to find in journalism a new pulpit, and in literature a mode of speech more suitable to living men.[77]

It is not clear how he financed this. What is evident is that he found happiness and a liberation of spirit, especially in the company of the other students. In a land 'seething with controversies' he learned from the professors 'that doubt was not sin but rather a growing pain of the soul, a means to a wider outlook and a clearer faith'.[78] One of those he heard was Simon's hero, Isaak Dorner, who later stated that 'of all the Scottish students he had known Fairbairn had most impressed him, on account of the union in him of the scientific

---

[75] See H. Escott, *A History of Scottish Congregationalism* (Glasgow, 1960).

[76] A. M. Fairbairn, introd. to O. Smeaton, *Principal James Morison: The Man and his Work* (Edinburgh, 1902), p. xxvi.

[77] A. M. Fairbairn, 'Experience in Theology: A Chapter of Autobiography', *CR* 91 (Apr. 1907), 558.

[78] Selbie, *Life of Andrew Martin Fairbairn*, 37.

mind and the sincerely pious heart'.[79] His later account[80] gives the impression not of one or two predominant influences, but of a host of stimulating teachers and ideas which helped him to formulate his own theological system, interpreted through the Eternal Son and the Eternal Father, a system which found its main expression in Fairbairn's *The Place of Christ in Modern Theology* (1893). The result was that 'theology changed from a system doubted to a system believed. But the system believed was not the old system which had been doubted.'[81] In place of a concentration on predestination, human depravity, and the possibility of free will, he learned to consider new questions concerning the nature of God, Christ, and their relationship. Thus strengthened and matured, he returned to Bathgate to preach a 'larger and nobler Christianity'. In 1870 the Evangelical Union elected him as its Chairman for the year.

In 1872 he began a five-year ministry at St Paul's Street Evangelical Union Church in Aberdeen. Here he wrote his first book, *Studies in the Philosophy of Religion and History*,[82] which revealed his lifelong interest in the historical development of religion, and first brought his work to the attention of F. Max Müller (whom he later knew in Oxford).[83] His Sunday evening lectures drew large audiences; among them was the young P. T. Forsyth,[84] destined to become Congregationalism's finest theologian of the early twentieth century. He continued his contributions to scholarly journals which he had begun in Bathgate, and turned his ambitions towards an academic post. His applications for the Chairs of Moral Philosophy at Aberdeen and St Andrews failed (his connection with the Evangelical Union was not a recommendation in that context), but there soon followed an invitation to be Principal of the Airedale College, the Congregational college in Bradford.[85] In July 1877 he moved south to Yorkshire.

Fairbairn thus entered the world of English Congregationalism just before the Leicester Conference. Airedale College was descended

---

[79] Quoted in the *British Monthly* (Christmas 1901).

[80] Fairbairn, 'Experience in Theology'.   [81] Ibid. 568.

[82] A. M. Fairbairn, *Studies in the Philosophy of Religion and History* (London, 1876).

[83] Friedrich Max Müller (1823–1900) was a Fellow of All Souls and Professor of Comparative Philology in Oxford. See *DNB XXII: Supplement*, 1023–9.

[84] Peter Taylor Forsyth (1848–1921). See W. L. Bradley, *P. T. Forsyth: The Man and his Work* (London, 1952), and *DNB: Missing Persons*, 230–1.

[85] Though it seems that he was not the first to be invited to that post. George Deane, tutor at Spring Hill, had received a prior invitation (which he declined) in the autumn of 1876. Minute Book of the Spring Hill College of Management and Mansfield College Council 1866–1916, entry for 6 Nov. 1876. MCA.

from a private Dissenting Academy; and like Spring Hill it offered a course which combined arts and theology. Fairbairn now achieved for Airedale what the Committee for College Reform had failed to do for other colleges; he separated the two courses and arranged for his students to take their arts courses in Edinburgh University. They returned from Edinburgh to face a rigorous theological training. With dour determination, Fairbairn then demanded the highest standards from his students. For him, ministry

> demanded the most strenuous virtues, and must be undertaken by those only who were prepared to pay the price of absolute devotion. Ignorant dogmatism, superficial sentimentality, puerile and unworthy handling of the sacred Scriptures, dependence on pulpit helps, and every other substitute for hard work he could not endure. Upon them he poured torrents of burning, blistering scorn with such fierceness that the memory of his look and tone no years can efface.[86]

He refused to enter his students for the examinations of the Senatus Academicus, on the grounds that the syllabus was too rigid and the standard too low.[87]

Not only within the College, but within the whole denomination, he quickly gained respect, not least at the Leicester Congregational Union Assembly.[88] Within three years he had been elected Chairman of the Yorkshire Congregational Union, and three years later still was elected to the Chair of the Congregational Union of England and Wales. He was brought to even wider notice. This man, Dale recognized, could represent Nonconformity in Oxford on equal terms with Anglicans.

On 7 October 1885 Fairbairn addressed an enthusiastic audience at the autumnal meetings of the Congregational Union in Hanley on 'The Sacerdotal and the Puritan Idea', contrasting the Catholic and Puritan conceptions of the Church, and recalling his hearers to the high ideals of Congregationalism.[89] One of the audience on that occasion, F. H. Stead, wrote of the way in which Fairbairn

---

[86] Quoted in Selbie, *Life of Andrew Martin Fairbairn*, 95–6.

[87] *Nonconformist and Independent*, 26 May 1881, 504–5.

[88] See ibid. 24 May 1877, 1065.

[89] Published in A. M. Fairbairn, *Studies in Religion and Theology* (London, 1910), 109–41.

gradually wound up the assembly to a pitch of enthusiasm that the most rapturous political meeting has rarely paralleled. The audience responded to every point with the wildest demonstrations of sympathy, until the cheering grew almost frantic and incessant. When Fairbairn at last sat down and the tempest of applause had subsided, Dr Dale turned to him and said, 'There now, you have built Mansfield, topstone and all.'[90]

The editorial in the next edition of the *Congregationalist* stated that 'By universal confession Dr Fairbairn's paper on the new Sacerdotalism was one of the most powerful utterances to which the Union has listened. . . . Those who heard it felt that Protestantism has no abler champion in our day.'[91] It was just three weeks later, on 31 October, that Fairbairn was in Oxford to address an extraordinary meeting of the Nonconformists' Union, with James Bryce in the chair, on the forthcoming foundation of Mansfield College in Oxford.

Dale had already enlisted the support of prominent members of the Congregational Union. He had convened a meeting on 7 July 1885 at the Memorial Hall in Farringdon Street in London, which led to the formation of a Building Committee, whose function was to raise the money for the site and buildings; the group included Alexander Hannay (Secretary of the Congregational Union),[92] Alexander Mackennal (Chairman of the Congregational Union in 1886), R. F. Horton, Henry Allon,[93] and two laymen, Albert Spicer[94] and Abraham Haworth, as well as Dale and Fairbairn.[95] Albert Spicer was appointed Treasurer for London, Jesse Haworth[96] for the north of England. Circulars were sent out appealing for money for a project 'not only of prime importance for the Congregational denomination', but one which 'can hardly fail to have a powerful effect on the theological thought and the religious life of the nation'.[97] Over the next four years, it drew into its orbit many of the wealthy Congregational families.

---

[90] Quoted Selbie, *Life of Andrew Martin Fairbairn*, 144–5.
[91] *Congregationalist* (Nov. 1885), 834.
[92] Alexander Hannay (1822–90). See *CYB 1891*, 176–80.
[93] Henry Allon (1818–92). See *CYB 1893*, 202–5.
[94] See *Albert Spicer 1847–1934* by one of his family (London, 1938).
[95] See Building Committee Minute Book, MCA.
[96] Abraham and Jesse Haworth were brothers, Manchester businessmen.
[97] Circular 5 Jan. 1886. Building Fund Book of Circulars etc. MCA.

Meanwhile in February 1885 the Spring Hill Committee of Management had sent a deputation to Oxford to seek a site for the new college. Dr Legge had first guided them to The Willows, a Private Hall run by the Revd H. J. Turrell, now in financial difficulties because of new University regulations, on the south-west side of Magdalen Bridge.[98] When negotiations for this property failed, their attention was focused on part of the fields of Holywell Manor belonging to Merton College.[99] The fact that Merton's Governing Body, presided over by Warden Brodrick, was liberal in sympathy must have eased the negotiations with Mansfield's representatives.[100] On 24 October Dale, Fairbairn, and other members of the subcommittee visited Oxford to inspect the site. A week later Fairbairn lunched with Jowett, dined with Bryce, and addressed a meeting of students and friends. On 2 November both the Spring Hill Committee of Management and the Building Committee meeting in London agreed to negotiate the purchase of the proposed site, and on 21 December they accepted Merton's terms—£3,000, together with £300 adjudged to be the cost of building a road through the site to join Holywell and South Parks Road (now Mansfield Road). It is doubtful whether they realized that the land they were purchasing included part of the remains of the 'royalist ramparts' which Charles I had persuaded the unwilling citizenry of Oxford to construct in 1642.[101]

A decision had to be made about the existing Spring Hill students. Fairbairn insisted that every student who entered the new Mansfield College should be properly qualified to begin a postgraduate theological course. He told the Committee of Management: 'The character of the College will be stamped even more by its first students

---

[98] See H. J. Turrell, *Letters 1887–96*, Bodleian Library. A few years later, The Willows was pulled down to be replaced by a boarding-house for Magdalen College School. See C. E. Mallet, *A History of the University of Oxford*, iii (London, 1927), 471.

[99] An area once known as 'Pinfold's Pasture'. The Oxford University Reform Act of 1854 and the Universities and Colleges Estates Acts of 1858–80 had greatly facilitated the sale of land by Oxford colleges, and much of this land had been sold already, not only for the University Museum and the nucleus of a University science area, but also for domestic houses on the south side of what is now South Parks Road. The land to the north of Holywell and to the east of Wadham College was now being developed, and during the 1880s was sold not only to Mansfield, but also to Balliol, to New College, and to the new Manchester College.

[100] I am indebted to Dr Roger Highfield of Merton College for much of this information.

[101] The Oxford Archaeological Unit did some excavation of the site before work began on the construction of a new residential building in 1992.

than by its first Professors: instruction must always bear some relation to the state of the instructed, and so this must be at a given degree.'[102] After each student was considered in turn, it was agreed that six should be supported in a University arts course to qualify them for admission to Mansfield, while of the remaining six, five would transfer to Cheshunt or Brecon Colleges, and one was to leave.[103] Dr John Massie was to move to Mansfield and join Fairbairn there. Dr Deane, whose expertise in science and mathematics was no longer needed, and about whom the students had raised several complaints, would leave the College, to live in retirement until his death a few years later.

Fairbairn took up residence in north Oxford after Easter in 1886, and was given leave to find temporary premises for the College for two years. He found rooms at 90 High Street; of the two main rooms, one had been Charles I's headquarters during the siege of Oxford in 1646, while the other formed the premises of the Oxford Union when Gladstone was a member. On 26 May the *Oxford Magazine* welcomed him and prophesied that 'Oxford Theology, and Oxford at large, should gain much from his residence here'.[104]

The new College moved to Oxford supported not only by the Committee of Management and Trustees of Spring Hill, and by many individual influential Congregationalists, but also by the Congregational Union and by many Anglican as well as Nonconformist members of the University. Hopes were high.

[102] Minute Book of Spring Hill College Committee of Management and Mansfield College Council 1866–1916, 20 May 1886. MCA.
[103] Ibid. 16 Sept. 1886.   [104] *Oxford Magazine* (1886), 199.

IV

Mansfield College, Oxford

An ornament of victory and a symbol of duty.[1]

MANSFIELD College opened in a mood of great optimism. The Burial Laws Amendment Act of 1880 had removed the last serious Nonconformist official social disability. In 1851 the Religious Census had revealed that attendances at Anglican and Nonconformist places of worship were almost equal in England. By 1901, almost half the active church-goers of the non-Roman Catholic churches in England and Wales were Nonconformists. Their wealth, the fact that they were the most powerful group supporting the Liberal Party, and their galaxy of famous preachers in London and elsewhere, all contributed to an optimism about their future which history did not finally bear out.[2] But the optimism of the time was reflected in the preparations made in 1886 and 1887 for the building of the new College, and in the celebrations planned for its opening.

The new College began work at 90 High Street in the first week of October 1886. Benjamin Jowett was about to finish his term of office as Vice-Chancellor of the University, and, as a friend of the new enterprise, made a point of welcoming Mansfield in his last official speech: 'Neque debemus omittere Collegium de Mansfield cuius etiam nunc fundamina ponuntur, institutum in usum scholarium ab Ecclesia Anglicana dissentientium: quos olim aversabatur Academia, nunc hospitio excipit.'[3] These words were reported in the *Oxford Magazine* for 20 October 1886.[4] The same issue referred to Fairbairn's inaugural lecture on 'The Study of Theology and the

---

[1] A. M. Fairbairn speaking in Liverpool as reported in *Liverpool Mercury*, 29 Mar. 1887.
[2] See James Munson, *The Nonconformists: In Search of a Lost Culture* (London, 1991) for a detailed portrait of Nonconformity during the last quarter of the 19th cent.
[3] 'Nor should we fail to mention Mansfield College, the foundations of which are even now being laid, an establishment for students dissenting from the Church of England: those whom the University once spurned it now warmly welcomes.'
[4] *Oxford Magazine*, 20 Oct. 1886, 301.

Theological Student' as a lecture of 'great breadth and power'; 'the ideal set forth in the lecture was a high one: if the studies of Mansfield College at all approach it, a very valuable element will have been added to Oxford life.'[5] Fairbairn himself was given a personal welcome by Exeter College, who elected him a member of their Common Room, where he frequently dined on Sunday evenings.[6]

Mansfield itself was not part of the University, but it was intended that all its students and staff, individually, would be matriculated members through another college. Those who were not already members of a college were to register through the Delegacy for Non-collegiate Students.[7] In order to avoid exclusiveness, Mansfield was to be non-residential.

Fairbairn was aware of the magnitude of the task facing him. At the end of the first term, he wrote in his report that the College had

> endeavoured to steal quietly into what is but a provisional state of being, feeling that nothing should be said or done to imply that it had actually begun to be. But newspapers reported, editors criticised, the *Times* approved, the *Saturday* reviled, the *Spectator*, in its superfinest manner, blundered or moralised; and we, in our poor provisional, unequipped, unhoused state, had to bear the counsels and criticisms of those who wished us so well that they insisted on our being born perfect, as well as the satire and the predictions of those who may even esteem it a compliment to be regarded as having wished us ill.[8]

He was able to provide the vision as well as the energy to create the institution:

> Mansfield is simply, in its own order, the greatest positive denominational enterprise on which our churches have entered since the

[5] Ibid. 290.

[6] Among his colleagues there were Professor Sanday, the classicist Ingram Bywater, and L. R. Farnell; William Ince, Regius Professor of Divinity, was an Honorary Fellow. William Morris and Edward Burne-Jones were also Honorary Fellows who occasionally dined in the College; it is interesting to speculate whether Fairbairn ever talked with them there. See L. R. Farnell, *An Oxonian Looks Back* (London, 1934).

[7] This was a society founded in 1868 for students not in membership of a college of the University, in an effort to widen the opportunities for the sons of less affluent families. See R. R. Trotman and E. J. K. Garrett, *The Non-collegiate Students and St Catherine's Society* (Oxford, 1962). In 1931 its name was changed to St Catherine's Society, and in 1956 it was transformed into St Catherine's College.

[8] A. M. Fairbairn, 'Our First Term and its Moral', Dec. 1886, Building Fund Circulars, MCA.

Act of Uniformity. It is not an assertion of right, but a performance of duty, and duty which rises out of conquered and conceded
rights.

. . . Mansfield is an attempt to raise the ideal and status of the
minister and the ministerial office.[9]

Students were not required to take the University Theology Schools
Examination,[10] but many chose to do so. Fairbairn himself lectured
on the philosophy of religion, and his colleague John Massie taught
New Testament. The students went out of College to attend lectures
and tutorials given by some of the more liberal Anglican theologians: William Sanday, Dean Ireland Professor, T. K. Cheyne, Oriel
Professor of the Interpretation of Holy Scripture, S. R. Driver, Regius
Professor of Hebrew, and Edwin Hatch, Reader in Ecclesiastical
History. Some students attended Dr Gore's[11] lectures at the newly
founded Pusey House.[12] At the end of the first term, Fairbairn reported that 'the Hebrew tutor G. J. Spurrell of Balliol and Drs Sanday
and Hatch have spoken most cordially of the character, energy and
work of the men'. It was a tribute to the close partnership and
friendship which Fairbairn established with these men that when
Edwin Hatch died shortly after the opening of the new building in
1889, leaving unpublished the manuscript of his 1888 Hibbert Lectures, it was Fairbairn who was asked to edit the work for publication;[13] that the College received 200 volumes from Hatch's library;[14]
and that a memorial service for Hatch was held in Mansfield College
Chapel.[15]

Just as Spring Hill first opened its doors to nine students, so did
Mansfield, though only five of these actually began their theological
course in 1886. But there were two radical changes from Spring Hill.
Every student of the College was already a graduate; and none was

---

[9] Ibid.

[10] For the BA degree in Theology, instituted by statute 27 May 1869 and first examined in 1870.

[11] Charles Gore (1853–1932), later Bishop of Oxford.

[12] Pusey House was founded in 1884 in St Giles in memory of E. B. Pusey. It was
originally known as the Dr Pusey Memorial Library, as it housed the former professor's
large theological library. In addition, the House offered, and still offers, pastoral care
and theological instruction to members of the University.

[13] Edwin Hatch, *Greek Influence on Christianity*, ed. A. M. Fairbairn (London, 1890).

[14] See W. B. Selbie, *The Life of Andrew Martin Fairbairn* (London, 1914), 189.

[15] Fairbairn's sermon on that occasion is printed in S. C. Hatch (ed.), *Memorials of
Edwin Hatch MA* (London, 1890), pp. xxxvii–xliii.

resident, even when the new building was opened. Lunch and dinner were provided, however, and every student was expected to dine in Hall at least five days each week during term. There was no charge for tuition, but students had to find the money for accommodation and University dues. In 1896 this was estimated to be just over £50: the cost of board and lodging for twenty-five weeks of the year was assessed at £43.15.0, and the dues at just over £9.[16] Several scholarships were available both for graduates starting their theological course, and for arts students intending to proceed to the ordination course. There was a steady flow of new applications, so that, by the time the new buildings were opened three years later, there were seventeen students at work, and several more admitted.[17] Fairbairn worked indefatigably to build up a Nonconformist centre for undergraduates. He frequently entertained them in his own home, and arranged regular Sunday evening services and lectures.

However valuable Mansfield's contribution, it was to be many years before the College was to take its full place in Oxford theological life. Though the Acts of Parliament of 1854, 1871, and 1877 had effectively broken the Anglican monopoly of Oxford, the seven Divinity Professorships, and Divinity degrees (that is, the degrees of BD and DD, as distinct from the new BA degree in Theology) were still restricted to clergy of the Church of England or of churches in communion with it; the ex officio places on the Theology Faculty Board were confined to Anglicans; the college chapels were Anglican foundations and were required to hold services of the Church of England; and the College Visitors, to whom appeals could be made, were usually Anglican bishops.

Among the Anglican theologians were many who were prepared to welcome a Nonconformist presence in Oxford. No one had been more welcoming than Edwin Hatch; 'at length he saw a chance of a true and scientific school of Theology springing up in the University.'[18] In an article in the *Methodist Times* (11 June 1885), written at the invitation of the editor (Hugh Price Hughes), Hatch had predicted that a Nonconformist presence in the University 'would show the possibility of a vigorous Christianity which believes in Christ and yet is not sacerdotal. It would stimulate those latent forces within the Church of England itself, which the want of a leader, and

---

[16] *Information for Intending Candidates* (1896), MCA.
[17] *Report of the Committee of Management, Mansfield College Oxford 1889–90*, 11.
[18] Article in *Christian World*, quoted in Hatch, *Memorials*, p. xxiv.

the want of a creed, have either crushed into quiescence or diverted into the insufficient channels of philanthropy.' It would provide a focus, or rallying point, for those of liberal, yet evangelical, views; while to Nonconformists, the University would offer culture, 'the special product of University life'. For the nation, it would ensure that the growing political influence of Nonconformists would be 'an educated influence'.[19]

There was now a new and more open approach to theology among the more conservative scholars. After the death of Pusey, the last survivor of the Tractarian movement in Oxford, in 1882, the more original Oxford minds within the orthodox theological establishment felt freer to express what they already believed. *Lux Mundi: A Series of Studies in the Religion of the Incarnation*, which appeared in 1889, shortly after the opening of Mansfield's new building, was a collection of essays by Oxford theologians who had met together regularly between 1875 and 1885; the authors, many of whom had been taught or influenced by Jowett or Green, wanted to mediate between the conservative view that religious truth was guaranteed by tradition and revelation, and the liberal view that knowledge and truth could be arrived at by human enquiry. The book, which marked a watershed in Anglican thinking, inevitably aroused vigorous controversy.[20]

Charles Gore, editor of *Lux Mundi*, and author of what proved to be its most controversial chapter on 'The Holy Spirit and Inspiration', was Principal of Pusey House. When Fairbairn had visited Oxford in November 1885 to make arrangements for the new Congregational College, Gore was one of many people he consulted: 'one of the finest and best was a High Churchman named Gore,' he wrote to his wife; 'I got some valuable hints from him as to what may be attempted and how.'[21]

It was considered essential that the buildings of the new College

---

[19] Quoted in *Mansfield College, Oxford: Its Origin and Opening* (London, 1890), 245–50.
[20] The book was refused by the Oxford University Press because some of the delegates thought it would 'open the floodgates'. See G. L. Prestige, *The Life of Charles Gore* (London, 1935). The contributors were taken aback by the hostility the book aroused in some quarters: 'we ourselves seemed to ourselves to have been saying those things for years; and to have heard everybody else saying them. Now suddenly we find it all spoken of as a bomb.' H. Scott Holland to Bishop Copleston, quoted in S. Paget, *Henry Scott Holland* (London, 1921), 281.
For a modern discussion, see Peter Hinchliff, *God and History: Aspects of British Theology 1875–1914* (Oxford, 1992), ch. 5.
[21] Quoted Selbie, *Life of Andrew Martin Fairbairn*, 193.

should express the confidence—a very new and as yet untested confidence—which Congregationalists now felt in establishing a presence in Oxford. Oxford had experienced much new building in the early 1880s, notably the new Examination Schools in the High Street: the architect was T. G. Jackson, who won the commission in competition with several other architects, among them Basil Champneys, the runner-up. Mansfield had to be able to hold its own in this environment. Two architects were invited to submit plans for the new Mansfield College: Alfred Waterhouse and Basil Champneys. The name of Alfred Waterhouse (1830–1905) was the suggestion of two Congregational Manchester businessmen, Abraham Haworth and Joseph Thompson;[22] Manchester was the place where most of Waterhouse's early work was done.[23] Basil Champneys (1842–1935) was suggested by other members of the Committee.[24] Waterhouse, the senior of the two, was offered £200 for his plan; Champneys was offered £120. Both had recently worked in Oxford: Waterhouse had designed a new range of buildings for Balliol, and in 1878 was responsible for the new Oxford Union Debating Hall; Champneys had recently extended the buildings of Lady Margaret Hall (following his extensive work for Newnham College in Cambridge), had developed the New College buildings along Holywell Street, and had designed the new Indian Institute on the corner of Holywell and Catte Street.

Waterhouse's plan (pl. 3)—a 'tired piece of French Renaissance'[25]—was rejected in favour of Champneys's ambitious but more harmonious Gothic plan.[26] When the Building Committee met on 31 January 1887, the purchase of an additional piece of land on the same site for a further £3,000 in order to give more space for building and grounds was agreed, and tenders were sought for the new building. Parnells of Rugby, who had worked on Keble College, were chosen, although the Oxford firm Kingerlees were employed to lay

---

[22] Alderman Joseph Thompson, a cotton spinner, was the future father-in-law of Mansfield's second Principal, W. B. Selbie.

[23] Waterhouse designed Manchester's new Town Hall, and Joseph Thompson was on the subcommittee responsible for it. He also designed Ancoats Congregational Chapel for Thompson, and other buildings for Abraham Haworth. See C. Cunningham and P. Waterhouse, *Alfred Waterhouse 1830–1903: The Biography of a Practice* (Oxford, 1992).

[24] See Building Committee Minute Book, MCA.

[25] J. C. G. Binfield, *So Down to Prayers: Studies in English Nonconformity* (London, 1977), 167.

[26] Waterhouse's original plans are in Mansfield College Library; Champneys's plans are in the Oxford City Library (and copies in Mansfield College Library).

3. Alfred Waterhouse's rejected design for Mansfield College

the foundation,[27] and work began in April 1887. The new building rising from its foundations caught the eye of the mathematics don at Christ Church, who included a walk down the new road between Holywell and Parks Road in *Isa's Visit to Oxford*: 'They saw "Mansfield College", a new College just begun to be built, with such tremendously narrow windows that Isa was afraid the young gentlemen who come there will not be able to see to learn their lessons, and will go away from Oxford just as wise as they came.'[28]

Two and a half years later Basil Champneys's 'most coherent and satisfactory achievement in the Gothic style'[29] was opened on what proved to be one of late nineteenth-century Congregationalism's proudest days. It aroused sufficient interest for the plans and drawings of the interior to be displayed at the Royal Academy in 1891.[30]

Champneys, who learned his architectural skills under John Prichard, diocesan surveyor of Llandaff, once wrote that the dogma according to which he had been trained was 'No salvation out of the thirteenth century'.[31] However, as he developed his own style, he preferred fifteenth-century Gothic; half his buildings, including Mansfield, were in Gothic, the other half in Queen Anne style. As an architect, he was 'refined and scholarly, rather than highly original',[32] and belonged 'to that unobtrusive school who do good work by stealth and blush to find it lionised'; 'there is a refined dignity about his buildings which but few of his contemporaries ever reach.'[33] The challenge he faced in designing Mansfield was to produce a collegiate building without student residential accommodation. He followed the traditional medieval style, preferring to employ a two-storey pattern (rather than the usual three-storey), since this showed the Chapel and Hall to better advantage.[34] Fairbairn was closely involved with the planning and received advice not only from the Building Committee, but from sympathetic Anglicans like Hatch, Jowett, and W. H. Fremantle.

[27] *Architect*, 21 Oct. 1887. The Kingerlee family was associated with George Street Congregational Church.

[28] Lewis Carroll, 'Isa's Visit to Oxford 1888', in 'Letters to Child Friends', *Works of Lewis Carroll*, ed. R. L. Green (London, 1965), 722.

[29] John Maddison, 'The Champneys Buildings, Mansfield College, Oxford', *MCM* 185 (1982–3), 32.

[30] See *Builder*, 13 June 1891, 467 and 27 June 1891, 509.

[31] *RIBA Journal*, 3rd ser. 19/16 (June 1912), 589.

[32] *The Times*, 6 Apr. 1935.   [33] *Builders' Journal*, 13 Aug. 1895, 10.

[34] See his article on 'The Planning of Collegiate Buildings', *RIBA Journal*, 3rd ser. 10/8 (21 Feb. 1903), 205–12.

The result was strikingly successful (pl. 4). The building, largely of Taynton stone, used three sides of a quadrangle facing south. A tower, or gatehouse (which, confusingly, led no further than the building in view), took the central position, flanked on one side by the Hall, and on the other by tutors' rooms and teaching rooms. Below a statue of John Milton were placed the College arms,[35] and above the doorway, flanked by the shields of the Spicer and Haworth families, was the College motto: DEUS LOCUTUS EST NOBIS IN FILIO (Heb. I: 2—'God has spoken to us in his Son'). The large and lofty Chapel took up another side of the quadrangle, while opposite stood the fine Library and the eleven-bedroom, four-storey Principal's Lodgings. Altogether, it was an imposing building for a college with fewer than thirty students.

The Chapel represented Mansfield's aspirations—on a scale to equal that of other Oxford college chapels, unsectarian, impressive, confident. But Mansfield Chapel was more than a college chapel— it was to be a place of worship for all Nonconformists in the University. It claimed its inheritance as a part of the whole Church, establishing a permanent Mansfield tradition. Thus Athanasius, Augustine, and Origen flank the entrance to the Chapel. At the formal opening of the College in 1889, Fairbairn declared that

> I would sooner that my right hand forgot its cunning and my tongue ceased to speak than that we should abate one jot or tittle of the large and comprehensive spirit that has made us seek, through pulpit and professor's chair, through chapel and lecture-room, to unite all branches of the Evangelical churches of the United Kingdom and the Colonies in this enterprise within the University of Oxford.[36]

But Bunyan standing guard outside the vestry, Milton in the centre of the tower, and Oliver Cromwell[37] in the Senior Common Room reflected Mansfield's own perception of its roots.

Inside, the Chapel (pl. 5) was a remarkably catholic 'commemoration of the saints': statues and windows representing many of the great figures of the Christian Church throughout the centuries. The

---

[35] It was later discovered that the College had no right to use these arms, which were not connected with the Mansfield family who founded it. See Ch. XII.

[36] *Mansfield College, Oxford*, 170.

[37] The portrait of Oliver Cromwell, a copy of a painting by Sir Peter Lely in the Pitti Palace in Florence, was presented by William Crosfield.

4. Mansfield College 1892

5. The College Chapel

statues inside represented great figures of the Reformed tradition from John Wyclif to Isaac Watts, together with George Whitefield and John Wesley; they were the choice of Dale and Fairbairn, and were executed by Robert Bridgeman of Lichfield.[38] Bridgeman's previous work was for Anglican churches, and this was his first introduction to the Reformed, Dissenting tradition. Fairbairn plied him with books to help him to understand the lives and backgrounds of the subjects, and he 'frankly acknowledged how ignorant he had hitherto been of these men and how great a piece of education his Mansfield work had proved'.[39]

The Chapel faced north rather than east, and the first stained glass windows to be inserted were those at the north and south ends. The south windows, presented by Mr and Mrs Jesse Haworth of Manchester in memory of their respective mothers, and executed by Messrs Shrigley and Hunt of Lancaster, represent scenes from Christ's ministry—the call of the first disciples, and the feeding of the multitudes; the north windows, the gift of Mr W. H. Wills (later Lord Winterstoke),[40] and executed by Messrs Joseph Bell and Sons of Bristol, represent Christ in glory supported by Paul and the apostles and the great figures from the Old Testament. The windows to east and west, executed by Messrs Powell and Sons of Whitefriars, London, were also the gift of Lord Winterstoke in 1906. Fairbairn found great satisfaction in completing the Chapel's 'commemoration of saints'. To some extent he was limited by the availability of portraits or other representations (he wanted to keep to 'historical, i.e. portrayed, persons'), for which he conducted extensive searches in the Ashmolean Museum and in the British Museum.[41] The final result is, for its time, a remarkably ecumenical selection: to the great figures of the Old Testament and of the Church of the New Testament there were now added representatives of the Greek and Latin Churches; the medieval Church in Britain and on the Continent; the Reformation in Britain

---

[38] Building Committee Minutes, 20 Nov. 1888, MCA. See also Dale's letters to Fairbairn on the subject in A. W. W. Dale, *The Life of R. W. Dale of Birmingham* (London, 1899), 503.

[39] *MCM* 10/14 (July 1918), 238–9.

[40] William Henry Wills, first Baron Winterstoke (1830–1911). He was a Congregationalist, Liberal MP 1880–5 and 1895–1900, chairman of the board of directors of the family tobacco firm in Bristol, and a great benefactor to Bristol and to national Nonconformist causes. See *DNB Second Supplement*, 684–5.

[41] For correspondence with Sir Alfred Dale on the choice of subjects, see Selbie, *Life of Andrew Martin Fairbairn*, 427–30.

and on the Continent; Puritanism and eighteenth-century Nonconformity (where Friedrich Schleiermacher[42] somewhat strangely found
a place); the American Church; and nineteenth-century Nonconformity, including some of those who had worked hard to establish
the college—Dale, James Legge, Alexander Hannay, and Alexander
Mackennal. It was 'the Catholic church looking in on the gathered
church'.[43] By the standards of the late twentieth century there are
limitations; but in 1906, commemoration of post-Reformation Roman
Catholic or Anglican 'saints' would have been too contentious.
Though much admired by Fairbairn, Newman was still too controversial a figure. The very small number of women commemorated
also reflects the assumptions of the time; and the choice (Martha
and Priscilla from the New Testament, Monica, mother of Augustine,
Helena, mother of Constantine, Margaret of Scotland, and Elizabeth
Fry) is interesting; Mary, the mother of Christ, the pre-eminent
woman of Christian tradition, is omitted from north and south; and
apparently no woman from the Congregational or Reformed tradition
was considered worthy of a place to east or west. Some other small
windows contain the arms of Oxford colleges, portraits of Sarah
Glover and of Alderman Manton, a prominent member of the Spring
Hill Council and later of the Mansfield Council,[44] and then at the
end of the right aisle, representations of Amos and Plato as exemplars
of prophecy and philosophy.

As time went on, memorial tablets were placed to succeeding
teachers and benefactors of the College, and to those killed on active
service in the two world wars. The fine organ, a three-manual Vowles
organ, was another gift from Lord Winterstoke. Chairs rather than
pews were chosen from the first, thus ensuring flexibility of seating.
Soon after the formal opening the oak screens at the north and
south ends of the chapel were added. The pulpit was placed in one
corner, rather than centrally, much to Dale's dismay; the reason lay
in acoustics rather than in liturgical principle. 'If it is quite certain
that the voice cannot be heard except from the corner, *cadit quaestio*;

---

[42] Friedrich Schleiermacher (1768–1834), German theologian who greatly influenced
Protestant theologians of the late 19th cent.

[43] J. C. G. Binfield, 'We Claim our Part in the Great Inheritance: The Message of
Four Congregational Buildings', in K. Robbins (ed.), *Protestant Evangelicalism: Britain,
Ireland, Germany and America* (Oxford, 1990), 203.

[44] Sir Henry Manton (1835–1924) was a Birmingham silversmith, and Deputy Chair
of Justices in Birmingham.

but it is a miserable humiliation that we have not been able to build a little place like that fit for its main purpose.'[45]

An equally fine building was the Library (pl. 6), with its pitched roof, said to have been inspired by a medieval barn at Harmondsworth, Middlesex. Twelve alcoves contained carved oak tables and chairs, many of which are still in use. Into this new Library was brought the large Spring Hill collection of books, many of them gifts from ministers and lay people in Birmingham since 1838.

In 1896 Powells were asked to add the delicate and attractive stencil plaster panels to the Library roof, ornamented with scrolls and Latin mottoes. By this time, a collection of portraits of ministers ejected from the Church of England in 1662 had been presented to the College, and most of them had been hung round the balcony— 'In this way our walls will lose their bareness, and we shall be constantly and happily reminded of that heroic age when our Free Churches were founded, and of those holy men of old into whose labours we have so largely entered.'[46] When Mrs John Rylands (whose husband, Manchester's first millionaire, had died in 1888, and who wished to endow a fitting memorial to him) saw the Library, she immediately commissioned Champneys to design a similar library, but on a grander scale, in Manchester—now the John Rylands University Library.[47] The College furnishings were the work of George Faulkner Armitage of Altrincham, designer and architect, brother-in-law of Jesse Haworth and Manchester agent for the firm of William Morris.[48] His work was in the Arts and Crafts tradition. In 1887 he had designed the interior decoration of the Manchester Jubilee Exhibition. A year later, he had redecorated the entrance gallery of

[45] Dale to Fairbairn, 5 July 1889, quoted in A. W. W. Dale, *Life of R. W. Dale*, 504. Dale to Fairbairn, 5 July 1889, quoted ibid. 504.

[46] *Mansfield College Report 1893–94*, 12. The collection of fifty portraits, copies made by a Mr Sintzenich of Exeter, was presented to Mansfield by J. H. Lloyd and other members of Highgate Congregational Church (where W. B. Selbie was then minister) in 1894. Fifteen further portraits were given by Mr H. R. Williams of Highgate. In 1912 J. H. Lloyd's daughter presented another six portraits of Puritan statesmen: Sir Edward Coke, Oliver Cromwell, Sir John Eliot, John Hampden, John Rogers, and Lord Saye and Sele.

[47] Fairbairn was guest speaker at the opening of the Library on 6 Oct. 1899. One may speculate as to whether he was inspired to complete the stained glass windows in Mansfield when he saw the fine windows at the Library, commemorating theologians and scientists and men and women distinguished in the arts and literature.

[48] See Binfield, *So Down to Prayers*, ch. 8 for an account of Armitage and his connections. See also Rosamond Allwood, 'George Faulkner Armitage 1849–1937', *Furniture History* (1987), 67–82.

6. The College Library

the Fine Art society in Bond Street, and at the Paris Exhibition he furnished the Council chamber of the British Section offices (for which he was awarded a gold medal). His work was now attracting public notice. This, together with his extensive Nonconformist connections and his recent redecoration of the smoking room of the Oxford Union no doubt led to the Mansfield commission, which proved to be a very happy one for the College. He was responsible for the furnishing of the Junior and Senior Common Rooms, and of the two professors' rooms. In addition, he was responsible for a large embroidered hanging of 'The True Vine' on the south wall of the Chapel, given in memory of his father. Many of his decorations at Mansfield are still extant, and others have been replaced only recently.

The total cost of the land, road building, buildings, furnishing, and gardens was £48,733 0s. 5d.[49] This money was all raised by the beginning of 1892 through the intensive efforts of Dale, Fairbairn, Albert Spicer, and others, all over the country. Spring Hill had drawn most of its support from the Midlands, though its alumni often persuaded the churches to which they ministered in different parts of the country to contribute. The Mansfield Building Fund, however, drew support from almost every part of the country, but much more from individuals than from churches. Eleven counties—Cheshire, Essex, Gloucestershire, Kent, Lancashire, Middlesex and London, Staffordshire, Surrey, Warwickshire, Worcestershire, and Yorkshire—each contributed more than £1,000; Lancashire headed the list with a contribution of £13,423 10s. 5d.[50] Manchester contributed £6,265; two-thirds of this sum came from the two brothers Jesse and Abraham Haworth.[51] Liverpool too was conspicuous in its support; it was in that city that Simon had first pleaded for support for an Oxford college. George Atkin, who had arranged Simon's visit to the Reform Club in 1883, presided at a similar meeting on 25 February 1886, at which Dale and Fairbairn spoke; over £1,000 was promised before the end of the evening. A special Liverpool committee was formed early in 1886 to raise more money from local supporters.[52] In other parts of the country, different members of the Spicer family were particularly generous, contributing together almost £5,000.[53] The

---

[49] See Building Fund Accounts, MCA.
[50] See Building Fund Circulars, MCA.   [51] Ibid.
[52] See Building Fund Minute Book (Liverpool District), MCA.
[53] See Building Fund Accounts, MCA.

support of the Haworth and Spicer families was acknowledged by placing their coats of arms on the outside of the tower.

It was hard work for both Dale and Fairbairn, touring the country in addition to their own regular work. Selbie accompanied Fairbairn on some of his tours, and in retrospect remembered 'the grasp, insight, sympathy, and vehemence with which Dr Fairbairn pleaded the cause, and the sheer weight of argument by which he bore down opposition and won men (and their money) to his side'.[54] The success of both Dale and Fairbairn in raising the necessary money was testimony partly to their own stamina and faith, and partly to the wealth and generosity of some of the leading Congregational families of the time. It reflected the confidence and optimism of Congregationalists as social and political barriers against them were removed, and freed them to take their place in the main arena of British life. The challenge now was to discover their role in that arena, and to justify their continued distinctive existence.

The celebrations at the formal opening of the College 14–16 October 1889[55] were not only an occasion of great munificence and celebration, far surpassing anything the College has seen since, but also an opportunity to declare to the world what Mansfield intended to offer to Oxford. There was a strong sense of 'returning home'. The invitation to those overseas included these words:

> Two hundred and fifty years ago your Fathers and ours learned in the English Universities those principles of religious and civil liberty we have ever since endeavoured to obey and to realize; and they felt no sacrifice harder or sorer than the being compelled, in 1662, for conscience' sake, to leave the stately Halls and historic Colleges where they had studied and taught, and where they had learned to seek and to love Freedom and Truth.[56]

A large marquee was hired to accommodate all the guests. On the evening of 14 October a service was held in the Chapel, with Dale as preacher. The following day there was a communion service at which Henry Reynolds,[57] President of Cheshunt College, was preacher; at 11.30 Fairbairn gave an inaugural lecture on 'Theology in the

---

[54] *MCM* 6/7 (Mar. 1909), 154.
[55] Only the *Rock* seems to have realized that 16 Oct. was the anniversary of the burning of Cranmer, Ridley, and Latimer in Oxford.
[56] Building Fund Minute Book, MCA.
[57] For Henry Reynolds (1825–96) see *CYB 1897*, 213–15.

Modern University'; this was followed by a luncheon, with eight speakers, presided over by Albert Spicer. Later in the day there were organ recitals, followed by a grand reception with over 1,000 guests. The good humour of the occasion is illustrated by a story recounted by the first Bursar, Norman Smith. Among those invited from the immediate neighbourhood was the Curator of the Pitt Rivers Museum, Dr E. B. Tylor, who 'regarded theology as a rather superfluous department of knowledge'. When he met the Principal, he explained his fear 'that there might be some dogmas lurking about the corridors'. 'Dr Fairbairn promptly informed him that all the dogmas were safely tied up for the night.'[58] The celebrations were completed by a breakfast the following morning with seven more guest speakers.

The guests included ten heads of Oxford colleges (and the 'Lady Principal' of Somerville Hall),[59] several Oxford professors and college Fellows, and many Oxford theologians; Free Church theologians from all over Britain, including representatives from the other English and Welsh Congregational colleges and the English Presbyterian College, from the Baptist College in Bristol and 'the Assembly's College' in Belfast, from the Free Church colleges in Aberdeen and Glasgow;[60] Dr Ray Palmer, representing the University of Yale (in which capacity he conferred an honorary Yale doctorate on Fairbairn), Andover Theological Seminary, and the National Council of Congregational Churches of the USA, who acknowledged the debt the United States owed to the Puritans; and other representatives from Australia, New Zealand, Canada, and India. Augustus S. Wilkins, Professor of Classics at Owens College, Manchester, considered himself a representative of Cambridge (he had been an active member of the Cambridge University Nonconformist Union and was later to be a member of the College Council). Letters and telegrams poured in from the United States and from the Netherlands, France, and Germany; one came from Fairbairn's old teacher, James Morison of Glasgow. Politicians, however, were not invited, not even Gladstone, for Dale had fallen out with him over Home Rule for Ireland.[61]

---

[58] Norman Smith, 'Further Memories of a Bursar', *CQ* (1927), 71.

[59] The colleges were Balliol (B. Jowett), Corpus Christi (T. Fowler), University (J. F. Bright), Oriel (D. B. Monro), Lincoln (W. W. Merry), Exeter (W. W. Jackson), Trinity (H. G. Woods), Brasenose (A. Watson), Merton (G. C. Brodrick), and Magdalen (T. H. Warren).

[60] Principal Angus of the Baptist College, Regent's Park and Professor Davison of the Wesleyan College, Richmond were invited but unable to attend.

[61] See Dale, *Life of R. W. Dale*, 505.

The speeches were celebratory, congratulatory, visionary. All agreed that Nonconformists would now have a centre for the study of theology 'in a spirit at once constructive, critical and devout', a service which Mansfield would be able to provide 'more thoroughly than any other institution in Great Britain'; it would provide 'a nobler training of the ministers of our Free churches'.[62] For Dale, the opening of Mansfield was an assertion of 'the duties and the rights of the intellect in religion'.[63] Fairbairn offered a magisterial survey of the history of Oxford University, and assessment of the nature of a university within modern society:

> A university has a two-fold relation—on the one hand to the people, on the other hand to knowledge; or, in other words, to the nation it serves, and to the nature it interprets. Conceived under the one relation, the university may be described as a society specially organised and equipped for the discipline and formation of men with a view to the better service of society and the State; conceived under the other, it may be defined as a body so constituted and qualified as to be best fitted for the creation, increase, and communication of knowledge. . . . In both respects the opposite or antithesis of the university is the seminary. The university is universal, is open to all the people without respect of persons or distinction of classes; but the seminary is a sectional or class institution, with no aims beyond those of the set or sect it was founded to serve.[64]

A university exists 'to teach and to enlarge the circle of the sciences'; its teachers must be 'inquirers, discoverers—men who deal with knowledge as living and not as dead'.[65] Yet 'there is nothing harder than to discover the forms and conditions under which it can live freely and justly within the academic'.[66] 'The theology that is to live in the universities must be the theology, not of legal definitions or academic formulae or civil statutes, more capable of evasion than of enforcement, but of free religious societies, or, simply, of men whose life is religion, and whose thoughts are the inchoate yet plastic material of theology.'[67] In Mansfield's pursuit of this theology students of every Church would be welcome (though in his mind the limits did not stretch further than Baptists, Methodists, Presbyterians, and Episcopalians).

---

[62] W. B. Selbie in *Mansfield College, Oxford*, 44–5. [63] Ibid. 70.
[64] Ibid. 121–3. [65] Ibid. 129–30. [66] Ibid. 111. [67] Ibid. 132–3.

Edwin Hatch took up a similar theme from an Anglican perspective (it was probably his last public utterance, for he died two weeks later). He saw Mansfield as 'intensifying the religious life of the University, pouring into it the free, fresh streams of evangelical religion',[68] 'helping to disabuse the members of the Church of England of the chimera of corporate unity',[69] and contributing to the ideal of the Church 'in which Judah shall not swallow Ephraim nor Ephraim Judah, but Judah and Ephraim shall live side by side, each working out its common purpose, but in which Judah no longer vexes Ephraim, nor Ephraim Judah'.[70]

The theme of reconciliation was taken up by others. Jowett spoke of the opening of Mansfield as 'a great festival of union and reconciliation'.[71] Henry Reynolds, who preached at the communion service, looked more deeply into the meaning of reconciliation:

> May we not cherish, and in this very service of reverence and love express, our profound conviction that the great Evangelical movement of the last century, and the Anglo-Catholic movement of this century, are co-operating to produce a greater movement than either? It is not impossible that even we may have something to do in stimulating its progress and development.[72]

> when the hour comes that the vigorous representatives of what are called Free Churches can see the kingdom of God in all its other manifestations, whether in Rome or Constantinople, Geneva or Canterbury, and when the most spiritual, devout, and conservative members of the historic Churches can recognise and act upon the recognition of the Divine life, of the brotherhood in Christ, of the supernatural order beyond the pale and boundary hitherto assigned, when the union between such as are one in Christ becomes a mutual indwelling such as that between the Father and the Son, then *all will be one* according to a higher ideal than has ever yet been powerfully embodied among men.[73]

The whole occasion was widely reported. A large news cuttings book in the Mansfield Archives is filled with reports from every

---

[68] Ibid. 184.   [69] Ibid. 185.

[70] Ibid. 185. Dean Stanley had referred to 'the long estrangements of Judah and Ephraim, of Jerusalem and Samaria' in a sermon in St Mary's, the University Church, after the abolition of religious tests, on 25 Feb. 1872. Quoted in E. Abbott and L. Campbell, *The Life and Letters of B. Jowett*, ii (London, 1897), 25.

[71] Ibid. 140.   [72] *Mansfield College, Oxford*, 88.   [73] Ibid. 90.

conceivable national and provincial paper. *The Times* of 15 October devoted an editorial to the subject:

> Apart from polemical differences, Anglican theologians in general, and Oxford divines perhaps in particular, long cultivated the habit of looking down upon their Nonconformist brethren as from a superior height of social and intellectual culture. Nonconformists returned the compliment by assuming a peculiarly aggressive and not too urbane type of Nonconformity. There could be no more signal illustration of the harmony and interdependence which nature herself ordains between the organism and its environment .... Anglicans and Nonconformists will still differ on the dogmatic points which divide them ... but it will no longer be possible for the Anglican clergyman to look down, as from a superior social and intellectual height, on the Nonconformist minister, educated in the same University and holding the same degree as himself, and inspired, like himself, with those most excellent traditions of urbanity, humanity, grace, and refinement which no true son of Oxford should ever permit himself to forget.

The *Church Times* (25 October 1889) hoped, like many others, that Mansfield's opening would contribute to an *increase* of religion in Oxford. It put this cogently by linking the aims of Mansfield with those of Pusey House, both of which had as their ideal 'the pursuit of Christian piety and sound learning':

> both aim at keeping alive the belief that the truth has been revealed to the world, and that it is possible to be known; both think that, in the verse which is to be seen engraved on the doorway at the new home of Nonconformist learning, *Deus locutus est nobis in filio,* and that theology is not a mere inquiry into the phenomenal characteristics of religious minds of all ages, but that it is engaged in the investigation of the results and working of principles which in the last result, are fixed and immovable, being the data permitted to us by revelation.

There were critics. Thomas Case, Wayneflete Professor of Moral and Metaphysical Philosophy, a frequent writer of letters to *The Times*, wrote to *The Times* on 16 October 1889 that 'this college has no connection whatever with the University. ... The truth is that Mansfield College is a Congregational seminary built within the precincts of the borough of Oxford'. Those who now began to refer to Mansfield as 'the dissenteries' were not intending a compliment. *John Bull* (19 October 1889) scoffed at the 'Liberal Churchmen of Oxford', who were now showing themselves in their true colours 'by taking part in the inauguration of an anti-Church institution'. The *Western Chronicle* (18 October 1889) warned of the temptations which would face the young Nonconformist students, and reflected that 'there is assuredly a school of bitter theological opposition to Dr Fairbairn in Oxford, who will sooner or later, be up and at him'. The *Scots Observer* (19 October 1889) thought the scheme too ambitious, and predicted that 'instead . . . of Mansfield conquering Oxford, it is a thousand times more likely that Oxford will swallow Mansfield'. Even the *British Weekly* predicted that Mansfield 'would become in a short time a pillar of the Church of England'.[74]

The Building Committee's work was now done, and the new College was launched. The building was handed over to the Trustees, now Trustees of the 'Spring Hill College Endowment', as stipulated in the Scheme of Management agreed by the Charity Commissioners in September 1885. A new governing body, the Mansfield Council, was to replace the Spring Hill College Management Committee, which had continued to meet in both Birmingham and Oxford. In 1899 this Scheme of Management was amended, in recognition of the fact that Mansfield was now a national, rather than a provincial, institution, and therefore should not be overweighted with Birmingham representation. This revised constitution remained the governing instrument until 1988. The Council was to have twenty-five members: two representatives elected by the College professors and tutors; six members elected by the Trustees; six members elected by the Congregational Union; eight members elected by the subscribers; two members elected by the registered life members; and the principal was a member ex officio. Of the Trustees, six each were to be elected by the subscribers, Council, and Congregational Union, two by the registered life members, and one by the professors and tutors.

There was a steady growth in the number of students, and in 1889 two further members were appointed to the Senior Common Room: James Vernon Bartlet and William Boothby Selbie. The Council, Trustees, and professors were now charged with working out in practice all that they had so eloquently described.

---

[74] Quoted in Selbie, *Life of Andrew Martin Fairbairn*, 181.

V

Andrew Martin Fairbairn

Principal of Mansfield College 1886–1909

LORD ACTON, Regius Professor of History at Cambridge at the end of the nineteenth century, once told Viscount Bryce that he doubted whether there was anyone in the University of Oxford whose learning was as great as Fairbairn's.[1] This judgement referred to a man who had had no secondary schooling at all, and whose ignorance of foreign languages at the age of 24 was such that he and a friend had a fierce argument over the meaning of the word 'Buffet' above a tea-room on their way to Paris; Fairbairn insisted, despite his friend's knowledge of French, that it was the name of the owner of the tea-room—'he would hear nothing to the contrary'.[2] In the intervening years, he had made good this deficiency, learning modern and ancient languages, and becoming a formidable exponent and interpreter of German theology. His scholarship was recognized in the award not only of an Oxford D.Litt., but of no less than seven honorary doctorates,[3] and in the part he played in the foundation of the British Academy (of which he was one of the original Fellows in 1902). Looking back, R. W. Macan considered Fairbairn to have been 'the most accomplished and profound exponent of systematic theology in the University since Mozley'.[4] Fairbairn's reading and his knowledge were encyclopaedic;[5] he had a passionate belief in

[1] Bryce's recollection is quoted in W. B. Selbie, *The Life of Andrew Martin Fairbairn* (London, 1914), 183. Lord Acton used to visit Fairbairn at his first Oxford home on the corner of Banbury and Bevington Roads. He later invited Fairbairn to contribute two chapters to the second volume of the *Cambridge Modern History*, on 'Calvin and the Reformed Church' and 'Tendencies of European Thought in the Age of the Reformation'.

[2] Letter from 'A.B.' to Selbie after Fairbairn's death, in News Cutting Book 4, MCA.

[3] From Edinburgh, Manchester, Leeds, Wales, Aberdeen, Yale, and Göttingen.

[4] R. W. Macan, *Religious Changes in Oxford during the Last Fifty Years* (Oxford, 1917), 14. J. B. Mozley (1813–78) was Regius Professor of Divinity at Oxford from 1871 until his death in 1878.

[5] To Hastings Rashdall and other friends he was known as 'The Encyclopaedia'. P. E. Matheson, *Life of Hastings Rashdall DD* (Oxford, 1928).

theology as the queen of the sciences, a subject which should only be approached by those whose minds have already been trained in another academic discipline. This he had learned through his own hard experience of trying to absorb theological principles without having first been trained to understand and evaluate them.

This awe-inspiring Scottish theologian was the towering figure of Mansfield's early years. Scotland had given him a profound respect for education and learning, and for the calling of the ministry, which he retained for the whole of his life. 'The spirit of John Knox and of the Covenanters always slept under those piles of erudition and that acquired moderation of language.'[6] At first, he and the classicist John Massie were the only members of staff; as time went on, most of those who joined them were themselves former pupils of Fairbairn, and thus reflected his influence. And so the early years of Mansfield's history are inseparable from Fairbairn, who shaped its early form and reputation and made a significant contribution to Oxford theology. His students (pl. 7), who greatly respected him, found him a dominant and dominating influence; he 'was inclined to play the earthly providence to his students, and to treat them as clay in the hands of the potter'.[7] He and his wife[8] and family (they had four children—two girls, Barbara and Helen, and two boys, John and Andrew—both boys were undergraduates, at Magdalen and Wadham, in 1889) settled in the spacious Principal's Lodgings in 1889. His salary was raised from £800 to 1,000 guineas in the following year, thus enabling him to live in some style.[9] He dined in College every weekday, and invited many distinguished visitors to share Mansfield's hospitality. Some came from the United States, where Fairbairn made many contacts on his frequent visits; many came from Scotland. James Bryce considered that 'Nowhere did one meet more interesting men or listen to better talk than in the Mansfield Common

---

[6] R. F. Horton, quoted in Selbie, *Life of Andrew Martin Fairbairn*, 388.

[7] A. E. Garvie, *Memories and Meanings of my Life* (London, 1938), 88.

[8] He married Jane Shields in Bathgate in 1868. It seems to have been a happy marriage; according to Fairbairn, she was 'content to be a wife and mother', though 'everything that I have done in public life has been made possible for me by my wife' (quoted in Selbie, *Life of Andrew Martin Fairbairn*, 43). College life at the turn of the century allowed little place for the wives of dons, but Mrs Fairbairn would have entertained guests in the Principal's Lodgings, and she seems to have taken a particular interest in some of the women students of Somerville. She outlived her husband by many years, and died in 1927.

[9] According to the Census of 1891, the household included a governess, a cook, a housemaid, and a parlourmaid, as well as the family.

7. **Staff and Students 1895** *Back row (left to right):* T. H. Cooper, J. M. Jones, W. D. Miller, S. A. Parsons, V. A. Barradale, W. D. Woods, T. Rees, A. Platts, E. W. Howes, H. E. W. Phillips, W. M. Harris *Middle row:* G. E. Phillips, J. T. Miles, F. Lenwood, R. J. Evans, D. M. Edwards, P. N. Harrison, R. M. Mofat, H. A. Cook, J. S. Griffith, W. M. Barwell *Front row:* E. W. Franks, H. W. Robinson, G. W. THATCHER, J. V. BARTLET, A. M. FAIRBAIRN, G. B. GRAY, R. S. Franks, R. H. Coats, W. P. Haines, L. H. Gaunt

93

Room during his [Fairbairn's] time.'[10] The most notable guest in 1890 was Gladstone, a keen reader of Fairbairn's books, who had expressed a wish to see the College in which he had taken an interest. He spent a week in Oxford at All Souls,[11] and on 6 February dined at Mansfield in company with Professor James Legge, Professor Cheyne, and others.[12] Fairbairn and Gladstone became engrossed in a conversation on hymnology,[13] after which Gladstone paid a visit to the JCR and impressed them with his 'dignified courtesy'.[14] The *Christian Commonwealth* (6 March 1890) reported that 'at a considerably late hour that night Mr Gladstone walked back to All Souls at such a pace as to render Principal Fairbairn, who was acting as escort, well-nigh breathless'; Gladstone was 80 and Fairbairn 51.

Fairbairn was stimulating to those who enjoyed a serious debate, and he in turn warmed to a sympathetic audience. It was his learning and his enthusiasm which were attractive; wit and humour were not a strong part of his character, though they found expression more readily when he felt relaxed with friends. One of his fellow members of Exeter College Senior Common Room referred not only to his 'Scottish loquacity', but also to his 'entrenched imperviousness to humour'.[15] Another friend wrote:

> His talk was interesting from the width of his reading and the masterful vigour of his mind, but he had not much light play either in conversation or debate: here, as in his writing, he never moved with great ease. Like some champion of the Middle Ages his thought often seemed to labour under the load of his rhetorical armour; and his weapon was the battle-axe more often than the rapier.[16]

He worked hard, teaching, writing, lecturing. But his life was not altogether without diversion, and he followed the contemporary Oxford custom of taking exercise after lunch. He liked walking along the river, especially if he could discuss theology with a companion.

---

[10] Quoted in Selbie, *Life of Andrew Martin Fairbairn*, 183.
[11] C. R. L. Fletcher, *Gladstone at Oxford 1890* (Oxford, 1908) makes no mention of the visit to Mansfield.
[12] The Visitors' Book, MCA carries Gladstone's signature, but no other, for that date.
[13] Selbie, *Life of Andrew Martin Fairbairn*, 297.   [14] Garvie, *Memories*, 68.
[15] L. R. Farnell, *An Oxonian Looks Back* (London, 1934), 100.
[16] P. E. Matheson, a Fellow of Magdalen, who had been an early member of the Oxford University Nonconformists' Union, quoted in Selbie, *Life of Andrew Martin Fairbairn*, 199.

He played golf every Saturday afternoon at Hinksey with three friends, a group known as the 'anti-Catholic foursome';[17] he played bowls on the lawn of the Principal's Lodgings; and in the mid-1890s he took up the new sport of cycling (pl. 8).

In 1895 he was made an honorary MA of the University. As an honorary MA Fairbairn was not a full member of the University and could not vote in Convocation. This deficiency was remedied on 17 March 1896 when he was elected MA by decree (though not without unexpected opposition from some who felt that voting rights should be confined to those directly engaged in teaching within the University). Though he was teaching men who were matriculated members of the University, and though he was a much respected figure in Oxford theological circles, he was never a member of the Theology Faculty.

Fairbairn's intellectual background in Scotland and in Germany meant that he laid great emphasis on philosophy as basic to theological thinking, and was greatly influenced by Hegel. Those of his students who had not studied philosophy before coming to Mansfield found his lectures difficult to follow at first. He set out his concept of the scope and range of theology in an article in the *Contemporary Review* in February 1887[18] on 'Theology as an Academic Discipline', making a distinction between divinity, a 'dead' subject, with 'the truth stated in well-balanced rigorous propositions, and proved by a series of cumulative arguments'[19]—no doubt remembering his own early theological instruction—and that theology which is proper to a university, which must engage with the thought of the age. Theology and the sciences should be brought into encounter 'that they may, as related and co-ordinated departments of knowledge, learn to know, respect, supplement, and explain each other. In other words, Theology ought to be an academic discipline and living science; and to be either, it must be both.'[20] The necessity for the agreement of faith and reason was one of the great principles underlying his thought. Reason stood over any other authority: 'in every controversy concerning what is or what is not truth, reason and not authority is the

[17] The friends were Percy Gardner, Professor of Classical Archaeology, and a leading member of the Oxford Society of Historical Theology; W. H. Fairbrother, Tutor in Philosophy for the Non-collegiate Society; and Sidney Ball, Fellow of St John's, a prominent member of the reforming group within the University, a founder of Toynbee Hall and Barnett House, and a leading socialist thinker who had earlier been a Vice-President of the Oxford University Nonconformists' Union.

[18] *CR* 51 (1887), 196–219.   [19] Ibid. 199.   [20] Ibid. 198.

8. A. M. Fairbairn and K. C. Anderson on a 'sociable'

supreme arbiter; the authority that decides against reason commits itself to a conflict which is certain to issue in its defeat'.[21]

He laid out three great themes for university theology. The first was 'the explication and articulation of the idea of God', a theme which would merge with and transcend philosophy. Fairbairn had loved to expound this theme ever since he had held audiences so attentive by his expositions in Aberdeen, and his thoughts on it were worked out finally and thoroughly in *The Philosophy of the Christian Religion* (London, 1902), one of his two greatest works. The second theme was applied or historical theology, which would include a study of the phenomenon of religion; he had been interested in the work of F. Max Müller, Professor of Comparative Philology at Oxford, since his Aberdeen days, and his *Studies in the Philosophy of Religion and History* (Edinburgh, 1876) had revealed him as a pioneer in the study of comparative religion. The third theme was to be special or Christian theology, with its sub-themes of biblical studies, ecclesiastical history, and constructive theology. On biblical studies, he rejected the fundamentalist attitude by the reminder that 'Christianity is the religion, not, as is often incorrectly said, of a Book, but of a Revelation. It has its sacred books, and it lives by faith in the God they reveal.'[22] On constructive theology, he held that 'the final function of theology is to unfold its ethical contents into an ideal of society and the state'.[23] This comprehensive range of study required the specialist teachers who could only be found in a university. Above all, 'Theology to be a real study must be loved.'[24]

Fairbairn had always argued that theology should be a study for graduates, and indeed every student who followed the Mansfield theological course had already taken a degree in another discipline.[25] But in order to promote serious study, the students were encouraged to take the Oxford Theology degree, the BA examination which could also be taken by undergraduates. This course did not altogether match Fairbairn's requirements. It included some elements of his three major themes, together with a study of liturgy, but the

---

[21] A. M. Fairbairn, *The Philosophy of the Christian Religion* (London, 1902), 18.

[22] *Contemporary Review*, 51 (1887), 206.

[23] Ibid. 216–17.   [24] Ibid. 218.

[25] When C. E. Mallet's *History of the University of Oxford* (volume i) was published in 1924, it was a Mansfield correspondent who pointed out in the *Mansfield College Magazine* (12/7 Dec. 1924) that it was as early as 1252 that Oxford University first passed a statute decreeing that no one should take a degree in Theology before graduating in arts.

large range of choice meant that a student could gain a degree after studying a limited area; for example in the field of doctrine he might be examined in the doctrine of the Holy Trinity, or of the Incarnation, or of Grace alone. When the Theology Faculty Board discussed revising the Regulations for the Honours School in 1897–8, suggestions were invited, and though Fairbairn was not a member, he was asked to submit ideas. He wrote a letter to Canon William Ince, Regius Professor of Divinity and Chairman of the Board, setting out his proposals.[26] He was prepared to recognize it as an arts course (though regarding it as a postgraduate course for his own students), but not as a professional qualification for the Anglican priesthood as it had been regarded in the past. He criticized the low standards of the examination; too many alternatives were offered, and the papers were often poorly set by the small number of examiners, who could not be expected to have specialist knowledge in every field. He wanted Hebrew, Greek, and Latin to be compulsory (Hebrew was then, as now, optional); and within each general subject, he favoured one paper covering knowledge of the field as a whole as well as further papers requiring more specialized knowledge of particular areas; further, he wanted apologetics to be more philosophical, and to include present, as well as past, obstacles to belief. The changes that were finally made in the regulations bore only indirect reference to Fairbairn's suggestions. The Mansfield course continued to be more rigorous than that followed in other colleges.

Fairbairn lectured to his own students on the philosophy of religion, theism, and homiletics. His enthusiasm was limitless, and his encyclopaedic knowledge illuminated every subject under discussion. He always began his course with a term's lectures on the 'Theological Encyclopaedia', according to the German custom, in which he introduced his students to the whole landscape of theological study, impressing on them its demands and its rewards. This was followed by lectures on theism and anti-theistic theories, and then 'a critical discussion of Agnosticism, Pantheism, Pessimism, Positivism, *et hoc genus omne*'.[27] There followed, according to Selbie, systematic theology in this sequence: The doctrines of God and the Godhead, the Person of Christ and the Holy Spirit, Man, Sin, the Atonement, Inspiration and Revelation, and the Church and the Kingdom. There

---

[26] This was printed as *Letter to the Regius Professor of Divinity on the School of Theology —8 March 1898* (Oxford, 1898).
[27] Selbie, *Life of Andrew Martin Fairbairn*, 184.

were also occasional courses on the philosophy of religion, comparative religion, and the history of English Puritanism.

His approach was not only philosophical but historical. R. S.
Franks, one of his most brilliant students, recollected that he and
his fellow students were made to realize

> the greatness of the problems of theology, and the amount of
> patient work necessary to understand them. We were made to feel
> too that only through a consistent tracing of the history of each
> problem could we understand the form it had assumed in our
> own time. We were brought fully to realize the relativity of the
> different traditional forms of doctrine.[28]

But several of his students were left wanting to be led on to something more constructive; 'it was tantalizing sometimes to be led to
the ends of the theological development in the Protestant orthodoxy, and not to be taken further.'[29] This criticism was more apt in
his later years, as he did not respond as vigorously to newer thinking
as he had to the crisis which led him to study in Germany in the
1860s. 'The enemies he had to meet were always clothed in the same
armour as those of his earlier days, and his mind was dominated to
the end by the influence of the problems with which he had himself
been compelled to wrestle.'[30]

However, he did publish two major works of theology while he
was at Mansfield. *The Place of Christ in Modern Theology* (London,
1893) went through twelve editions in the succeeding fourteen years,
and was widely read. It was an attempt to provide the groundwork
for a system of theology through the historical records of the life of
Jesus, and so through the consciousness of Christ's relationship to
God as Son of the Father—'the determinative idea of theology is not
the Church, but the Christ'.[31] Historical criticism, both of the Scriptures and of the Church's doctrinal development, had made it possible
for the first time since the earliest years of the Church to stand 'face
to face with the historical Christ'. The first part of the book is a

---

[28] R. S. Franks, 'In Memoriam: A. M. Fairbairn', *MCM* 8/1 (Mar. 1912), 24–5.
[29] Ibid. 26.   [30] Selbie, *Life of Andrew Martin Fairbairn*, 185.
[31] A. M. Fairbairn, *The Place of Christ in Modern Theology* (London, 1893), 188. Fairbairn
was criticized by his contemporary Robert Watts, Professor of Theology in the Presbyterian College, Belfast, for subordinating God's sovereignty to his 'fatherhood', and thus
'merging the Divine attributes and prerogatives in a universal Divine fatherhood'. See
R. Watts, *Professor Drummond's 'Ascent of Man' and Principal Fairbairn's 'Place of Christ in
Modern Theology' Examined in the Light of Science and Revelation* (Edinburgh, 1894), 147.

brilliant critical survey of Christian thinking about Christ, from the second down to the nineteenth century, set side by side with a discussion of the differing Christologies of the New Testament (this last was an approach ahead of its time). It revealed Fairbairn's thought at its best.

The later, more constructive part of the book is less successful. Fairbairn stood within the tradition of Liberal Protestantism, which emphasized the search for the 'historical Jesus', whom it tried to disentangle from Christian tradition, to use as the key to an understanding of the heart of Christianity. Thus Fairbairn tried to distinguish between the 'authentic, historical, Jesus' on the one hand, and the interpretation and doctrine of the Church on the other.

> Theology as well as astronomy may be Ptolemaic; it is so when the interpreter's Church, with its creeds and traditions, is made the fixed point from which he observes and conceives the truth and Kingdom of God. But theology may also be Copernican; and it is so when the standpoint of the interpreter is, as it were, the consciousness of Jesus Christ, and this consciousness where it is clearest and most defined, in the belief as to God's Fatherhood and His own Sonship.[32]

He criticized Newman's doctrine of development for being abstract rather than historical, and for taking as its starting-point too late a date.

More fruitfully, Fairbairn went on to claim that the Christian notion of God, and the Christian understanding of the Atonement, had been too forensic, under Latin influence—'the Godhead has tended to become mainly significant as a convenient mode of carrying out a legal process which the legalised notion of God had made necessary'.[33] This failed to express the real nature of God:

> Personal and therefore moral relation was of the very essence of His being. A God who could not be without a Son was a God who could not be without moral qualities in exercise. . . . Father and Son do not here denote a Paternity and a Sonship that begin to be, for in the region of the eternal all the categories of time cease; but they denote states, relations, that ever were and ever must be in God.[34]

---

[32] Fairbairn, *The Place of Christ*, p. viii.   [33] Ibid. 429.   [34] Ibid. 406.

From this there followed a challenge to the orthodox doctrine of the impassibility of God:

> Theology has no falser idea than that of the impassibility of God. If He is capable of sorrow, He is capable of suffering; and were He without the capacity for either, He would be without any feeling of the evil of sin or the misery of man. The very truth that came by Jesus Christ may be said to be summed up in the possibility of God.[35]

> We may then construe the sufferings and death of Christ as if they were the sacraments, or symbols and seals, of the invisible passion and sacrifice of the Godhead.[36]

If this is what the Mansfield students heard, they were not entirely deprived of constructive, challenging theology.

His other major work was *The Philosophy of the Christian Religion* (1902), in which he attempted a philosophical justification for the argument of *The Place of Christ in Modern Theology*. 'The end of the argument is the establishment as a truth of reason of that supremacy of Christ as the revealer of God which forms the first principle of the dogmatic theology contained in *The Place of Christ in Modern Theology*.'[37]

These two books in particular established Fairbairn's reputation as one of the great theologians of his time; the *Chicago Post* (17 November 1902) called him 'easily chief of living theologians'. The *Literary Digest* of New York (25 October 1902) quoted the view of the *Nineteenth Century and After* that Fairbairn was 'the ablest of living English Nonconformist theologians'. *The Philosophy of the Christian Religion* was regarded as his greatest book—'The book for which all his previous books, lectures and discourses have been preliminary studies and preparations.'[38]

The students whom Fairbairn was training were preparing for the Christian ministry, and on this he held very firm ideas. He was a most articulate and vigorous exponent of the Puritan understanding of ministry. This he first set out in a lecture at the opening of the new college buildings of Airedale Independent College, Bradford in

---

[35] Ibid. 483.   [36] Ibid. 485.
[37] R. S. Franks, 'The Theology of A. M. Fairbairn', *Transactions of the Congregational Historical Society*, 13 (1937–9), 146.
[38] *Methodist Times*, 19 June 1902.

1877.[39] There were, he noted, two concepts to be considered, the priestly and the prophetic—

> as either a speaker to God on behalf of men, or a speaker to men on behalf of God. In the priest they see a man holier than themselves, who can in their stead offer to God the services and sacrifices they themselves are too sinful to present; in the prophet they see a man skilled in divine things, so penetrated by divine truths and ideas as to be, as it were, a physical voice of God.... through the priest man seeks God, but through the prophet God seeks man; the essential aim of the first is by gifts and sacrifices to propitiate God, but the essential aim of the second is to make man so see and feel the divine truth and righteousness as to be lifted into fellowship with the Eternal.[40]

As the greatest Hebrew literature was prophetic, so the first followers of Christ were preachers and prophets, not priests. And preachers had to be formed by long and patient, hard study, so that they could stand in living relation to the truth which was of God.

These ideas found even more vigorous expression in that lecture to the Congregational Union meeting at Hanley, Staffordshire in 1885 on 'The New Puritanism and the New Sacerdotalism' which had aroused such rapturous applause. He contrasted the two opposing conceptions of the Christian Church which laid claim to allegiance in late nineteenth-century England, the sacerdotal and the puritan. According to the puritan conception,

> the church is the kingdom of God, or of the truth, created and governed directly by Christ, composed of His saints, with vassals, but without princes, civil or ecclesiastical, by its nature invisible, omnipresent, ideal, incapable of realization in any or in all forms of polity, existing in part in all the churches, fully embodied in no one singly or even in all combined.[41]

> The ultimate truth ... through which we live and on which we build, which governs all our thoughts and determines all our ideals and endeavours, is the Eternal and Sovereign Fatherhood, which is absolute and universal in its grace.[42]

---

[39] A. M. Fairbairn, *The Christian Ministry and its Preparatory Discipline* (London, 1877).
[40] Ibid. 4–5.
[41] A. M. Fairbairn, 'The Sacerdotal and the Puritan Idea', a reprinted version of the lecture in *Studies in Religion and Theology* (London, 1910), 109–10.
[42] Ibid. 129.

He found inspiration in 'our Puritan age' of the seventeenth century, which

> lasted but a generation, but in great men, great questions, great conflicts, great issues, simple heroism and magnanimous patriotism, it was the most fruitful and illustrious age in our annals. Without it the English people, neither here nor beyond the sea, would have been in liberty, in enterprise, in civilization, in progress, in religion, what they are today.[43]

But 'at the very moment when the Providence of God has so ruled our history as to leave us free to realize our characteristic religious idea, we are confronted by its very antithesis—a resurgent sacerdotalism'.[44] Sacerdotalism he defined as

> the doctrine that the man who ministers in sacred things, the institution through which and the office or order in which he ministers, the acts he performs, the sacraments and rites he celebrates, are so ordained and constituted of God as to be the peculiar channels of His grace, essential to true worship, necessary to the being of religion, and the full realization of the religious life.[45]

While opposing this doctrine, he recognized that 'the spirit and inspiration of this resurgent Sacerdotalism is religious', and the creation of 'a living faith, of a splendid and self-forgetful zeal'.[46] But the 'cardinal truth' of sacerdotalism was ecclesiological, while that of Puritanism was theological. Fairbairn said he wanted Congregationalists to eschew controversy as 'a rude and impotent weapon'; controversy should be with false systems, not with 'men'. He therefore wanted them to build churches which, as priestly bodies, would work for the reconciliation of humanity and God, proclaiming faith in Christ who 'sanctifies all places, makes everything sacramental' and in 'the continuity of religious life, which makes us possess the truth and hold communion with the saints of all the churches, share in and sympathize with all the good of all the ages'.[47] The moment had come which would determine 'whether we are a people called of God to do the work that now needs to be done in England'. That work was 'the creation of the new Puritanism'.[48] His final rallying cry was:

---

[43] Ibid. 114.   [44] Ibid. 117.   [45] Ibid. 119.   [46] Ibid. 124.
[47] Ibid. 138–9.   [48] Ibid. 118.

If we so interpret our mission, then we shall accomplish a work that will make it impossible for the sceptre that controls English destinies ever to pass into the hands of a disestablished sacerdotal church, and we shall help to keep it for ever in the hands of the risen and reigning Christ.[49]

That lecture actually revealed that Fairbairn was fascinated by 'sacerdotalism'. He had always been fascinated by Newman and by the Tractarian movement, and they often came up in his conversation; he had the greatest respect for Newman as a person ('the one man in all England on whose lips the words of the dying Polycarp sit with equal grace and truth'[50]) but believed that the doctrines of Newman and the Anglo-Catholics concerning the Church and the priesthood laid the emphasis in the wrong place. His further reflections on Newman and on Anglo-Catholicism were printed in several articles in the *Contemporary Review*, written both before and after he had come to Mansfield, and later collected together in a volume entitled *Catholicism: Roman and Anglican* (London, 1899). They included his challenge to Newman in an article entitled 'Catholicism and Modern Thought' (first published in the *Contemporary Review* in May 1885). His basic criticism that Newman's philosophy rested on scepticism—'He who places the rational nature of man on the side of Atheism, that he may better defend a church, saves the church at the expense of religion and God'[51]—indicated that he and Newman were using 'reason' in different senses, and that their views were developed from different first principles. Newman had replied to Fairbairn in the *Contemporary Review* (October 1885), and Fairbairn published a rejoinder in December; Newman published a final response for private circulation only. The debate was not creative, in the sense that neither man in any way modified his view.[52]

His views on ministry and priesthood were put to more creative purpose in the last few days of the nineteenth century when he, William Sanday (Regius Professor of Divinity), and R. C. Moberly (Regius Professor of Pastoral Theology) organized a conference jointly at the Principal's Lodgings at Mansfield and at Christ Church on 'Different Conceptions of Priesthood and Sacrifice'. Its proceedings

---

[49] Ibid. 141.

[50] A. M. Fairbairn, 'Reason and Religion', *CR* 48 (Dec. 1885), 842.

[51] A. M. Fairbairn, *Catholicism: Roman and Anglican* (London, 1899), 140.

[52] See Sheridan Gilley, *Newman and his Age* (London, 1990), 416–18 for a discussion of this controversy.

were published,[53] and in the preface Sanday explained: 'The Conference arose out of the idea that the bitterest part of modern ecclesiastical controversy turned upon the associations of what is called
"sacerdotalism"; and the further idea that much of this bitterness
might be preventible by mutual explanations.'[54] Fifteen participants,
representing broadly three groups (High Churchmen, Nonconformists, and 'Churchmen who would not be called "High"'), gathered
together for two days to discuss questions which had already been
circulated. Fairbairn was supported on the Nonconformist side by a
Methodist, Dr T. W. Davison, and by two Congregationalists, Arnold
Thomas[55] of Bristol and P. T. Forsyth, soon to be Principal of Hackney College, London. The Anglican representatives included three
of the contributors to *Lux Mundi*, R. C. Moberly,[56] Charles Gore, and
Henry Scott Holland,[57] and also a recent convert to Anglicanism,
Cosmo Gordon Lang,[58] the future Archbishop of Canterbury. The debate was fair and friendly and did remove some misunderstanding.
'If there was just the lightest touch of asperity now and then in our
debates it must be confessed it came from our friend [Fairbairn]',[59]
who certainly ensured that the Puritan understanding of ministry was
known in Oxford.

Fairbairn shared other ideas with Oxford theologians through the
Oxford Society of Historical Theology. Following the example of
Mansfield, the Unitarians moved their Manchester College (via London) to Oxford in 1889, occupying for a time the rooms at 90 High
Street vacated by Mansfield. They in turn built a new college further
down Mansfield Road, and contributed scholarship in the tradition
of James Martineau to liberal theological thinking in Oxford.[60] The
Taylerian Society of Manchester College was disbanded in 1891, and
replaced by the Oxford Society of Historical Theology, which was
to form a meeting-ground for Oxford theologians of more than one

[53] W. Sanday (ed.), *Different Conceptions of Priesthood and Sacrifice* (London, 1900).
[54] Ibid., p. viii.
[55] Arnold Thomas (1848–1924) was Chairman of the Congregational Union in that
year.
[56] Robert Campbell Moberly (1845–1903), Regius Professor of Pastoral Theology.
[57] H. S. Holland (1847–1918), Canon of St Paul's Cathedral, later Regius Professor of
Divinity 1910–18.
[58] C. G. Lang (1864–1945), then Vicar of Portsea.
[59] Sanday, *Different Conception*, 252.
[60] See V. D. Davis, *A History of Manchester College* (London, 1932) and B. Smith, *Truth,
Liberty, Religion: Essays Celebrating Two Hundred Years of Manchester College* (Oxford,
1986).

denomination or school of thought, to promote discussion of historico-critical issues. As the first President, Professor T. K. Cheyne, remarked in his opening address, 'We are now as a body only in course of assimilating the fruitful idea that there is a theology which is independent of ecclesiastical connexions.'[61] In practice, it was the more liberal-minded Anglicans, together with Congregationalists and Unitarians, who attended, joined in later years by both Roman Catholics and, occasionally, Jews. Fairbairn was the second President, Max Müller the third; the scholarly J. Estlin Carpenter, Vice-Principal and later Principal of Manchester College, was secretary until he was replaced by Fairbairn's pupil J. Vernon Bartlet, jointly with Hastings Rashdall,[62] in 1894. Some of the ideas in *The Place of Christ in Modern Theology* were shared with the Society at its annual meeting, held at Mansfield on 26 May 1892, the year before the book was published, when Fairbairn delivered the essence of the first two chapters as a paper on 'Development as a Law in Theology and the Church'. Many of the more creative English theologians and biblical scholars tested their ideas out at the Society in early career, and for the Nonconformists in particular it was one of the most stimulating arenas for discussion.

Fairbairn's influence not only reached other Oxford theologians, and Mansfield students, together with those few outside the College who enrolled for certain lectures; it also reached many of the growing number of Oxford Nonconformist students reading other subjects. The Chapel had from the start been intended as a focus of Nonconformist worship for the whole University, and Fairbairn ensured that the preaching was always of a high standard. He himself preached at regular intervals, and invited other distinguished English Nonconformists, representatives of the Church of Scotland, the United Free Church of Scotland, and the Presbyterian Church of England, and American Protestants to preach on other Sundays. It was stimulating for both preacher and congregation. The ageing J. Guinness Rogers wrote of his own experience of preaching in the Chapel:

---

[61] Oxford Society of Historical Theology, *Abstract of Proceedings 1891–92* (Oxford, n.d. [1892]), 7.

[62] Hastings Rashdall (1858–1924) was a Fellow of New College, and later Dean of Carlisle.

Of course one preaches to larger audiences, but I have seldom
addressed one more impressive in its aspect or more inspiring in
its influence. A man must be callous indeed who is not moved by
the sight of the young people massed before him. On the one side
are the Mansfield students, with a large gathering of members of
other colleges; on the other are grouped a considerable contingent
of lady students, chiefly, I believe, from Somerville Hall. It does
not need much exercise of imagination to conceive of the far-
reaching influence possible for the words addressed to such a
company of those who must play an important part in the future
of the nation.[63]

An even larger number of people was brought under Fairbairn's
influence, as well as that of other liberal Oxford theologians, through
the Summer Schools of Theology based at Mansfield in 1892 and
1894.[64] Selbie believed that Fairbairn first conceived the idea after
his visits to Chautauqua, the American Summer School, in 1884 and
1890, where he had enjoyed lecturing on comparative religion and
the philosophy of religion. The Mansfield Summer Schools were a
great success, in that each attracted more than 350 'students' (ministers of many denominations who wanted to keep up to date with
theological thinking and biblical criticism), and lecturers came from
Scotland and the USA as well as Oxford.[65] Lectures were held in
Mansfield and in Balliol, and the participants stayed in Wadham
and Exeter Colleges as well as Mansfield. Distinguished heads of
houses were persuaded to show the participants round their own
colleges. Fairbairn enjoyed every minute of it; 'Taking him all in all,
Dr Fairbairn has impressed the ministerial students at the Summer
School of Theology in Oxford as the greatest among the great men
they have met there'—so wrote one of the participants.[66] The School
had its critics among those fearful of biblical criticism, but Fairbairn
was undeterred. 'The times of sifting are always the times of clari-
fying. It is the gold that endures.'[67] His ideas had also reached a

---

[63] J. G. Rogers in *Independent and Nonconformist*, 13 Dec. 1894.
[64] For details of the Summer Schools, see the *Mansfield College Reports* for 1892–3 and
1894–5.
[65] The lecturers included George Adam Smith, Marcus Dods, James Orr, and A. B.
Bruce from Scotland, and Francis Brown and C. A. Briggs from Union Theological
Seminary, New York.
[66] Quoted in Selbie, *Life of Andrew Martin Fairbairn*, 226.   [67] Quoted ibid.

wider audience in July 1891 when he took a leading part in the first meeting of the International Congregational Council in London.[68]

Fairbairn was much involved in educational reform; he was an active member of the Bryce Commission on Secondary Education 1893–5, and was one of the most influential opponents of state support for denominational schools, proposed in the 1902 Education Bill, though his opposition was of no avail.[69] More effective was his contribution to the establishment of Theology degrees in the new University of Wales. It was primarily due to his influence that the Welsh BD was a postgraduate degree, and a degree of high standing. One of his old students, Thomas Rees, who became Principal of the Bala-Bangor Independent College in Bangor in 1909, wrote that 'The theological faculty of the Welsh University is no less Dr Fairbairn's monument and the incarnation of his spirit than Mansfield itself.'[70] Fairbairn visited all the Welsh theological colleges three times between 1894 and 1896; he lectured frequently in Wales, and his books were widely read there. When he retired he said he hoped he would be best remembered for his work for Mansfield and for the Welsh Theological Faculty.[71]

His longest visit away from Oxford[72] was to India in 1898–9, when he was Haskell Lecturer (a University of Chicago appointment) in Calcutta, Bombay, and Madras. He was the second Haskell Lecturer, the first from Britain. His brief was to expound the philosophical ideas underlying Christianity—a task to which he warmed—while taking the opportunity to develop further his long-standing interest in Indian religion. On his return he published two articles in the *Contemporary Review*, recounting his experiences and reflections.[73]

---

[68] See International Congregational Council, *Authorised Record of Proceedings* (London, 1891). On 20 July Fairbairn addressed the Council on the theme 'Congregationalism and the Church Catholic'. Four days later he was one of the speakers at the unveiling of a tablet to John Robinson at Leiden.

[69] On 12 June 1902 Fairbairn led the National Free Church Council's deputation to Balfour to protest against the Bill; on 23 Sept. he deputized for the Chairman of the Congregational Union with an address to the Assembly on 'Congregationalists and the Education Question' (*CYB 1903*, 34–46). But he did not support the 'Passive Resistance' which led many to refuse to pay local rates. News Cuttings Book V, MCA chronicles Fairbairn's part in the agitation in some detail through press reports.

[70] Quoted in Selbie, *Life of Andrew Martin Fairbairn*, 221.

[71] *MCM* 6/7 (Mar. 1909), 164.

[72] He frequently visited the Continent, including a visit to St Petersburg in 1892.

[73] 'Religion in India', *CR* 75 (June 1899), 761–81, and 'Race and Religion in India', ibid. 76 (Aug. 1899), 153–73.

Perhaps the most eloquent testimony to Fairbairn's standing with his own students was shown by the welcome they gave him when he returned from India:

> We met the carriage at the gates. The horse was taken out, and ropes were attached to the Carriage. At a given signal the quad was brilliantly illuminated by Bengal lights, which flashed from the Doctor's house, the tower, the turret, and the south-west corner of the chapel. Each man was provided with a torch, and these also were lit. Then we went in procession twice round the quad, and finally landed the Doctor and his party safely at the steps of the house. By this time the torches were all blazing merrily, and we stood cheering lustily and singing 'For he's a jolly good fellow.' The Doctor was evidently much moved, and could not speak to us. We too could scarcely speak, but managed to tell him, by our enthusiasm mainly, that we were very glad to see him back again.[74]

This was probably the height of Fairbairn's reputation. From this point on, his influence began to wane as he grew older and as his isolation from the newer theological currents became more frustrating to his students. In retrospect, it seems that his permanent influence has been most strongly expressed through the constructive work that he inspired in others, rather than in his own theological work. One of his greatest students, R. S. Franks, thought the reason lay in the fact that 'his theology is "mediating theology" in the unsatisfactory sense of the word', and in a failure to work out his system in detail: 'in the working out of the details of his theology he uses the traditional Trinitarian and Christological conceptions, while at times he throws doubt on their validity: moreover, in the interpretation of Scripture, and especially of St Paul, he often reads his own meaning into the passage and modernizes it in a way that is impossible as sound exegesis.'[75]

Fairbairn's emphasis on the Fatherhood of God did not lead him into a false optimism—'As Fairbairn himself says over and over again, the Father judges sin even more strictly than the sovereign'[76]—but it did lead him to interpret the Kingdom in this-worldly terms and

---

[74] Quoted in Selbie, *Life of Andrew Martin Fairbairn*, 364.
[75] Franks, 'Theology', 147. [76] Ibid. 149.

so to neglect that eschatological element in the New Testament which Schweitzer[77] was soon to revive.

Fairbairn's was the strongest influence on the development of the new College, but not the only one. The contribution of all those other people who formed the early Mansfield community must now be considered.

[77] Albert Schweitzer, *Von Reimarus zu Wrede* (Tübingen, 1906), trans. W. Montgomery as *The Quest of the Historical Jesus* (London, 1910).

VI

Mansfield Creates its Tradition

THE College had begun in confident and optimistic mood. It opened at a time when Congregationalists were beginning to think of themselves as Free Churchmen rather than as Nonconformists or Dissenters. Fairbairn had always preferred the term 'Free Church' (a Scottish term), which he contrasted with 'Established Church'. A 'Free Church', he claimed, was 'more of a dynamic force in society', 'a voluntary society created by affinities of thought and light', while an Established Church 'is a Church politically created and legally guaranteed'.[1] While Fairbairn was Principal, there was a great rallying of Free Church opinion in opposition to the Education Act of 1902 (in which he played a major role); and four years later 185 MPs returned at the General Election belonged to one of the Free Churches, 73 of them Congregationalists (including one former Mansfield student, Silvester Horne, and one former member of staff, John Massie).

But beneath the surface the optimism was not entirely justified, for 'the seeds of the numerical, and what many saw as a theological, decline were already present (though this was not officially and publicly recognized until well into the twentieth century[2]). Although the number of Congregational churches, members, and ministers in England and Wales continued to increase until 1908, the increase was not proportionate to the increase in the population as a whole.[3]

[1] A. M. Fairbairn, *Studies in Religion and Theology* (London, 1910), 102–3.

[2] The *British Congregationalist*, 13 Feb. 1913, ran a symposium on 'The Decline in Church Membership'. In his Chairman's address in May 1905 P. T. Forsyth told the Congregational Union that 'the Free Churches have been gaining more in public attention than in public weight.' *CYB 1906*, 16.

[3] See R. Currie, A. Gilbert, and L. Horsley, *Churches and Churchgoers: Patterns of Church Growth in the British Isles since 1700* (Oxford, 1977), and James Munson, *The Nonconformists: In Search of a Lost Culture* (London, 1991). The reasons for this decline, which has continued ever since, have been much debated. See particularly J. Cox, *The English Churches in a Secular Society* (Oxford, 1982), 265–76; Munson, *The Nonconformists*, 290–306; and R. Helmstedter, 'The Nonconformist Conscience', in Peter Marsh (ed.), *The Conscience of the Victorian State* (Hassocks, 1979).

The achievement of political, and to some extent social, equality left Nonconformists without one of their main driving forces, a force which had been particularly strong (to the detriment of theology and churchmanship) in the second half of the nineteenth century. In 1897 Fairbairn wrote:

> It is perhaps harder to be a Nonconformist today than it has ever been in the history of England. The very decay of the disabilities from which our fathers suffered has made it harder for us than for them to dissent. But while it has become harder it has also become more necessary: for the need of the testimony to a Church in which Christ is supreme was never so great as now. The less sharply principles have to be suffered for, the more the conveniences and the conventionalities of life prevail; and there is nothing so dangerous to the Church as to follow the expedient rather than the right.[4]

Mark Johnson has suggested that, in founding Mansfield, 'Nonconformists had no other well-defined purpose than to find an acceptable place for themselves in the mainstream.'[5]

The challenge facing Mansfield in the last years of the nineteenth century was to discover how to share in Oxford's culture, how to contribute to it, and yet how to retain a distinctive identity and remain loyal to the principles of Puritanism as they had been refined into the Dissenting tradition. In what ways was Mansfield to be *different*, different both from Anglican theological colleges in and around Oxford, and from other Oxford colleges which were part of the University?

It was different from other Oxford colleges in being small—twenty-five was the average number of Mansfield students in the first years (though the building itself conveyed the impression of a much larger community)—and in being non-residential. The latter fact made it all the more important to foster a sense of loyalty and community, and a reading of the *College Magazine* and of the JCR Minutes for the first twenty years of the college's life suggests that this was quickly achieved. The students, as graduates, were more mature than their contemporary undergraduates, and, perhaps more important, they shared a common vocation to the ministry. They were conscious of sharing in 'an epoch-making enterprise'.

[4] Quoted in W. B. Selbie, *The Life of Andrew Martin Fairbairn* (London, 1914), 257–8.
[5] Mark Johnson, *The Dissolution of Dissent 1850–1918* (New York, 1987), 224.

At the same time, the figures represented in the windows which were put in the Chapel at the end of Fairbairn's Principalship witnessed to the non-sectarian, ecumenical (by the understanding of the time), international ideals of the College. The ethos was 'evangelical Protestant'; the vision was catholic. The *Annual Report* for 1889–90 predicted, with some measure of truth, that the College 'promises to be a force for international Christian unity as well as a centre of usefulness'.[6]

One hundred and sixty-two men were admitted to Mansfield for a course lasting at least two years while Fairbairn was Principal; as most of the future Mansfield staff were chosen from their ranks, they played a significant role in setting the standard and creating the ethos of the College. All candidates for admission were interviewed by the College's Board of Education. Most, but not all, were Congregationalists; fourteen were Baptists, two were Welsh Presbyterians, two were Welsh Independents, and three were Primitive Methodists. Fairbairn had always hoped that the college would be open to all Nonconformists.[7]

The first five students to be admitted in 1886 may be taken as an initial sample of the kind of men who came up to Mansfield, of the work they did subsequently, and of their impact on the world outside. At least four of them were the sons of Congregational ministers: William Boothby Selbie, educated at Manchester Grammar School and Brasenose College, Oxford, where he graduated in Literae Humaniores, went on to pastorates in London and Cambridge, and finally succeeded Fairbairn as Principal of the College; Dugald Macfadyen,[8] also educated at Manchester Grammar School, and then at Merton College before coming to Mansfield, was minister of three churches (he followed Selbie at Highgate) before settling in Letchworth to give his time to social and political issues; Charles Silvester Horne,[9] a graduate of Glasgow University, went on to become the famous minister

---

[6] *Mansfield College Annual Report 1889–90*, 15.

[7] In 1891 J. H. Shakespeare, soon to become Secretary of the Baptist Union, urged his fellow Baptists to establish a college in Oxford or Cambridge; this did not happen until the 1930s. See R. E. Cooper, *From Stepney to St Giles': The Story of Regent's Park College 1810–1960* (London, 1960). The Presbyterian Church of England had discussed the possibility of moving its college to Cambridge from 1873 onwards, but the move did not take place until 1899, with the foundation of Westminster College. See R. Buick Knox, *Westminster College Cambridge: Its Background and History* (Cambridge, n.d. [c.1979]).

[8] Dugald Macfadyen (1867–1936). See *CYB 1937*, 699 and *MCM* 110 (Dec. 1936), 437.

[9] His contemporary W. B. Selbie wrote his biography—*Charles Silvester Horne* (London, 1920). See also *DNB: Missing Persons*, 329.

first of Kensington Chapel and then of Whitefields Tabernacle in Tottenham Court Road, London, and MP for Ipswich in 1910, before his premature death in 1914; and Thomas Wolfendale,[10] educated at Caterham School and Cambridge, was a minister in Durham before working for many years as a Secretary of the British and Foreign Bible Society in several parts of England. All that is known about the family background of the fifth, J. A. Robinson, is that he was born in Portugal; he moved from Airedale with Fairbairn to Oxford, then returned to mission work in Portugal, where he had hoped to establish a National Protestant Church; but he died within eighteen months.[11] These earliest students had no common room, and so their rooms in Walton Street were the focus for socializing—they would meet in each other's rooms in the evenings for cocoa and singing the latest Gilbert and Sullivan songs.

Those who followed came not only from Britain, but from the United States, Canada, South Africa, Australia, and New Zealand. In 1887 Howard Bliss came from the United States for one year. He eventually followed his father as Principal of the American College in Beirut, where he made a deep impression. He made a similar impression on his fellow students, for one them wrote later that 'when Howard Bliss came to Mansfield the sons of the morning sang for joy. . . . He came across the Atlantic like a breath of fresh air and his year with us will never be forgotten by those who survive.'[12] The British (by far the majority) came mostly from grammar schools, though some came from Nonconformist boarding-schools such as Mill Hill and a few from the traditional public schools. Those with little secondary education, like Fairbairn himself, were the exception. All were graduates before starting the College course; out of the 154 students admitted by Fairbairn for a course, which was completed, of at least two years, 54 were graduates of Oxford and Cambridge, while the rest came from fifteen different universities. Thirty-nine are known to have been the sons of ordained ministers.[13]

---

[10] Thomas Arthur Wolfendale (c.1864–1938). See *CYB 1939*, 718 and *MCM* 113 (July 1938), 530–1.

[11] See *Mansfield College Annual Report 1891–92*, 12.   [12] *MCM* 11/5 (Dec. 1920), 57.

[13] This proportion (25%) is higher than the 20% of all Nonconformist ministers in the late 19th cent. proposed by K. D. Brown, *A Social History of the Nonconformist Ministry in England and Wales 1880–1930* (Oxford, 1988), 29. The relevant information was collected from the *Mansfield College Magazine*, the *Congregational Year Books*, the Board of Education Minutes, Charles E. Surman's 'Directory of Dissenting Ministers' at Dr Williams's Library, London, and from individual biographies.

It may be wondered how it was that the sons of ministers, most of whom lived on small salaries, were able to take advantage of such a lengthy education. The Franks family, who provided more Mansfield students than any other, may be taken as a not untypical example.[14] Whereas Fairbairn in the 1890s was enjoying a salary of 1,000 guineas, on a level with that enjoyed by Alexander Mackennal as minister of the affluent Bowdon Downs Congregational Church, Manchester, the Revd W. J. Franks was receiving a salary of £200 as minister of Redcar Congregational Church, Yorkshire (his sole pastorate 1865–1902).[15] Born in 1838, he had trained for the ministry at Cotton End Academy in Bedfordshire at a time when only a tiny handful of Nonconformists were entering Oxford and Cambridge. There were four Franks sons, all of whom eventually followed their father into the Congregational ministry. All attended Sir William Turner's Grammar School at Coatham, Redcar. The eldest, Robert Sleightholme Franks, was a very able mathematician who outgrew what his school could teach him before he was ready to take the Cambridge Scholarship examinations. His father therefore arranged for him to go to live with the family of a fellow minister known to be a good mathematician, in Somerset. The result was that Robert Franks gained an exhibition to Cambridge in mathematics. The exhibition was not sufficient to cover his expenses; it was therefore supplemented by a discreet subsidy from a wealthy deacon in Redcar Church. After Cambridge, and a year back in Yorkshire, Robert Franks applied to enter Mansfield in 1893. Here he was given one of the twelve theological scholarships (it was worth £50–£60, sufficient to cover tuition fees and accommodation for the 24 weeks of University term), and would have been able to supplement this by modest fees from preaching engagements. His three brothers all followed him to Mansfield: John Franks was an exhibitioner in classics at Cambridge, Ernest Franks (whose son Richard also studied at Mansfield in the 1920s) took his first degree in Edinburgh, and Richard Franks won a Dr Williams' Scholarship to study first at Glasgow. Robert Franks, the eldest, became in later life not only one of Mansfield's, but also one of Congregationalism's, greatest theologians. In general, the students came from homes of modest means, but homes where education was valued, and they were supported by the generosity, expressed

[14] Much of the information in this paragraph came from personal communication from Lord Franks, son of R. S. Franks, 17 Oct. 1991.
[15] For William James Franks, see *CYB 1929*, 215.

either individually, or through endowments for scholarships, of the wealthier Congregational families. They had to live frugally and they had to work hard.

Mansfield's intellectual reputation was important from the beginning. Fairbairn the systematic theologian set the standard. He set out to educate scholars who could combine an understanding of modern critical developments with a mature Christian faith, and who could defend that faith with sharpened intellectual tools. At first, he had only one colleague, John Massie. Massie was the chief link between Spring Hill and Mansfield, spending half his teaching career in each. When he moved from Birmingham, he became a member of the Common Room at Corpus Christi College, and it was said that he was able to help Fairbairn to avoid '*faux pas* in good [Oxbridge] form'.[16] He could not have been called an *exciting* teacher, for he loved the most detailed examination of texts, and his 'microscopic methods' taxed even the patience of J. V. Bartlet, himself a most exact, not to say pedantic, scholar:

> A truly religious man, [Massie] yet felt it enough that the interpreter of the New Testament writings should handle them much as the great classics of Greek literature were handled at Cambridge, viz. on a basis of searching linguistic and grammatical accuracy, with such attention to historical and archaeological references as to make the text of each writing, both in the detail and as a whole, yield up its original meaning with clarity and sobriety.[17]

Massie produced a commentary in the Century Bible series, on Corinthians. In 1901 he was honoured with the degree of DD when he attended the Yale Tercentenary celebrations as the College representative.

However, he was more than a meticulous scholar. He was a keen cricketer and played for the College Eleven. And in the spirit of Dale and T. H. Green he was also a good citizen. He served as a local magistrate, a county councillor, and chairman of the county education committee, as well as on Congregational committees, and when he resigned from the Mansfield staff in 1903 at the age of 62, it was in order to enter politics. He represented Wiltshire North as a Liberal MP from 1906 until 1910.

---

[16] J. V. Bartlet in *MCM* 12/9 (Dec. 1925).   [17] Ibid. 220.

The opening of Mansfield coincided with the general recognition among both Nonconformist and Anglican scholars of the significance of biblical criticism. From the first, Mansfield students were introduced to the critical 'scientific' study of the Bible. Whereas in 1873 Henry Rogers had delivered the Congregational Lecture to the Congregational Union on 'The Superhuman Origin of the Bible Inferred from Itself' without reference to higher criticism, by the end of that decade the critical study of the Bible was steadily gaining ground in Nonconformist academic circles (though not without resistance).[18] While Fairbairn himself did not fully incorporate biblical criticism into his own thinking, he welcomed it and ensured that his students were introduced to it through the best critical scholars. In Bradford, he had appointed Archibald Duff, an 'advanced' Old Testament scholar, to teach Hebrew and Old Testament. In Oxford he arranged for his students to be taught by the recently appointed Old Testament scholars T. K. Cheyne and S. R. Driver.[19] T. K. Cheyne, Oriel Professor of Holy Scripture 1885–1908, had studied briefly in Göttingen, and along with A. B. Davidson[20] and William Robertson Smith[21] laid the basis for British critical scholarship on the Old Testament.[22] Samuel Rolles Driver succeeded Pusey as Regius Professor of Hebrew in 1883. He had already shown himself to be a first-class scholar with the publication of *A Treatise on the Use of the Tenses in Hebrew* (London, 1874); he went on to write commentaries on nearly half the Old Testament, and was regarded as a sound guide through the mass of critical work on the Old Testament then being published. It was a matter of pride for Mansfield that its early students and members of staff included two who were to become pre-eminent in Old Testament study—George Buchanan Gray and

---

[18] See W. B. Glover, *Evangelical Nonconformists and Higher Criticism in the Nineteenth Century* (London, 1954). R. F. Horton's *Inspiration and the Bible* (London, 1888) accepted the critical approach. The fact that it came out before the 'Down Grade Controversy' (see Glover, *Evangelical Nonconformists*, 163–76) had died down meant that he lost some church members and provoked much opposition; had the book been published a few years later, it would not have aroused such controversy.

[19] Regius Professor of Hebrew and Canon of Christ Church.

[20] Andrew Bruce Davidson (1831–1902), Professor of Hebrew and Oriental Languages, New College, Edinburgh. See *DNB Second Supplement*, 471–2.

[21] William Robertson Smith (1846–94), Semitic scholar, removed from his Chair at Aberdeen Free Church College for allegedly undermining belief in the inspiration of Scripture. See *DNB* xviii. 568–70.

[22] See T. K. Cheyne, 'Reform in the Teaching of the Old Testament', *CR* 56 (Aug. 1889), 216–33. After *c.*1900 Cheyne's ideas passed beyond the original into the fanciful with his 'Jerahmeelite' theory, and he was no longer taken seriously as a scholar.

H. Wheeler Robinson[23]—and that a scholar who was to produce one of the great biblical commentaries of his generation, A. S. Peake,[24] began his teaching career at Mansfield.

Fairbairn also issued frequent invitations to Scottish Old Testament scholars such as Marcus Dods,[25] A. B. Bruce,[26] and George Adam Smith[27] to preach, teach, and lecture at Mansfield, thereby providing a means of interchange between Oxford and Scottish scholars. The way in which Old Testament biblical criticism could invigorate preaching can be discerned in the published lectures of George Adam Smith, whose frequent visits to Mansfield during the years 1894–1900 as College Pastor and College Chapel preacher gave him the opportunity to contribute to the intellectual and religious life of the College.

In Aberdeen Smith had given a pioneering series of lecture-sermons on Isaiah, later published as the *Book of Isaiah* (2 vols.; London, 1888–90), which drew out the contemporary relevance of the prophetic insights. During the academic year 1894–5 he gave a series of lectures at Mansfield on 'The Pastor's Use of the Old Testament'. Though the text of these lectures is not available, a series of lectures delivered at Yale in 1899 was published as *Modern Criticism and the Preaching of the Old Testament* (London, 1901), and provides examples of his thinking. While he acknowledged that biblical criticism had challenged some prophetic authorship (to the dismay of many), it had renewed the authenticity of the words of the prophetic books 'as vision, as truth and as the revelation of God' (217). The social preaching of men like Kingsley and Maurice in an earlier generation had foundered, he believed, because it was not 'sustained

---

[23] See E. A. Payne, *Henry Wheeler Robinson: A Scholar, Teacher, Principal: A Memoir* (London, 1946); *MCM* 128 (Jan. 1946), 157–61; and *DNB 1941–50*, 727–79.

[24] Arthur Samuel Peake (1865–1929). See L. S. Peake, *Arthur Samuel Peake* (London, 1930); J. T. Wilkinson, *Arthur Samuel Peake: A Biography* (London, 1971); and *DNB 1922–30*, 657–8.

[25] Marcus Dods (1834–1904), Professor of New Testament Criticism and Exegesis at New College, Edinburgh. See *DNB Second Supplement*, 510–12.

[26] Alexander Balmain Bruce (1831–99), Professor at the Free Church College, Glasgow. *DNB Supplement*, 321–2.

[27] George Adam Smith (1856–1942). He had temporarily undertaken tutorial work in Hebrew and Old Testament studies at Aberdeen in 1881 in place of William Robertson Smith. In 1882 he began a ten-year ministry at Queen's Cross Free Church, Aberdeen. In 1892 he was elected Professor of Old Testament Language, Literature, and Theology at the Free Church College, Glasgow. See Lilian Adam Smith, *George Adam Smith* (London, 1943); *DNB 1941–50*, 792–4; and *Proceedings of the British Academy* (London, 1942), 325–6.

upon a thorough historical criticism of the Prophets' (219). This criticism enabled the Christian scholar to understand the contemporary relevance of the prophets; they spoke to a generation experiencing the transformation of Hebrew society from an agricultural to a commercial economy, emphasizing the responsibility for justice as well as 'charity', and evoking an altruism that transcended 'a *merely* national religion'. In Glasgow Smith was involved in community work in inner-city areas, particularly in the city's Toynbee House Settlement, and as the Chairman of the Scottish Council for Women's Trades. His teaching and personal example would have tuned well with the concerns of the Mansfield students of the 1890s, and provided them with a deeper theological and scriptural foundation.

New Testament Greek and exegesis was the responsibility of John Massie, but for interpretation and more advanced study the Mansfield students were sent to the lectures of William Sanday, Dean Ireland (1882–95), then Lady Margaret (1895–1919), Professor. As a Fellow of Exeter College Sanday came to know Fairbairn as a fellow member of the Senior Common Room and the two were clearly on warm personal terms.[28] They frequently went on walks together in Fairbairn's earlier years in Oxford. Sanday's fortnightly New Testament seminar became both a collaborative scholarly enterprise and a training ground for some of the leading New Testament scholars, both Anglican and Nonconformist, of the early twentieth century. In this enterprise Mansfield men and members of Pusey House worked at a table side by side 'engaged in collecting, verifying, and tabulating data bearing, however remotely, on the history and theology of the New Testament'.[29] The members of the seminar eventually produced *Oxford Studies in the Synoptic Problem* (Oxford, 1912). Sanday himself always intended that the sum and culmination of all his researches would be a *Life of Christ*, but this never materialized. Though he appears not to have spent any prolonged period of study in Germany, he read almost everything that was written on the New Testament in German as well as in English, and was the chief interpreter of German New Testament study to British scholars of his generation. Many Mansfield men were privileged to share in his seminar.

---

[28] As witness correspondence from Fairbairn to Sanday in the Bodleian Library, MS Eng.misc.d.140, fos. 119–29, d.123, fo. 1 and fos. 196–232. For Sanday's appreciation of Fairbairn's work at Mansfield, see his letter to the *Guardian*, 4 June 1892, quoted in Selbie, *Life of Andrew Martin Fairbairn*, 223–4.

[29] See W. Sanday, 'The Future of English Theology', *CR* 56 (July 1889), 52.

Edwin Hatch, whose 'smiling greeting as we entered was like a ray of sunshine',[30] lectured on canon law and church history as Reader in Ecclesiastical History. Hatch was a fine scholar whose contribution to the understanding of the Hellenistic background of the New Testament has not received full recognition. He believed in a 'scientific' rather than a 'dogmatic' approach to his subject, in a historical rather than a metaphysical method.[31] His Bampton Lectures of 1880 on *The Organization of the Early Christian Churches* were published in 1881, and were soon translated into German by Harnack— Hatch was one of the few English theologians whose work was known and respected on the Continent. As they cast doubt on the divine authority of episcopacy, they were popular with Congregationalists. 'We may say . . . the Divine right of episcopacy is dead; it died in the light created by historical criticism,' wrote Fairbairn in 1882.[32] Hatch's death at the early age of 54, at the peak of his intellectual powers, only days after the opening of Mansfield's new building, was a great loss. But he had already had a permanent influence on some of the early Mansfield students.

In 1889 one of those students, James Vernon Bartlet, was appointed Lecturer in Early Church History at Mansfield (and in 1900, Professor). Bartlet became one of the great Mansfield characters, affectionately called 'the last of the Early Fathers' and, on account of his considerable height, 'the elongated saint'. 'Tall and spare, with a piquantly Spanish appearance and an amusingly oracular and erudite manner of utterance',[33] he was genuinely and deeply respected by his students, both for his scholarship and for his personal integrity. Many in later life spoke of him as their 'father in God'. He gave the whole of his adult life to Mansfield and to scholarship.

As a lecturer he was hardly a success. Convoluted sentences seemed to come more naturally to him than simple ones, whether in or out of the lecture room. When he played tennis, he would suggest a knock-up with his opponent by saying, 'Before we start the match proper, I will knock the ball to you, and you will knock the ball back

---

[30] T. H. Martin in *MCM* 137 (July 1950), 26.

[31] See E. Hatch, 'From Metaphysics to History', *CR* 55 (June 1889), 864–72.

[32] A. M. Fairbairn, 'Ecclesiastical Polity and the Religion of Christ', in *Jubilee Lectures: A Historical Series Delivered on the Occasion of the Jubilee of the Congregational Union of England and Wales* (London, 1882), p. xxv.

[33] W. T. Pennar Davies, *Mansfield College, Oxford: Its History, Aims and Achievements* (Oxford, 1947).

to me, but, as it were, without contention.'[34] When he wanted to point out that religion was common to the whole variety of human beings, he would say, 'What I may call the *polupoikilos sophia* of God is nowhere more remarkable than in the unsophisticated undifferentiated simplicity of religious life.'[35] His students used the time during his lectures for activities other than note-taking: some wrote letters, while one at least translated his dictated paragraphs into Latin.

Bartlet (1863–1940) was the son of a Scottish schoolmaster who was headmaster of Mill Hill School for a short time. The home was narrow in outlook, typical of 'a rather grim school of Scottish pietism' and characterized by 'dour obscurantism';[36] but his education at Highgate School and Exeter College, where he gained a First in Theology, after initially reading Classics, and even more his years of study at Mansfield, enabled him to reach a faith which did not contradict his intellectual convictions. Learning from Fairbairn, Sanday, and Hatch, he became a champion of the 'historical method' in biblical and theological study. One of his pupils who learned and accepted this method from him wrote:

> He had a theory of his own by the help of which he believed he was able to bridge the gulf of antagonism between differing theological schools. He pleaded for the distinction between what he called 'idea' and what he called 'conceptions'. The 'idea' was the deep underlying religious reality common to all believing Christians, apprehensible in experience and imperfectly desirable in speech, but not capable of being run into any mould of formal definition. 'Conceptions' on the other hand were the formulated doctrines in which men endeavoured—and rightly endeavoured—to expound the significance of the idea.[37]

He believed that the path to church unity was through an 'objective' study of church history, and devoted his life to writing, research, and teaching on this theme. His contributions to the Oxford Society of Historical Theology followed the same motif. In later

---

[34] Interview with Eric Shave, May 1990. The transcript is in Mansfield College Library.
[35] H. Wheeler Robinson, *MCM* 118 (Jan. 1941), 638. [36] *CYB 1941*, 392.
[37] C. J. Cadoux, introd. to J. V. Bartlet, *Church Life and Church Order during the First Four Centuries* (Oxford, 1943), p. xvii.

years, as a Director of the London Missionary Society, he was 'a specially valued consultant' on the negotiations for church union in South India.[38] *The Apostolic Age* (London, 1899) was his major contribution to church history during Fairbairn's Principalship.

His fellow student, Selbie, was appointed Tutor in the same year that Bartlet was appointed Fellow. But Selbie remained for one year only, until he was called to be minister at Highgate. His contribution to Mansfield, as Principal nineteen years later, belongs to a later chapter.

The third early student who contributed to the establishment of the Mansfield academic tradition was George Buchanan Gray.[39] Gray was the son of a Dorset Congregational minister. His first theological study was undertaken at New College, London, where the teacher who recognized his ability in Hebrew recommended that he move on to Oxford to study with S. R. Driver. He came to Mansfield in 1888; a fellow student, T. H. Martin, remembered that 'At first, Dr Fairbairn was a little afraid of his radical and iconoclastic tendencies.' But after achieving a First in Oriental Languages, and collecting all the University prizes and scholarships for which he was eligible, and a period of study at Marburg, he settled down to the life of a scholar, and 'the Doctor's fears subsided'.[40] He was appointed Tutor at Mansfield in 1892 and then in 1900 Professor of Hebrew and Old Testament Exegesis.

Gray came to be recognized as the greatest Old Testament scholar of his generation in the English-speaking world. It was to Gray that Professor Driver entrusted the completion of his final work on Job; and it was Gray whom Driver would have liked to see as his successor as Regius Professor. But only an Anglican could be appointed to that position. Gray's first major work was *Studies in Hebrew Proper Names* (1896); there followed several commentaries in the series of International Critical Commentaries. He loved the Hebrew language and the Hebrew Scriptures, and like Bartlet dedicated his life to his chosen subject, and to helping others to a deeper understanding. His books were 'learned but sagacious, lively but reverent'.[41] As a teacher, the standards he set were higher than most could reach. Among the less academically inclined 'the preparation of unseens

[38] N. Goodall, *A History of the London Missionary Society 1895–1945* (Oxford, 1954), 537.
[39] George Buchanan Gray (1865–1922). See *CYB 1923*, 107; *MCM* 12/3 (Dec. 1922), 51–3 and 12/4 (June 1923), 75–9; *CQ* (1923), 26–30; and *DNB 1922–30*, 356–8.
[40] *MCM* 12/3 (Dec. 1922), 51.   [41] G. R. Driver in *DNB 1922–30*, 357–8.

for Buchanan Gray was the most hilarious hour of the week'.[42] A strong Independent, he lived a full life, preaching in country churches like those he had known in his boyhood, energetically supporting the Liberal Party, and giving time and effort to promoting social work (especially at Mansfield House Settlement).

Another who gave long service to the College was Norman Smith,[43] who had come to the College from New College, London (with a Cambridge degree) within six weeks of its opening; his father had died suddenly and he wanted to support his widowed mother. Recognizing his practical gifts, Fairbairn made him his private secretary within a year, a post which developed into that of Bursar. In his years of service to the College his knowledge of the place was such that he was affectionately nicknamed 'Bradshaw'—'the universal guide'. Bernard MacDonald (son of George MacDonald, the Victorian novelist who began his career as a Congregational minister) visited the College regularly to teach 'Elocution'.

These long-serving major figures were joined by a succession of other scholar tutors, all but two of them Mansfield-trained. Griffiths Thatcher (student 1889–93, Hebrew Tutor 1893–1909) was an Australian whose first visit to Mansfield was as a representative of Australian Congregationalists at the opening of the College buildings. He acquired exceptional learning in Semitic languages. Before he died, he told a friend that he had a reading knowledge of thirty-seven ancient and modern languages. In 1910 he returned to his native land as Warden of Camden College, Sydney and remained in that office until 1933.[44] R. S. Franks (student 1893–8) was Tutor from 1898 until 1900 before moving to a church in Birkenhead.[45] Thomas M. Watt (student 1901–4), a graduate of Aberdeen University, lectured in philosophy, and philosophy of religion and theism, from 1904 until 1909.[46] From Oxford, but not from Mansfield, came A. S. Peake, the first Nonconformist to become a Theology Fellow of an Oxford College,

---

[42] *MCM* 133 (July 1948), 178.

[43] Norman Hardwick Smith (1859–1932). See *CYB 1933*, 245–6 and *MCM* 101 (June 1932), 123–6, and his articles in the *CQ* (1926), 191–201 and (1927), 64–74.

[44] Griffiths Wheeler Thatcher (1865–1950). See *MCM* 137 (July 1950), 23–4 and J. Garrett and L. W. Farr, *Camden College: A Centenary History* (Sydney, 1964).

[45] Robert Sleightholme Franks (1871–1964) was one of Mansfield's most distinguished students, whose main work was as Principal of Western College, Bristol 1910–39. He continued to write substantial theological works until he was almost 90. See *CYB 1964–65*, 439–40 and *DNB 1961–70*, 392.

[46] Thomas M. Watt (1878–1938) spent the later part of his career as a minister of the Church of Scotland. See *MCM* 113 (July 1938), 528–9.

a Methodist scholar whose main life work was in Manchester; he was Tutor in Hebrew and Old Testament Studies at Mansfield from 1891 until 1893.[47] From Aberdeen and Cambridge, in succession to John Massie, came Alexander Souter as Yates Professor[48] in 1903. His best-known standard work, *Novum Testamentum Graecae*, was published in 1910 while he was still at Mansfield, and before his return to Aberdeen as Regius Professor of Humanity.[49]

There were refreshing links with the outside world through occasional visiting lecturers such as Sir William Ramsay[50] and George Adam Smith, through the system of 'College Pastors', introduced in 1892; through serving ministers like R. F. Horton and P. T. Forsyth[51] who lived in the College for short periods; and above all through the Sunday morning preachers in Chapel. Most of the leading Nonconformist scholars and preachers were invited to Mansfield at least once. In the academic year 1901–2, for example, the preachers included R. F. Horton, George Adam Smith, J. H. Shakespeare (Secretary of the Baptist Union), Marcus Dods, and the Revd Cuthbert Hall (President of Union Theological Seminary, New York).

If Mansfield was not a part of the University, it had to show by its academic achievements that it was worthy to be so. Within three years, Mansfield men had five prizes;[52] and G. B. Gray had won the Pusey and Ellerton Hebrew Scholarship. It was rewarding to Fairbairn when the College carried off an impressive number of University scholarships and prizes. As all its students were matriculated members of the University, many of them through the Non-collegiate Delegacy, they were eligible for its open awards. Mansfield men

---

[47] See Wilkinson, *Arthur Samuel Peake*. From 1904 until his death in 1929 Peake was Professor of Biblical Criticism and Exegesis at Manchester University. In 1908 he presented Fairbairn to receive the first honorary DD of Manchester University. In 1920 he himself was one of the first Nonconformists to receive the honorary Oxford DD.

[48] W. E. Yates of Leeds had endowed this post in 1896.

[49] Alexander Souter (1873–1949). He finally retired to Oxford, and used to attend Mansfield College Chapel regularly on Sundays in the last years of his life.

[50] Professor of Humanity, Aberdeen University 1886–1911. In 1907 he gave the second series of Dale Lectures (endowed in memory of R. W. Dale), and subsequently published as W. M. Ramsay, *The Cities of St Paul: Their Influence on his Life and Thought* (London, 1907).

[51] P. T. Forsyth was College Pastor in 1893, while he was minister at Clarendon Park, Leicester.

[52] W. B. Selbie won the Senior Septuagint Prize in 1888. H. T. Andrews won the same prize as well as the Ellerton Theological Essay Prize; and J. V. Bartlet won the Hall-Houghton Senior Greek Testament Prize. G. A. Wood, who was still following his arts course, won the Stanhope Historical Essay Prize.

regularly won the University Greek Prizes, the Septuagint Prizes, the Ellerton Theological Essay Prize, the Pusey and Ellerton University Scholarship, the Denyer and Johnson Theological Scholarship, the Kennicott Hebrew Scholarships, and the Hall Houghton Scholarships. R. S. Franks was the first to earn the new B.Litt. degree for a theological subject—'The Theories of the Atonement of Anselm and Grotius', which formed the basis of his book *A History of the Doctrine of the Work of Christ*.[53] In 1895, the year in which Fairbairn was elected an honorary MA, G. B. Gray was elected to the Board of Oriental Studies.

For practical experience, the students served local rural churches, sometimes for several weeks during vacations. Altogether they were worked very hard; more than once there were complaints about the excessive number of lectures. But it was not all hard work. Although the college was not residential, the Oxford college model was followed in many respects. From the beginning there was a Junior Common Room, in which a regular weekly social meeting took place, and whose business meetings were faithfully recorded in a JCR Minute Book; and dinner was taken in Hall each weekday evening (the chef 'had the interesting name of Pusey'), preceded by a short devotional service in the Chapel. The traditional Oxford custom of 'sconcing'[54] must have been established, for moves to abolish it failed regularly. The 'arts men', men who had been accepted by the College but had not yet begun their theological training, were required to dine in Mansfield at least once a week. When all were present, therefore, there was a community of about twenty-five students and four or five members of the SCR dining together in Hall, the senior members sitting as in other Oxford colleges at a separate high table, though not on a dais.

Sport played a considerable part in college life: there was a tennis court which was regularly used in the summer, and in 1898 a cricket and football ground was rented. Rowing too soon found a place in college life. Those Mansfield men who had matriculated through the Delegacy for Non-collegiate Students often took part in the Delegacy's sporting activities. Two of the earliest students remembered that

---

[53] As a non-Anglican, he was ineligible for the BD degree.

[54] An ancient custom, by which undergraduates compelled any of their number who broke certain rules (e.g. mentioning a woman's name in Hall) to drink a large tankard of ale without pausing for breath, under pain of paying for beer for the accuser.

Wolfendale had rowed at Cambridge, and he helped to create and foster the habit of rowing together on the Upper River which was a marked feature of the 'Early Fathers' of Mansfield and an element in their *esprit de corps*—especially when it took the form of a picnic outing far up the river in boats, in one of which Dr Fairbairn himself pulled a strenuous if not exactly a skilful oar.[55]

The first recorded 'smoker' (pl. 9) was held on 13 November 1895. It became an important Mansfield institution for years. Members of the Junior Common Room invited friends from other colleges to an entertainment, provided by themselves, at which ample provision was made for an evening's relaxation with cigarette or pipe. On one or two occasions these evenings were shared with the students next door at Manchester College.

On Sundays the service was held at 11.30 a.m., thus allowing people to attend the University sermon at 10.00 a.m. and then proceed down Holywell and Mansfield Road to the Mansfield Chapel without rush. The services were attended by large congregations from University and town, considerably depleting the congregation at George Street Congregational Church during term time. In the evenings, the men would frequently cycle out into the Oxfordshire countryside to take services in the small rural churches.

No college can run smoothly without the loyalty and work of the college servants, a remarkable group of men and women about whom too little has been recorded in the past.[56] However, later *College Magazines* tell us about two of the early 'servants'. William Collins came from Christ Church in 1889, when the new building was opened, and served the College well until his death in 1925; a loyal Anglican, he was a sidesman at St Cross Church.[57] Charles Symonds came to Mansfield straight from an orphanage at Witley, moved to Queen's after a few years, but took a drop in income to return to Mansfield as chef. During the First World War he had leave from the College to take administrative responsibility for the hospital in the Examination Schools.[58] In 1905 William Buckingham came to the College and served for forty-two years under three Principals until his death in 1947.

[55] *MCM* 113 (July 1938), 530.
[56] See D. C. M. Platt, *The Most Obliging Man in Europe: The Life and Times of the Oxford Scout* (London, 1986).
[57] See *MCM* 12/8 (June 1925), 187.   [58] *MCM* 12/9 (Dec. 1925), 230–1.

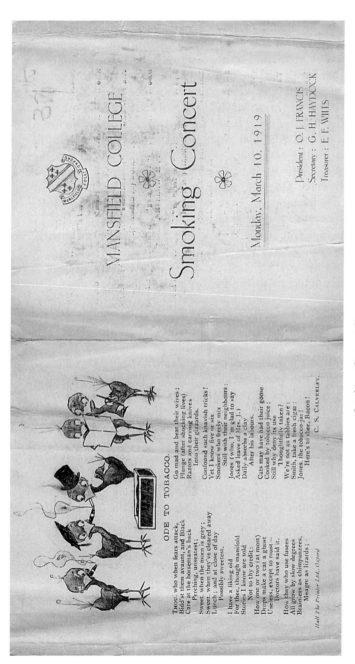

9. Smoking Concert Programme 1919

It was an almost exclusively male institution at first, according to the custom of the time. The Chapel windows, commemorating ninety-one men and seven women, reflected the common assumption that men were the natural leaders of the Church. But changes were afoot. The first women's colleges were founded at the end of the 1870s,[59] and some of their students attended Mansfield Chapel services. In the *Annual Report* for 1894–5 there was reference to 'two lady students' who had attended certain courses; in 1900 the June edition of the *Mansfield College Magazine* referred to the 'new precedent' established by having invited a woman (Dr Margaret Alden, wife of Percy Alden) to speak. And in 1904 the JCR agreed, though not by a unanimous vote, to allow 'ladies' to play tennis on the College courts at certain specified times.

The founding of the *Mansfield College Magazine* (for private circulation) in 1895, and the institution of 'Registered Life Members' in 1899, further strengthened the ties of loyalty to the College. Former students returned to the College each summer to meet their contemporaries and former tutors, and to 'recharge their batteries'. The articles in the *Magazine* in succeeding years convey something of the strength of the College community and of the loyalty which its members felt.

Most of the men (117 out of 162) who studied under Fairbairn went out into the pastoral ministry of Congregational or Baptist churches, and 80 of these served in that ministry for more than twenty-five years (some went to Australia and New Zealand).[60] One-fifth (32) spent at least part of their careers as university or college teachers. Edward Anwyl was Professor of Welsh and Comparative Philology at the University College of Wales in Aberystwyth and was knighted for his contribution to Welsh education;[61] E. R. Hughes was Reader in Chinese Religion and Philosophy at Oxford from 1933 until 1947, after a career as a missionary with the London Missionary

---

[59] The Association for the Education of Women in Oxford was founded in 1878. Lady Margaret Hall and Somerville Hall were opened as Halls of Residence a year later, and the group of women students living in private homes became known as the 'Society of Oxford Home Students' (later St Anne's College).

[60] Of these, four eventually moved to the Church of England, three to the Church of Scotland, two to the Unitarians, two to the Society of Friends, and one to the Scottish Episcopal Church.

[61] See *MCM* 9/3 (Dec. 1914), 33–41 and J. E. Lloyd and R. T. Jenkins (eds.) *Dictionary of Welsh Biography* (London, 1959), 12–13.

Society (LMS) in China.[62] The most distinguished theological scholar amongst them, R. S. Franks, was Principal of Western College, Bristol for twenty-nine years, 1910–39, and wrote several significant theological books.[63] A. E. Garvie[64] was Principal of New College, London for twenty-six years (1907–33). Several Mansfield men taught in the Faculty of Theology in the University of Wales which Fairbairn had helped to establish.[65]

Eighteen men went overseas as missionaries, to China, India, or the South Seas, almost all under the auspices of the LMS.[66] Sidney Berry[67] was Secretary of the Congregational Union for twenty-five years; Leyton Richards[68] was an outstanding pacifist leader; Malcolm Spencer[69] was an ecumenical leader in his own individual way, as was Frank Lenwood.[70] 'Fairbairn's men' made their mark. Mansfield's position in Oxford, and the personal intellectual stature of Fairbairn, gave the College a pre-eminent place among Congregational theological colleges. And its Principal held a position of authority, in a denomination which had no bishops, of much greater significance than that of Anglican college principals (whose recognition might come later when appointed to the episcopate).

Fairbairn's influence began to decline after the opening of the new century. His students felt that he had not kept abreast of newer theological thinking and was unable to guide them through the new explorations of the current German theology. T. M. Watt wrote after Fairbairn's death of his waning influence:

[62] See *MCM* 150 (Jan. 1957), 322–3.

[63] e.g. *A History of the Doctrine of the Work of Christ*, 2 vols. (London, 1918; reissued in 1 vol. as *The Work of Christ* in 1962), *The Atonement* (Oxford, 1934), originally delivered as the Dale Lectures at Mansfield in 1933, and *The Doctrine of the Trinity* (London, 1953).

[64] Alfred Ernest Garvie (1861–1945). See A. E. Garvie, *Memories and Meanings of my Life* (London, 1938) and *MCM* 128 (Jan. 1946), 440–1 and *DNB* 1941–50, 289–90.

[65] These included Joseph Jones, John Morgan Jones, J. D. V. Lewis, and Thomas Rees. See also App. I.

[66] Fairbairn gave long service as an Honorary Director of the LMS. See Goodall, *History of the London Missionary Society* and Irene Robbins, 'Mansfield and the LMS', *MCM* 127 (July 1945), 134–6.

[67] Sidney Malcolm Berry (1881–1961). See *CYB 1962*, 449–50 and *MCM* 160 (Jan. 1962), 93–4 and 161 (July 1962), 123–4, and *DNB* 1961–70, 99–101.

[68] Leyton Richards (1879–1948). See Edith Ryley Richards, *Private View of a Public Man* (London, 1950) and *CYB 1949*, 503.

[69] Malcolm Spencer (1877–1950). See M. Lawson, *God's Backroom Boy: The Story of Malcolm Spencer* (London, 1952), and *CYB, 1951*, 520–1.

[70] Frank Lenwood (1874–1934). See R. C. Wilson, *Frank Lenwood* (London, 1936); *CYB 1935*, 282–3; and *MCM* 106 (Dec. 1934), 293–301.

It may have been, amongst other reasons, that since the wine of Ritschlianism had been introduced into the College, the older vintage of Hegelianism had grown out of favour. The fine and broad culture which the historical method in theology gives was neglected in favour of a too uncritical reliance on the experience of the religious consciousness, and its pragmatic interpretation . . . The interest of many men in the College was turned aside from theology, to what they held to be the more direct cause of religion, and the Doctor's influence as a thinker began to wane.[71]

Fairbairn remained a Hegelian and disappointed his students by maintaining silence on the theology of Albrecht Ritschl, who was so influential in Germany and whose books were now being translated and read in England. He was not able to help his later students to work out an adequate theological response to the intellectual problems of the new century.

Ritschl (1822–89) had been appointed Professor of Dogmatic Theology at Göttingen in 1864, and published his main work *The Christian Doctrine of Justification and Reconciliation* in three volumes between 1870 and 1874. Volume i was translated into English in 1872; volume iii was finally translated in 1900; volume ii has never been translated. Ritschl had broken with the Hegelianism of his youth and training to found a new school of thought which came to dominate progressive Christian thinking, at Mansfield as elsewhere among Liberal Protestants. He agreed with Schleiermacher that the facts of Christian experience must be the starting-point for theology, but disagreed as to the nature of experience. For Schleiermacher it was essentially personal feeling; for Ritschl it was 'value-judgement'. This contrasted with Fairbairn's Hegelian emphasis on reason. 'The knowledge of God can be demonstrated as religious knowledge only when God is conceived as securing to the believers such a position in the world as more than counter-balances its restrictions,' wrote Ritschl.[72] As the Kingdom of God was central to the teaching of Jesus, so Ritschl saw this Kingdom as the moral goal of human beings.

Ritschl had several important disciples: Wilhelm Herrmann (1846–1922), professor at Marburg, Julius Kaftan (1848–1926), professor in Berlin, and Adolf Harnack (1851–1930), also professor in Berlin. Harnack's

---

[71] T. M. Watt, *MCM* 8/1 (Mar. 1912), 31–2.
[72] A. Ritschl, *The Christian Doctrine of Justification and Reconciliation*, vol. i, trans. J. S. Black (London, 1872), 8.

Das Wesen des Christenthums was published in Germany in 1900, and its English translation, by T. B. Saunders, *What is Christianity?*, published in 1901, was widely read. Mansfield men went to both Marburg and Berlin to 'taste the wine of Ritschlianism', and Bartlet liked to refer to himself as 'a liberal of the Harnack or right-wing Ritschlian type'.[73]

When Fairbairn was invited to spend time in India he asked his old student A. E. Garvie to lecture at Mansfield in his stead. Of the suggested subjects which Garvie submitted, Fairbairn chose Ritschlianism. The interest of the JCR, as of the senior men, had already been stimulated by a paper by Garvie on Ritschlianism at a College reunion in 1897. Thus the Mansfield men of 1898–9 were given a *critical* introduction to Ritschl's thought; and the lectures were so well received that a special request led to their being published as *The Ritschlian Theology* in 1899—the first study of Ritschl in English.[74]

There are hints in their Minutes that the Council was aware that Fairbairn was losing his grip and that his teaching had become somewhat stale. In 1904 a special subcommittee was asked to review the College studies. Its report recommended that the Principal should be asked to submit a scheme of subjects for each term to the Board of Education[75] before term started; and that no tutor or lecturer should continue in office for more than five years, thus providing a regular opportunity for promising students to continue study beyond a third year, in conjunction with a tutorship.

The Ritschlian theology which was gaining ground in Mansfield was compatible with the interests of the men in the new ecumenical movement, especially as it was developing through the British College Christian Union (BCCU), to become the Student Christian Movement (SCM) in 1905. The SCM, which developed from a meeting at the Keswick Convention in 1893, was destined to become one of the greatest influences on generations of future church leaders. Mark Johnson has described it as 'the avenue by which the Mansfield students entered the ecumenical movement'.[76] The leading SCM figure at Mansfield was Frank Lenwood (Mansfield 1897–1900).

[73] W. H. Coats, for example, wrote about his experiences in Marburg in *MCM* 6/1 (Dec. 1907), 55–60.

[74] A. E. Garvie, *The Ritschlian Theology* (Edinburgh, 1899).

[75] The Board of Education, which included some Council members and some co-opted members, was responsible to the Council for admissions and for the College curriculum.

[76] Johnson, *The Dissolution of Dissent*, 227.

At a theological colleges conference organized by the BCCU in Birmingham in April 1898, Fairbairn was one of the speakers. It was at this conference that Frank Lenwood, still a Mansfield student, emerged as a leader; he was elected chairman of the Theological Committee. It was Lenwood who had introduced the Travelling Secretary of the BCCU (Fred O'Neill) to Fairbairn in 1897; O'Neill found Mansfield's Principal 'greatly interested in the BCCU and the World's Student Christian Federation but thought there ought to be much more union between colleges, especially between colleges in the same place, as, for instance, Wycliffe Hall and Mansfield College. He would much like to see missionary study started in Mansfield College.'[77]

Lenwood, like Horton before him, had charisma, social confidence, and great ability. Like Horton, he had been to a public school, and was President of the Union during his undergraduate career. He and six of his contemporaries at Mansfield formed 'The Context'— a group which met for five days a year for over fifty years in order to share ideas and experience.[78] He won several prizes during his Mansfield career, sharing the Senior Greek Testament Prize with the future New Testament scholar B. H. Streeter. He was much impressed by the way in which Anglican and Roman Catholic chaplains cared for undergraduates, and eagerly accepted Fairbairn's invitation to become the first Chaplain to Nonconformist undergraduates in the University, as well as Tutor in New Testament Greek to Mansfield men, in 1901, and remained for the next five years. He had an intensity of conviction which could evoke great dedication (though some found it overpowering), and which he used to influence men (and women—he was always supportive of the value of women's contribution to the SCM, missionary work, and church life in general), encouraging them to take part in this 'interdenominational fellowship' which he believed would prepare the way for the ultimate unity of the Christian Church. In 1909 he was Chairman of an influential conference on 'The SCM and the Social Question' in Matlock in which William Temple took part.

---

[77] O'Neill's diary, quoted in T. Tatlow, *The Story of the Student Christian Movement* (London, 1933), 118–19.

[78] Apart from Lenwood, the members were Henry Child Carter, Percy Neale Harrison, Thomas Henry Cooper, Godfrey Edward Phillips, William Morton Barwell, and James Shaw Griffith. They took the name of their group from a sermon preached by G. E. Phillips on 'The Eternal Context'.

Lenwood was not the only Mansfield man who was active in the SCM in these pre-war days. Malcolm Spencer (Mansfield 1900–3) was Travelling Secretary of the Theological Department from 1906 to 1909, when his place was taken by Martyn Trafford (Mansfield 1905–8), a Baptist who served until his sudden death in 1910.[79] Lenwood felt the call to work with the LMS in India for three years at the end of the decade, and subsequently as LMS Foreign Secretary for ten years. He was more far-sighted than some of his contemporaries in realizing that missionaries should be laying the foundations of indigenous churches, a task that could not and would not be done in a hurry.

It was a great disappointment to him that, despite his own considerable standing in the SCM, he never persuaded the Mansfield JCR to associate formally with the Theological Colleges Department of the SCM; this did not happen until March 1912, the month following Fairbairn's death. Lenwood was a complex personality with a deep concern for the poor and for those outside the Church. But it does seem that his social and religious ideas had a weak theological foundation. While working as Foreign Secretary at the LMS he abandoned belief in the divinity of Christ, and to avoid embarrassment to the Society resigned his position. His views were made public in his book *Jesus: Lord or Leader?* (London, 1930). For the last years of his life, until he was killed in a climbing accident in 1934, he was minister of Greengate Congregational Church, Plaistow.

The advent of the SCM, and the accompanying impulse to missionary work through the Student Volunteer Missionary Union, was associated with that 'Social Gospel' which found expression in the work of the Mansfield House Settlement. It is to the foundation, work, and influence of that Settlement that we must now turn.

[79] For Trafford, see *MCM* 7/3 (Dec. 1910), 49–55 and T. Tatlow, *Martyn Trafford: A Sketch of his Life and his Work for the SCM* (London, 1910).

VII

Mansfield House Settlement

'THIS is no other enthusiasm of humanity than the one which has travelled the common highway of reason—the life of the good neighbour and the honest citizen.' These words of T. H. Green engraved above the entrance to the Mansfield House Residence at 89 Barking Road, Canning Town exemplified both the inspiration and the aim of the Settlement—to provide the conditions for a good life, economically, socially, aesthetically, intellectually, and spiritually, for all groups in society.

The Mansfield Settlement was inaugurated on 21 May 1890 (the day after the annual meeting of the College's Trustees and subscribers) at a breakfast meeting in the College Hall.[1] Twenty people were present, including students and members of Council, and the offer of Percy Alden,[2] who was just completing the second year of his course at the College, to act as Warden, was accepted. The Committee which was then elected soon arranged for the purchase of two houses in the Barking Road, Canning Town, and work began in September. Though it has undergone many changes of emphasis, and moved in and out of several different houses in Barking Road, and though its work is on a much smaller scale than in its first decade, Mansfield House still serves the local community.

The idea of a College settlement in London arose in the first place among the students themselves: 'I ought to say, to the credit of the Mansfield students, that the movement originated entirely among the men themselves without, in the first place, any official interference on the part of the College.'[3] This was borne out by the reference to the founding of Mansfield House in the College Report for 1890–1: 'Although the movement has not originated with the

---

[1] See Minute Book of the Executive Committee of Mansfield House, Canning Town, microfilm, Stratford Library, Newham, London.

[2] Percy Alden (1865–1944). See *MCM* 127 (July 1945).

[3] Percy Alden in *Christian Commonwealth*, 29 Mar. 1894.

Council, and is not under their control, yet in their judgment it calls for this special notice, and they heartily commend it to the sympathy and support of their constituents.'[4]

What were the influences which led up to this enterprise, influences sufficiently strong to keep the Settlement alive for so long? Like the foundation of the College itself, the initiation of the Settlement owed much to the inspiration of T. H. Green. Percy Alden himself was personally influenced by both Green and Arnold Toynbee. Aged 15, he had been sent as a messenger to Green's house on business connected with the Oxford Local Examinations. 'What a kind friend Green was to every young man who showed that he had a craving for something higher and better than the satisfaction of a few selfish desires!', he wrote later.[5] On the same occasion he met Arnold Toynbee, and later affirmed that 'it was to Green that Toynbee most frequently resorted for advice or counsel'.[6] Largely through Green's influence, Alden eventually went up to Balliol in 1884 to read Greats. Green was now dead, and though Benjamin Jowett, Master of Balliol, was in general sympathy with Green's ideals, in practice these ideals were often in conflict with a more worldly ambition for Balliol men.

In 1888, aged 23, Alden applied to Mansfield with the intention of preparing for the Baptist ministry, the first applicant who was not intending to prepare for the Congregational ministry. This caused some considerable discussion, and it was not until the Board of Education had a further meeting that he was admitted as a 'non-foundation' student, a fact which was 'not to be noted in the College's published report'.[7] In the event, Alden became a Congregational minister 'without pastoral charge' for some years, but eventually joined the Society of Friends, and went on to have a distinguished career in social and political work. Green's ideal of the 'good citizen' remained with him, and it was Green's portrait which hung in the Warden's office at the new Settlement.

In the spirit of Green was the influence of Arnold Toynbee,[8] and of those associated with Toynbee Hall, founded in his memory, in

---

[4] *Mansfield College Report* (1890–1), 9.
[5] *Mansfield House Magazine* (1884), 49.   [6] Ibid.
[7] Board of Education Minute Book 1881–1943, entry for 16 Oct. 1888, MCA. Alden was the first of many Baptists who studied at Mansfield.
[8] Arnold Toynbee (1852–83). See *DNB* xix. 1063–5 and Alon Kadish, *Apostle Arnold: The Life and Death of Arnold Toynbee 1852–1883* (Durham, NC, 1986).

particular Samuel Barnett, first Warden of the Hall. Arnold Toynbee was another Balliol man who had come under the influence of Green, and who followed Green's example in living a life in which intellectual striving and good citizenship were constructively inter-active. As an undergraduate he had taken part in Ruskin's experi-ment in road-making in Hinksey, and in vacation had lived alongside a few other undergraduates in Whitechapel helping Canon Barnett,[9] then Vicar of St Jude's Church. This experience convinced him that it was necessary to have a proper understanding of the actual needs of the poor before they could be helped; and that social reform was the proper expression of one's religious obligation. 'For the sake of religion he had become a social reformer; for the sake of social reform he became an economist,' wrote his friend Alfred Milner.[10] Never in robust health, his activities proved too great for his physique, and he died in 1883 just before he was due to be elected a Fellow of Balliol.

In his memory, Toynbee Hall was founded in Whitechapel with Samuel Barnett as Warden, and with considerable support from Oxford. Toynbee Hall was a 'settlement' rather than a 'mission', and in many respects proved a model for the Mansfield Settlement. In a paper read at St John's College, Oxford on 17 November 1883, Barnett had argued against college missions, which in practice quickly devel-oped into autonomous parishes, and lost touch with the founding college; in addition, the opportunity to work in them was confined to Anglicans. A settlement, offering the opportunity for graduates and undergraduates to live and work together in East London, pre-sided over by a clergyman, but without sectarian restrictions, would, he argued, be more appropriate for a university or college.[11] In the rooms of a future Archbishop of Canterbury, Cosmo Gordon Lang of Balliol, following the lecture, a group of undergraduates pledged themselves to support Barnett's plan, and within a few months they and a few others raised sufficient money to buy an old building in Whitechapel. The first residents moved in before the end of 1884, and Toynbee Hall was launched. From the outset, education and social investigation were prime functions, and it soon established itself as a centre of intellectual exploration and challenge in a hitherto

---

[9] Samuel Augustus Barnett (1844–1913), priest and social reformer. See *DNB 1912–21*, 31–2.

[10] Alfred Milner, *Arnold Toynbee: A Memoir* (London, 1895), 39.

[11] See S. Barnett, *Settlements of University Men in Great Towns* (Oxford, 1884).

educationally and socially desolate part of London. Amongst those who came to live in the Hall, Barnett noticed that those who had felt Green's influence had the strongest motivation for social reform.[12]

In the same year as the foundation of Toynbee Hall, another group of Oxford men, mainly associated with Keble College, founded Oxford House (Settlement) in Bethnal Green. This was more overtly Christian and missionary in purpose (though T. H. Green's influence was not entirely absent), and its residents included a higher proportion of men who intended to become clergymen. Its object was summed up by the Warden of Keble, E. S. Talbot, as 'the preparation of character for . . . the reception of the religion of Christ'.[13] Meanwhile the group of Anglican Oxford scholars whose discussions were to lead to the publication of *Lux Mundi* in 1889 included men who were influenced by the Christian Socialists, and the book broke new ground for such a volume by including an essay on 'Christianity and Politics' by W. J. H. Campion.

Interest in social reform was thus strong in Oxford, among Nonconformists as well as among Anglicans. R. F. Horton himself was influenced by the ideas of Green and the ideals of Toynbee. The Oxford University Nonconformists' Union included social reform among the topics discussed at its meetings. An occasional speaker at the Nonconformist Union was Canon W. H. Fremantle, Chaplain of Balliol, whose Bampton Lectures on 'The World as the Subject of Redemption', published in 1885, were a significant theological contribution to Christian social thinking; their purpose, the author wrote, was 'to restore the idea of the Christian Church as a moral and social power, present, universal, capable of transforming the whole life of mankind, and destined to accomplish this transformation'.[14] Fremantle had done pioneering work as Rector of St Mary's, Bryanston Square in introducing lay participation in the church's affairs, and

---

[12] See W. Reason (ed.), *University and Social Settlements* (London, 1898) 12. See also Kadish, *Apostle Arnold*, 227–9 and A. Briggs and A. Macartney, *Toynbee Hall: The First Hundred Years* (London, 1984).

[13] In *The Times*, 21 Jan. 1891, 13, quoted in K. S. Inglis, *Churches and the Working Classes in Victorian England* (London, 1963), 157. See M. Ashworth, *The Oxford House in Bethnel Green: A Hundred Years of Work in the Community* (London, 1984).

[14] W. H. Fremantle, *The World as the Subject of Redemption* (London, 1885), 1. William Henry Fremantle (1831–1916), a friend and correspondent of Henry Allon, was a former student of Jowett's who served as Chaplain of Balliol 1882–94. He was Dean of Ripon 1895–1915. See *Recollections of Dean Fremantle* (London, 1921).

in developing an extensive social programme for all classes. For a time Samuel Barnett had been his curate.[15]

When Mansfield began work at 90 High Street in 1886, two ministers from London were involved in introducing students to the problems of working-class areas. One was Andrew Mearns, the Secretary of the London Congregational Union, and 'editor' of *The Bitter Cry of Outcast London*, a pamphlet which created a deep impression, expressing 'exactly that mood of corporate guilt and apprehension which stirred some members of the comfortable classes after 1880 to lend a hand to their poorer brothers'.[16] 'Whilst we have been building our churches and solacing ourselves with our religion and dreaming that the millennium was coming,' the pamphlet stated, 'the poor have been growing poorer, the wretched more miserable, and the immoral more corrupt'.[17] The pamphlet was read widely, in Oxford and elsewhere.[18] As a result the London Congregational Union proposed to establish three Mission Halls, to undertake both practical and religious work.

The 'mood of corporate guilt' had been growing among Congregationalists, whose support lay mostly among the middle classes. Times had changed since Thomas Binney's assertion to the Congregational Union in 1848 that Congregationalism had a special mission 'neither to the very rich nor to the very poor', but to 'the thinking, active, influential classes . . . the modern movers and moulders of the world'.[19] J. Guinness Rogers wrote in an editorial in the *Congregational Review* in 1888 that many working-class people believed that 'they had not the sympathy from the churches and their ministers, which, from the teaching of Christ, they had a fair right to anticipate; that, on the contrary, their leanings, like those of the

[15] See L. E. Nettleship, 'William Fremantle, Samuel Barnett and the Broad Church Origins of Toynbee Hall', *Journal of Ecclesiastical History*, 33 (1982), 564–79.

[16] Inglis, *Churches and the Working Classes*, 69. The exact authorship of *The Bitter Cry of Outcast London* has been disputed; it seems that while it was prepared under the direction of Andrew Mearns, it was actually written by W. C. Preston, a Congregational minister out of pastoral charge living in south-east London, and drew on work by G. R. Sims, author of *How the Poor Live* (1883). See *CYB 1903*, 193–4 and *CYB 1926*, 170.

[17] *The Bitter Cry of Outcast London* (London, 1883), 2.

[18] Sir Frank Tillyard later claimed to have been the first person in Oxford to read it, and remembered that it had been read by undergraduates in boathouses as well as by 'leaders of thought' in Oxford; 'it struck the right note at the right moment.' Tillyard also detected the influence of 'the Maurice school of thought'. See 'Congregational and Social Service: Retrospect 1831–1931', in A. Peel (ed.), *Essays Congregational and Catholic* (London, 1931), 339, 340.

[19] *CYB 1848*, 9.

world outside, are to the wealthy, the influential, the successful classes'.[20]

The second London minister who worked with Mansfield students was Frederick William Newland, two years senior to R. F. Horton when he was an undergraduate at Merton, and a member with Horton of the Oxford University Nonconformists' Union in the early 1880s. In 1884, after further study at New College, London, Newland began a ministry at Canning Town. His original intention of preparing for missionary work in China was challenged by reading *The Bitter Cry of Outcast London*, and he was persuaded that work in east London was no less important. He spoke at conferences at 90 High Street, and invited pairs of students to work with him for two weeks at a time during the Christmas and Easter vacations. One of those students was Percy Alden, the future first Warden of Mansfield House Settlement. It was this connection which led to the founding of the College's Settlement in that particular part of London—the Borough of West Ham, which lay beyond the reach of the existing settlements. Newland worked closely with the Settlement until he left Canning Town for Grimsby in 1894.[21]

Though Fairbairn did not initiate the Settlement, he fully supported it. His own father was a working man, and he had spent much of his boyhood years working for shops and for a miller. Fairbairn never lost his innate sympathy for working men, and in spite of his formidable learning and rather severe appearance in later life, always retained his ability to communicate with them. According to his biographer, it was his reading of Ruskin's *Unto This Last* at Bathgate which first alerted him to the significance of social questions, and as minister in a town with considerable poverty and unemployment, he learned early in his ministry that social questions should not be ignored in the pulpit.[22] His lectures to working men in Bradford in the 1870s on 'Faith and Modern Free Thought' attracted large audiences, and convinced him not only that working men were alive to religious questions, but also that the lecture was one of the best means of reaching them.[23]

---

[20] *Congregational Review* (July 1888), 603.

[21] See F. W. Newland, *Newland of Claremont and Canning Town* (London, 1932).

[22] W. B. Selbie, *The Life of Andrew Martin Fairbairn* (London, 1914), 49.

[23] These lectures were later published as *Religion in History and in the Life of Today* (London, 1884). The 4th edn. was given the title *Religion in History and in Modern Life* (London, 1894) and included an essay on 'The Church and the Working Classes'.

In later years, Percy Alden looked back and reflected that 'we probably should not have realised our ambitions in respect of the Settlement, had it not been for the encouragement which Dr Fairbairn gave to the project from the very outset'.[24] Fairbairn was President of the Settlement for the rest of his life, and paid frequent visits. He showed the same gift as in Bradford for communicating with working men:

> He would hold an audience of working men spellbound by the scope and breadth of his learning. They regarded him as a sort of walking encyclopaedia. His speeches, erudite and sympathetic, delivered without notes, appealed very much to the working men of Canning Town, who were no mean judges of either oratory or learning. . . . He never ceased to exhort the churches to take a deeper and wider interest in the social welfare of the people, and on many occasions he argued that what was wanted was more of the spirit of service in the Church and less of that worldly materialistic atmosphere in which churches were apt to stagnate. 'Whatever concerned the weal of man,' I remember his saying in Mansfield Hall, 'was essentially religious'; and he asked us to remember that the one thing we could do was to fill life with good materially as well as morally, and that a life so lived would not be lived in vain.[25]

Though Fairbairn was much more cautious than Alden in encouraging residents at the Settlement to become involved in civic committees, he did recognize the duty of the churches to prepare 'the right kind of men' to serve in Parliament and County Councils.[26] Fairbairn would not have committed himself as far as Alden did to the principles of the Labour movement, but he regularly supported Alden against uninformed critics of the work of Mansfield House, and his heart was always in its work.

Mansfield House was a settlement and not a mission. Inglis describes it as 'one of the few settlements in London or elsewhere which on Barnett's definition was not in some aspects a mission'.[27] This was in accord with Fairbairn's own convictions. In his lecture to the Congregational Union as Chairman in October 1883 he had told his audience:

---

[24] Quoted in Selbie, *Life of Andrew Martin Fairbairn*, 301.
[25] Percy Alden, ibid. 302–3.   [26] Ibid. 303.
[27] Inglis, *Churches and the Working Classes*, 160.

It is not enough to organize evangelistic missions, however excellent and fit these may be. It is not the distinction of the industrial classes to be in peculiar need of conversion; it is the need of the so-called upper classes in a still more eminent degree. What is necessary to reach and affect both is a more fully realized Christianity, the resolute endeavour to bring the religion professed of the churches into completer harmony with the mind of Christ.[28]

and

Religion ought to feel that social and industrial questions are peculiarly its own, and cannot be wisely or justly determined without its help. . . . Secularism should have had no excuse for its being; religion ought to be secular, and would be all the more spiritual and eternal for so being.[29]

Thus Canon Barnett's definition of a settlement during his speech at the meeting following the laying of the foundation stone of the new Mansfield House Residence in 1896 was in no way in contradiction to Fairbairn's ideas:

A settlement is not a mission. A mission exists for a definite purpose, for the promotion of [a] fixed set of principles, such as Christian doctrine, teetotalism, socialism, or may be individualism . . . The settlements do not exist to promote any set of principles, but to make a stand for the unity of society. We do not mean by this uniformity; I want to see the settlements make a stand for unification, and strive to bring about such a good understanding between all classes that they may become workers together.[30]

This in turn was echoed theologically by Fairbairn in his essay on 'The Church and the Working Classes' in the 1894 edition of *Religion in History and Modern Life*: 'churches composed exclusively of rich and poor mean the reign of the conditions and categories of time within the realm of the eternal.'[31] This essay was a plea to overcome the alienation of the Church (rather than religion) from the working classes, for which the Church had to bear the chief responsibility. Fairbairn had rejected any individualistic interpretation of the

---

[28] 'The Christian Religion in the Nineteenth Century', pub. in A. M. Fairbairn, *Studies in Religion and Theology* (London, 1910), 97.
[29] Ibid. 99.   [30] Quoted in *Mansfield House Magazine* (Jan. 1897), 5.
[31] Fairbairn, *Religion in History and Modern Life*, 4th edn. 62.

gospel. Like Dale, his view of the Atonement involved the whole of the human race. The Kingdom of God, not the Church, was the primary focus of Christ's teaching: 'the Church must be construed through the Kingdom, not the Kingdom through the Church.'[32] The signs of the Kingdom are spiritual and ethical, and 'relate to gracious helpfulness and service, never to officers or acts of ceremonial'.[33]

Barnett's concept of the settlement was that adopted by Percy Alden when he was Warden. 'The working classes must be influenced in other ways than by sermons delivered from the pulpit'; the underlying conception of the Settlement's work 'is not individualistic, but co-operative; we are not a collection of individuals, or atoms, or units; we are all members of one living organism, every member with its functions to discharge, the happiness of every member necessary to the whole'.[34] He quoted F. D. Maurice, whose Christian Socialism had inspired an earlier generation: 'Not land and capital, not labour and goods, but right human relations lie at the root of all social reform.'[35] It was Maurice's theology of *The Kingdom of Christ*,[36] as much as any, which inspired the work of Mansfield Settlement. Though each settlement had its individual ethos and emphasis, there was a modicum of consultation and co-operation. In July 1894, for example, there was a conference for representatives of all London settlements and college missions at Toynbee Hall, at which Percy Alden chaired one of the discussions.[37] Another model for the Mansfield Settlement was Hull House, Chicago (though actually three months 'younger' in foundation), which Percy Alden visited in 1895. A year later, Jane Addams, Warden of Hull House and herself a Congregationalist, paid a reciprocal visit, and made a great impression: 'she won all hearts by her earnest, clever, and witty speech, and her own unassuming manner.'[38]

Whereas Toynbee Hall and Oxford House were both within the Metropolitan area, Canning Town was the southern part of the separate Borough of West Ham (now Newham). It lay between London and the Essex marshes, a desolate area of dockland, where much of

[32] A. M. Fairbairn, *The Place of Christ in Modern Theology* (London, 1893), 515–16.
[33] Ibid. 517.   [34] Percy Alden, *MCM* 2/14 (June 1899), 91.
[35] Ibid. 92.   [36] F. D. Maurice, *The Kingdom of Christ* (1st edn. London, 1838).
[37] *Mansfield House Magazine* (1894), 143.
[38] Ibid. (1896), 104. See J. Addams, *Twenty Years at Hull House* (Chicago, 1910) and Albert Peel, *The Congregational Two Hundred 1530–1948* (London, 1948), 263–4.

the work was casual. An anonymous writer in the *Mansfield House Magazine* described it thus:

> A flat, marshy expanse, a muddy stream, a few ill-looking trees, were originally the prospect that pleased, and man has shown more than his customary vileness in dealing with it. Shooter's Hill in the distance, the masts of shipping that one catches here and there, and the gas works that decorate the low-lying, mist-barred flats, are artistically the redeeming features; and of these the first two are frequently lost to view through the haziness of the atmosphere, and the charm of the last, after all, a doubtful one.[39]

As a district outside the Metropolitan area, West Ham was unable to share in the minimal benefits offered by the Metropolitan Common Poor Fund. The great dock strike of 1889[40] was followed by several periods of unemployment in the area, and the problems of West Ham became a focus for dealing with the problems of unemployment nationally. Percy Alden played a key role in identifying the problems and suggesting solutions; but 'while we are waiting for the reorganisation of industry upon a more ethical basis, we must do what we can to relieve the distress'.[41]

Work for the Settlement began in the autumn of 1890 in the two houses 143 and 145 Barking Road, while a house at 179 was taken as temporary premises for the Warden. The Executive Committee which had been appointed to raise money and generally support the enterprise met regularly, usually monthly; it included F. W. Newland (minister of Canning Town Congregational Church), J. Spencer Curwen (Liberal candidate for West Ham until 1890), Joseph King (a former member of the Oxford University Nonconformists' Union), who was elected Treasurer, Norman Smith (student, then Bursar of the College), and Arthur Marshall (a Congregational layman), who was elected Chairman. Plans were soon drawn up for building a hall at the rear of the houses by F. W. Troup,[42] and these were put into effect before the end of 1891. A Men's Club was started in the Hall,

---

[39] *Mansfield House Magazine* (1897), 87–8.
[40] F. W. Newland had supported the cause of the dockers. See *CYB 1939*, 708.
[41] *Mansfield House Magazine* (1893), 1.
[42] Francis William Troup (1859–1941) had Congregational connections. In 1906 he designed a house for A. M. Fairbairn at Lossiemouth. See Neil Jackson, *F. W. Troup: Architect 1859–1941* (London, 1985).

and grew steadily in numbers. By December 1891, Will Reason, an old Mansfield man who was working at the Settlement, was reporting 600 members in the Club.[43] A Boys' Club, started by J. Grafton Milne, was opened in the Shipwrights' Hall, Swanscombe Street.

The work developed rapidly. One of those who came to help was Frank Tillyard, a Balliol-educated lawyer who had been a member of the Oxford University Nonconformists' Union. He found that much legal help was needed, and began to set aside one evening a week, first on his own, and later with a colleague, Arthur Blott, for assisting with legal problems. His 'clinic' soon earned the title 'The Poor Man's Lawyer', and proved a pioneering effort in free legal aid; representatives from other settlements came to see what was being done, with a view to setting up something similar. It led one docker to comment: 'If Christianity means a lawyer what don't charge nothink, then there's summut in it.'[44] A few years later Toynbee Hall adopted a similar scheme.[45]

In 1893 two new premises were acquired. The Wave Lodging House at 234–5 Victoria Dock Road was taken over and run as an adjunct to the Settlement, with 120 beds available each night: 4*d.* a night in the main building and 6*d.* a night in the smaller, quieter cottages at the rear. And a disused public house, the Walmer Castle, Woodstock Street, was bought as a new home for the Boys' Club. This proved to be in poor condition, and early in 1895 the Club moved into 310 Barking Road, previously known as Brennan's Boxing Saloon, soon renamed Fairbairn House. This was rebuilt in 1900 with the help of a generous donation from Passmore Edwards.[46] Finally, after a fire in the Warden's Residence, and a special building fund appeal, a further site—two cottages at 89 Barking Road—was purchased; the cottages were pulled down, and F. W. Troup was asked to draw up plans for a new Residence to house twelve Residents and twenty visitors. The new building was a four-storey block, red brick with Portland stone trimmings. It was on the foundation stone of this building that the quotation from T. H. Green at the beginning of this chapter was

---

[43] Minute Book of the Executive Committee of Mansfield House, Canning Town, 15 Dec. 1891, microfilm, Stratford Library, London.

[44] Quoted in an interview with Percy Alden, *Christian Commonwealth*, 29 Mar. 1894.

[45] See Briggs and Macartney, *Toynbee Hall*, 50.

[46] For Passmore Edwards (1823–1911), editor and philanthropist, see *DNB Second Supplement*, i. 612–14. This is now, in premises rebuilt and recently extensively modernized, the site of the present Mansfield Centre, together with the nearby 30 Avenons Road. Most of the original Settlement buildings were destroyed during the Second World War.

engraved. Thus, within a decade, the Settlement was operating in four premises: the Lodging House in Victoria Dock Road, and the Hall, the Boys' Club, and the Residence and Office in three separate buildings in Barking Road.[47] In these premises an amazing number of activities were taking place. A pamphlet dated 1893 (*A Week at Mansfield House*, London, 1893) lists the following: Mutual Improvement Society, Pleasant Sunday Afternoon, Happy Sunday Evenings for Children, Sunday Evening Discussions, Sick Benefit Society, Loan Society, Penny Bank, Mansfield House Club (for working men), Youths' Club, Orchestral Society, Poor Man's Lawyer, Local Parliament, Gymnastic Society, Mansfield House Ramblers Cycling Club, Mansfield House Federation Football Team, and the Brotherhood Society, as well as several classes of instruction.

The example of Canon Barnett, who organized a Picture Exhibition in Whitechapel, was followed by Percy Alden, when an exhibition of 200 pictures on loan was mounted in the Hall of the Boys' Club in 1895, and attracted great numbers. This precedent was followed each summer for some years.

Sunday evening services were held in the Hall, attended by a small minority of those attracted to the Settlement. The inspiration for the Settlement was always the Christian faith, but its expression, for Alden particularly, involved social and political activity alongside those who were not closely involved with church life. At a public meeting in 1892, Percy Alden stated:

> I have always been very anxious that the religious basis on which we work at Mansfield House should be made as broad as possible, and I have come to the conclusion that there are an enormous number of religious men outside the churches—men imbued with a religious spirit, and having at their hearts the welfare of the community—who, if banded together, might do a vast amount of good. I regard the Labour movement as a religious movement, and can honestly say that I have found more unselfishness among working men than among any other class.[48]

His own emphasis was becoming more strongly political.

---

[47] The present sites of Mansfield House are at 310 Barking Road and the nearby 30 Avenons Road.

[48] Quoted in *Twenty-One Years at Mansfield House 1890–1911* (London, 1918). No author given.

Alden believed that some kind of political activity could not be avoided if there was to be any improvement in social conditions. In the year in which the Settlement was founded, James Keir Hardie was nominated as the Independent Labour parliamentary candidate for West Ham South, and visited the constituency for the first time. In 1892 he was elected MP, with support from the Liberals. Alden, then a Liberal but not an individualistic one, campaigned for him and supported his ideas on unemployment. Hardie spoke at the Settlement on several occasions, as did Ben Tillett and Ramsay MacDonald. When Lord Rosebery, the Prime Minister, queried the estimate of a deputation which visited him in December 1894 at Stratford Town Hall that there were 5,000 unemployed workmen in West Ham, it was Alden who was asked to conduct a census of the unemployed for the local trade union, together with the Independent Labour Party and Social Democratic Federation. He found 10,000.[49] A few months later he gave evidence to the Select Committee on Distress from Want of Employment.[50] During those same months he gave interviews to several daily papers during the period of great unemployment, successfully appealing for donations to relieve suffering amongst the unemployed. Two years later, after serving on the Borough Council for some time, he was elected Deputy Mayor of West Ham. He also encouraged other Mansfield House residents to serve on School Boards and the Board of Guardians.

In 1901 Alden became editor of the Liberal *Echo* for a short time and resigned his position as Warden, though he remained in residence as Honorary Warden for some months longer. In that year also he joined the Society of Friends, and became Organizing Secretary of the Friends' Social Union from 1903 until 1911; and for four years he served on the Fabian Society Executive. 'A born organizer, he tended to take over the administration of almost every movement with which he became connected.'[51] In 1905 his book *The Unemployed: A National Question* (London, 1905) aroused considerable interest, and the following year he was elected Liberal MP for Tottenham. In 1903 he had become a member of the Rainbow Circle,[52] at

---

[49] See José Harris, *Unemployment and Politics: A Study in English Social Policy 1886–1914* (Oxford, 1972), 89.

[50] Ibid. 92.

[51] Peter d'A. Jones, *The Christian Socialist Revival 1877–1914* (Princeton, 1968), 335.

[52] See *Minutes of the Rainbow Circle 1894–1924*, ed. Michael Freeden, Camden Fourth Series 38 (London, 1989).

whose meetings he sometimes contributed papers; after the First World War he moved over to the Labour Party. Until his death in an air raid in June 1944 his time was devoted to various political and social reform movements (for which he was knighted in 1933).

Others followed in his footsteps, particularly two of his Mansfield contemporaries, Will Reason and Henry Cubbon. Will Reason,[53] who married Alden's sister, worked at the Settlement for seven years, and later in life took a leading role in COPEC.[54] Henry Cubbon[55] followed Alden as Warden from 1902 until 1913. Like Alden, Cubbon believed that

> The competitive system, in so far as it operates in the sphere where the necessaries of a decent physical existence are provided, ought to be replaced by the co-operative system—the system that is ethical and spiritual, that is concerned with 'the Father's business', that is the natural expression of love to God and to man. What is needed is that the Christian *spirit* should find its correspondence in the Christian *system*.[56]

William Blackshaw[57] was Co-warden from 1926 until 1930.

Educational work, though not perhaps as ambitious as at Toynbee Hall, was important in the Settlement. Help was provided in preparation for the examinations of the Society of Arts, London Matriculation, and the St John's Ambulance Society. One of the most enterprising activities was the 'Local Parliament', in which men met in the Warden's room, formed themselves into a mock debating chamber, and debated public and social issues.

Throughout these early years, the Settlement and College were in close touch. It was Fairbairn's idea that every weekend a Mansfield student should spend three days in Mansfield House. When the formal constitution was drawn up in 1896, the College was given formal representation on the Executive Committee. One of the most active College members in the Settlement's affairs was G. B. Gray—

---

[53] For Will Reason (1864–1926) see *CYB 1927*, 150–1 and *MCM* 12/11 (Dec. 1926). See also his article in *MCM* 4/25 (Mar. 1903), 21–8. He wrote frequently for the *Mansfield House Magazine*.

[54] Conference on Politics, Economics and Citizenship, held in Birmingham in 1924.

[55] For Henry Cubbon (1864–1933) see *CYB 1934*, 257–8 and *MCM* 103 (June 1933), 183–4.

[56] *MCM* 5/31 (Mar. 1905), 159.

[57] William Blackshaw (1866–1953). He had been Warden of Croft House Settlement, Sheffield from 1901 until 1913. See *CYB 1954*, 505 and *MCM* 144 (Jan. 1954), 189–90.

a regular attender at committee meetings, and frequent lecturer. A highlight of the year for the Settlement was the Whit Monday outing to Oxford, when students showed visitors round the colleges, and Settlement and College fielded cricket teams against each other. In 1894, a special train was even hired to bring the visitors to Oxford.

The description given so far implies that the work of the Settlement was confined to men exclusively. That is how it began. But within two years of the foundation of the Settlement, a Women's Settlement was formed, with premises nearby in the Barking Road, and though this was not formally linked with Mansfield College, the two Settlements worked closely together, and the *Mansfield House Magazine* carried regular reports of the Women's Settlement. It was a happy event when Percy Alden married one of the medical advisers to the Women's Settlement, Dr Margaret Pearse.

The inevitable tension between religion and politics in an enterprise such as Mansfield Settlement was leading some into politics and social activity rather than pastoral ministry. But the main function of the College in these years was to prepare men for the latter, and it is to that purpose and activity that we must now return.[58]

[58] The connections between College and Settlement have waxed and waned in the years since 1909. During the early years of the 20th cent. the Settlement boasted the largest boys' and men's club in Europe. In 1930 Fairbairn Hall was built in Barking Road.

In the early 1960s the Settlement received unwelcome publicity when its Warden since 1923, Sir Ian Horobin, was convicted of indecent offences against boys in the Club. Since that time, the earlier paternalistic attitudes have evolved into a more democratic ethos, and under its present Warden, the Revd Geoffrey Hooper, the Settlement has found a continuing role among the people of Newham. The premises in Canning Town have been reduced, and a rural outdoor centre developed at Lambourne End. In recent years the links between College and Settlement have been strengthened, and undergraduates have taken a particular interest in the Settlement.

VIII

The End of Optimism: 1909–1920

On 4 November 1908 Fairbairn celebrated his seventieth birthday. He had already told the Mansfield Council in the preceding June that he intended to retire before Easter 1909. He did so with some reluctance, but told Sir Alfred Dale, Chairman of Council, that he felt that the good of the College 'calls for this last sacrifice'.[1] Others had felt for some time that a failing grasp of intellectual and practical affairs was making him more autocratic, and therefore more remote from students and colleagues; and that he was no longer alert to the intellectual challenges of the time. The Fairbairn era had been one of outstanding achievement, and his men had looked to him as 'a strong tower', but it was now time for a new leader and new ideas.

Fairbairn's formal letter of resignation to Sir Alfred Dale expressed pride and optimism as well as sadness at severing his leadership of the College:

> At this moment its reputation stands higher than ever before; it has more students than at any past period in its history; its sons can be reckoned amongst the foremost men of the colleges and Free Churches of England; and its influence is acknowledged in the University as well as in the country at large. The congregations in the chapel on Sundays are steady, the preaching is excellent, the services as a rule are honourable to the simple faith and worship of our churches. When the college was founded in Oxford there were many things which gave cause for anxiety, but these were all overcome through the generous policy of the Council and the loyal co-operation of the men associated with me. I can therefore hand over my responsibilities in the full confidence that the wisdom which helped in the past will not fail in the future.[2]

[1] Quoted in W. B. Selbie, *The Life of Andrew Martin Fairbairn* (London, 1914), 432.
[2] Quoted ibid. 433.

Something of his achievement was demonstrated in the volume of essays presented to him as a Festschrift[3] on his seventieth birthday. The essays, all by former students, showed an enormous range, from biblical studies, patristic studies, the philosophy of religion, Reformed history, Islamic studies, to Celtic studies. At least three authors were present or future university professors;[4] and four were present or future principals of theological colleges.[5] Although the book lacked any real unifying theme other than an indebtedness of the authors to the person honoured, it was living proof of the intellectual standards which Fairbairn had practised and taught.

As Fairbairn was neither an official lecturer nor even a recognized teacher of the University, there was no formal University ceremony in his honour when he retired. But a group of his friends, in particular his two golfing companions Sidney Ball and Percy Gardner, arranged a farewell dinner for him on 8 March 1909 in St John's, presided over by the Rector of Exeter College, Dr W. W. Jackson.

Fairbairn left Oxford after the end of Hilary Term, having given most of his large and important library, including a valuable collection of pamphlets, to the College.[6] He spent the remaining three years of his life either at his house in Lossiemouth or staying with one of his children. He told his students that he had 'no intention whatever of being silent or of acting as if my active life was ended. While I have something to say I shall say it, at least so long as there are people willing to hear.'[7] But his hopes of making further contributions to theological thought were not realized, and all he achieved was the publication of a collection of earlier essays and addresses, published as *Studies in Religion and Theology* (London, 1910).

Fairbairn died on 9 February 1912. His funeral took place in the College Chapel, conducted by Selbie, Bartlet, and Gray, attended

---

[3] *Mansfield College Essays* (London, 1909).

[4] A. S. Peake (Professor of Biblical Exegesis, Victoria University, Manchester), E. Anwyl (Professor of Welsh Comparative Philology, University College of Wales, Aberystwyth), and Alexander Souter (Regius Professor of Humanity, University of Aberdeen).

[5] R. S. Franks (Western College, Bristol), A. E. Garvie (New College, London), H. W. Robinson (Regent's Park College), and W. B. Selbie (Mansfield).

[6] Much of this library was later either sold to the Bodleian Library or otherwise dispersed. Some of the dispersed books were later acquired by the Bodleian, and placed with the others in a separate section classified as 'Mansfield'. Altogether 511 books which once belonged to Fairbairn, Mansfield, or Spring Hill are in this collection. I am indebted to Paul Morgan for this information.

[7] *MCM* 6/7 (Mar. 1909), 147.

not only by his own students, but by many representatives of the University, City, Congregational Union, and British Academy; his body was then buried in Wolvercote cemetery, next to that of his old friend James Legge.

His old students gave a memorial tablet for the Chapel in his memory. At its unveiling Charles Silvester Horne gave a magnificent tribute to his former teacher, claiming that, during the twenty-four years since he had left the College, 'something of Dr Fairbairn's personality and teaching has entered into every sermon I have ever preached, and every view I have tried to take of truth and duty'.[8] And while he was speaking, W. A. Powicke, another former student, 'pictured the old man as he used to issue from the vestry, screwing up his face and planting his feet as though the devils of unbelief were barring his way'.[9]

The Council established both a Fairbairn Essay Prize and a Fairbairn Scholarship. At Mansfield House a Fairbairn Studentship enabled one student each year to spend twelve months at the Settlement in order to gain practical experience in social work. Selbie, his successor and former student, set to work on a substantial biography of Fairbairn, which later gained added importance from the fact that Fairbairn's papers were all destroyed during the Second World War.

When Fairbairn had announced his retirement, the College Council looked to North America as well as Britain in its search for a worthy successor. G. B. Gray was actually sent to the United States to make enquiries about possible people who could maintain and enhance Mansfield's reputation. Eight names, including three from the USA, were brought to the Council's joint meeting with the Board of Education on 15 January 1909; these were discussed and eventually reduced to three—G. Buchanan Gray, W. B. Selbie, and George Adam Smith. At the first vote George Adam Smith polled slightly fewer votes than his two rivals and was eliminated;[10] at the second vote, Selbie received nine votes, and Gray received eight. Selbie was therefore declared elected, and appointed with an initial salary of £800 a year.[11] The Council had chosen the candidate with considerable

---

[8] Quoted in Selbie, *Life of Andrew Martin Fairbairn*, 447.

[9] *MCM* 8/5 (June 1912), 101.

[10] In 1910 George Adam Smith became Principal of the University of Aberdeen.

[11] Entry for 15 Jan. 1909, Minute Book of the Spring Hill Committee of Management and Mansfield College Council, MCA.

pastoral experience and a growing reputation for preaching, rather than the practising scholar.[12]

Selbie[13] was a Lancashire man, the son of a minister, educated at Manchester Grammar School and Brasenose College, where he read Greats. He was one of the first five students interviewed and accepted for admission to Mansfield at 90 High Street in 1886, and so was one of the pioneering junior members of the College. When he had completed his course, he remained for a further year as a Tutor in Hebrew, before being called to be minister of Highgate Congregational Church in London, where he remained for twelve years. During his last three years in London he belonged to a lively discussion group who called themselves the 'Minor Prophets', where he shared ideas with some of the most creative minds in Congregationalism, such as P. T. Forsyth and A. E. Garvie.[14] In retrospect, he realized that, although the group was 'living on the brink of a volcano', they were 'wholly blind to the signs of the times', and 'had none of the vision and insight of true prophets'.[15] Nevertheless he felt there had been great value in men of very diverse theological viewpoints (P. T. Forsyth and R. J. Campbell could hardly have found much common ground) being able to meet together in friendly discussion.[16]

In 1902 Selbie had moved to Cambridge in succession to Forsyth as minister of Emmanuel Congregational Church, a church which by that time fulfilled something of the same role in Cambridge as did Mansfield Chapel in Oxford, in that it was a centre for Nonconformist undergraduates.[17] His powers as a preacher were maturing, as was his understanding and practice of Congregational churchmanship. A volume of his sermons at Cambridge was published in 1910.[18] A. H. Fowler, who was an undergraduate in Cambridge and

---

[12] Gray was respected within his denomination, but appears not to have preached in Mansfield College Chapel.

[13] William Boothby Selbie (1862–1944). He destroyed all his papers before his death, saying that he (the biographer of Fairbairn and Horne) did not want his own biography to be written. See *DNB 1941–50*, 768–9.

[14] Nine of the 'Minor Prophets' were later elected Chairmen of the Congregational Union, and five became principals of theological colleges.

[15] W. B. Selbie, 'Some Very Minor Prophets', *CQ* (1943), 32–6.

[16] See the 'Minute Book of the Minor Prophets', MCA.

[17] It had a long and distinguished history dating back to the late 17th cent. The first undergraduate to be admitted as a church member was John White in 1851. See B. L. Manning, *This Latter House: Emmanuel Church, Cambridge 1874–1924* (Cambridge, 1924).

[18] W. B. Selbie, *Aspects of Christ and Other Sermons* (London, 1910).

attended Emmanuel Church 1901–4, remembered the electric effect of Selbie's preaching after a year without a regular minister:

> when Selbie came the whole atmosphere changed. He seemed suddenly to bring you face to face with reality. His words would stab your spirit broad awake. He spoke directly to your condition and your need. His sermons were challenging, fortifying, a tonic to the spirit. The fact that he stood there and spoke to the impressive congregation of town and gown without a note, or with but half a sheet of note-paper, unconsciously added to the impression his words made. The effect upon me was electric. I had never known preaching like this before. It gave me a new idea not only of what preaching could be, but of what the Christian life demanded.[19]

It was a notable ministry, and gave Selbie many lifelong friends.

Thus he brought to his new responsibility an experience of Mansfield's pioneering years, eighteen years in the pastoral ministry in London and Cambridge, and the vigour of a man of 46. In retrospect, one can see that whereas Fairbairn had matched the needs of Mansfield in 1886 with his great intellectual stature, in 1909 Selbie the preacher offered a spiritual fervour which could challenge the darkness about to spread over Europe. Those who had voted for Gray had been rightly concerned about scholarly standards. Selbie was a scholar too, though 'only a third of him was persuaded that scholarship really mattered'.[20]

His reputation within the denomination was recognized by his election to the Chair of the Congregational Union for 1914–15. His address to the Union's May meetings in 1914 had as its theme 'The Church of the Redeemed', a plea for a renewal of Congregational churchmanship—'It has long been our boast that, as Congregationalists, we are the highest of High Churchmen'[21]—but 'How can we bring our Churches up to the standard we profess?'[22] There was a need for Congregationalists to know what they stood for, to make church membership more of a reality, and to restore the primacy of the Church Meeting, so that they could contribute constructively to the reunion of the Church. Whatever prophetic word Selbie intended to deliver in the autumn was never heard, because the outbreak of war caused the cancellation of the CU Autumnal Meetings.

---

[19] *MCM* 125 (Aug. 1944), 102.   [20] E. R. Micklem, ibid. 104.
[21] *CYB 1915*, 34–5.   [22] Ibid. 39.

'The pulpit was his throne.' So wrote Nathaniel Micklem, one of Selbie's former students, who was eventually to succeed him.[23] 'The inspired mouse' (in spite of his small stature and his high-pitched voice, he 'took hold' of a congregation in a way few others could) drew the largest congregations on Sunday in Oxford. 'Mansfield Chapel under Selbie was no retreat for spiritual invalids.'[24] His determination to turn out men who above all could preach the gospel meant that the weekly sermon class was regarded with some apprehension. Certain phrases had a habit of reappearing and became part of Mansfield's folklore—'that wouldn't save the soul of a tomtit'; 'if the Gospel of Christ is not the power of God unto salvation, it's the merest flapdoodle'; 'you may preach like the Angel Gabriel, but if your congregation can't hear you, you might just as well be a monkey chattering in a tree.' He told his students: 'The ideal is to know beforehand *what* you are going to say, but not exactly *how* you are going to say it; but you won't get to this stage until you have had at least ten years at the job.'[25] When he himself was preaching on a Sunday, he would be in his study by six o'clock in the morning.

Following in the footsteps of Fairbairn, and as a graduate of the University in both Greats and Theology, Selbie more readily found an acceptable place in the University Theology Faculty. In 1913 he was co-opted on to the Theology Faculty Board along with Darwell Stone, Principal of Pusey House, and thereafter re-elected each time his term expired. And in the following year, his lectures, along with those of his Mansfield colleagues, and of the Principals of Manchester College and of Pusey House,[26] were placed on the official lecture lists.

But it was not until 1920, when Selbie was honoured with a DD by decree, the first to be given to a Nonconformist since 1662, that he could really feel accepted as an equal among other Oxford theologians.[27] It was the culmination of a long struggle both to open Divinity degrees beyond the priesthood of the Church of England, and to raise their standard. In the past, Oxford Divinity degrees (BD

---

[23] N. Micklem, *The Box and the Puppets* (London, 1957).

[24] *MCM* 13 (June 1932), 128.

[25] A. Thomas, 'Notes of Selbie's Lectures on Preaching', MCA.

[26] Pusey House, originally the Dr Pusey Memorial Library, founded in 1884, offered library facilities, pastoral care, and theological instruction to members of the University.

[27] This was reinforced with his appointment as the first Free Church examiner in the Theology Schools in 1924 and his election as an Honorary Fellow of Brasenose College in 1926.

and DD, to be differentiated from the Honours School of Theology which led to a BA) had been normal requirements for many positions in the Church of England, and had implied a teaching authority; it was customary for newly appointed bishops of the Church of England to be given an honorary DD automatically. Attempts at reform foundered for many years because it was difficult to gather sufficient support for both the reform of standards *and* the opening of the degrees to a wider constituency; when the one issue was raised, so was the other, and those who supported one did not always support the second. Further, even when the support of both the Theology Faculty Board and the Hebdomadal Council was secured, it was impossible to persuade Convocation,[28] a very conservative body, which consisted of all MAs who had paid their dues and remained on the books of their colleges, of the wisdom of such reforms.

The first attempt in 1894 had failed. In 1912, the Theology Faculty Board, now presided over by Henry Scott Holland, Regius Professor of Divinity, sought to remove restrictions on examiners for the Honours School in Theology, and to abolish the requirement that candidates for BD/DD should be in priests' orders of the Church of England; in 1913 their proposals were passed by Congregation in February, after being amended to the effect that a BD thesis should 'bear a definite relation to some department of Christian Theology',[29] but rejected by Convocation on 29 April (placet 334, non-placet 763).[30] At this stage, A. C. Headlam, then Principal of King's College, London, who was to succeed Scott Holland as Regius Professor in 1918, proposed in an article in the *Church Quarterly Review*[31] that the best way to safeguard the Christian character of the degrees was to have two 'schools' within the Faculty, one Anglican and one Nonconformist. This idea had already been proposed by the theology professors. Headlam had even suggested that Nonconformist leaders should, like bishops, automatically receive a DD; but it was Selbie who 'earnestly and successfully persuaded him to refrain from seeking approval of such a plan'.[32]

[28] It was Convocation which had deprived Horton of the right to examine in 'The Rudiments of Faith and Religion' in the 1880s.
[29] This was to placate those anxious to ensure the Christian character of the degree. See *Oxford University Gazette*, 12 Feb. 1913, 475–6 and 19 Feb. 1913, 492.
[30] Ibid. 30 Apr. 1913, 708–9.
[31] 'Degrees in Divinity', *Church Quarterly Review*, 76 (July 1913), 357–70.
[32] R. Jasper, *A. C. Headlam: Life and Letters of a Bishop* (London, 1960), 130.

When Headlam gave his inaugural lecture as Regius Professor, he remarked that Oxford Divinity degrees were 'still distinguished by that absence of merit which, as in the case of the Garter, is so dear to the English heart'.[33] He it was who in February 1920 in the more liberal post-war climate finally successfully steered through Hebdomadal Council, Congregation, and Convocation a reform of the statutes relating to Divinity degrees.[34] There were to be proper standards for the BD, with an initial qualifying examination as well as a thesis; and for the DD, published work or an original thesis of a high standard was required. In addition, the denominational restrictions were removed. Selbie was appointed to the Committee which was to consider the award of honorary Divinity degrees at the Encaenia following this reform. Thus on 23 June 1920 honorary DDs were bestowed on the Roman Catholic Baron von Hügel, the Presbyterians John Skinner, George Adam Smith, and James Cooper, and the Methodist A. S. Peake.[35] But on 8 June Convocation had already conferred on Selbie a DD by decree—the greatest academic honour Oxford could offer him.[36] On 12 June, the JCR held a special breakfast in his honour; the next month the *Mansfield College Magazine* offered its congratulations, and referred to the added pleasure the honour gave to the College 'because of the distinguished way in which it was conferred—by special decree, on the first possible occasion after the new statute came into force, and in splendid isolation'.[37]

Throughout the early years of his Principalship Selbie was fortunate to be supported by Gray and Bartlet in Old Testament studies and church history[38] respectively, and in New Testament studies by Souter, James Moffatt, and C. H. Dodd successively. When Gray died suddenly in 1922, Selbie said he felt as if 'the linchpin' of the College had been removed. Though Selbie may have been the right choice as Principal in 1909, it was Gray above all who upheld the College's

---

[33] A. C. Headlam, *The Study of Theology* (Oxford, 1918), 24.

[34] Congregation approved the alteration of statutes on 3 Feb., Convocation on 24 Feb. 1920. See *Oxford University Gazette*, 4 Feb. 1920, 382, 25 Feb. 1920, 434–5.

[35] Ibid. 14 July 1920, 822.

[36] Ibid. 9 June 1920, 748. Unlike an honorary doctorate, a DD by decree gave all the privileges of an Oxford doctorate, equivalent to a present-day 'degree by special resolution'.

[37] *MCM* 11/3 (July 1920), 48.

[38] In 1909 Bartlet's Chair was named the Mackennal Chair of Church History, in honour of Alexander Mackennal, Chairman of the College Council 1891–1904.

intellectual reputation. He was not only a great Old Testament scholar, but also a person of clear and balanced judgement, an Independent of the old tradition. In 1905 Oxford had recognized his scholarship with the award of the D.Litt. degree. In 1912 his second commentary in the International Critical Commentary series, on Isaiah 1–39, was published; his first commentary in the series was on Numbers (1903). He was pouring out a steady stream of smaller works, articles and contributions to encyclopaedias. In 1914 he was the first Nonconformist to be invited to give the Speaker's Lectures in Biblical Studies; the lectures, on 'Sacrifice', were edited and published after his death as *Sacrifice in the Old Testament* (London, 1925). And in 1919 he was appointed Grinfield Lecturer in the Septuagint. Like Selbie, he was a member of the Theology Faculty Board, as well as being appointed an examiner for the Board of Oriental Studies.

Bartlet too was producing a steady flow of articles both for journals and for encyclopaedias on biblical and early Christian subjects.[39] In 1917 he produced a major work in collaboration with the Anglican scholar A. J. Carlyle, his friend and contemporary at Exeter College: *Christianity in History: A Study in Religious Development* (London, 1917). Bartlet wrote the earlier sections on 'Beginnings' and 'Ancient Christianity', and contributed towards the later chapters. The book illustrates well Bartlet's historical approach to doctrinal problems and differences, and his own eirenic (a favourite word) approach to them, which was to make a valuable contribution to discussions on reunion after the end of the war.

Selbie, Gray, and Bartlet formed the solid triumvirate of this second phase of Mansfield's life. Two distinguished New Testament scholars successively joined the Mansfield SCR for a time: James Moffatt and C. H. Dodd. Moffatt, who was the youngest man ever to be awarded the DD degree in a Scottish university, was lured from Scotland to take Souter's place as Yates Professor in 1912, but only stayed for three and a half years before returning to Glasgow as Professor of Church History at the United Free Church College.[40] It was during his stay in Oxford that his translation of the New

---

[39] See the extensive bibliography in J. V. Bartlet, *Church Life and Church Order during the First Four Centuries, with Special Reference to the Early Eastern Church Orders*, ed. C. J. Cadoux (Oxford, 1943), 177–97.

[40] James Moffatt (1870–1944) had already published *The Historical New Testament* (Edinburgh, 1901) and *Introduction to the Literature of the New Testament* (Edinburgh, 1911). See *DNB 1941–50*, 602.

Testament was published.[41] He presented a copy to each member of the JCR, inscribed 'with the author's compliments', and suggesting that they could all improve on it.

His successor, Charles Harold Dodd, was as great a scholar of the New Testament as Gray was of the Old Testament. The difference was that whereas Gray spent his entire teaching career at Mansfield, Dodd learned his craft at Mansfield and then went on to academic posts at Manchester and Cambridge.[42] Dodd had entered Mansfield as a student in Fairbairn's last year, and was therefore taught during his course by Souter, Moffatt, and Gray, as well as by Selbie and Bartlet. He had a short ministry in Warwick 1912–15, but was clearly destined for an academic career, and Mansfield was fortunate to have him as Yates Lecturer, then Professor, for fifteen years. He was a great practitioner of the historical criticism which he had learned at Mansfield (and in his earlier classical studies at University College, Oxford). A Mansfield scholar in the succeeding generation wrote that Dodd's leitmotif was 'the conviction that God is Lord of history, and that the word of God spoken in Scripture is so inextricably interwoven into the fabric of historical events that it can be let loose into the modern world in the fullness of its relevance and power only through historical criticism exercised with the utmost integrity and thoroughness'.[43] It was during the years he was teaching at Mansfield that Dodd began to publish his magisterial works on the New Testament (see Chapter IX).

There was another important position held in connection with Mansfield, that of Chaplain to Congregational students. After Frank Lenwood's departure, this post, combined with an assistant Lectureship in Greek New Testament Studies, was held successively by R. K. Evans (1907–11),[44] Allan Gaunt (1911–15),[45] and Nathaniel Micklem (1919–21); the significance of their work was increasingly recognized.

---

[41] *The New Testament: A New Translation* (London, 1913).

[42] See F. W. Dillistone, *C. H. Dodd: Interpreter of the New Testament* (London, 1977) and *DNB 1971–80*, 243–4.

[43] G. B. Caird, 'C. H. Dodd', in M. E. Marty and D. G. Perman (eds.), *A Handbook of Christian Theologians* (Cambridge, 1984), 321.

[44] Robert Kenneth Evans. See his articles 'The Present Religious and Ecclesiastical Situation in Oxford', *MCM* 7/3 (Dec. 1910), 55–9 and 'The Sacraments' in *MCM* 7/4 (Mar. 1911), 83–8. For the rest of his career, mostly in China, where he served as Professor of Christian Philosophy and New Testament Theology at Yenching University, see *CYB 1926*, 164; *MCM* 12/8 (June 1925), 225–30; and *MCM* 12/9 (Dec. 1925), 227–30.

[45] Allan Gaunt (Mansfield 1907–10) died prematurely in 1917. See *MCM* 9/10 (Apr. 1917), 163–4.

In 1914 Wilfred Bradley (Mansfield 1909–12) was appointed Tutor in Philosophy and Chaplain to Baptist students (with part of his post financed by the Baptist Union), based at Mansfield; after Allan Gaunt's departure in 1915 he continued to look after the Congregational students until the end of the war, and carried on an extensive correspondence with men at the front. There was now a responsibility not only to British students but to the Rhodes Scholars who since 1902 had begun to arrive in England, most of them from the United States, but others from the British colonies, and a few from Germany. Many of them came from non-episcopal backgrounds, and Mansfield made a special effort to offer them friendship and a spiritual home.[46] From this time there began a tradition for Mansfield to hold a Thanksgiving Day Service and Dinner in November.

Allan Gaunt had estimated that there were at least 400 non-Episcopalian students in residence 1911–12, half of them Presbyterians and Methodists, who had their own chaplains or ministers, the other half Congregationalists, Baptists, and Quakers, for whom Mansfield took some responsibility.[47] They were offered many opportunities for service to the community outside the University, particularly through Mansfield House and through the Free Church Camps for Schoolboys. Many of them also took the opportunity to attend the SCM Swanwick Conferences.

The JCR Minute Book for these years speaks of a well-established and lively common-room life. Frequently, at the end of the academic year, those who were going down spoke warmly and appreciatively of what the JCR had meant to them, and of how much they would miss it. When Selbie first became Principal, there was a much-discussed approach to the SCR for better relations between junior and senior members of the College, for more flexible teaching arrangements, and for regular daily services. The response to the last suggestion was positive; daily services, each evening, were instituted, and were considered to have contributed to 'a happier tone' within the College. The relations between junior and senior members gradually improved.

The tradition of regular JCR Conferences was now well established,

[46] See C. K. Allen, *Forty Years of the Rhodes Scholarships* (Oxford, 1944). W. M. Macmillan, in *My South African Years: An Autobiography* (Cape Town, 1975), recounts how welcoming and welcome was Mansfield College Chapel to a South African Rhodes Scholar of Scottish background.

[47] *Mansfield College Annual Report 1911–12*, 12.

and the surviving JCR Conference Book in the College Archives gives a full account of the talks and discussions. In January 1907 Bartlet had spoken critically about 'the new theology' in response to the reported views of R. J. Campbell, minister of the City Temple in London, views which were soon to be published in a book of the title.[48] Campbell was 're-interpreting' Christianity for the modern age by stressing the immanence of God to the point that he found no essential difference between humanity and divinity, by claiming that sin was more a 'blunder' than a real alienation, and by reducing the Incarnation to a position more consonant with Unitarianism.[49] His views seem to have found favour with some of the students, which may account for the fact that Campbell himself was invited to lead a JCR Conference on 30 November 1909 on 'The Mystical Element in Christianity'. Earlier that year, on 9 June, a young Fellow of Queen's, William Temple, spoke on 'Incarnation and the Modern Mind'. W. E. Orchard,[50] minister of the Presbyterian Church at Enfield and a friend of Campbell, though one who was beginning to move theologically in a very different direction, spoke on 'The Modern Mind and How to Reach it' on 8 March 1912. Later that year, on 27 November, Charles Gore, then newly appointed Bishop of Oxford, spoke about 'Original Sin'. The author of the JCR Notes in the next *College Magazine* wrote that 'the Bishop of Oxford visited the JCR and read a paper on Original Sin; that ancient dogma, clearly and brilliantly treated in the paper, was much tattered and assaulted in the discussion. It may be of interest to know that his Lordship characterized the House as "a very unpauline lot".'[51]

On 26 November 1914 the speaker was Maude Royden, then editor of *Common Cause*, the journal of the National Union of Women's

---

[48] R. J. Campbell, *The New Theology* (London, 1907). R. J. Campbell (1867–1956) had studied at Christ Church 1891–4. He was then an Anglican, much influenced by Gore; but he also attended, and occasionally preached at, Free Church congregations in and near Oxford. He consulted Fairbairn before deciding to accept a call to Union Street Church, Brighton in 1895. See R. J. Campbell, *A Spiritual Pilgrimage* (London, 1916).

[49] It should be said that the publicity given to Campbell's views meant that he was pressed to write his book too quickly and therefore without thinking the issues through sufficiently. Several years later he repudiated his extreme liberalism and returned to communion with the Church of England. See Campbell, *A Spiritual Pilgrimage* and ch. 2 of K. W. Clements, *Lovers of Discord: Twentieth Century Theological Controversies in England* (London, 1988).

[50] For Orchard, see W. E. Orchard, *From Faith to Faith* (London, 1933) and Elaine Kaye and Ross Mackenzie, *W. E. Orchard: A Study in Christian Exploration* (Oxford, 1990).

[51] D. W. Langridge in *MCM* 8/3 (Dec. 1912), 70.

Suffrage Societies, already a noted supporter of the women's movement, and later a powerful preacher.[52] Her subject was 'The Spiritual
Significance of the Women's Movement'. Her fundamental point
was the recognition of women's claims to be regarded as human
beings in their own right; she also perceived as 'tragic' the supportive
attitude of most women to the war which was already three months
old. Her views did not find universal and unqualified approval within
the College, but at least she was given a hearing. The chair at this
meeting was taken by Constance Todd, Mansfield's first woman
student.

Constance Todd was the first woman to be ordained to the Christian ministry in Britain.[53] She was brought up in a Presbyterian family
in London, and, after school in Southwold, came up to Somerville
College to read History in 1908. Becoming convinced of a calling to
the ministry, she approached Selbie about the possibility of entering
Mansfield as a student. He recognized her academic suitability, as
she had gained good second-class honours in the History Schools
(she could not call herself a graduate since women were not yet able
to take degrees); but he also recognized her calling as genuine, and
saw no reason to reject her solely on the grounds that she was a
woman. His confidence was well justified, for she distinguished herself
academically, and, when she had completed the course, not only received a call to the Darby Street Mission of the King's Weigh House
Church, but gained recognition from the London Congregational
Union as a fully accredited Congregational minister. She also married a fellow student, Claud Coltman, the day after their ordination,
and together they went on to exercise a joint ministry in several different churches.[54] Constance Coltman was the first of a small number
of women who subsequently passed through Mansfield.[55] It is note-
worthy that the group of Oxford dons who had supported the founding of Mansfield were the same group who had helped to further the
cause of women's education in Oxford. Thus when Selbie joined the

---

[52] For Maude Royden, see Sheila Fletcher, *Maude Royden* (Oxford, 1989).

[53] The first woman to be called to pastoral charge of a church in England was Gertrud
von Petzold, a student of Manchester College 1901–4. She was minister of Narborough
Road Free Christian (Unitarian) Church in Leicester 1904–8.

[54] See Elaine Kaye, 'Constance Coltman: A Forgotten Pioneer', *JURCHS* 4/2 (May 1988),
134–46.

[55] There were only four other women who took the ministerial course at Mansfield
while Selbie was Principal: May Bradley (1927–30), Irene Robbins (1930–3), Joyce Rutherford
(1928–31), and Dorothy Wilson (1924–7).

Council of Somerville College (Constance Coltman's old college), in 1919, he was following in an honourable tradition. T. H. Green had been a leading figure in the foundation of Somerville Hall.[56] Professor James Legge was one of the earliest members of the Committee of the Hall in 1879, R. F. Horton joined it (by this time called the Council) in 1883, and when Horton resigned, Fairbairn had taken his place from 1888 until 1907.[57] The JCR responded well to its first female member. At first, she was invited to make use of the JCR except during house meetings, and the Principal, presumably having enquired, was informed that 'no objection was felt to Miss Todd being present at Sermon Class'. Some months later, on 6 May 1914, an extraordinary house meeting was held when it was resolved 'to place on record its approval of the admission of women to the college, and its belief that women as being by right of Christian principle members of the Christian church on full equality with men, should be accorded full facilities for the study of theology and as far as practicable full enjoyment of the advantages afforded by theological colleges'.[58] A woman student was to be admitted to full membership of the JCR, except that she was not to attend meetings 'open to members of the University unconnected with the College and not to women'. All this was quite unusual in the context of the University life of the time, when for example women undergraduates still had to be chaperoned to lectures as well as social events. When Constance Todd came to the end of her course, she referred to her years in the College as 'among the most wonderful in all her experience' and she thanked the JCR.[59]

During the long vacation of 1914 events took place which were to change the face of Europe, though few realized it at the time. When the College re-assembled for Michaelmas Term, the members were divided in their response to the war which had broken out in August. Most supported it, in common with the majority of Congregationalists, and many left Oxford during that autumn in order to take part. The most popular form of service was with the YMCA, at home or overseas; some worked in the YMCA Tent at White City, A. P. Cullen worked in Rouen and Le Havre,[60] and P. G. Simmonds went

[56] The status of Somerville was changed to that of college in 1894.
[57] See M. St Clair Byrne and C. H. Mansfield, *Somerville College 1879–1921* (Oxford, 1922) and Minutes of the Council I, Somerville College Archives.
[58] Entry for 6 May 1914, JCR Minute Book 1909–17, MCA.   [59] Ibid. 21 June 1916.
[60] He wrote about his experiences in 'The Romance of Service', *MCM* 9/4 (Mar. 1915).

to Cairo. The College Manciple and chef, J. C. Symonds, was called to organize a base hospital in the Examination Schools.

There was a small group of at least four pacifists who opposed the war, and they were vigorously supported by C. J. Cadoux, who stayed on as Hebrew Tutor after finishing his course in 1914.[61] On 2 March 1915 W. E. Orchard, now the minister of the King's Weigh House Church, an outspoken pacifist, returned to speak to the JCR on 'The Church and Militarism'. This provoked considerable discussion, in which some objections were raised to Orchard's thesis that while the Church had organized 'our worship and emotions' it had not organized 'our life', and so had let hatred build up to war. The objections he swept aside as 'pseudo-philosophical, pseudo-evolutionary, or pseudo-exegetical'.[62] Orchard and Cadoux were both founder members of the Fellowship of Reconciliation,[63] and Cadoux proved to be one of their chief intellectual spokesmen. He served briefly in the Friends' Ambulance Unit in France in 1915, but otherwise used his research time for writing a thesis on 'A History of the Christian Attitude to Pagan Society and the State, down to the Time of Constantine', part of which was published in 1919 as *The Early Christian Attitude to War* (London, 1919)—a scholarly work in support of the thesis that the pre-Constantinian Church was opposed to Christian participation in war. It was recognized as the standard work on the subject for more than fifty years. C. H. Dodd was also a pacifist, though in more muted fashion.[64]

Selbie himself had little sympathy with the pacifists, though he was greatly saddened by the enmity between Britain and the Germany which had contributed so much to the development of theology; he regretted that there was 'a real divorce in Germany between theology as a science and its social and religious purpose'.[65] When he read in the *Oxford Chronicle* on Rugby station that 'Mr C. John Cadoux of Mansfield College Oxford' had supported a conscientious objector at a tribunal, he wrote a tart note to Cadoux warning him to give his private address and not compromise the College.[66] Bartlet, with his

---

[61] See Elaine Kaye, *C. J. Cadoux: Theologian, Scholar and Pacifist* (Edinburgh, 1988), 49.

[62] JCR Conference Minute Book 1912–16, MCA.

[63] See Jill Wallis, *Valiant for Peace: A History of the Fellowship of Reconciliation 1914 to 1989* (London, 1991).

[64] See Dillistone, *C. H. Dodd*, 72–3, 83–4.

[65] W. B. Selbie, *The War and Theology* (Oxford, 1915).

[66] 25 Mar. 1916. See Cadoux Archives, Bodleian Library.

eirenic personality, was more sympathetic to, though not himself a supporter of, the pacifist position.[67]

On 2 March 1916 conscription was introduced, but theological students in training for the ministry could at first claim exemption, though this was later cancelled. The eight Mansfield theological students still in training at the time were all declared exempt by the Oxford Tribunal. Three however had already volunteered for military service, and others were to follow. It was only to be a matter of time before the College would experience the tragedy that had already descended on others. The first war death to affect the College was that of Selbie's eldest son Robert Joseph Selbie, a frequent visitor at Mansfield House, and for the previous two years a private tutor to an American family, at Ypres on 13 June 1916. Many felt that that bereavement affected Selbie for the rest of his life. He and his wife gave a carved lectern to the Chapel in his memory, made under the supervision of those responsible for the original work in the Chapel (Basil Champneys and Robert Bridgeman). Less than three weeks after Joe Selbie's death, Percy Simmonds fell in battle on the Somme: 'the JCR loved him and had great hopes for him.'[68] The following year, Eric Claxton, an arts man who had intended to begin theological training at Mansfield as soon as he had taken his degree, was also killed. Both these students are commemorated in the College Chapel.

By 1916 the College, depleted in numbers, had placed two of its class-rooms at the disposal of the Serbian Relief Committee for the use of about forty Serbian boys who had fled from Turkish persecution and reached Oxford. A marquee on the upper lawn in summer and the large lecture room in winter were used by a Garden Club for Wounded Soldiers, organized by 'a representative Committee of Oxford ladies'; the Club was very popular, with a regular daily attendance of 400 to 500 men, and in the three years of its existence served over a quarter of a million teas.

In 1916 a parade service was arranged in the College Chapel for cadets and men of the Royal Flying Corps each Sunday before the usual service, and Selbie was appointed Honorary Chaplain. The normal Chapel services continued, despite the much depleted gathering of undergraduates, and the smaller numbers contributed to closer contact between students of different denominations. In his annual

---

[67] See Bartlet, *Church Life*, introd. by C. J. Cadoux, p. xxviii.

[68] *MCM* 9/9 (Dec. 1916). His letters from the front 1914–16 were privately printed as *For his Friends: Letters of Second Lieutenant P. G. Simmonds*, ed. F. C. Bryan (Oxford, 1918).

report on 'Pastoral Work in the University' in June 1918, W. S. Bradley reported that 'some of the best attended meetings in recent terms have been those of a theological society with a senior and junior membership embracing Roman Catholics, Free Churchmen and Anglicans of various types', and predicted that 'it will only be in line with what is going on elsewhere, if in future Oxford men of the most diverse religious traditions became increasingly anxious to understand one another'.[69]

In this ecumenical movement, already developing before war had broken out, Mansfield was to play a leading part. The College had never been sectarian, and Fairbairn's vision had always encompassed a larger Church in England. Three Mansfield men had played a significant role in the British College Christian Union, which became the Student Christian Movement (SCM) in 1905: Frank Lenwood, Malcolm Spencer, and Martyn Trafford. The Mansfield JCR had hesitated about joining the Theological Colleges Department of the SCM in Fairbairn's time because there was a statement of belief as qualification for membership.[70] In 1912 a compromise was reached. The SCM Executive was prepared to accept Mansfield 'as a recognized College of a Christian Church and not because of any expressed or implied attitude towards the basis of the Student Movement', on the understanding that Mansfield's hesitation applied to a basis of any kind, and not to the particular basis of the SCM.[71] Through the SCM in Oxford and its national conferences, the future leaders of the British non-Roman Catholic churches began to meet and form valuable friendships.

In his report to the College Council in 1911, just before leaving Mansfield for China, R. K. Evans had written of the SCM as 'the strongest moral and religious force in the University': 'in it High Churchmen, Low Churchmen, Free Churchmen meet in living spiritual fellowship and Christian service.' He went on:

> If I were asked to select the outstanding feature of the situation in Oxford this year in so far as it concerns the work for which I am specially responsible, I should have no hesitation in saying that it is the emergence of a corporate consciousness, a new sense of

---

[69] *Mansfield College Annual Report 1917–18*, 7–8.
[70] It was about the *principle* of having a statement, rather than the statement itself, that Mansfield was hesitant.
[71] Entry for 12 Mar. 1912, JCR Minute Book 1912–16, MCA.

churchmanship on the part of young Free Churchmen in the University—a new sense of common membership in, and loyalty to, the church of their fathers, firstly denominationally, as Baptists, Congregationalists, Presbyterians, Methodists; and secondly interdenominationally, as members of the Free Evangelical Churches.[72]

The Free Churches had already seen the value of a closer association. In earlier years, Nonconformists had met together in order to promote political action for the removal of disabilities. By 1890 more positive ideas of federation were being discussed, and the Lambeth Quadrilateral of 1888, laying down a basis for corporate union between Anglicans and Nonconformists, gave an added impetus to ecumenical discussions. Alexander Mackennal, Chairman of the Mansfield Council (1892–1904), attended the informal ecumenical conferences at Grindelwald,[73] organized by the Methodist Henry Lunn, between 1892 and 1894, and was one of the Special Editors of the *Review of the Churches*.[74] In 1896 he played a leading part in the foundation of the National Free Church Council. Selbie was already a notable member of the Council before coming to Mansfield, and in the year 1917–18 served as its President.[75]

Mansfield students, and Vernon Bartlet, played the leading Congregational role in the founding and development of the Free Church Fellowship. The Fellowship had its origin in a group of a dozen young men who met at Mansfield just before Easter 1911. They drew up plans for a conference at Swanwick, the recently opened conference centre in Derbyshire, in the summer. One hundred men, most of them friends of the founding group, came together at Swanwick and shared what they later referred to as 'a Pentecostal experience'. One of the participants wrote later that 'Many of us... had eaten our hearts out in a dreary isolation, but that week we walked into a new world and things have never since been quite the same to any of us.'[76] The following April the gathering re-convened and adopted

---

[72] *Mansfield College Annual Report 1910–11*, 12.

[73] Those who attended, including several Anglicans, did so in a personal capacity.

[74] Henry Lunn was General Editor; the other Special Editors were Archdeacon Farrar (Anglican), Donald Fraser (Presbyterian), John Clifford (Baptist), and Percy Bunting (Methodist).

[75] See E. K. H. Jordan, *Free Church Unity: History of the Free Church Council Movement 1896–1941* (London, 1956).

[76] Richard Roberts, quoted in *The Free Church Fellowship 1911–65: An Ecumenical Pioneer* (Royston, 1967), 9.

a formal 'Covenant', which was actually drafted by Nathaniel Micklem, then in his first year at Mansfield. It included this sentence:
'Our desire is to cultivate a new spiritual fellowship and commun-
ion with all branches of the Christian Church; our hope is of a Free
Church so steeped in the spirit and traditions of the entire Church
Catholic as to be ready in due time for the reunion of Christendom.'[77]
Mansfield men were elected as General Secretary (Malcolm Spencer)
and Secretary to the Committee (G. E. Darlaston), and all but one of
the Congregational members of the Committee (including Mansfield's
Chaplain, R. K. Evans).

The greatest impetus towards a closer relationship between all the
churches stemmed from the World Missionary Conference in Edin-
burgh in 1910. Frank Lenwood and W. B. Selbie (and a former student,
T. H. Martin) from Mansfield attended as official delegates of the
LMS. It was in the wake of that conference that a series of well-
attended lectures were delivered at Mansfield in Hilary Term 1911 on
'Evangelical Christianity: Its History and Witness'. The speakers represented Anglicanism (A. J. Carlyle), Presbyterianism (John Oman),
Baptist Churches (Newton Marshall), Methodist Churches (A. S.
Peake), and the Society of Friends (Edward Grubb) as well as Congregationalism (F. J. Powicke). Those who attended included 'a certain
number of High Churchmen, especially senior men in the University, e.g. the Principal of Pusey House [Darwell Stone]'.[78] When the
lectures were published in 1911, Selbie, the editor, defined Evangelical
Christianity as 'that type of Christian life and truth which regards
as primary and determinative, alike for the individual and for the
Church, living faith in Christ as all-sufficient mediator of God's
grace'.[79] The intention of the volume was to promote 'the real spiritual unity of Christendom'. Selbie wrote:

> It is indeed true that the times seem to be ripe for a better spirit
> among the Churches. They need to stand together, both for the
> defence and propagation of the Gospel. The world outside cannot
> understand their divisions and will never take their efforts seriously,
> unless they can show that they are really one in Christ Jesus. While
> this is no reason for abandoning positions conscientiously held, it

[77] The Covenant is quoted in *The Free Church Fellowship 1911–65*. See also J. W.
Grant, *Free Churchmanship in England 1870–1940* (London, n.d. [1955]), 217–20.
[78] *Mansfield College Annual Report 1910–11*, 12.
[79] W. B. Selbie (ed.), *Evangelical Christianity: Its History and Witness* (London, 1911),
p. v.

is a reason for seeking better relations with those who are all aiming at the same goal, but seeking to reach it by different roads.[80]

To the published volume Bartlet contributed an essay on 'The Protestant Idea of Church and Ministry as Rooted in Early Christianity', in which he traced the development of the 'charismatic' (based on 'gifts' rather than 'orders') ministry of the apostolic age through the local ministry of 'bishops and deacons' into the later 'historic episcopate'. He affirmed that 'there is *no doctrine of succession to apostolic grace*, but only of *continuity in apostolic order*'.[81]

Bartlet wrote and taught tirelessly on this theme, contributing towards a better understanding between churches through historical study. He was recognized by his contemporaries as 'one of the most learned scholars of our generation in Oxford in the New Testament and the early Patristic literature'.[82] His pamphlet *The Validity of the Congregational Ministry* (London, 1916) pursued the same theme. He played a leading part in three conferences which were held at Mansfield in January 1918, 1919, and 1920 between Anglicans and Free Church representatives. He contributed a paper on 'Corporate Authority' which was published in *Towards Reunion*[83] after the first two conferences. Another Mansfield man, A. E. Garvie, contributed a paper on 'The Reformed Episcopate'. The conference of 1920 reached a considerable area of agreement in preparation for the Lambeth Conference later in the year, and contributed to the issuing of *An Appeal to All Christian People* at that conference.

Was this leading to the subsuming of everything Mansfield had stood for in a united Church? Was the ecumenical movement an admission of weakness, a moving together of weakened Churches in a desire to renew strength? This all depended on the theology which was to underpin it; and this was the challenge to the next generation of Congregational theologians. The inspiration for the Edinburgh Conference was pastoral and evangelistic; the theological dimension came later. At this stage, it was from P. T. Forsyth, a one-time member

---

[80] Ibid., p. x.   [81] Ibid. 28.

[82] A. J. Carlyle in CQ 19/1 (Jan. 1941), 26–7.

[83] *Towards Reunion: Being Contributions to Mutual Understanding by Church of England and Free Church Writers* (London, 1919), ed. A. J. Carlyle (Chaplain and Lecturer, University College and Rector of St Martin's and All Saints, Oxford), S. H. Clark (Vicar of Tonbridge), J. Scott Lidgett (Superintendent, Bermondsey Settlement), and J. H. Shakespeare (Secretary, Baptist Union).

of the Mansfield Council (1896–1902, elected by the subscribers) and now Principal of Hackney College, who had sat at Fairbairn's feet in Aberdeen, that the most original, profound theology was emerging from within the Reformed tradition. He sought to delineate the essential character of the Church, and to call all Christians and all denominations to be faithful to the gospel character.[84] A generation later, Mansfield men played a leading role in working out the theological dimensions of the ecumenical movement from a Reformed perspective.

Mansfield itself experienced a renewal of life in 1919. In the last year of the war, the number of students had declined to two. But by Trinity Term 1919, there were twenty. The fact that there had been serious concern about numbers of students before the war[85] was forgotten in the enthusiasm of men returning from the war to enter the ministry.

The new Chaplain,[86] Nathaniel Micklem, presented the Council with a challenge in his report in the summer of 1919. Behind the relief and superficial optimism of peace he discerned a great spiritual malaise to which the ministers of the future and those responsible for training them would have to respond:

> when I consider the carelessness, the pleasure-seeking, the insensibility of men to the great issues of the day and to the almost universal suffering of mankind; when I recollect, as how can I forget? that those who are here are but a remnant out of a great company who freely gave their lives for ideals for which these men now here, 'else sinning greatly', should be and should know themselves to be 'dedicated spirits'; when I see both in the town here and in the country generally a growing indignation at the discrepancy of the life actually lived here with the needs and duties of the hour—how can I but be gravely concerned about the future?[87]

[84] See e.g. P. T. Forsyth, *The Charter of the Church* (London, 1896), *Lectures on the Church and the Sacraments* (London, 1917), and 'Unity and Theology', his contribution to *Towards Reunion*, 51–81.

[85] *Mansfield College Annual Report 1912–13*, 6.

[86] W. S. Bradley died suddenly, of pneumonia, in 1918.

[87] *Mansfield College Annual Report 1918–19*, 8.

IX

Whither Congregationalism?
The 1920s

THE mood of the early 1920s has been characterized by Adrian Hastings as 'confident agnosticism'.[1] Oxford shared fully in this mood, despite the strong Anglican presence. Relief at the end of the slaughter was combined with a certain light-hearted hedonism which had little time for religion. More seriously, the intellectual challenges of Darwin, Marx, Nietzsche, Freud, and Durkheim to orthodox Christianity were too strong for many intelligent enquirers to resist.

The spiritual malaise of which Micklem warned the College Council was accompanied by a decline in church-going and church membership in almost all denominations, but in Nonconformist churches in particular. The peak year for Nonconformist church membership as a whole was 1906; for membership of Congregational churches, it was 1908.[2] From that year on, the number of Congregational churches, members, and ministers declined. This had two almost immediate effects on the College: a shortage of candidates, and a shortage of money.

Although the number of students at Mansfield in 1920 was larger than ever before, the increase was short-lived. The College Report for 1923–4 referred to 'the smallness of the numbers who are coming forward', and shared 'in the anxieties of the leaders of all the great branches of the Christian Church at the gravity of this problem'. The Congregational Union appointed a Commission on the Colleges in 1921, and asked it to consider how an adequate supply of suitable ministerial candidates could be encouraged, while at the same time examining the feasibility of an amalgamation of colleges. Their

[1] Adrian Hastings, *A History of English Christianity 1920–85* (London, 1985), 221. See ch. 12 for a witty and penetrating survey of the intellectual climate of the 1920s.

[2] Nonconformist church membership as a whole was 2,020,000 in that year. See R. Currie, A. Gilbert, and L. Horsley, *Churches and Churchgoers: Patterns of Church Growth in the British Isles since 1700* (Oxford, 1977). The number of members of Congregational churches in 1910 was 453,138—*CYB 1911*, 602–4. By 1930 it was 312,216—see *CYB 1931*, 582–3 (statistics for 1920 are not available).

findings were presented in 1923 and 1925.[3] They were approving of the union of Hackney and New Colleges in London in 1924, but regretted that other proposals for amalgamation foundered, often through provincial loyalty and prejudice. Mansfield was exempt from any proposal of amalgamation partly because of its unique position —it stood alone (apart from Cheshunt College, Cambridge, which as a legal entity was associated with the Countess of Huntingdon's Connexion rather than the Congregational Union and which was open to candidates for the ministry in other denominations) as an exclusively postgraduate college; and because, with a distinguished staff, it had set the highest intellectual standard for ministerial training within the denomination.

There was some concern about quality too. One of Selbie's colleagues thought that he was occasionally too lenient in standards of admission in an effort to fill the places.[4] And at the end of the decade Dodd referred to his concern in a letter to his former teacher Alexander Souter, now in Aberdeen:

> I am not altogether happy about the college. We don't seem to get the type of men offering for the Ministry to which we were formerly accustomed, and the simple fact is that a good many of our men are not really up to the Mansfield course. However we keep hoping for better times, and I do think that two or three of our First Year are better than we have been having recently.[5]

However, one also has to bear in mind that twenty-one of Selbie's students became theological teachers themselves.

A denomination declining in membership meant diminishing financial resources. This was reflected in a decline in subscriptions to the College; as original subscribers died, they were not being replaced by new ones.[6] This meant that little could be put aside for repairs and maintenance.

Underlying these concerns was the fact that none of the Free Churches was producing a theology adequate to the situation described by Nathaniel Micklem in his report to the College Council

---

[3] *CYB 1924*, 16–18, *CYB 1926*, 55–9. See also the 'Report of the Council on the Supply of Ministers' in *CYB 1926*, 15–19.

[4] E. R. Micklem in *MCM* 125 (Aug. 1944), 105.

[5] C. H. Dodd to A. Souter, 18 Jan. 1930. Bodleian Library MS Eng.lett.c.603 fo. 96.

[6] The respective amounts received through subscriptions and donations in 1920–1, 1924–5, and 1929–30 were (to the nearest pound) £946, £836, and £679. See *Mansfield College Annual Reports*.

in 1919;[7] the voice of P. T. Forsyth (who died in 1921) had not yet been heeded. The most challenging critic after Forsyth's death was not a minister, but a Congregational layman who taught history at Cambridge, Bernard Lord Manning. In 1923 he wrote in the new journal, the *Congregational Quarterly*,[8] that Nonconformity looked to many undergraduates like 'Anglicanism and water'; 'It seems to contain nothing but what Anglicanism contains, whilst Anglicanism contains some things that it lacks.'[9] When its political significance declined, so did its zest. In a fierce and uncompromising article in the *Congregational Quarterly* in 1927 on 'Some Characteristics of the Older Dissent' he challenged 'Dissent' to recover its heritage of orthodox theology, of churchmanship and ministry, and of solemnity of worship, a heritage which he claimed had been obscured by the disintegration of Calvinism, the Evangelical Revival, and the alliance of Nonconformity and Liberalism. 'If Dissent is to survive it must survive not as a degenerate form of Anglicanism or a despiritualized form of Quakerism; it must survive as *sui generis*, because it can believe in itself.'[10] The admission of Nonconformists to Oxford and Cambridge had often benefited Anglicans more than Dissenters. 'Our forefathers who drove the Established Church step by step from its privileged position conferred on it benefits much greater than those that they won for dissenters.'[11] Thus he quoted G. M. Trevelyan's verdict that 'the men who would formerly have been the leaders of a militant Nonconformity have been absorbed in the general stream of national life', leading to 'the diminution of the Dissenting bodies both in self-consciousness and power'.[12]

As yet there was no strong voice from Mansfield to take up Manning's challenge. No doubt Selbie himself would have said that the preaching of the gospel, supported by scholarship but unfettered by ecclesiastical pronouncements, was Mansfield's central task, and the essence of Congregationalism's contribution to the Church Catholic. This was no doubt the view of many of those, Nonconformist and Anglican, who flocked to hear Selbie preach. His colleagues meanwhile were making a substantial contribution to biblical scholarship.

---

[7] See the end of Ch. VIII.

[8] Founded by Albert Peel in 1923, and edited by him until 1945.

[9] 'Nonconformity at Cambridge', *CQ* (1923), 179–87.

[10] *CQ* (1927), 300.   [11] *CQ* (1923), 185.

[12] G. M. Trevelyan, *British History in the Nineteenth Century and After* (London, 1937), 284.

One of Selbie's former students and colleagues wrote after his death that 'his was the one prophetic voice in the University' in the years immediately following the First World War.[13] He preached, powerfully and without a note, on alternate Sundays during term, always drawing large congregations, not only College students and members of staff and their families, but undergraduates of varied religious background and allegiance, and prominent members of the University. It was not unknown for people to be turned away from the Chapel when he was preaching. Not until Chavasse came to St Aldate's in 1922, and F. R. Barry to St Mary's in 1928, did the Mansfield congregations cease to be the largest in Oxford.

Senior members of the University were often invited to lunch in the Principal's Lodgings to meet visiting preachers. Junior members were welcomed to the 'Open House' tea later in the afternoon, and forty or so attended each Sunday during term. These occasions were presided over by Mrs Selbie 'with the *eclat* of the *grande dame*'.[14] Though she played no official part in College life, in her role as hostess she was 'one of Oxford's great women characters'. She had a wonderful memory, and retained her interest in Mansfield until her hundredth birthday in 1964.

In vacations Selbie travelled all over the country preaching each Sunday in a different congregation, thus becoming very well known in the denomination. He wrote a weekly column in the *Christian World*—'Answering Questions'—with his photograph at the head of each contribution. His interest in psychology, and in 'the new psychology' emanating from North America and from Germany, deepened his understanding of religious experience, and added to the power of his preaching and his conduct of public prayer. This interest led to his most substantial book, *The Psychology of Religion* (Oxford, 1924), a printed version of his Wilde Lectures in the University. In addition, he was a 'natural' pastor, one to whom people of many different temperaments and needs turned at times of crisis. To his students likewise he was always available: 'his door was always open, you walked in, knocked on his study door and he was there; and if you wanted any advice, he was always willing to give it to you.'[15]

---

[13] E. R. Micklem in *MCM* 125 (Aug. 1944), 106.

[14] See *MCM* 166 (Apr. 1965), 228–30. Mildred Mary Selbie was the daughter of Joseph Thompson, the Manchester Nonconformist shipping magnate who had served on the College Building Committee.

[15] Eric Shave (Mansfield 1920–7), taped interview May 1990, MCA.

Because of his extensive pastoral and preaching activity, his published work, apart from *The Psychology of Religion*, tended to consist of revised lectures, sermons, and articles, or short commissioned works, rather than substantial works of scholarship. During the 1920s he published books such as *The Difference Christ Has Made* (London, 1921), *The Christian Ethic in the Individual, Family and State* (London, 1929), and *Religion and Life* (Oxford, 1930). He was chosen to write the book on *Congregationalism* (London, 1927) in the Methuen series on 'The Faiths; Varieties of Christian Expression' edited by L. P. Jacks.

In *Congregationalism* he set out his view of ordination:

> Among Congregationalists ordination is not the conferring of a Grace, but the recognition and ratification by the Church of the Call of God, and the commissioning and setting apart of the man so called to the ministry of a particular church. With God's call to the individual the Church has nothing to do. That is a matter between God and the individual soul. But the Church can convince itself of the reality of the call by putting a man through a long course of preliminary study and training before committing to him the sacred charge of the Church which has called him to its ministry.[16]

That ministry was prophetic rather than priestly. It was Selbie's task to enable such men (and women) to become effective preachers.

As a theologian he had limitations. One of his students recollects: 'His lectures were not his own ideas, they were just the theology that had been thought out before, which was handed to us. It was certainly systematic, and we got very good stuff from him. But you felt as though it just saved you from reading a lot of books, that's all.'[17]

It was George Buchanan Gray more than anyone who represented the academic standing of Mansfield. The second day of November 1922 was therefore a devastating one for the College. Gray had set out in the afternoon to attend a meeting of the Theology Faculty Board in the Clarendon Building. He rushed up the stairs, sat down at his appointed place, then suddenly collapsed and died. He was 56, in his intellectual prime, with much work unfinished: his most

---

[16] W. B. Selbie, *Congregationalism* (London, 1927), 186.   [17] Shave, interview.

valuable book, *Sacrifice in the Old Testament: Its Theory and Practice* (Oxford, 1925), appeared posthumously.[18]

Selbie's choice as successor to Gray would have been Nathaniel Micklem. But the Council decided to appoint John Paull Naish, who had undertaken a special period of study at Mansfield in oriental languages between 1918 and 1921 and had won the University Syriac Prize, as Lecturer. He was a member of the Society of Friends, 'a strangely mercurial personality, who shone his eyes and bared his teeth with enthusiasm when he spoke, but whose learning and scholarship were unrivalled'.[19] He was reputed to know fifty languages, and regularly reviewed foreign literature for the *Congregational Quarterly*.[20]

It was Dodd, the New Testament scholar, on whom the reputation of the College for biblical studies now stood. His graceful, lucid exposition of the Bible appealed to scholar and lay person alike. He aroused a lifelong interest in the Greek New Testament among many of his students, who were constantly amazed at the speed of his thought, the extent of his knowledge, and the accuracy of his memory (pl. 10). He published his first book, *The Meaning of Paul for Today*, in 1920, and several years later in 1928 came his magisterial and much-awaited *The Authority of the Bible*, to be followed by a steady flow of authoritative scholarly works. In 1926 he had been appointed University Lecturer in New Testament, and in that year and in 1929 he was Grinfield Lecturer in the Septuagint. It was while he was at Mansfield that he began to develop his most original and distinctive idea—'realized eschatology'—first in an article in the *Interpreter* (1923) on 'The Eschatological Element in the New Testament and its Permanent Significance', and then more specifically in a paper which he read to the first Anglo-German theological conference organized by Adolf Deissmann and George Bell at Canterbury in 1927.

In that year he spent a few months at Yale, lecturing on 'Development in the Thought of Paul'. It was known that the University was looking for a successor to Benjamin W. Bacon as Professor of New Testament Studies; it was also known that Dodd was regarded

[18] See A. S. Peake, 'Dr G. B. Gray's Contribution to Semitic Scholarship', *MCM* 12/4 (June 1923), 75–9.

[19] Information from Geoffrey Nuttall.

[20] Naish left Mansfield in 1931 to become Chief Oriental Reader for the Oxford University Press. He published many books in the field of oriental studies. See *Who Was Who 1961–70*.

10. **Staff and Students 1927** *Back row (left to right)*: [?], A. Lidster, G. C. Batten, [?], G. V. Jones, A. A. Kremenlieff, J. Bromley *Second row*: C. E. Dean, [?], D. Wilson, [?], F. H. Brown, L. A. Simpson, A. F. Bayly, R. L. Franks, J. R. Theobald, H. A. Wilson, [?], A. P. Tory *Third row*: E. C. Shave, G. C. Edmonds, J. H. MILNES, J. P. NAISH, J. V. BARTLET, W. B. SELBIE, C. H. DODD (with his dog Anubis), E. R. MICKLEM, W. H. CADMAN, E. A. Payne *Front row*: E. Rees, J. W. Richards, C. E. Norwood, E. W. McKeeman

176

as a strong candidate. Before the end of the year, he received a formal invitation to succeed Bacon, accompanied by strong, warm, persuasive, informal pressure. But partly for family reasons, and partly through loyalty to Mansfield, he decided to remain in Oxford for the time being.[21]

Successive rises in salary and his appointment as Vice-Principal (with a possible interpretation that it was the prelude to further promotion when Selbie retired) in 1929 were not to anchor him to Mansfield for much longer. In any case, scholarship and teaching had more appeal than administration. The only theological chair in England open to Nonconformists unexpectedly became available when A. S. Peake died suddenly in August 1929. The committee responsible for finding his successor as Rylands Professor of Biblical Criticism and Exegesis at Manchester University agreed unanimously to invite Dodd to accept nomination. This time he agreed to move, regarding it as an honour for the College as well as for himself. He wrote to Alexander Souter: 'I do indeed feel it to be a great honour, and all the more so since the vote was unanimous. I am glad too for the sake of the College, as I know you will be, since I believe your loyal attachment to Mansfield as well as personal friendship for me lies behind your persistent advocacy.'[22] One of his friends wrote that 'you would be astonished how my thought of Mansfield is like that of Hamlet without the prince of Denmark'.[23] It was at this time that Aberdeen University awarded him the first of his eleven honorary degrees.

Mansfield's reputation was further enhanced by the publication of P. N. Harrison's *The Problem of the Pastoral Epistles* (Oxford, 1921), a detailed and scholarly discussion of the authorship of the pastoral epistles, a work which has never been superseded. Harrison was a former Mansfield student who wrote scholarly books and articles in such time as could be spared from his pastoral ministry.[24] Another outstanding former student, Nathaniel Micklem, serving a five-year appointment as Chaplain and Tutor, was now clearly destined for an outstanding career in the church of his inheritance.[25] A pacifist

[21] See F. W. Dillistone, *C. H. Dodd: Interpreter of the New Testament* (London, 1977), 99.
[22] C. H. Dodd to A. Souter, 18 Jan. 1930. Bodleian Library, MS Eng.lett.c.603, fo. 97.
[23] Quoted in Dillistone, *C. H. Dodd*, 104.
[24] For Percy Neale Harrison (1897–1900) see *CYB 1965–66*, 442 and *MCM* 165 (July 1964), 210.
[25] His grandfather Thomas Micklem had become a Dissenter early in life. Other sections of the family remained Anglican. See *The Box and the Puppets* (London, 1957), 14.

and liberal (in both politics and theology) during the First World War, he was already writing books which marked the first stage of his theological journey: *The Open Light: An Enquiry into Faith and Reality* (London, 1919), *A First Century Letter: An Exposition of I Corinthians* (London, 1920), *The Galilean: The Permanent Element in Religion* (London, 1920). He was general editor of a series called 'The Christian Revolution' (published by Headley Brothers), in which Mansfield authors were well represented. As well as his own first books, the series included Dodd's book on *The Meaning of Paul for Today* (London, 1920) and C. J. Cadoux's *The Early Christian Attitude to War* (London, 1919). These books were written

> with an exhilarating sense of confidence in Christianity, with fresh insights into the understanding of Scripture and the ways of grace, and they were unswervingly centred on Jesus Christ as the way, the truth and the life. Their substance and style brought a sense of liberation from what had come to be regarded as the imprisoning —even deadening—effect of traditional theological language.[26]

Much to Selbie's disappointment, Micklem had decided to leave Mansfield after only two years, in favour of a post teaching Old Testament studies at the Selly Oak Colleges in Birmingham. He was replaced by his younger brother, Romilly Micklem, a gentle, artistic man who brought grace and sensitivity to the regular College worship —'the very man whom the JCR would have chosen for themselves'.[27] He acted as Chaplain to all Congregational students, and also as senior friend to the Livingstone Society for Free Church undergraduates.[28] Like Selbie, he was interested in psychology, and used his developing understanding in an unusual book on *Miracles and the New Psychology: A Study in the Healing Miracles of the New Testament* (London, 1922).

This interest in psychology, which Selbie shared, was reflected in J. A. Hadfield's Dale Lectures on 'The Contribution to Ethics and Religion of Psychotherapeutics', which attracted crowded audiences, and which were later published as *Psychology and Morals* (London,

---

[26] Norman Goodall, 'Nathaniel Micklem CH 1888–1976', *JURCHS* I/10 (Oct. 1977), 289.

[27] *MCM* 11/5 (Dec. 1920), 64. For Edward Romilly Micklem (1892–1960) see *CYB 1961*, 444–5 and *MCM* 157 (July 1960) 23–5.

[28] The Society, originally founded to promote interest in mission work at home and abroad, often met in the Mansfield JCR. See the Minute Books of the Livingstone Society 1893–1930, MCA.

1923, and subsequently reprinted fifteen times until 1964). Hadfield was a former student of Mansfield (1903–6) who had been influenced by William McDougall, and had gone on to medical training in Edinburgh after study in Oxford. He gained first-hand experience of nervous disorders during the First World War, and instead of going into the ministry set up his own psychotherapeutic practice in Harley Street. Both C. H. Dodd and C. J. Cadoux consulted him over a considerable period of time about their own personal problems; no doubt other ministers, as well as lay people, did so too.

Two years later, Albert Schweitzer gave the Dale Memorial Lectures on the theme 'The Struggle for the Ethical Conception of the World in European Philosophy'. He and Madame Schweitzer stayed in the Principal's Lodgings.

> He had a little room upstairs allocated to him for a study, and on lecture days he would shut himself up there in a developing frowst engendered by a peculiarly smelly gas-fire, preparing his lecture up to the very last moment in German. He would then walk across to the lecture-room and deliver the lecture without a note in (*pace* George Seaver) French. There was no hesitating for a word. He spoke slowly, but flowingly, and gave us a beautifully ordered discourse.[29]

The lectures were eventually published in English in 1923 as *The Decay and the Restoration of Civilization* (translated by C. T. Campion) and *Civilization and Ethics* (translated by J. P. Naish; the 1929 edition was translated by Campion). It was in these lectures that Schweitzer first formulated and made public his ethic of 'reverence for life', a concept which has continued to exercise a significant influence.

Relations with the Baptist Union had always been good, and several Baptist ministerial students had chosen Mansfield for their theological training.[30] In 1926, under the will of James Neobard, a new scholarship was founded for students preparing for the Baptist ministry at Mansfield (though tenable by a Congregationalist if no suitable Baptist candidate appeared). A closer relationship with the Baptists began in the following year when Henry Wheeler Robinson,

---

[29] E. R. Micklem, 'Dr Albert Schweitzer and Mansfield', in *MCM* 146 (Jan. 1955), 255. Schweitzer was so sensitive about the use of the German language that he would not even allow the German titles of Bach chorale preludes to be printed in the programmes for his organ recitals.

[30] Sixteen Baptist students studied at Mansfield while Selbie was Principal.

Principal of the Baptist Regent's Park College in London, moved to 55 St Giles to prepare the way for the removal of his College to Oxford. Selbie had heard of a site on the corner of St Giles and Pusey Street owned by an Anglican Evangelical who was anxious to sell it, but not to a Roman Catholic. He sent a message to this effect to Wheeler Robinson, who was known to favour a move to Oxford.[31] Robinson managed to carry his College Committee with him, and the site was purchased. At first the College operated in both Oxford and London, with Robinson commuting between the two. Mansfield immediately offered hospitality to the Regent's Park men, and from 1928 until the completion of the new Baptist College buildings in 1939 the Baptist students and staff shared Mansfield's common rooms, Chapel, and lecture rooms. Wheeler Robinson was invited to teach Old Testament theology to Mansfield men. Many on Mansfield's side hoped that the two colleges could either unite or at least share their teaching resources, but in spite of periods of joint teaching, this did not come about, largely because of doubts on the Baptist side.

Wheeler Robinson was one of Fairbairn's students; he was at Mansfield from 1895 until 1900. He won several University prizes and was marked as a future Old Testament scholar. He owed a great debt to Gray: 'Gray became to the men he taught an externalised conscience, an intellectual ideal in exegesis and philosophy, a continuous though unseen censor of the pretentious and the vague.'[32] His own scholarship was recognized by his election as President of the Society for Old Testament Study in 1929, and in the following decade by his election as the first Free Church Chairman of the Board of the Oxford Faculty of Theology.[33]

The College records for the 1920s convey an impression of settled and confident routine: Mansfield had established its place within Congregational denominational life on the one hand, and Oxford theological life on the other. Its association of former students was strong. It was the only fully postgraduate college within the denomination; and although it was not officially part of the University

[31] See R. E. Cooper, *From Stepney to St Giles: The Story of Regent's Park College 1810–1960* (London, 1960), 86.

[32] Quoted in E. A. Payne, *Henry Wheeler Robinson: Scholar, Teacher, Principal: A Memoir* (London, 1946), 33.

[33] Among his publications were *The Christian Doctrine of Man* (Edinburgh, 1911), *The Religious Ideas of the Old Testament* (London, 1913), and *The Christian Experience of the Holy Spirit* (London, 1928).

its contribution was recognized by the inclusion of the lectures of its theological teachers in the University lecture lists. Further recognition came to Selbie when he was elected to an Honorary Fellowship at his old college, Brasenose.

Students from overseas continued to find a welcome at Mansfield, as did missionaries on furlough. Among the many American visitors was Amos Wilder (1922–3), whose prowess at tennis took him to the centre court at Wimbledon and into the Oxford, and Oxford and Cambridge, tennis teams.[34] Among German visitors was Adam von Trott (Hilary Term 1929), a law student who combined his visit to the SCM Quadrennial Conference in Liverpool with a term's experience of an English theological college; the Mansfield JCR 'were refreshed and cheered by his amazing and amusing personality',[35] although other Oxford circles were more attractive to him. From Japan came S. Endo, K. Kawabe, and Tokutaro Takakura, later to become one of Japan's foremost Christian scholars and ministers. From China came Hsu Ti-shan (T. S. Hsu 1924–6), later Professor of Chinese at Yenching and Hong Kong Universities.[36] And from Bulgaria, Paul Christoff and A. Kremenlieff.[37] On furlough from missionary service with the LMS in Central Africa came Mabel Shaw.[38]

Although there were only three full-time women students at Mansfield during Selbie's Principalship, he and the denomination were committed to the principle of equality.[39] Constance Coltman contributed a perceptive article on 'Protestantism and the Ministry of Women' to the *College Magazine* in June 1924, foreshadowing

---

[34] Amos Wilder (1895–1993) became a distinguished writer and biblical scholar at Harvard. See *MCM* 195 (1992–3), 55.

[35] JCR Notes, *MCM* 12/16 (July 1929), 419. John Marsh, who was President of the JCR during Adam von Trott's visit, helped him to return later to Balliol as a Rhodes Scholar. Adam von Trott later lost his life because of his part in the plot against Hitler in 1944. See Christopher Sykes, *Troubled Loyalty: A Biography of Adam von Trott zu Solz* (London, 1968) and Giles MacDonogh, *A Good German: Adam von Trott zu Solz* (London, 1989).

[36] See *MCM* 136 (Jan. 1950), 5–6.

[37] Paul Christoff was a Congregational minister in Bulgaria for four years before practising as a barrister. A. Kremenlieff was a Congregational minister in Bulgaria for thirty years. See *MCM* 175 (Dec. 1972), 18–19.

[38] Mabel Shaw served with the London Missionary Society at Mberishi, Northern Rhodesia from 1915 until 1941.

[39] A resolution affirming that the ordination of any woman who had complied with the requirements of college training laid down for male candidates for the ministry and who received a call to a congregation which belonged to the Congregational Union would be recognized had been passed by the General Purposes Committee of the Congregational Union in 1909. See the reports in the *Christian World*, 18 Mar. 1909 and 4 Oct. 1917.

much of the argument half a century later, and ending with a plea that the Free Churches 'may reveal to others the mind of Christ as concerns the place and function of women in His Church'.[40] The following term, Dorothy Wilson began a three-year course at Mansfield, where her 'vivacious and friendly personality' made a considerable impact. Like Constance Coltman, she was brought up in a Presbyterian family, and did not consider ministry within Congregationalism until the General Assembly of the Presbyterian Church of England unanimously rejected her request for permission to prepare for the ministry in 1924.[41] 'Dr Selbie then invited me to Mansfield, bless him!', she wrote in 1956. She had to struggle against ill health throughout her life, but went on from Mansfield to several pastorates and much work for religious education.[42] She once wrote very warmly in the *College Magazine* about Selbie's support for women students, how 'kind and fair and wise' he had been, 'never hiding from them the fact that life for a woman minister is as yet bound to be difficult, but also making clear his conviction that God can speak through a woman as well as through a man, that she, too, may be called to His service in the ministry and can then do nothing but answer the call'.[43] Selbie was one of the earliest Vice-Presidents of the Society for the Ministry of Women.[44]

There was a break with the past with the death of Sir Alfred Dale, Chairman of the Council and Board of Education, and son of R. W. Dale, in 1921. He was for many years Vice-Chancellor of Liverpool University and a distinguished educationalist. Within the same year came the resignation of Sir Albert Spicer, Treasurer for more then thirty years. However, their successors belonged to the same tradition. Sidney Berry, who was elected Chairman of the Council, was not only an old Mansfield man, but the minister of Carrs Lane Church in Birmingham; and the new Treasurer was Sir Arthur Haworth,[45] whose father and uncle had been great benefactors to the new college in the 1880s. In 1923 Sidney Berry was elected Secretary of the

[40] *MCM* 12/6 (June 1924), 142.

[41] See J. Field-Bibb, 'Women and Ministry: The Presbyterian Church of England', *Heythrop Journal*, 31 (1990), 159.

[42] See the obituary in *MCM* 150 (Jan. 1957), 325–6.

[43] *MCM* 101 (June 1932), 135.

[44] The interdenominational Society for the Ministry of Women was founded in 1929 under the presidency of Maude Royden.

[45] Sir Arthur Adlington Haworth (1865–1944). He was Liberal MP for South Manchester 1906–12.

Congregational Union, and he held that position for the next twenty-five years. This meant that Mansfield and the Union were kept in close touch.

Mansfield men were influential in the denomination through the pages of the *Congregational Quarterly*. During these years it was a forum for debate and discussion among Congregational ministers and scholars, and its quality and interest were outstanding. Selbie was on the editorial board and a contributor from the beginning. It was in the pages of the *Quarterly* for 1926 that R. F. Horton made a plea for Free Churchmen to come together to meet the needs of the time for 'a presentation of Christianity equally removed from Romanism and from Fundamentalism, a presentation which the intelligence and reason and knowledge of modern men can whole-heartedly accept, a presentation which, starting from the Christ Who is ever the same, shows clearly what He has to say to new times and new truth.'[46] In August 1925 the Union of Modern Churchmen had met in conference in Oxford. They had, wrote Horton, shown 'great courage', but, as 'nonconformists' *within* the Church of England, they were hampered by inevitable restrictions. The Nonconformists *from* the Church of England, he suggested, should be attempting the same work; they were free to 'use their liberty in accepting new truth and discarding outworn formularies and modes of thought' and indeed it was their duty to do so. Selbie welcomed the challenge, and in a later number of the *Congregational Quarterly* in the same year wrote that 'the task of the moment' was 'to discover a modernist gospel, to preach the Christian message in terms which modern men can receive and understand, and yet retain all its saving and sanctifying power'.[47]

The result was a series of annual conferences from 1927 onwards, the first two of which were held at Mansfield, before migrating to Cheshunt College, Cambridge in 1929. The first, in July 1927, with R. F. Horton in the chair and 130 participants, took as its theme, 'The Christian Faith in the Light of Modern Science and Criticism'. Most of the speakers were Mansfield men. Selbie spoke on 'Psychology and the Validity of Religious Experience', C. H. Dodd on 'The Fourth Gospel', R. S. Franks on 'Towards a Metaphysic of Religion'.[48]

---

[46] R. F. Horton, 'Free Churchmen and the Modern Churchmen', *CQ* (1926), 171.
[47] *CQ* (1926), 359.
[48] These lectures all anticipated major published works: W. B. Selbie's *The Validity of Christian Belief* (London, 1939), C. H. Dodd's *The Interpretation of the Fourth Gospel*

Warnings of the divergence of outlook which was to prove so difficult for Mansfield in the 1930s first came into the open when Nathaniel Micklem, about to leave England for a new teaching post in Kingston, Ontario, spoke on 'Congregationalism and Modernism'; while agreeing that faith had to be re-interpreted in modern terms, he warned that Congregationalism and Modern Protestantism in general were in danger of disintegration 'through the presentation of a vague and sentimental religiosity without justice, without judgement, without a soul-shattering mercy, without a Redeemer and without God'.[49] Christian experience could not be separated from Christian dogma and historic facts, and Christianity itself depended on *revealed* truth.[50]

In 1931 the centenary of the Congregational Union was marked by a volume edited by Albert Peel entitled *Essays Congregational and Catholic* (London, 1931). Of the seventeen contributors, nine were old Mansfield men (including four members or former members of staff), one was an old Spring Hill student, and another was R. F. Horton, who could be considered an honorary Mansfield man. Selbie's contribution on 'Congregationalism and the Great Christian Doctrines' was a summary of his theological position, and indeed that of most of his Congregational contemporaries in the closing years of his Principalship.

Representatives of Mansfield had continued to take a leading part in the ecumenical developments of the 1920s. The University's recognition of the Principal through the conferring of the DD degree further increased Selbie's reputation and confidence, and he played a significant role in the ecumenical conversations of the 1920s. At the 'Old Men's Meetings' in the summer of 1920 there was a concentrated discussion on the subject of 'Reunion'. R. K. Evans, returned to England after several years in China, told the assembly that he now found a much more hopeful situation among the churches; but crucial issues had to be faced. 'We Free Church men could not compromise about Apostolic or Episcopal succession, which is the pivot

---

(Cambridge, 1953) and *Historical Tradition in the Fourth Gospel* (Cambridge, 1963), and R. S. Franks's *The Metaphysical Justification of Religion* (London, 1929). The proceedings of the conference were published in *CQ* (1927), 505–68.

[49] *CQ* (1927), 552.

[50] The second conference, also held at Mansfield, took as its theme 'Our Authority: The Church; The Bible; Our Lord Jesus Christ; Science'. Bartlet gave one of the main papers on 'The Bible as Authority'. See *CQ* (1928), 517–51.

of the "Catholic" position;' but he urged that they go on trying to 'transcend the antithesis between Catholic and Evangelical'.[51]

In July 1920 the Lambeth Conference issued its 'Appeal to all Christian People', expressing a more understanding and appreciative attitude towards Nonconformists, moving beyond friendly co-operation to a proposal that the Nicene Creed should provide a doctrinal basis for reunion.[52] The Anglican bishops invited representatives of other churches to join them in conference to promote dialogue and co-operation. In the following edition of the *College Magazine*, W. E. Ireland (Mansfield 1888–93), minister of the Congregational Church in Macclesfield, wrote of his reflections on the Lambeth proposals and how they would affect him in practice. Again the stumbling block was over 'orders': 'It has seemed to us that the refusal to recognise the non-episcopal ministry was a refusal to recognise the manifest gifts of the Spirit.' He pleaded for a vision 'of what yet lies far ahead—"the idea of Christ as the true ideal for a Christian church"'.[53]

In January 1921 a gathering of Free Church representatives met at Mansfield for three days to discuss their response to the Lambeth Appeal. Subsequently the Federal Council of the Evangelical Free Churches of England and the National Free Church Council appointed a committee to draw up a formal response. Selbie and Bartlet were two of the Congregational representatives on that committee, and when it met, Selbie was appointed chairman. After their report, *The Free Churches and the Lambeth Appeal*, was published in 1921, the Archbishop of Canterbury, Randall Davidson, invited the Free Church representatives to continue in dialogue with Anglican delegates at Lambeth Palace. These discussions eventually foundered on that problem of (re-)ordination which had so concerned the Mansfield men.[54]

While this dialogue was continuing, Selbie, along with Cosmo Gordon Lang, J. Scott Lidgett, P. Carnegie Simpson, and A. C. Headlam, participated in a series of lectures in London during November and December 1922, published in 1923 as *The Lambeth Joint Report*

[51] *MCM* 11/3 (July 1920), 46.

[52] For the 'Appeal' see G. K. A. Bell (ed.), *Documents on Christian Unity 1920–24* (London, 1924), 1–14.

[53] 'The Lambeth Proposals and Congregational Practice', *MCM* 11/5 (Dec. 1920), 55–7.

[54] See Adrian Hastings, *A History of English Christianity*, 97–9.

on Church Unity: A Discussion. His lecture on 'The Free Churches and Reunion' welcomed the Lambeth Appeal—'it had never before been stated openly that those who belonged to the Free Churches were Christians in the same sense as others'[55]—but explained that those in the Free Churches approached the question of reunion from a different position from Anglicans. Free Church men and women did not consider themselves schismatics. The Anglican emphasis on creeds and episcopal ordination might yet prove a stumbling block to reunion; he hoped that the creeds, which Congregationalists had always regarded as 'excellent declarations of the faith', would not be made a *test* of membership, and expressed a continuing concern that questions remained about 'a commission through episcopal ordination' for existing Free Church ministers. The burning question for Selbie, in a decade which can now be viewed as a golden age of Anglo-Catholicism, was whether the Church of the future was to be Protestant or Catholic: 'If the Anglo-Catholic view of Church tradition and of orders and of episcopacy is to prevail, it is quite unthinkable that either we, or indeed the liberals and evangelicals within the Church [of England], will ever be able to come to anything like an agreement.'[56] In his address from the chair of the Congregational Union he had earlier declared: 'Believing as we do that it is not the Church that makes Christians, but Christians that constitute the Church, we can accept all Christians as brethren, whatever be their Church or their creed.'[57]

A few years later, one of his old students who kept in constant touch with him, C. J. Cadoux, published *Catholicism and Christianity: A Vindication of Progressive Protestantism* (London, 1928), a vigorous and lengthy defence of Liberal Protestantism, so exhaustive in treatment that the editor of *Essays Catholic and Critical*, E. G. Selwyn, wrote in the preface to the third edition in 1929 that 'It is a great thing to have the case thus presented within the covers of one volume. If Dr Cadoux fails to establish it, probably no other attempt will succeed' (p. vii). Cadoux was an active participant in the ecumenical discussions at Mansfield, and an eager controversialist.[58]

Mansfield men played an important role in the ecumenical Conference on Christian Politics, Economics, and Citizenship (COPEC)

---

[55] *The Lambeth Joint Report on Church Unity* (London, 1923), 68.
[56] Ibid. 83.   [57] *CYB 1915*, 44.
[58] See Elaine Kaye, *C. J. Cadoux: Theologian, Scholar and Pacifist* (Edinburgh, 1988), 88–92.

in Birmingham in April 1924. The three Mansfield Professors—Selbie, Bartlet, and Dodd—all contributed to the reports of the Commissions, A. E. Garvie was an acting Vice-President, and Malcolm Spencer helped to organize it. Several others participated.

Of the 145 students who completed a course lasting at least two years, having entered when Selbie was Principal, 20 were Baptists, 5 were Methodists, and 1 was a Welsh Presbyterian; 25 are known to have been the sons of ministers; 5 were women. Information is available about the future careers of 126 of them. Seventy-one spent their entire careers in pastoral ministry. Sixteen served as missionaries, while 21 taught theology in higher education. Fourteen eventually moved into the Church of England.

Selbie reached the age of 65 in 1928, but was invited by the Council to continue for a possible further five years. Bartlet's term, on the other hand, was not extended, but he was given the title of Professor Emeritus. A successor to Bartlet had to be found as soon as possible, to be in position before a successor as Principal had to be sought. There must also have been a sense that Dodd would soon be drawn away to a university appointment. Mansfield posts were not advertised, to the disappointment of some possible candidates, but 'feelers' were put out along the appropriate English, Welsh, and Scottish grapevines.

It was J. S. Whale, one of his former students, who was appointed to succeed Bartlet; he began work at Mansfield in April 1929. He came from a brief pastorate at Bowdon Downs, near Manchester. During his equally brief four years at Mansfield he brought a new influence to the College. Whereas Selbie was a quintessential 'Free Churchman',[59] Whale stood in the tradition of Reformed theology, and took the Reformation as the defining element of and justification for Congregationalism. He had to teach early church history, as Bartlet had done, because his students had to take examinations in it, and he did it conscientiously. But his greater interest was in the Reformation period, and he gave this the greater emphasis, thereby reviving interest in Calvin and the Genevan tradition.[60]

---

[59] Selbie wrote in *Essays Congregational and Catholic* that 'the theological Odyssey of Congregationalism has been a process of gradual emancipation from the stern unbending Calvinism of early Independents' (131), and was the author of *Positive Protestantism* (London, 1926) and *The Freedom of the Free Churches* (London, 1928).

[60] John Seldon Whale (1896–   ) moved to Cambridge in 1933 as President of Cheshunt College.

When Dodd was appointed Vice-Principal in 1929, many may have seen this as a prelude to his succeeding Selbie as Principal. His resignation a year later in order to move to Manchester put an end to any such speculation. Within another month, the subcommittee appointed to find a successor reported its recommendation that Nathaniel Micklem should be invited to return from Canada, to which he had gone from Selly Oak in 1927, to become Yates Professor and Vice-Principal. This was agreed after a special meeting of the Council and Board of Education; and in November, the Council expressed the 'hope and expectation' that he would in due course succeed to the Principalship. In 1931 he returned to England to begin teaching at Mansfield; and in 1932 he succeeded Selbie as Principal. A new era had begun.

X

Nathaniel Micklem and the Challenge to Faith: 1932–1939

NATHANIEL MICKLEM became Principal of Mansfield in March 1932, after a year as Yates Professor, Vice-Principal, and, unofficially, Principal-elect. His father Nathaniel Micklem, KC, had tactfully resigned from the Council as soon as the appointment was made.

Micklem returned to Mansfield at the beginning of an ominous decade. Economic problems at home had led to the formation of a National Government in 1931. But worse was developing on the European scene. Within a year of Micklem's becoming Principal, Hitler came to power as Chancellor in Germany, and the country which had nurtured so many great biblical scholars and theologians was soon to be enmeshed in a demonic struggle into which almost every European country, as well as some outside, was eventually to be drawn; Christian Europe was on trial. The new Principal of Mansfield was to prove one of the minority of Christian leaders who tried to warn the Church what was happening, and to respond to the challenge.

He had enjoyed many advantages in his early years. His father, who with R. F. Horton had been one of the earliest Nonconformist undergraduates in Oxford, was a notable barrister, and for a time a Member of Parliament. He and Horton were friends, and it was Horton who baptized the young Micklem and influenced him in his sense of calling to the ministry. The son came up from Rugby to New College, his father's old college, to read Greats, and like his father was elected President of the Oxford Union (unopposed in the case of the son). He was a natural advocate, with a great gift for language, and with a questing mind, which often found its most profound expression in poetry;[1] and these gifts were combined with a lifelong deep personal faith. This privileged background and inheritance gave him a self-confidence which left him free to devote his

---

[1] See e.g. *The Labyrinth* (Oxford, 1945) and *The Labyrinth Revisited* (London, 1960).

energy to the tasks before him. He revealed a remarkable gift for identifying the main issue in a debate, for seeing through to the heart of
every controversy. His confidence, his wit, his intellect, and his charm
made him a most acceptable representative of Mansfield in a wide
sphere, not only among theologians, but also in political and literary
circles.

He had entered Mansfield in 1911, before Fairbairn's death but
when Selbie was already Principal. He characterized the atmosphere
of his own theological education (1911–14) thus:

> The bonds of rigid dogmatism were being thrown off; Seeley in his
> *Ecce Homo* had enabled thousands to realize for the first time the
> true humanity of our Lord, while Harnack from Germany was
> demonstrating, as we supposed, that Church history between the
> apostolic age and the Reformation was the sad story of a Hellenizing
> and paganizing of the Gospel, and was offering us a version of the
> essence of Christianity which accorded well with the Liberalism of
> the period. The early Fathers of the Church, as we were disposed
> to think, were guilty of obscuring and institutionalizing a simple
> and spiritual Gospel; the theologians of the Middle Ages were hair-
> splitting logicians; Calvinism was no longer credible nor in any
> way attractive; the Roman Church was passing through the throes
> of its dissolution.[2]

At this stage he had no problem in identifying himself with this
outlook. But at some time between leaving the College as a student
and his return as Vice-Principal he came to realize the inadequacy
of the theology which had replaced the 'rigid dogmatism' of an
earlier age, and was to play a leading part in the recovery of a more
adequate 'dogma'.

In those years as a student, his ecumenical vision was already taking shape. He joined the Intercollegiate Christian Union (later to become the SCM) and attended its conferences at Swanwick; he was a
representative at a World Student Christian Conference in 1908; and
he shared in the excitement and inspiration of the beginnings of the
Free Church Fellowship, whose Covenant statement he helped to draft.[3]

He had a varied career between finishing his course at Mansfield
and returning as Principal. In October 1914, two months after the
outbreak of the First World War, he was ordained in Highbury Chapel,

---

[2] N. Micklem, *What is the Faith?* (London, 1936), 11.   [3] See Ch. VIII.

Bristol, where he served as assistant minister to the saintly Arnold Thomas for two years. His pacifist views, which the Bristol church had tolerated, proved unacceptable in his succeeding ministry at Withington, Manchester, and in 1917 he and his wife (Agatha Frances Silcock[4] of Bath, whom he married in 1916) spent several months organizing a YMCA centre behind Dieppe.

In 1918 he embarked on what was to become a brilliant academic and public career, combining writing, teaching, journalism, and preaching with participation in public affairs. His spell as Chaplain of Mansfield at the end of the war was short. There followed six years as Professor of Old Testament studies at the Selly Oak Colleges, Birmingham, until he was lured away to Canada, this time to teach New Testament Studies at Queen's Theological College, Kingston, Ontario. By the time he returned to England in 1931, he had published six theological works, as well as memoirs of Arnold Thomas and of his father-in-law Thomas Ball Silcock. Two of these works, *Prophecy and Eschatology* (London, 1926)[5] and *A First Century Letter: An Exposition of Paul's First Epistle to the Corinthians* (London, 1920), his only essays in the field of biblical studies, reflected what he had been teaching; neither claimed to be original. But *Christ and Caesar* (London, 1921), which he wrote jointly with an older ex-Mansfield friend with whom he had shared digs in Bristol, the Baptist Herbert Morgan,[6] foreshadowed a major concern of his later life: how is the Christian to act responsibly in the arena of an imperfect—or even (apparently) demonic—world? His comment that when the Hebrew prophets had to oppose the government of their day they were 'not disowning their people but standing for their people's true destiny and for those principles upon which alone their people could find true blessedness'[7] leads the reader to reflect how Micklem himself, less than two decades later, stood alongside German leaders trying to recall the Church and people of Germany to their true vocation, and how he tried to do the same in his own country.

In Canada, Micklem had found himself worshipping in a United Church of Congregationalists, Presbyterians, and Methodists.[8] He

---

[4] See 'Agatha Micklem', *MCM* 159 (July 1961), 69–70.

[5] A study of the Old Testament prophets and the contemporary significance of their message.

[6] Herbert Morgan (Mansfield 1902–6) was a strong pacifist and supporter of the Labour Party. See *MCM* 130 (Jan. 1947), 201–3.

[7] N. Micklem and H. Morgan, *Christ and Caesar* (London, 1921), 207.

[8] The United Church of Canada was formed in 1925.

was happy in this ecclesiastical milieu, as well as in his college (a Presbyterian foundation), and his later description of those years in his autobiography, *The Box and the Puppets* (London, 1957), suggests that he enjoyed a good deal of freedom to think and write, the results of which were to appear after his return to England. He paid at least one visit to Europe during that time, for in 1928 he attended the second British–German theological conference at the Wartburg, and contributed a very liberal essay—'I said there . . . that the traditional doctrines of the Person of Christ were as venerable and useful as the tattered banners of past battles that decorate old churches'[9]— to the volume of essays which emerged from the gathering.[10]

When he took over at Mansfield, the College affairs had suffered neglect because of Selbie's ill health in the preceding two or three years, and a vigorous lead was needed. But more serious still, Micklem detected a general spiritual malaise within the denomination which called for challenge.[11] He felt the change from Canada particularly strongly; the United Church of Canada was a vigorous, young, partly ecumenical church, while the Congregational Union which celebrated its centenary in 1931 seemed to him to be a complacent, even self-satisfied, denomination, oblivious to the real challenge before it. He later described his dismay at the situation in this way:

> Theological liberalism had run to seed. This was particularly noticeable in the Congregational denomination which in England had fought the battle of theological freedom as it had been fought in Scotland by the Presbyterians. But the Presbyterians were anchored, if not very securely, to the Westminster Confession as the Anglicans to their Prayer Book; the Congregationalists with the break up of Calvinist orthodoxy and their new free attitude to the Scriptures had no anchor. I was quite certain that the religion being taught in many of our churches was a form of Christianity so watered down that it could not be called the religion of the New Testament, and that it was no proclamation of the Gospel as our fathers and all previous generations knew it.[12]

---

[9] N. Micklem, *The Religion of a Sceptic* (London, 1976), 52.

[10] 'A Modern Approach to Christology', in G. K. A. Bell and Adolf Deissmann (eds.), *Mysterium Christi* (London, 1930).

[11] There was said to have been a stock SCM joke: 'Yes, I like Congregationalists, I don't believe much either.'

[12] Micklem, *The Religion of a Sceptic*, 53.

In response to this situation, which compared so badly with his experiences in Canada, a prophetic strain was evoked from his mind and personality, a personality which always warmed to debate and controversy. As he later admitted, 'I lifted up my strident voice or dipped my pen in some corrosive ink'[13] and wrote and said things in a way which in later years he would have modified. The stage was set for confrontation between the comparatively young, dynamic, mercurial Principal, and the older men, brought up in the years of Nonconformist optimism, loyal to what they understood as their Congregational heritage, who, by and large, made up the membership of the Council.

What Micklem regarded as the weakness of theological thinking among Congregationalists was epitomized by the recent book by Frank Lenwood, the charismatic leader of Micklem's own student days—*Jesus Lord or Leader?* (London, 1930); for Micklem and many others, this book showed just how far a contemporary Congregationalist could stray from the historic faith.[14]

Lenwood was a member of a group of Liberal Modernists which gathered around Thomas Wigley,[15] minister of Blackheath Congregational Church. Wigley had given a series of lectures in Blackheath on Modernist themes between 1928 and 1930. The group of ministers who had been drawn to these lectures decided to convene a meeting at the May Assembly of the Congregational Union in 1932, and about seventy-five attended. In time, the group issued a statement (drafted by Wigley) which was published in the *Christian World* on 9 February 1933 (a revised version was issued on 13 October of the same year).[16] It was described as 'a reasoned restatement of the grounds of Christian belief, couched in terms better suited to the educational standards and scientific apprehensions of the present day'.[17]

The three serious critics of the statement in the columns of the *Christian World* were Micklem, Bernard Manning, and Ebenezer

---

[13] Ibid.

[14] It needs to be said that Lenwood's personal character and inspiration were greater than his professed theology; and that few Congregationalists were willing to follow him so far away from 'the historic faith'. In a critical review of the book in CQ (1931), 54, J. S. Whale wrote that his 'Christian character and life have been a priestly means of grace to many'.

[15] Thomas Wigley (1891–1961). See *CYB 1962*, 476–7.

[16] See Blackheath Group, *A Re-statement of Christian Thought* (London, 1934) for the resulting correspondence.

[17] Quoted J. W. Grant, *Free Churchmanship in England 1870–1940* (London, n.d. [1955]), 303.

Griffith-Jones (who had recently retired as Principal of the Yorkshire United Independent College[18]). Micklem's immediate comment was that the group's 'rather jejune *credo* represents, I take it, a modern Christian philosophy or the conclusion of rational discussion unassisted by revelation'.[19]

The day after the Blackheath statement had appeared in the *Christian World*, C. J. Cadoux[20] had been appointed Mackennal Professor of Church History at Mansfield in succession to J. S. Whale, and shortly afterwards was also appointed Vice-Principal. Cadoux was never a member of the Blackheath group, but his Liberal Protestant allegiance, firm to the end of his life, made him unsympathetic to Micklem's attitude. The two men differed greatly in temperament and background as well as in theology, and though each tried to be fair to the other, their partnership was always tense and a cause of anxiety to both. Cadoux had the thinner skin and perhaps suffered more.

Cadoux had been an exact contemporary of Micklem at Mansfield (though Cadoux was older) and they were friendly as students. Cadoux, like Micklem, was a pacifist throughout the First World War, but, unlike Micklem, continued to be so to the end of his life. He too spent some early years on the staff of Mansfield as Hebrew Tutor (1914–19), then went to Bradford to join the staff of the Yorkshire United Independent College as Professor of New Testament Studies. Here he was happy in his teaching and writing, sharing in the intellectual life of Bradford, greatly admired as a scholar, warmly appreciated for his ministry among the churches of the Yorkshire Congregational Union. A keen apologist for Congregationalism and Liberal Protestantism, he shared in discussions concerning church reunion, but took a more extreme line than Micklem on the virtues of Congregational churchmanship. He was committed to Christian unity, but believed in Congregationalism as 'the true catholicity', and had little sympathy with the way Micklem's thought was developing.

In Bradford, he published two substantial scholarly volumes, *The Early Church and the World: A History of the Christian Attitude to Pagan Society and the State down to the Time of Constantine* (Edinburgh,

---

[18] An amalgamation of Airedale and Rotherham Colleges in 1888.
[19] N. Micklem in *Christian World*, 16 Feb. 1933.
[20] See Elaine Kaye, *C. J. Cadoux: Theologian, Scholar and Pacifist* (Edinburgh, 1988).

1925), and *Catholicism and Christianity: A Vindication of Progressive Protestantism* (London, 1928), in addition to smaller books and numerous articles. Though happy in Bradford, he longed to return to Oxford and had hoped to succeed his revered teacher J. V. Bartlet. That was not to be; but when Bartlet's successor J. S. Whale left to become President of Cheshunt College in Cambridge, Cadoux was appointed in his place by unanimous vote of the Council. When his appointment was announced in the JCR, a cheer went up.[21] Some of those who so greatly welcomed Cadoux did so in part because they felt he would be a significant counterweight to the Principal's allegedly un-Congregational ideas and practices.[22] And Cadoux, who always greatly venerated his own old teachers, felt a deep loyalty to the Congregational principles he had learned from Selbie, and to the 'historic method' of interpreting Christianity which he had learned from Bartlet. He was and remained devoted to the College and its traditions to the end of his life.

Micklem had been invited back to Mansfield to teach the New Testament. But when he became Principal he had to take over the teaching of systematic theology and the philosophy of religion instead (unwillingly, according to his account in *The Box and the Puppets*). Though modest about his own capacity in this field, his searching, questing mind brought enrichment not only to his students, but eventually to Congregationalism as a whole.

New Testament studies were passed to the Presbyterian scholar T. W. Manson, whose first and probably best book *The Teaching of Jesus* (Cambridge, 1931) had just been published. He was a worthy successor to Dodd, and it was Mansfield's loss that he only stayed for five years, leaving Mansfield in order to succeed Dodd in Manchester as Rylands Professor.[23] A. M. Hunter[24] came from the Manse of Comrie in Scotland to succeed him in 1938; he had studied with Bultmann in Marburg, and had some experience of lecturing at Glasgow University. He was working on a thesis which was published

[21] See letter from the secretary of the JCR, Cadoux MSS Box 47, fo. 146, Bodleian Library.

[22] The letters in the Cadoux MSS Box 47, Bodleian Library make this clear.

[23] Thomas Walter Manson (1893–1958) remained in Manchester for the rest of his life. See *DNB 1950–60*, 688–9.

[24] For Archibald Macbride Hunter (1906–91) see *MCM* 194 (1991–2), 54. From 1945 until 1971 he was Professor of New Testament Exegesis in Aberdeen University. He published numerous books and articles on New Testament themes.

in 1940 as *Paul and his Predecessors*. Meanwhile W. H. Cadman continued to work as Research Fellow in the New Testament; it was to Micklem's regret that the Council did not agree to appoint him to a Chair at Mansfield. Old Testament studies remained in the hands of the revered H. Wheeler Robinson, whose Baptist students continued to use Mansfield as their base until their own college (Regent's Park College) was built in Pusey Street in 1939. He was assisted in the teaching of Hebrew by the Baptist Tutor L. H. Brockington, one of his former pupils.

There was continuing regret that 'it should seem necessary to have two colleges in Oxford for purposes so closely allied as those of Regent's Park and Mansfield',[25] and it was difficult for two college communities to coexist in the same building, neither entirely separate nor yet united. But representations from the Mansfield Council for closer co-operation did not find favour with the Baptist Council.

The practical side of the College's affairs was in the hands of John Harrison Milnes,[26] who had succeeded Norman Smith as Bursar in 1924, after three pastorates (the last at George Street, Oxford). He remained in this post until 1946, a warm and encouraging presence and a steady support to the Principal.

In *The Box and the Puppets*, Micklem echoed Abelard in entitling his description of the early years of his Principalship 'Historia Calamitatum'; and it was quite clear that, even though he was then writing after retirement, the scars from those early struggles were not healed. The differences with the JCR (over liturgical prayer and the concentration on teaching Aquinas, for example) were much reduced after the first two or three years; the difficulties with the College Council lasted longer.

The first clash with the Council came over what Micklem called 'that terrible house', the Principal's Lodgings. There were four floors to be looked after—large, cold, draughty, and ill-designed for life without several servants. The Selbies had had four maids, and the Micklems found that it was very difficult to fulfil their commitments with fewer. The Council was not very sympathetic to the problem, and it took two years to reach an agreement on some necessary alterations; eventually central heating was installed, and the lowest and highest floors of the Lodgings were sealed off, so that the

---

[25] Minute Book of Mansfield College Council 1917–43, entry for 19 June 1936, MCA.

[26] John Harrison Milnes (1876–1964) had studied at Mansfield from 1901 until 1904. See *MCM* 165 (July 1964), 211 and *CYB 1964–65*, 444–5.

Principal and his family were left with accommodation on two floors only.

The more serious difference between Micklem and many members of the Council was theological. Though there are many themes which remained consistent in his writing from the 1920s to the 1970s, his theological thinking undoubtedly underwent a major change in the late 1920s—'not in principle but in stress', he wrote later.[27]

A comparison of Micklem's first book, *The Open Light* (London, 1919), with his writing fifteen years later shows how far his thinking had changed. In *The Open Light*, he assumed 'that which is the postulate or condition of all thinking, that Reason is sovereign and that there can be no appeal beyond Reason; for by Reason every appeal must commend itself';[28] and urged the reader to 'help deliver Christianity from the jargon of theology and dead metaphysics'.[29] His contribution to the Congregational Theological Conference in 1927 on 'Congregationalism and Modernism' foreshadowed the marked change of emphasis in his thinking: 'My contention is that an undogmatic Christianity is a contradiction in terms . . . The Christian Church is built not on reason but on dogma.'[30] Undogmatic Congregationalism was in danger of ignoring justice, judgement, mercy, and redemption.[31]

His article on 'The Theological Watershed' in *Queen's Quarterly*[32] seven years later in 1934 showed how much his emphasis had changed: although 'the faith once stated can be seen to be rational as alone making intelligible the world of human experience', 'the core of the Christian faith is something to which the human reason of itself could never attain'.[33] Reason remained important to his faith and thinking, but the emphasis shifted; it was no longer the source, but rather the means of expression, of faith. The issue was between a religion of 'Reason' and a religion of 'Grace'. Contemporary Protestantism he regarded as 'an unstable mixture of Aufklärung and Reformation. The fundamental idea of the Aufklärung is that everything may and must be fathomed, penetrated and grasped by the human intellect.'[34] On the other hand, the motif of historic Christianity was 'not evolution but crisis, not illumination but redemption,

---

[27] Micklem, *The Religion of a Sceptic*, 53.
[28] N. Micklem, *The Open Light* (London, 1919), 18.
[29] Ibid. 166. [30] CQ (1927), 551. [31] Ibid. 552.
[32] *Queen's Quarterly* (Kingston, Ontario), 41 (1934), 100–17.
[33] Ibid. 111. [34] Ibid. 100.

not a hope deferred but a victory achieved, not process but trans-figuration, not a development of earth but the irruption of heaven'.[35] The phrases 'historic Christianity' and 'orthodox Christianity' were beginning to appear frequently in his writing.

This was the moment when the writings of Karl Barth were first published in English. Sir Edwyn Hoskyns's translation of Barth's *Commentary on the Epistle to the Romans*, a powerful indictment of liberal immanentist theology, was published in 1933. *Credo*, which appeared in German in 1935, was translated into English (by J. McNab) in 1936; and the Gifford Lectures, under the title *The Knowledge of God and the Service of God*, were published in 1938 (translated by J. L. M. Haire and I. Henderson). Barth was already being discussed among the theologians who read German and kept up to date with German scholarship. Selbie had chosen as the theme for his pres-idential address to the Oxford Society of Historical Theology in 1928 'Some Recent German Theology', and had concentrated on a dis-cussion of Barth. He viewed Barth as a prophet who had 'caused a stirring among dry bones', and his theology as one of 'crisis'—'so much so that it might almost be called an *interim* theology'. 'He has seen the vision of God, of sin and of salvation, and his theology is a cry out of the depths.' But he felt that Barth's objections to reli-gious experience and his neglect of the historical were taken too far. It is a pity that we have no record of the discussion following Selbie's address.[36]

Barth had a growing influence on Congregational and Presbyterian theologians, and in the later 1930s many Mansfield students were deeply influenced by him. In 1935 Barth's disciple Günther Dehn, recently ejected from his Chair at Halle, was invited to give the Dale Lectures at Mansfield; his theme was 'The Gospel of the Reformers and the Modern Man'.[37] Micklem always denied that he was ever a 'Barthian',[38] though he was charmed by Barth the man, whom he entertained at Mansfield in 1938, on the occasion of his receiving an Oxford DD. But clearly Micklem's thinking was part of that same movement of theology.

---

[35] Ibid. 115. The sentence carries allusions to the contemporary work of Karl Barth, Gustav Aulén, and A. N. Whitehead.

[36] Oxford Society of Historical Theology, *Abstract of Proceedings 1928–9* (Oxford, n.d. [1929]), 5–16.

[37] Published as *Man and Revelation* (London 1936), with a foreword by N. Micklem.

[38] See *British Weekly*, 1 Dec. 1955.

What is the Faith? (London, 1936) was Micklem's considered statement of what the Church ought to be proclaiming. A considerable
section of Protestantism had, he believed, been

> so eagerly advancing into new country that it has almost over-
> looked its duty to maintain communications with its base, or, to
> drop the military metaphor, it has been so concerned to accom-
> modate the Christian faith to the modern mind that it has been
> relatively careless to make sure that it is the Christian faith, and not
> merely some mutilated fragment of it, which it has been restating.[39]

And so his book was concerned with 'dogma'—its nature and content
—taking the clauses of the Apostles' Creed one by one. He turned
to the Reformers to seek understanding of the distinction between
'the Bible' and 'the Word of God'. The Bible *declares* the Word of
God, which is to be expounded by the Church: 'The Church is em-
powered and required to define and expound the Word which con-
stitutes it. . . . But the Church's definitions and expositions of the
Word may be tested by the Word itself declared in Scripture.'[40]

For English Congregationalists, this was part of that rediscovery
of the Reformed tradition which Bernard Manning, and P. T. Forsyth
before him, had already tried to foster. Micklem had a very influential position from which to promote it; the Principal of a Congregational theological college had a standing which could in some
ways be compared to that of a bishop in an episcopal communion;
and the Principal of Mansfield had the strongest of those positions,
since he was educating those future ministers who wished to continue
with research, who were most likely to predominate among college
staffs in the future, and who were therefore most likely to influence
the future thinking of the denomination. In addition, from 1932
until 1962 he wrote a weekly column in the *British Weekly* under the
name 'Ilico'.[41]

On 12 March 1939 he joined with seven other Congregational
theologians in signing an 'Open Letter' 'To the Ministers of Christ's
Holy Gospel in the Churches of the Congregational Order', recalling
them to their Reformed principles.[42] It is among this group that

---

[39] Micklem, *What is the Faith?*, 13.   [40] Ibid. 108.

[41] Some of these articles were published in *No More Apologies* (London, 1940).

[42] This is quoted in full in *The Box and the Puppets* (London, 1957), 93–9. The Letter
was drafted by Bernard Manning, and revised by Micklem and J. S. Whale. The other
signatories were Sydney Cave, J. D. Jones, H. F. Lovell Cocks, E. J. Price, and J. Short.

we can trace the beginning of the movement which was to result almost forty years later in the formation of the United Reformed Church. Many of those chiefly responsible for the negotiations which brought that church into being were pupils of Micklem at Mansfield. This rediscovery of Reformed principles involved a renewed emphasis on churchmanship.[43] An important article appeared in the *College Magazine* in June 1933 by K. L. Parry on 'Our Debt to the Oxford Movement'.[44] Its theme was 'that the real influence of the Oxford Movement was to send us back behind the Evangelical Movement to the earlier traditions of seventeenth century Congregationalism',[45] for the Oxford Movement itself was a revolt from Evangelicalism. Fairbairn had reminded Congregationalists that 'the Puritan theology was remarkable for its high and Catholic doctrine of the Church; ... the high Anglican rather than the Evangelical has been here the Puritans' heir';[46] and, again quoting Fairbairn, 'we are Churches devoted almost by pre-eminence to the realisation of religion in the whole life of man'.[47] These have been threads in Mansfield's tradition of theology to this day.

A few years later, Micklem's booklet *Congregationalism Today* (London, 1937) reminded Congregationalists of their tradition of church order, traced back through John Owen to Geneva, of the offices of minister, deacon, and elder (the office of elder had latterly been subsumed under that of deacon and largely forgotten). Later he was to urge recognition of synodical authority within Congregationalism— 'the sacred principle of the church meeting applied to the wider fellowship', its purpose 'to seek and declare the will of him who is the sole Head of the Church'.[48] Whereas the existing denominational structure, with its County Unions and Congregational Union, was 'an expediency structure', synodical structure was 'a faith structure', with a theological foundation.

His thinking led him to the belief that church divisions were not

---

[43] See Grant, *Free Chirchmanship in England*, ch. vii for a detailed account of this. See also D. W. Norwood, 'The Case for Democracy in Church Government: A Study in the Reformed Tradition with Special Reference to the Congregationalism of Robert William Dale, Peter Taylor Forsyth, Albert Peel and Nathaniel Micklem' (London Ph.D. thesis, 1983).

[44] *MCM* 103 (June 1933), 195–200. Kenneth Parry (Mansfield 1906–9) had been one of 'Fairbairn's men'.

[45] Ibid. 196.   [46] Quoted ibid. 197.   [47] Ibid. 199.

[48] N. Micklem, *Congregationalism and the Church Catholic* (London, 1943), 47.

only unhappy, but also sinful. He found obstacles within Nonconformity—small-mindedness, inertia, inherited bitterness, deep misunderstanding, and 'that element in Nonconformity which, consciously
or unconsciously, derives its ancestry not through Wittenberg or
Geneva but from the so-called Age of Reason'.[49] In the face of com-
munism, fascism, and atheism, Christians 'ought to be Catholics before we are Protestants or Romanists, and Protestants before we are
adherents of our particular persuasions'.[50] There was need for a new
attitude to the past. Nonconformists tended to forget that the ministers ejected from the Church of England went out 'in sorrow and
in tears'; 'the sad thing is that their descendants have inherited their
principles but not their sorrow'.[51]

This recovery of what Micklem believed was the true Congregational, Puritan, Reformed inheritance, expressed with a confidence
which few could emulate, brought him into conflict with those who
took a different view of the tradition, not only those immediately
connected with the College, but others outside. Some, like Cadoux
and Albert Peel (editor of the *Congregational Quarterly*), were able to
produce an eloquent intellectual defence of their differing positions;
others, including a few of the lay members of the Council, were
essentially clinging to the Congregationalism of their youth without
any clear theological understanding of the issues involved. Cadoux
had written two articles in the *Christian World* (18 and 25 October
1934) under the heading 'Dogma and Truth: The Doctrinal Task of
the Church', which were in effect though not in name criticisms of
a paper which Micklem had read at the Congregational Theological
Conference the previous summer.[52] They led to a difficult encounter
between Principal and Vice-Principal.[53] It cannot have helped that
Cadoux was in the habit of discussing his problems with Bartlet and
Selbie, both of whom still lived in Oxford; but though sympathetic
to Cadoux's viewpoint, each acted as a restraining influence on his
instinct to protest. Cadoux's lectures delivered in Bangor in 1938,
published as *The Case for Evangelical Modernism: A Study of the Relation between Christian Faith and Traditional Theology* (London, 1938),

---

[49] Micklem, *The Church Catholic: Addresses to the Friends of Reunion* (London, 1935),
64.

[50] Micklem, *What is the Faith?*, 20.   [51] Micklem, *The Church Catholic*, 46.

[52] Published in the *CQ* (1934) under the title 'The Holy Spirit and a New Creed'.

[53] See Kaye, *C. J. Cadoux*, 155.

represented the traditional Liberal Protestant position with 'both pugnacity and persuasiveness'.[54] Albert Peel (whose book on *Inevitable Congregationalism* had provoked Micklem's *Congregationalism Today*) somewhat unwisely used his review of the book in the *Christian World* (17 November 1938) as an opportunity to compare the variety of teaching offered to Mansfield students by the Principal and Vice-Principal with that offered to the congregations of the Temple in the reign of Elizabeth I by Richard Hooker and Walter Travers:

> In the Temple there was Canterbury in the morning and Geneva in the afternoon, so that, in old Fuller's words, 'What Mr Hooker delivered in the forenoon, Mr Travers confuted in the afternoon . . . the nails and pins which one master builder drave in were driven out by the other.' The brains of Mansfield students must be sharpened as they ponder the writings of their learned members.

The next week's issue of the *Christian World* carried not only a pacificatory letter from Bartlet, but also a sharp denial from the representatives of the Mansfield JCR.

Micklem's reaction to the current theological liberalism had led him to read deeply in Origen, John of Damascus, Aquinas, Calvin, and Schleiermacher. His duty was to teach the philosophy of religion to students whose acquaintance (if any) with philosophy was not likely to include any knowledge of 'the great age of the Christian synthesis'. In his view the first three books of Aquinas' *Summa contra Gentiles* offered 'an incomparable starting point for young philosophers'.[55] When, in the late 1930s, he devised a course on systematic theology, which included an apologetic concern, he borrowed from Aquinas the method adopted by that theologian in his *Summa theologica* of posing selected questions, stating arguments against and for the answer to be given, discussing the issues raised, then answering the counter-arguments. These lectures, so he told the College's Board of Education in 1945, were 'designed to coach those who can understand them in the way to tackle the simpler questions likely to be put to them on their soap-box in Hyde Park'.[56] This teaching did not

---

[54] *The Times*, 3 Oct. 1938. See also C. J. Cadoux's article in *CQ* (1942) on 'The Present Theological Cleavage in Congregationalism', 230–9.

[55] Micklem, *The Box and the Puppets*, 75.

[56] Memorandum on the College Curriculum, attached to Board of Education Minutes, 1 Oct. 1945, Minute Book of the Mansfield College Council and Board of Education 1944–53, MCA.

meet with a warm reception from some of the students, who threatened to complain to the Council, where they would have found many sympathetic ears. The argument that Aquinas, as a writer before the Reformation, belonged to the whole Western Church would have carried little conviction; and the recent 'defection' of W. E. Orchard, minister of the Congregational King's Weigh House, to the Roman Catholic Church had increased suspicion of 'Romanizing tendencies'.[57]

Micklem's position was not helped by some aspects of the report of the Commission on the Colleges of the Congregational Union which was presented to the Congregational Union Assembly in October 1936, published in the *Congregational Year Book* in 1937.[58] The Commission was prompted by the need for greater efficiency and economy in ministerial training; its Chairman was Sir Arthur Haworth, one of Micklem's chief critics on the Mansfield Council. An appendix to that report analysed the average costs of training a student at each of the Congregational colleges in the academic year 1934–5. Mansfield was by far the most expensive at £374; all other colleges averaged less than £166, and at Western College, Bristol the average cost was only £88.[59] These figures looked embarrassing, but Micklem pointed out in his *Annual Report* for 1937–8 not only that Mansfield's expenses included the cost of the Chapel and the Chaplaincy, but that the college, uniquely among Congregational colleges, offered specialized theological teaching and supervision for research students.

One of the reasons for the high figure for Mansfield was that there was a particularly small number of students in the academic year 1934–5. When Professor Oliver Franks (later Lord Franks) drew the attention of the Council to this problem at its meeting on 4 May 1937, he was asked to prepare some detailed comments and proposals. Accordingly, on 21 June he raised some searching questions about the relationship between Mansfield and the University, and Mansfield and Congregationalism. One outcome of the succeeding discussion was the suggestion that a Congregational church should

---

[57] W. E. Orchard left the King's Weigh House in Apr. 1932, and was received into the Roman Church in June of that year, in Rome itself. See W. E. Orchard, *From Faith to Faith* (London, 1933) and Elaine Kaye and Ross Mackenzie, *W. E. Orchard: A Study in Christian Exploration* (Oxford, 1990).

[58] *CYB 1937*, 137–60. This Commission was the recommendation of the Ministerial Training Committee, which had replaced the old College Board in 1930.

[59] Ibid. 158–9. The figures are given to the nearest pound.

be associated with the College Chapel; but this proved too difficult. Another, whether as a direct result or not, was an increase in students, so that in June 1939 the Principal was able to report that the College was about to have a larger number of students than for twenty years.[60]

A further cause of contention between Micklem and the Council arose over proposed alterations to the College Chapel. An unsatisfactory feature of the Chapel was the fact that, in practice, its focus of attention was the Principal's stall. Lionel Pearson, architect, had been asked to suggest some way in which a more appropriate focal point could be provided. His report included a recommendation that a cross should be placed on the communion table. Sir Arthur Haworth felt this would be 'contrary to customary usage in Congregational places of worship'.[61] Micklem was asked to draw up a memorandum explaining the proposed changes. His response was

> that Mansfield Chapel is not, and never has been, a typical Nonconformist Chapel in the line of our tradition, and nothing can make it such. We may very much regret that we have not a chapel of Puritan austerity and simplicity. What we have is a highly ornate and decorated building. Since we have this, we must see to it that the ornamentation and decoration express our real meaning.
>
> . . . and since we are by the building committed to much symbolism, it is perfectly appropriate to take and use that which is recognized as the universal Christian symbol.[62]

The matter was referred to the Old Men's Meetings, and fully discussed, but the outbreak of war put the whole matter into abeyance.

How the JCR coped in practice with these differences is suggested by the comment by its President in the *College Magazine* for December 1938 that 'Providence has been very good to us this term in supplying us with sources and materials.'[63] The resulting theological pantomime, with 'suitable eschatological music', featured three sisters: Liberella, 'Quiney whose home is the Vatican', and 'Barthy the Revelation fan'. As the programme note explained, the three sisters

---

[60] The outbreak of war meant that some of these students were not able to come to Mansfield until much later.

[61] Minute Book of the Board of Education, entry for 30 Sept. 1938, MCA.

[62] 'Memorandum drawn up by the Principal at the request of the Board meeting on 30 September 1938 to explain why some alteration is necessary in the Chapel and what is the meaning of the proposal of Mr Lionel Pearson', MCA.

[63] *MCM* 114 (Dec. 1938), 576.

represented 'the three most powerful theological tendencies in the College today'. Some of those who took part went on to distinguished theological careers, for the late 1930s was a vintage era for Mansfield students. In many cases, their own convictions were challenged and eventually strengthened by encountering these two different expressions of faith, each maintained through strong conviction.[64]

Tensions and differences notwithstanding, the College's intellectual life was flourishing in the 1930s. Micklem, Cadoux, and Wheeler Robinson were all writing and publishing books. In 1936, the year in which the College celebrated its Jubilee, the reviews in the *College Magazine* reveal what a rich contribution to theological and biblical study was being made by men trained at Mansfield: C. H. Dodd's *Parables of the Kingdom* and *The Apostolic Preaching and its Development*, Nathaniel Micklem's *The Church Catholic* and *What is the Faith?*, J. S. Whale's *The Christian Answer to the Problem of Evil*, W. B. Selbie's *The Fatherhood of God*, and Malcolm Spencer's *Economics and God* were all reviewed in the *Magazine* in 1936.

And as part of the Jubilee commemorations, a volume entitled *Christian Worship: Studies in its History and Meaning*—an interpretation and a vindication of 'the common tradition of our Reformed Churches'—edited by Nathaniel Micklem (and dedicated to Selbie), was published by the Oxford University Press in 1936. The breadth of range of the essays, all by past and present students or members of staff, indicated something of what Mansfield had achieved. It contained three sections: biblical studies, historical studies, including more detailed studies of Reformed traditions of worship, and contemporary studies. While the volume rightly emphasized the importance of the preaching of the Word, it also exemplified the renewal of Congregational worship as a whole—prayer, hymnody, sacrament —in which Mansfield took such a leading part.

The sense of Mansfield as one extended community was greatly encouraged by Micklem. He began the practice of writing a piece in each issue of the *Magazine* 'To the Brethren of the Dispersion', with news of the College and recommendations for reading. And the sense of community within the College (which was still non-residential) was fostered by the happy tea-parties to which all members of the staff and their families invited students.

---

[64] See e.g. John Huxtable, *As It Seemed to Me* (London, 1991), 13–14.

The life of the College community was deepened and strengthened through Micklem's introduction of morning, rather than evening, prayers. The JCR Notes described this as 'probably the most memorable feature of our life together this term. . . . We wish to express our deep appreciation of the way in which the Principal has conducted it.'[65] He turned the chairs in the antechapel to face east, and used that area for the worship of the College community, while the main body of the Chapel was used for Sunday worship. His brother Romilly Micklem, who remained as College Chaplain until 1938,[66] lent a small chamber organ (which he subsequently gave to the College); a deacon at Rodborough Tabernacle gave a table, built round a pillar, and a prie-dieu; others gave appropriate pictures. Copies of the privately printed *Rodborough Bede Book*, a compilation of liturgical prayer drawn up by C. E. Watson, minister of Rodborough Tabernacle, a Cotswold Congregational church, in 1930, were acquired for regular use.[67] The Principal conducted prayers himself, using liturgical as well as extempore forms of prayer.[68] Horton Davies has commented that 'under the inspired leadership of Nathaniel Micklem, as Principal of Mansfield College, this one institution may be said to have provided in its College Chapel a standard of worship that led all the English Free Churches from 1933 onwards'.[69]

One of the purposes of those morning prayers was 'to join in the priestly intercession of the universal Church'.[70] And no country was more in need of such intercession than Nazi Germany. Micklem's concern for Germany under the Nazi regime was initially prompted by the visit of Professor Dehn in 1935; it was strengthened when Dr Birger Forell, a Swedish Lutheran minister who was Chaplain to the

---

[65] *MCM* 102 (Dec. 1932), 180. See also John Wilding, 'Morning Prayers', *MCM* 103 (June 1933), 202–4.

[66] He left quietly for a pastorate at Gerrards Cross. 'It is surprising that a man of his musical talent should be so incapable of blowing his own trumpet,' commented his brother in his *Annual Report* in 1939. He was succeeded by John Marsh.

[67] The book, which was reissued by the Independent Press in 1943, made 'a protest against disordered spirituality' (Horton Davies, *Worship and Theology in England: The Ecumenical Century 1900–65* (Princeton, 1965), v. 369). The compiler used the word 'bede' in its meaning of 'a short form of service'. For C. E. Watson (1869–1942) see A. T. S. James, *A Cotswold Minister* (London, 1944). In the later years of Micklem's Principalship the *Rodborough Bede Book* was replaced by Romilly Micklem's *Responsals*.

[68] His books on prayer, *A Book of Personal Religion* (London, 1938), *Officia Brevia* (Oxford, 1939), and *Prayers and Praises* (London, 1941), illustrate the significance he attached to the devotional life of the minister, and therefore of his students.

[69] Davies, *Worship and Theology in England*, 373.

[70] Micklem, *The Box and the Puppets*, 76.

Swedish Embassy in Berlin, visited Mansfield in 1936 and told him that he ought to visit Germany to make personal contact with the Confessing Church, for it was now cut off from any communication with the other churches of Europe. By early 1937 he was in touch with Dorothy Buxton, and encouraged her campaign of letters to the press concerning the German situation.[71] The result was that Micklem, who had studied in Germany before coming up to Oxford in 1911 and spoke German fluently, paid two visits to Germany in 1937 and 1938.[72]

The first visit, to Düsseldorf, Barmen, and Berlin, took place during the Easter vacation of 1937. In Düsseldorf he shared in the officially illegal ordination ceremony of a young minister; in Barmen he learned how news of persecuted members of the Church was disseminated; and in Berlin he took part in the clandestine theological school of the Confessing Church. 'I sometimes think that no one really knows what is the Church of the living God till he has had fellowship with it in the catacombs,' he later reflected.[73] Few, if any, other English visitors were privileged to share so fully in the daily life of the Confessing Church. He brought home an invaluable collection of pamphlets and leaflets produced by the underground press, together with assorted letters and press cuttings, which he later entrusted to the Bodleian Library.[74] In Germany, these had to be destroyed as soon as they were read, and therefore now only exist outside that country. And he reported at some length to the Archbishop of Canterbury, Lang, on his experience. In Oxford, he was generally regarded as the authority on the German church situation.[75] He had offered Mansfield hospitality to enable representatives of the Confessing Church to attend the Life and Work Conference in Oxford

---

[71] See 'Church and Politics: Dorothy Buxton and the German Church Struggle', in Keith Robbins, *History, Religion and Identity in Modern Britain* (London, 1993).

[72] The other British churchmen who visited Germany in 1937 and 1938 included the Bishop of Chichester (George Bell), the Dean of Chichester (A. S. Duncan-Jones), Dr A. J. Macdonald, and the Bishop of Gloucester (A. C. Headlam). Church leaders did not agree in the interpreting of the German situation.

[73] Micklem, *The Box and the Puppets*, 106.

[74] This large collection includes twenty volumes of published pamphlets etc., and two volumes of 'underground literature'. It has now in addition been catalogued with a further collection of documents donated by Richard Gutteridge, and made available on microfiches. See *Der Kirchenkampf: The Gutteridge–Micklem Collection at the Bodleian Library, Oxford* (London, 1988).

[75] On 24 Feb. 1938 he spoke to the Oxford Society of Historical Theology on 'The Theological Issues in the German Church Struggle'.

on the theme 'Church, Community and State' in July 1939, but in the event they were not allowed to travel.

A year later he visited Germany again (where he spent his fiftieth birthday), this time taking with him one of his college students, Alec Whitehouse, who was also fluent in German. By this time, the German church struggle had gained a higher profile in Britain, partly through the trial and imprisonment of Martin Niemöller. Will Moore, a Fellow of St John's and member of Mansfield's Board of Education, had travelled to Berlin with the Dean of Chichester for the trial, but they were not allowed in the court room. 'Never, I think, since the early days of the Reformation have the British been so aware of Continental Christianity as at this time,' reflected Micklem later.[76] This would surely have been part of the conversation at the reception which Mansfield gave for Karl Barth on the occasion of his receiving an honorary degree in Oxford on 4 March 1938.

The Royal Institute of International Affairs commissioned Micklem to write a report on the conflict between the German Government and the Roman Catholic Church over the previous five years, and presumably felt that a non-Catholic might be able to write with more objectivity than a Roman Catholic. So, while Alec Whitehouse made contacts with the Confessing Church, Micklem visited Berlin (where 'I have never felt evil as a physical, almost tangible, thing as I did on that visit to Berlin'[77]), Munich, Freiburg, Cologne, Düsseldorf, Hanover, and experienced briefly what it was like to live in a police state—'a nerve strain of which the British can have no idea'.[78] In Berlin he and Alec Whitehouse 'agreed that a thundercloud seemed to be hanging over Berlin, and no one knew when it would burst'.[79] In Birger Forell's study they had the impression that it was 'the Protestant religious centre of Europe'. And Alec Whitehouse wrote in his diary of 'some bedtime meditations on the uselessness of sectarianism to deal with a situation like this, and the general littleness of English Free Churches as at present conceived'.[80]

In Berlin they met a young German pastor, Hans Herbert Kramm. Alec Whitehouse thought of him at the time as 'the young Athanasius, for he is putting every ounce into this struggle, and has plenty of ounces to put in'.[81] When Kramm managed to escape to England, he was welcomed to Mansfield, and was offered the use of the College

---

[76] Micklem, *The Box and the Puppets*, 109.   [77] Ibid. 111.
[78] Ibid. 112.   [79] Alec Whitehouse, private diary entry, 4 Apr. 1939.
[80] Ibid. 4 Apr. 1939.   [81] Ibid. 3 Apr. 1939. See also *MCM* 147 (July 1955), 257–8.

Chapel for the worship of a small group of German-speaking Christians he had gathered together.[82] This was the nucleus of the Oxford German-speaking Lutheran Congregation which still meets regularly in the University Church.

Micklem later told a young research scholar that people would not really believe what he said he had experienced and seen in Germany.[83] His friendship with the Dominicans at Blackfriars in Oxford enabled him to arrange to stay at Dominican houses in Germany, where 'we discoursed together with great freedom on politics and theology and religion'.[84]

On their return Alec Whitehouse prepared *Christendom on Trial: Documents of the German Church Struggle* for publication by the 'Friends of Europe'. Nathaniel Micklem maintained what contact he could with the Confessing Church, and in the autumn of 1938 gave a letter to John Marsh (who hid it under his shirt) to be delivered secretly to the wife of Hans Lilje, then imprisoned in Berlin. Meanwhile for Chatham House he wrote *National Socialism and the Roman Catholic Church* (Oxford, 1939), a full, thorough, and objective assessment of 'National Socialism' and the way in which it was being interpreted and established in Germany.[85] He could not reveal until after the war that his collaborator was Dr Heinrich Rommen, whose wife and children were at the time still in Germany. He warned that a 'ferocious and illimitable anti-Semitism' was 'an integral element in the National Socialist *Weltanschauung*' and would put a bar to any acceptance by the Church of its philosophy and policy. And there could be no compromise with 'political Catholicism': 'National Socialism as a philosophy or religion is a pure Immanentism; it recognizes no God outside, or other than, its own inner demands and wishes. The Church claims to speak to the nation in the name of the transcendent God whose law is eternal, above all nations, and part of the structure of the universe.'[86] The Nazi regime was 'the negation of

---

[82] When Mansfield was taken over by a government department at the beginning of the war, the congregation was invited to use the University Church, and actually held their first service there on 3 Sept. 1939, the day war broke out.

[83] M. D. Hampson, 'The British Response to the German Church Struggle' (Oxford D.Phil. thesis, 1973), 252 n. 1.

[84] Micklem, *The Box and the Puppets*, 111.

[85] The Roman Catholic writer Adrian Hastings has called it 'a most generous work'; 'Which English Catholic of the 1930s could have written such an objective study of the plight of German Protestants?', in *A History of English Christianity 1920–85* (London, 1985), 272.

[86] N. Micklem, *National Socialism and the Roman Catholic Church* (London, 1939), 61.

God erected into a system of Government'.[87] By the time the book was published, Kristallnacht had illustrated how this was likely to work out in practice. The book was smuggled into Germany—in false dust wrappers supplied by Blackwells.

At the end of the book, he wrote: 'With the passing of 1938 the Christian Church in Germany enters into a dark cloud, but it is unafraid. *Nubicula est; transibit.*'[88]

That cloud was about to envelop the whole of Europe.

[87] Ibid. 37, quoting Gladstone's comment on the government of Naples.
[88] Ibid. 237.

XI

The War and its Aftermath:
The Future of Congregationalism
1939–1953

ON 24 August 1939 the Principal of Mansfield received a telegram from the Government to say that most of the College buildings were to be requisitioned the following day; only the Chapel, Library, and Principal's Lodgings would be left for College use. He had already discussed with the University Registry arrangements for such a contingency. Fortunately Regent's Park College, to which Mansfield had played host for so many years, had just moved into its new buildings in Pusey Street, and immediately offered Mansfield staff and students the hospitality of the dining-room, common rooms, and lecture rooms of the College, half a mile away from Mansfield. And so the Mansfield students commuted between the two colleges, using their own Chapel during daylight hours (it was impossible to black it out satisfactorily),[1] a temporary Junior Common Room in the basement of the Principal's Lodgings, and the Library until that too was taken over by the Codes and Cyphers branch of the Foreign Office in 1942 (the Mansfield books were moved under Bodleian supervision to the old library of New College until 1946). Meanwhile the rest of the College buildings were taken over by the Admiralty for secret work, and carefully guarded day and night.[2] The result was that wartime students never saw the dining hall or common rooms in the main building.[3]

'The Christian ethic is essentially one which has to deal with the

---

[1] The Chapel was used for the occasional wedding. In 1 Jan. 1940 the Principal officiated at the wedding of the future Prime Minister Harold Wilson and Gladys Mary Baldwin, the daughter of a Congregational minister. Harold Wilson had often attended both the Chapel services and the meetings of the Congregational Society at Mansfield.

[2] A Registry File in the Oxford University Archives UR-SF-CQ-11-MAN contains all the correspondence between the College, the University Registry, and the relevant government departments relating to the requisitioning and occupation of the College.

[3] At least one of these never dined in the College Hall until twenty years later, at Commemoration. See *MCM* 167 (Oct. 1965), 256.

rampant evil of the world'; so wrote C. J. Cadoux at the beginning of the war.[4] The College staff was divided on the application of that ethic to the current situation, though the differences were mutually respected and did not cause harsh feelings. The Principal had now abandoned his earlier pacifism and regarded armed resistance to Nazi Germany as justified because of its flouting of all civilized norms of behaviour. In the *College Magazine* he wrote:

> For myself I think of this war as *bellum justum* (so far as there can be such a thing) in a way I could never so clearly judge the last war, I feel sure that God is calling whom He will to refuse all military service as He may call another to 'sell all that thou hast and give to the poor', but I should distinguish a personal vocation of this kind from an absolutely clear principle of duty immediately binding upon all Christians.[5]

The case for pacifism had not been destroyed. But 'the judgement of most men of moral seriousness will be against [the pacifist], and he may not claim that the New Testament is on his side'.[6]

At the very beginning of the war, he had been asked to write a book offering guidance to Christians in the moral dilemma they now faced. *May God Defend the Right!* (London, 1939, reprinted 1940) was written and published very quickly: the preface was dated 27 September 1939, and the book itself was published in October. The tension between the belief that war can never be the will of God, and the conviction that the particular war in which Britain was now involved was nevertheless the will of God, illustrated for Micklem the tension which lies at the heart of the New Testament in the Cross. National Socialism represented 'an open rebellion against the Christian tradition'; 'we may without impropriety speak of Anti-Christ.'[7] Yet there was a spiritual peril in armed resistance—'that we shall suppose ourselves to be righteous because our cause is righteous'; 'the ecumenical Church of Christ must see this war as a judgment upon a civilization in which we are all involved and for which we must all take responsibility.'[8] 'When the war broke out, people like Professor Micklem . . . never stopped preaching the difference

---

[4] C. J. Cadoux, *Christian Pacifism Re-examined* (Oxford, 1940), p. x.
[5] *MCM* 116 (Jan. 1940), 616.
[6] N. Micklem, *The Theology of Politics* (Oxford, 1941), 139.
[7] N. Micklem, *May God Defend the Right!* (London, 1939), 120.   [8] Ibid. 28.

between the Nazis and the German people,' remembered a member of the German Lutheran congregation in Oxford.[9]

The Vice-Principal had also put pen to paper. On 6 September 1939 he began writing what was published several months later as *Christian Pacifism Re-examined* (Oxford, 1940), in which he considered afresh the arguments against Christian participation in war, as well as the counter-arguments, and remained convinced that the Christian's duty was to refuse to fight. The republication of his *The Early Christian Attitude to War* (which first appeared in 1919) in 1940 reinforced his case. As had happened during the previous war, many young men who felt they must make a stand as conscientious objectors came to seek his help. While Micklem's three sons were still small and were sent to Canada for most of the war, Cadoux's two sons were old enough to be called up; both joined the Friends' Ambulance Unit as conscientious objectors, and one of them was taken prisoner.[10]

Other members of staff took no public role in the issue. Ministerial students were exempted from military service and so were not necessarily faced with making a decision. But one student, Philip Johnson, was given leave of absence in order to join the armed forces, and was killed in action in 1944. A former student, the Baptist E. W. McKeeman (Mansfield 1926–8), was reported missing at sea while serving as a chaplain in the Navy; another, Herbert Pugh (Mansfield 1920–4), was drowned in the Atlantic while serving as a chaplain to the RAF, and was posthumously awarded the George Cross.

Morale was high in spite of the war, and despite the threat of invasion and the strong possibility that the Principal and some others were on Hitler's death list.[11] Micklem was beginning to receive more general recognition in Oxford, in the denomination, and in the country at large. In 1940 he was elected President of the Oxford Society of Historical Theology, and gave his presidential lecture under the title 'The Relations of Orthodoxy and Revelation Historically Considered'; in 1945 he was Chairman of the University Theology

[9] Quoted in F. L. Müller, *The History of German Lutheran Congregations in England 1900–1950* (Frankfurt, 1987), 108.
[10] Many North American families offered a home to the children of Oxford academics. A large group of them travelled together across the Atlantic in 1940. After careful consideration, the Cadoux family decided against sending their two daughters.
[11] N. Micklem, *The Box and the Puppets* (London, 1957), 115.

Faculty Board. He was involved in the work of the Royal Institute of International Affairs (Chatham House), which was temporarily settled at Balliol. In 1942 the Archbishop of Canterbury, William Temple, asked him to write the Archbishop's Lent Book for 1943; the result was *The Doctrine of our Redemption* (London, 1943), a discussion of the meaning and biblical foundation of that redemption which represents 'the transfiguration of our common life' so that it becomes 'a glad and free offering in love to God'. In reviewing the book in the *College Magazine*, R. S. Franks found it 'felicitous in its combination of sound historical learning, devotional spirit and literary grace'; the author, he considered, was 'entirely at home with those doctrines which emphasize the immanence of God in Christ and the effect of that immanence upon mankind', but, in spite of wide sympathies, was unable to 'accommodate himself to a transactional theory of the Atonement'.[12] However, Micklem granted that Anselm 'for all his impersonal and legalistic language, saw deeper into the mystery of sin than Abelard'.[13]

In the year in which that book was published, Micklem was elected Chairman of the Congregational Union for 1944–5 (pl. 11)—a recognition both of his personal stature, and of the standing of the College. When he was invited to broadcast a regular Christian News Commentary on Sunday afternoons for the BBC, with news of Christian communities in Occupied Europe, his name and voice were brought to a still wider constituency.

His relations with the Council were slow to improve. In *The Box and the Puppets* he relates that the Council passed, but did not minute, a vote of censure on him. This seems to have been in the wake of a complaint from the Vice-Principal (which Selbie, whom Cadoux frequently consulted, had done his best to restrain) to the Council that his functions were undefined and therefore his position unsatisfactory. In response the Council requested the Senior Common Room to suggest an appropriate arrangement; this was referred back to the Council, which then agreed that 'the Vice-Principalship of the College carry with it the right and the duty of acting for the Principal whenever he is prevented from fulfilling any engagement or performing any duty as Principal of the College'.[14] These discussions were echoed in the Principal's letter in the *College Magazine* in

[12] *MCM* 123 (July 1943), 69–71.
[13] *The Doctrine of our Redemption* (London, 1943), 75.
[14] Mansfield College Council Minute Book 1917–43, entry for 21 Nov. 1942, MCA.

11. **Staff and Students 1944** *Back row (left to right):* Miss Hawkridge, H. Wanbon, H. Greenwood, Dorothy Havergal-Shaw, R. S. Paul, H. Hirschwald, D. James, V. Thomas, A. Green *Front row:* L. H. BROCKINGTON, W. H. CADMAN, C. J. CADOUX, N. MICKLEM, J. MARSH, W. A. WHITEHOUSE, T. Hawthorn (*Absent:* G. Beck, T. P. Brooks, W. Brown, G. ZUNTZ)

July 1942, which referred to the fact that Council members 'seem to be appointed for life', and that many of them 'recollect at least the echoes of the flaming campaign of Fairbairn and Dale'.[15] He appealed to former students to use their influence, when the opportunity arose, to elect new members who would be ready to face the challenge of the future. After Dr Will Moore[16] was elected the new Chairman of the Council in 1947, relations between Principal and Council greatly improved.

Micklem's relationships with the students were particularly happy during the war. He told the Annual Meeting in 1940 that 'I have never been more happy about the religion and temper of the Junior Common Room,'[17] and in the *College Magazine* he wrote that 'my frequent anxieties about the future of our churches are allayed when I contemplate the men who are now coming forward for the ministry'.[18] The Principal and his wife were 'at home' to JCR members on Saturday evenings, when the preacher for the following day was often present. The JCR had settled down comfortably into its 'eschatological existence in the catacombs',[19] and the witty reports of its 'formal' meetings in the JCR Minute Book convey the impression of a lively and energetic atmosphere. The President for 1942–3 wrote in the JCR Notes in the *Magazine*:

> it is with mixed feelings that I have to record that with the departure of the most vociferous disciples of Barth and Brunner the theological atmosphere of the JCR is considerably less blue. The Reformed theology is still sustained with quiet strength by Dr Hirschwald . . . it is to George Caird, perhaps, that we have to look for the Grand Synthesis.[20]

Herbert Hirschwald (he later changed his surname to Hartwell) was a German Lutheran who had fought for his country in the First World War (for which he was awarded the Iron Cross) and had then become the youngest judge of the Prussian Supreme Court. In 1934 he joined the Confessing Church, and in the following year was dismissed from his public position under the Nuremberg Regulations. He then helped in the Ecclesiastical Emergency Office for

[15] *MCM* 121 (July 1942), 41.
[16] Will Grayburn Moore (1905–78) was Fellow, Tutor, and Lecturer in Modern Languages (French and German) at St John's College.
[17] *Mansfield College Annual Report 1940–41*, 26.   [18] *MCM* 118 (Jan. 1941), 646.
[19] *MCM* 116 (Jan. 1940), 619.   [20] *MCM* 122 (Jan. 1943), 63.

Non-Aryan Christians, which brought him in touch both with George Bell, Bishop of Chichester, and later with John Marsh. He finally escaped from Germany with his family a month before war broke out. John Marsh invited him to Mansfield, where he took the ministerial training course, and eventually earned a doctorate for a thesis on Karl Barth, published as *The Theology of Karl Barth: An Introduction* (London, 1964).[21] A learned and humble man, he was a personal symbol of the suffering of German and non-Aryan Christians and Jews (though the extent of that suffering was not fully grasped at the time). Hans Herbert Kramm, the young pastor whom Micklem and Alec Whitehouse had met in Berlin, was another refugee who found a home in Mansfield; the College gave him hospitality for the two years 1938–40 as a token of support for the Confessing Church. In the first month of the war, the Principal had accompanied him to a tribunal appointed to decide the status of aliens; this did not prevent him from being interned for some months in 1940–1.[22] He spent his time at Mansfield writing a thesis which was eventually published in 1947 as *The Theology of Martin Luther*. He was instrumental in establishing German-speaking congregations, not only in Oxford, but in other parts of Britain, and in the publication of an English edition of the Barmen Declaration. He was officially a member of the Senior Common Room; but as he 'had fallen between two common rooms, it was decided to issue to him a season ticket to the JCR'.[23]

The wartime generation of Mansfield men distinguished themselves in sport, contributing not only to the teams of St Catherine's, but also to those of the University. Donald James played rugger for the University; Basil Sims played hockey; Geoffrey Beck played both hockey and cricket.[24]

John Marsh had joined the staff as Chaplain and Tutor in Philosophy in 1938. A former student of the College (1928–31), he was

---

[21] After ordination he worked as a chaplain to German prisoners of war, then secured a post as secretary for German affairs with the British Council of Churches Inter Church Aid and Refugee Service. He died in 1989. See *MCM* 192 (1989–90), 6–7.

[22] When he was released he addressed the JCR on 'The Confessions of No. 40469' —an account of his prison experiences.

[23] JCR Minute Book 1930–57, entry for 17 Oct. 1941, MCA. After the war he returned to Germany, and died at the premature age of 45 in 1955.

[24] John Marsh's comment on Geoffrey Beck's performance in the Oxford v. Cambridge cricket match: 'There will be those in the denomination who will say that it is a change for a Mansfield man to be on the Lord's ground.'

destined to follow Micklem as Principal, and to develop into an ecumenical statesman within the World Council of Churches. He had achieved high honours in Philosophy at Edinburgh, and was a great support to the Principal in the teaching of philosophy of religion. In addition, he was a leading senior figure in the Oxford SCM, and an energetic Chaplain to all Congregational undergraduates through the Congregational Society (successor to the Dale Society). 'I doubt whether since the days of Frank Lenwood Mansfield has contributed so much to the SCM as it has through all the past year through Mr Marsh,' declared the Principal in his *Annual Report* in 1941.[25]

When A. M. Hunter decided to return to Scotland at the end of 1942, Wheeler Robinson had already retired and a temporary arrangement had been made for the teaching of Hebrew. The opportunity was now taken to reorganize the teaching of the Bible so that two tutors shared the teaching of both Old and New Testament. J. C. Ormerod (Mansfield 1906–10) was invited to move from the Yorkshire United Independent College in Bradford to share jointly the teaching of biblical studies with W. H. Cadman, who was also given an official teaching position. This arrangement was a salutary reminder that in contradistinction to the dangerous and effectively anti-Semitic teaching of the 'German Christians', the Hebrew Scriptures are an integral part of the Christian Bible. Micklem warned in 1944: 'We have virtually let the Bible shrink to the New Testament (and Psalms) because we have let our ideas of religion shrink to mere personal piety.' Deuteronomy was quite as important as St John's Gospel for European civilization, for 'Deuteronomy deals with questions of civilization, and St John's Gospel does not.'[26] However, this particular plan for biblical teaching soon foundered because Ormerod had a serious breakdown in health only weeks after beginning his teaching at Mansfield. John Marsh was asked to step into the breach and add biblical studies to his existing teaching. In order to ease his burden, Alec Whitehouse, a student at Mansfield 1937–40, was asked to return as Chaplain and Tutor in Theology and the Philosophy of Religion in 1944.[27]

---

[25] *Mansfield College Annual Report 1940–41*, 26.

[26] N. Micklem, *Europe's Own Book* (London, 1944), 30.

[27] In the interim he had been minister of Elland Congregational Church in Yorkshire. Subsequently W. A. Whitehouse was Reader in Divinity at the University of Durham 1947–65 before moving to the new University of Kent as Professor of Theology 1965–77, and Master of Eliot College 1965–9 and 1973–5.

C. J. Cadoux's health was deteriorating, and he had to abandon his responsibility for the library at the same time as A. M. Hunter retired. The opportunity was taken to invite another refugee from Nazi Germany to come to Mansfield. Dr Günther Zuntz was a classic-ist already living in Oxford who was glad to undertake the cataloguing of the very considerable bequest of books from Vernon Bartlet (who had died in 1940), and to take a leading role in the reorganization of the library planned for the return to the College Library after the war. He was also pleased to be invited to give occasional lectures on ancient manuscripts in the College. From Mansfield he moved to the University of Manchester in 1947, eventually being appointed Professor of Hellenistic Greek.[28]

As the tide of the war began to turn, the thoughts of Principal, Council, and staff began to focus on the need for change and reconstruction after peace was achieved. Micklem was developing his thinking on the relation between theology and law, and between religion and politics. In *The Theology of Politics*, published in 1941, he examined the idea of Christendom, which 'surveys the intermediate country between theology and politics': 'All political problems are at bottom theological . . . a man's political outlook is coloured or even determined by his real thought, or thoughtlessness, about God and man and the meaning of human life.'[29] He warned that post-war problems would be theological and religious as well as economic and social. In *Europe's Own Book* (London, 1944) he claimed that 'where there is no spiritual valuation of man there is no freedom'. His ideas were worked out more fully in the Wilde Lectures which he was invited to give in the University of Oxford in 1949, published in 1952 as *Law and the Laws*—an examination of the mutual relations of theology, moral philosophy, and jurisprudence. That concern with law and politics, drawn in part from his own family background, was to come to the fore in the years of his retirement, when he served as President of the Liberal Party.

The war came to an end in the summer of 1945. But a government organized for war could not immediately be turned into an administration for peace, and it was a further year before the College regained its building, and before potential students on active service were released. As the war was about to end, Micklem felt bound to

[28] He was Professor of Hellenistic Greek 1963–9. In 1956 he was elected a Fellow of the British Academy. He died in 1992.
[29] Micklem, *The Theology of Politics*, p. xi.

stake the claims of the College in the post-war world. He told the Council:

> I think it fair to say to you, and true, that Mansfield is able to afford to Congregational students and to students of all the Free Churches advantages which no other College is in a position to offer, and I venture to think that the maintenance of our standards and traditions is a matter of the very greatest importance to the religious life of this country.[30]

In its own specific way, the College was moving into a new era, because so many of those connected with its beginnings had now died. Selbie, not only the second Principal of the College, but one of the first generation of Mansfield students, died in 1944. Dr Cadoux spoke at his funeral in the College Chapel, paying tribute to one who 'worthily cherished and garnered the harvest' planted by Fairbairn, and referring to the new generation as one 'into whose imperfect hands the maintenance of this great heritage has been entrusted'.[31] Sir Arthur Haworth, second Treasurer of the College, and son of one of the original benefactors, died in the same year (he was succeeded by Howard Gosling); and in the following year Wheeler Robinson, pupil of G. B. Gray, died. C. J. Cadoux died in the summer of 1947 after a long illness, a year before his official retirement was due. His memorial in the College Chapel—'Pro Regno Christi Molitor'[32]— was a fitting acknowledgement of his loyalty and devotion. Micklem himself, as a son of one of the earliest Oxford Nonconformist undergraduates, was now one of the few links with the origins of the College.

Cadoux's death left the Mackennal Chair in Church History vacant. As was the practice of the time, the post was not advertised, but a subcommittee of the Council, consisting of J. S. Whale, W. G. Moore, and the Principal, was asked to suggest a name or names. The subcommittee was unable to agree on one name, but invited three candidates to appear before the next meeting of the Council and Board of Education as possible successors: W. T. Pennar Davies (Mansfield 1941–3, Professor of Church History at Bala-Bangor), Geoffrey F. Nuttall (Mansfield 1929–36, Lecturer in Church History, New College, London),

---

[30] *Mansfield College Annual Report 1945–46*, 22.
[31] C. J. Cadoux, 'Address Delivered at the Funeral Service of W. B. Selbie, 1 May 1944', MCA.
[32] 'A Striver for Christ's Kingdom'.

and Aubrey Vine (minister of Broad Street Congregational Church, Reading). Pennar Davies declined the invitation on the grounds that he felt his vocation lay in Wales;[33] the other two were both interviewed. When it became clear that neither candidate had the wholehearted support of either Council or Principal, other names were brought forward of candidates who might be considered for a more junior post for a limited time; after discussion, and without interviewing him, the Council agreed to appoint Erik Routley, whom Micklem recommended, as Lecturer, rather than Professor, for a period of five years.[34]

In celebration of the Diamond Jubilee of the College in 1946, Pennar Davies was asked to write a short history of Mansfield, which was published as *Mansfield College Oxford: Its History, Aims and Achievements* (Oxford, 1947). He wrote idealistically of the College 'marching on to new victories'.

The growing practical challenge to the College was the need for more money, and for new sources of income. The College had depended for its income not only on the revenue from the Spring Hill Endowment and legacies, but on subscriptions from Congregational churches and from individuals. The decline in membership of Congregational churches was reflected in a diminishing income from these sources. In the year 1945–6, individual subscriptions amounted to just £194 7s. 6d. and donations from churches £46 12s. 9d. There had been a steady decline since 1900–1, when the comparable figures were £1,737 16s. 3d. and £227 6s. 3d. Three years later, in 1947–8, for the first time, the College had an excess of expenditure over income.

A copy of Pennar Davies's history was sent to all old students together with an appeal for subscriptions to the College. After sixty years, the College buildings, on which little had been spent since the opening, were in need of substantial repair; the stonework was beginning to crumble, and the roofing was in need of renovation. Yet

---

[33] He was appointed Principal of Memorial College, Brecon soon afterwards.

[34] For E. Routley, see below, Ch. XII. Aubrey Vine was appointed Tutor at the Yorkshire United Independent College in 1951.

Geoffrey F. Nuttall remained at his post in London until New College was closed in 1977; from 1977 until 1980 he was a Visiting Professor at King's College, London. His writings, which include *The Holy Spirit in Puritan Faith and Experience* (Oxford, 1946), *Visible Saints: The Congregational Way 1640–60* (Oxford, 1957), and *Richard Baxter* (London, 1965), have established him as one of the foremost ecclesiastical historians of his generation, and as one of Mansfield's most distinguished scholars. He was elected a Fellow of the British Academy in 1991.

nothing had ever been set aside for structural repair. What might be done to generate more income, apart from appealing to churches and former students?

Already in August 1944 a building subcommittee of the Council had been asked to consider more efficient use of the space available, and the provision of residence for twenty to thirty students. The following summer it recommended to the Council that a new Principal's house should be built opposite the tower, enabling the existing Principal's Lodgings to be converted into a hostel for seventeen students. It was even suggested that the Chapel floor might be raised to allow eight students' rooms to be provided underneath.[35] The architect Thomas Rayson was asked to prepare appropriate plans, which were then presented to the Council at its next meeting.[36]

This meant a reversal of the College policy adopted in 1886 of a non-residential institution. But times had changed. 'I have for myself long been of opinion that the advantages of a residence would clearly outweigh the disadvantages,' wrote the Principal in the *College Magazine*.[37] In the following edition of the *College Magazine* the College Treasurer, H. W. Gosling, outlined these plans to the old students, claiming that 'the menace of seminary', feared by the original founders, would be countered by the presence of non-theologians from outside the College. Out of term, the premises could generate income by providing hospitality for conferences. Moreover, 'a dream that might then come true is of every Mansfield man knowing that so long as he remains in the ministry he and his wife might be invited at stated intervals to be guests of Mansfield for a month'.[38] Meanwhile, capital had to be found. 'Suffice it to say that if any of our men can introduce me to anybody who is prepared to consider giving me £25,000 for this purpose, I will cancel most engagements to pay a visit in the indicated quarter.'[39]

Another yet more radical idea was stirring in the mind of a future Principal. On 19 June 1947 'Dr Marsh in reviewing the present building

---

[35] The plan for providing rooms in the Chapel was abandoned in favour of a hostel for eighteen students to adjoin the proposed new house for the Principal. This plan would allow residence for thirty-five students all together, enabling the College to offer accommodation to students from outside.

[36] Council Minutes 28–9 June and 1 Oct. 1945, MCA.

[37] *MCM* 127 (July 1945), 148.

[38] H. W. Gosling 'Some Desirable Developments at Mansfield', *MCM* 128 (Jan. 1946), 164.

[39] Ibid.

situation outlined a suggestion that Mansfield should become a Hall of this University, with accommodation for some 70 men, and therefore a total undergraduate population of about 200.'[40] This suggestion was received with sufficient interest to lead to the appointment of a subcommittee to consider it, but no more was heard of the proposal at the time. It was at the same meeting, though on the following day, that W. G. Moore was nominated as new Chairman of the Council.

That benefactor whom the Treasurer sought was not forthcoming, and for the time being the College had to struggle on with inadequate resources. Any thought of structural alterations to the Chapel had to be abandoned. A temporary experiment of turning the chairs and other movable furnishings round to face south during 1946–7 was abandoned as unsatisfactory: instead, the use of the stalls was discontinued, an open Bible was placed on the Communion Table, and a Cross at the front of the original Principal's stall. Plans for new building were shelved, but the existing structure was adapted to form a temporary hostel for ten or eleven students. Most of these were unmarried ordination students; any surplus rooms were occupied by Congregational students preparing for other careers.

The change to a residential college, even in this rather makeshift fashion, brought problems for women students, for their status was still ambiguous, and they were now rarely allowed either to use the JCR or to dine in Hall. The outgoing President of the JCR in 1953 wrote in a record book for his successors of this problem: 'When this whole question comes up again, please recognize it as a matter of great moment, and try to contribute something constructive to the thinking of the Council, which is inhibited.'[41]

The shortage of money brought great pressure to bear on the staff. In 1947 there was insufficient money to continue the Chaplain's post; fortunately for the existing holder of the post, Alec Whitehouse, he was appointed Reader in Divinity at the University of Durham. John Marsh, who was now promoted to the status of 'Professor'[42] of Systematic, Dogmatic and Philosophical Theology, undertook to assume again the role of Chaplain to the Congregational Society, as

[40] Minute Book of the Mansfield College Council and Board of Education 1943–53, entry for 19 June 1947, MCA.

[41] JCR President's Book 1952–66, MCA.

[42] The old courtesy title used for the teachers in Nonconformist theological colleges. This was no longer possible in colleges which became part of a university.

well as continuing to act as Bursar (a responsibility which he had assumed in 1946). He and his wife and family moved into the tower, and regularly entertained Congregational undergraduates there.[43] W. H. Cadman was now officially appointed Professor of Biblical Studies.

John Marsh did not remain with the College much longer, for in 1949 he was appointed the first Professor of Christian Theology at the University of Nottingham. It was the College's inability to afford a successor, and therefore to provide adequate teaching and tutorial provision, that brought the crisis facing Mansfield even more acutely before the Council and staff. The Principal was at pains to explain to those outside that his students were not all preparing for the same qualification, nor following the same curriculum; in the academic year 1950–1, for example, one student was preparing for the Oxford BD, four for the B.Litt., one for the D.Phil., five for Theology Schools, and eight were taking the basic College course.[44] This put a tremendous strain on the three members of staff; Micklem continually pleaded, with 'some bitterness of spirit',[45] that a staff of four was a minimum basic requirement. The situation was temporarily alleviated in 1951–2 by the presence of Dr Nels Ferré, Professor of Philosophical Theology at Vanderbilt University in Nashville, Tennessee, whose year in Oxford was financed by the Fulbright Foundation. His help with the teaching of philosophy of religion was much appreciated.

One possible solution to the crisis was an amalgamation with another Free Church college, especially in the light of declining numbers of students in theological colleges generally.[46] A suggestion made in August 1944[47] that Mansfield should consider union with Cheshunt College in Cambridge came to nothing. A later proposal for a closer link with Regent's Park College did at least lead to the appointment of a joint Lecturer (Horton Davies, a Mansfield student 1940–2) in Church History in 1953, but that arrangement was short-lived.

Despite the difficulty of promoting even minimal co-operation between Baptists and Congregationalists in ministerial training in

---

[43] John Marsh was an enthusiastic participant in the Congregational Society walking parties in the Lake District each Easter.

[44] *MCM* 138 (Jan. 1951), 59.   [45] *Mansfield College Annual Report 1952–53*, 4.

[46] See *Congregational Year Books* for the years 1948 to 1953 for numbers.

[47] Minute Book of Mansfield College Council and Board of Education 1943–53, entry for 9–10 Aug. 1944, MCA.

Oxford, College staff and former students were contributing substantially to the ecumenical debate. John Marsh represented the Congregational Union at the inaugural meetings of the World Council of Churches in Amsterdam in 1948. Nathaniel Micklem drafted the statement on Congregationalism for the Sixth International Congregational Council Meeting at Boston in 1949, which was later included in 'A Statement on Congregationalism to the Faith and Order Commission of the World Council of Churches' in 1951.[48] He also played a leading role in responding to the Archbishop of Canterbury's agenda for church unity in England in a sermon preached at Cambridge in 1946. The Church of England offered to make a 'Concordat' with each of the Free Churches, accepting full intercommunion and mutual recognition of ministers, while the Free Churches would be asked to 'take episcopacy into their own systems'. In response to this, Anglican and Free Church representatives met each year for the next three years under the joint chairmanship of the Principal of Mansfield College and the Bishop of Derby (A. E. J. Rawlinson, himself from a Congregational background), and produced the report *Church Relations in England.*[49] As an introduction, Micklem wrote an essay which was also published separately as a pamphlet, *Congregationalism and Episcopacy* (London, 1951). He did not reject the acceptance of episcopacy out of hand; after all, Nonconformists already accepted the principle of *episcope* (in the New Testament connotation of the word). But there would be grave difficulties over the recognition of women ministers and occasional lay administration of the Sacrament. What Micklem did try to emphasize was the great change in attitude on the part of the leaders of the Church of England towards Nonconformists, which provided a new atmosphere for discussion. 'The truth is, we are all being driven back to search the Scriptures, and we are all finding that to some extent the Scriptures confirm and to some extent condemn our traditional ideas and usage.'[50] He even

[48] See R. N. Flew (ed.) *The Nature of the Church: Papers Presented to the Theological Commission Appointed by the Continuation Committee of the World Conference on Faith and Order* (London, 1952).

[49] *Church Relations in England: Being the Report of Conversations between Representatives of the Archbishop of Canterbury and Representatives of the Evangelical Free Churches in England* (London, 1950). The Free Churches represented included the Baptists, Methodists, Independent Methodists, Wesleyans, Moravians, Presbyterians, Churches of Christ, and the Countess of Huntingdon's Connexion, as well as Congregationalists. The Congregational Union was represented by Nathaniel Micklem, K. L. Parry, and H. F. Lovell Cocks. Archbishop Fisher's sermon was printed with the Report.

[50] *Congregationalism and Episcopacy* (London, 1951), 21–2.

wondered whether Congregationalists might not experiment with their own form of episcopacy for a trial period.[51]

As already observed, Micklem had warm and friendly relations with many Roman Catholics, in Oxford and elsewhere.[52] It was with much distaste and regret that he agreed to write a pamphlet criticizing certain aspects of the Roman Catholic Church for the Congregational Union Life and Work Committee in 1952. Under the title *The Pope's Men* it was published both as a separate pamphlet and also as an article in the *Congregational Quarterly*.[53]

It was to the debate which finally led to the union between Congregationalists and Presbyterians that Mansfield men made the greatest contribution. The suggestion of such a union had been made in the 1930s, and was revived during the later years of the war.[54] The issue was first brought to the May Assembly of the Congregational Union in 1945. On that occasion C. J. Cadoux had spoken against the proposal, and came to be regarded as the chief spokesman of the 'anti-union' party. When he went home from those meetings, he sat down to write a 10,000-word pamphlet entitled *The Congregational Way*, published by Blackwells in January 1946. He set forth a plea for mutual co-operation rather than organic unity, believing that the emphasis on the ordained ministry, on synodical government, and on baptism as an absolute requirement for membership would cause essential Congregational principles to be lost. Cadoux recognized the need for specially trained and dedicated ministers to be set aside for 'a peculiarly-sacred office', usually and 'wisely' marked by ordination. But 'it ought never to be forgotten that, according to the Congregational way, he is still essentially a Christian layman', not marked off from others by any 'sacerdotal stamp' empowering him to perform functions which others were 'inherently debarred' from performing.[55] He accepted that the plea of Micklem and others for a more significant role for church councils in Congregationalism did not challenge

[51] Ibid. 23.

[52] Campion Hall, the Jesuit College established in 1895, was actually built on the site of Micklem Hall, once owned by a 'brewer kinsman' of Nathaniel Micklem.

[53] *CQ* (1952), 218–30; *The Pope's Men* (London, 1953).

[54] See Arthur Macarthur, 'The Background to the Formation of the United Reformed Church (Presbyterian and Congregational) in England and Wales in 1972', *JURCHS* 4/1 (Oct. 1987), 6.

[55] *The Congregational Way* (Oxford, 1945) 27. Though an accredited minister of the Congregational Union, Cadoux was never ordained, and never had a permanent pastorate. R. F. Horton, too, was never ordained, despite a long pastoral ministry.

the independence of the local church; but the trend 'needs watch-ing'. He wrote in similar vein in his regular contributions to the weekly *Christian World*. His vision of unity was based on fuller co-operation and enlarged mutual recognition.

Micklem however felt that negotiations could be conducted in such a way that essential Congregational principles were not lost:

> The really crucial issue is this: if the Presbyterians are willing to recognize that all authority in the Church of Christ is ministerial, not magisterial, or spiritual, not legal, and if the Congregationalists will recognize the spiritual (not legal) authority of the finding of synods (or whatever they are called) reached after prayer and spir-itual conference, we shall find a way through.[56]

In 1945 a Joint Presbyterian/Congregational Conference was set up, and a long series of discussions between the Congregational Union and the Presbyterian Church of England on their possible union began. As an aid to the deliberations, Micklem wrote a back-ground booklet, *Towards Union? The Facts* (London, 1946), in which he pointed out how the two denominations could draw strength from each other:

> I suspect that those are most concerned for union who most deeply realize the weakness of the churches and their failure to rise to the great calls of the hour and who see that both sides here have principles which are of value and so complementary that together we could find a church order richer and more satisfying than either of us know in isolation.[57]

The Scheme of Union which the Conference produced in 1947 led not to union at that stage, but to a covenant relation between the two bodies.

Following on the Open Letter of 1938 (see Chapter X) a group of younger ministers had formed the Church Order Group. They began to explore the roots of Congregationalism and discovered a stronger tradition of association than many realized. Thus John Marsh, for example, wrote on 'Unions and Associations: Some Historical Notes' in the *Congregational Quarterly*,[58] drawing on evidence from the time of Robert Browne (*c.*1550–1633) onwards: the vital question for

---

[56] *MCM* 128 (Jan. 1946), 170.   [57] Quoted in *Presbyter*, 4/3 (1946), 25.
[58] *CQ* (1952), 321–35.

Congregationalists was now not whether or not there should be any centralized power—the Congregational Union had to take and use it in order to carry out its functions—but under what authority it was exercised. In the 1940s John Marsh had edited a series of short works entitled 'The Forward Books', 'for the sake of "the Church which is to come" '.[59] Even more radical were the articles appearing in the *Presbyter*—'A Journal of Confessional and Catholic Churchmanship', which ran, in printed form at least, from January 1943 until 1950.[60] Daniel Jenkins, the editor for much of its life, had been a Mansfield student in the late 1930s, and was in the mid-1940s serving as SCM Secretary in Birmingham.[61] In a remarkable series of books and articles, he and others attempted to work out the implications of Reformed theology for life and worship in the later twentieth century.[62] But for Cadoux the *Presbyter* was identifying itself with 'a trend in modern religious thought which, in common with most Mansfield men and most Congregational ministers I know, I regard as definitely reactionary and erroneous'.[63] Within Mansfield itself, however, it was Cadoux, rather than Micklem, who was feeling isolated on this issue.

In 1948 the Oxford University Press published *A Book of Public Worship: Compiled for the Use of Congregationalists*, edited by John Huxtable, John Marsh, Romilly Micklem, and James Todd (the first three were Mansfield men). In the introduction, John Marsh set out the principles of Christian worship and recalled Congregationalists

---

[59] They included Micklem's *Congregationalism and the Church Catholic* (London, 1943, repr. 1944), John Huxtable's *The Ministry* (London, 1943), and others by former Mansfield men.

[60] The *Presbyter* began as a monthly broadsheet among Birmingham ministers of the Presbyterian Church of England in 1939. At the end of 1942 James Clarke and Co. offered to take over the publishing responsibility, and Daniel Jenkins and Alexander Miller were appointed joint editors. John Marsh was an adviser. The journal's supporters and contributors were not confined to Congregationalists and Presbyterians. After 1948 the new *Scottish Journal of Theology*, founded by T. F. Torrance and J. K. S. Reid, provided a forum for the discussion of Reformed theology and churchmanship, and the *Presbyter* lapsed.

[61] It should be noted, however, that the most formative influences on Daniel Jenkins came through his studies at the University of Edinburgh, at a time when Karl Barth was better known in Scotland than in England, and under Lovell Cocks, a former student of P. T. Forsyth, at the Yorkshire United Independent College, rather than through Mansfield.

[62] See particularly Daniel Jenkins, *The Nature of Catholicity* (London, 1942), *The Gift of Ministry* (London, 1947), *Tradition and the Spirit* (London, 1951), and *Congregationalism* (London, 1954).

[63] Letter to Alec Whitehouse, 2 Feb. 1944.

to the liturgical principles of their tradition. The early Congregationalists 'were concerned, not that they might do as they pleased,
but that they might worship as they ought'.[64] In common with other
liturgical scholars,[65] the compilers reminded readers that Calvin and
other Reformers had stressed that both Word and Sacrament were
needed for a full order of worship. The book included orders for
such worship, as well as services for special occasions such as baptism
and ordination. While in no way prescriptive, it was intended to
foster a deeper and more informed understanding of the principles
of public worship. It reflected that revival of ordered worship in which
Mansfield took a leading part.

The number of students who took a course of at least two years,
having entered when Micklem was Principal, was 106; of these seven
were known to have been the sons of ministers; four (one fewer
than under Selbie) were women. Seven were Baptists, three Methodists, two were Welsh Independents, one was Welsh Presbyterian, and
three were Lutherans. Of the ninety-seven for whom career information is available, thirty-eight (39 per cent) spent at least twenty-five
years in pastoral ministry, and thirty-eight (39 per cent) spent lesser
time in pastoral ministry. Nine were missionaries, twenty-one were
theological teachers in higher education; four moved to the Church
of England.[66]

Micklem was due to reach the age of 65 in 1953. The Council felt
it was particularly important to appoint a new Principal to succeed
him well in advance of the retirement date, because of the financial
crisis facing the College, which was to require very important discussions and decisions. Several names were discussed, none of them
recorded in the Council's minutes. The name that was finally agreed
unanimously was that of John Marsh, who accepted the appointment.

So in June 1953 Nathaniel Micklem gave his last speech (but one
of his wittiest) as Principal of Mansfield at the gathering of Old
Men. His portrait, painted by Archie Utin, was formally presented to
him by one of the oldest surviving students, the 87-year-old William
Blackshaw (Mansfield 1890–3).[67] Martin Krapf presented him with a
Festschrift by some of his German admirers. John Huxtable wrote of
him in the *College Magazine* that he had done more than any other
to change the face of Congregationalism in the previous twenty-five

[64] *A Book of Public Worship*, p. vii.
[65] The Liturgical Movement of the 20th cent. has been ecumenical and international.
[66] See also App. II.   [67] W. H. Blackshaw died only a few weeks later.

years.[68] After sharing in his father's hundredth birthday celebrations in the autumn, he and his wife set out for the United States, where they spent two terms at Vanderbilt University, Tennessee before settling in their new home in Princes Risborough, where he continued to write both poetry and prose, and to take part in public life.[69] In his later years he 'appeared to have a special ministry to those who found faith difficult'.[70] 'Ever a seeker was I, but ever in secret a finder.'[71]

At Mansfield, John Marsh was left to face the problems.

[68] *MCM* 143 (July 1953), 165.

[69] In 1957–8 he was President of the Liberal Party. His books in retirement included *Ultimate Questions* (London, 1955), his autobiography *The Box and the Puppets*, *Faith and Reason* (London, 1963), and *A Religion for Agnostics* (London, 1965), and some volumes of poetry. In 1974 he was made a Companion of Honour for his services to theology.

[70] J. Huxtable, *MCM* 179 (1977), 25.

[71] N. Micklem, *Waifs and Strays* (Princes Risborough, 1972), 28.

XII

The Crisis Challenged: 1953–1962

W HEN John Marsh became Principal, he knew that only a bold new initiative would enable Mansfield to overcome its financial crisis. The College Auditor told him that he had four years in which to 'get things moving'.[1] The accounts were balanced only at the expense of overloading the teaching timetable of the academic staff while simultaneously offering them salaries well below those of other university teachers. This was not a state of affairs which could continue for long.

The new Principal, his wife Gladys,[2] and their three children moved into the Principal's Lodgings. John Marsh was 48, in full vigour and apparently undeterred by the immense difficulties facing the College. The fourth Principal in an eminent succession, a Mansfield-trained man like his two immediate predecessors, he was drawn back from Nottingham to Oxford by affection for his own college and his old teachers, and by a commitment to the Reformed churchmanship and ministry of Congregationalism. For the previous four years he had effectively established the Department of Christian Theology at the newly constituted Nottingham University (elevated from the status of a constituent college of London University in 1949). His important work of theology *The Fulness of Time* (London, 1952; based on his Oxford D.Phil. thesis) had recently been published.[3]

He was firmly rooted in his own tradition[4] and was known as a

---

[1] John Marsh, 'A Mansfield Principalship 1953–70', *MCM* 188 (1985–6), 51–4.

[2] John Marsh married Gladys Walker of Cockermouth in 1934. Gladys Marsh was and has remained a member of the Society of Friends.

[3] The relationship between time and eternity was a lifelong interest, and in later years he continued to write and lecture on the subject. Alongside this, he continued to work as a biblical scholar, in the tradition of Rudolf Bultmann, with whom he had studied in Marburg 1931–2, and whose *The History of the Synoptic Tradition* he translated (Oxford, 1963).

[4] His mother was a Congregationalist, his father an Anglican. In his childhood he attended the local parish church and sang in its choir, but became a Congregationalist by conviction in adolescence.

well-informed and determined apologist for the Reformed basis of Congregationalism.[5] He viewed this as a contribution to 'the Church which is to come', and was already recognized as a leader of the ecumenical movement. He was one of the delegates of the Congregational Union to the inaugural meeting of the World Council of Churches in Amsterdam in 1948 and was due to attend its second meeting at Evanston in 1954. In addition, he was well known on both sides of the Atlantic as a lecturer, writer, and preacher. He was already Chairman of the British Council of Churches Commission on Broadcasting, and was soon to play an important role as adviser to the Independent Television Authority on religious television, and as a member of the Central Religious Advisory Committee of the BBC. Now his skills as an administrator were to be tested as well.

When he arrived back in Mansfield, the wartime stringencies were at last coming to an end. Food rationing finally ended in July 1954. 'The age of affluence' was dawning. With it came a continuing decline in the membership of Congregational churches.[6] Although the number of ministerial students was just being maintained, ordinary subscriptions and contributions from the churches to the colleges were still very low, and the likelihood of any growth in support was small unless some special appeal was launched. A further cloud on the horizon was the fact that the new Censor of St Catherine's Society (Alan Bullock, now Lord Bullock) warned that, in spite of much goodwill towards Mansfield, his Society's plans for change and expansion might mean their being unable to accept and matriculate Mansfield students in the future.

An Appeal had already been launched by the College Council as John Marsh assumed his new responsibility, and finance was a major subject of discussion at his first Council meeting. He had already realized that the College would have to expand if it were to become an economically viable institution in the post-war world. This could provide the opportunity to broaden its intellectual atmosphere, all the more necessary now that the College was largely residential. In his inaugural lecture at Nottingham, he had called for theology to engage with other subjects on the frontiers of knowledge—'giving

---

[5] He had edited the 'Forward Books' in the 1940s, and edited and contributed to *Congregationalism Today* (London, 1943).

[6] Between 1930 and 1952 the number of members of the Congregational churches of England and Wales had dropped from 312,216 to 223,008. See *CYB 1931*, 582 and *CYB 1953*, 361.

and being given, no shelter but the truth'. It was in that spirit, with that aspiration, and with the experience of Nottingham behind him, that he set about a 're-foundation' of Mansfield within, rather than outside, the University.

He was asked by the Council to consult the University Registrar, Sir Douglas Veale—the key figure in University plans for development —about Mansfield's dilemma. At the end of May 1954 John Marsh had a discussion with the Registrar and reported his conversation to the Council on 18 June. The Registrar had informed him that, while the University had access to money for new building in Oxford through the University Grants Committee,[7] particularly for post-graduate accommodation, none could be made available before 1960. However, both the Censor of St Catherine's and the Registrar had pointed out that Mansfield might benefit substantially by becoming a Permanent Private Hall (PPH),[8] for with that status its students would be eligible for local authority grants and supplementary scholarships from the Ministry of Education; this would widen the possible supply of students and make it unnecessary for the College to supplement meagre grants.

Action was taken swiftly. A subcommittee was appointed to investigate the proposal, and presumably given authority to act, for by the time the Council next met on 6 December, it was reported that an application to become a Permanent Private Hall had already been submitted to the University's Hebdomadal Council[9] on 30 November, and that it was an item on their agenda that very day. It was fortunate that the Chairman of Council was Dr Will Moore, Fellow of St John's and a prominent figure in the University; he knew and understood much about the 'byzantine' structure of the University,

---

[7] The University Grants Committee had been formed in 1919 as a way of channelling government funding to universities while still maintaining their independence from direct government control. After 1945 it had earmarked a certain amount of money for student accommodation. Such money could only reach Mansfield via the University itself.

[8] Private Halls, with 'Licensed Masters', had been originally established as private ventures from the middle of the 19th cent. Permanent Private Halls, in practice educational institutions supported by non-Anglican religious denominations, had been established under a University Statute of 1918. Their students had the same privileges and obligations as those of colleges, but the University retained certain control over numbers and organization. At the beginning of 1955 there were two Permanent Private Halls in the University: Campion Hall for Jesuits, and St Benet's Hall for Benedictines. Regent's Park College and Greyfriars Hall were both made Permanent Private Halls in 1957.

[9] The University's 'cabinet', which prepared legislation for Congregation. During the 20th cent. it became the chief formulator of University policy.

and his support for the proposal carried weight. The formal application set out to show that Mansfield fulfilled all the requirements of a 'PPH': that it had a proper constitution recognized by the Charity Commissioners, that it was not run for profit, that its Principal was a graduate (MA, D.Phil.) of the University, that it lay within the permitted $2\frac{1}{2}$-mile radius of Carfax, and that its buildings were inspected and approved by the Delegates of Lodging. A further note added that while the College preferred to keep the title by which it had been known for sixty-eight years, it would accept the description 'Mansfield Hall' if directed by Convocation.[10]

The application was accepted by Hebdomadal Council, and put on the agenda for the meeting of Convocation on 22 February 1955. It was agreed not to ask the College to change its name. The actual decree was then proposed in Convocation by the Senior Proctor, Michael Maclagan of Trinity College, as follows:[11]

Insignissime Vice-Cancellarie,

Collegium de Mansfield anno millesimo octingentesimo octogesimo sextoque statutum intra civitatem sed extra Universitatem per multos annos exstitit. In orbe alumni eius fidem Christi doctrinasque ecclesiarum anglice Independent nominatarum et propagunt et ornunt. Cis Universitatem viri praeclari in facultate Sacrae Theologiae, quorum inter ceteros nomino Vernon Bartlet et Nathaniel Micklem, studia nostra libenter et valde quasi candelae inluxerunt, legendo disputando et cetera omnia faciendo.

Collegium nunc statum et dignitatem aulae privatae quaerit, quo applicationi concilio hebdomadali jam assentiri placuit. Insuper concilium hebdomadale statuit ut nomen de Mansfield College per tot annos bene notum decreto approbato continuetur. Praeterea propositum est ut Johannes Marsh, in artibus magister, hodie ejusdem collegii principalis novae aulae magister sit.

Insignissime Vice-Cancellarie hoc decretum proponere volo.[12]

---

[10] *Oxford University Hebdomadal Council Papers*, 219: 339–41.

[11] Quoted *MCM* 147 (July 1955), 273.

[12] 'Most distinguished Vice-Chancellor,

Mansfield College, founded in 1886, has existed for many years within the community but outside the University. In the outside world its alumni promote and honour the faith of Christ and the teachings of those churches known as "Independent". Here in the University men eminent in the Faculty of Theology (among others I would mention Vernon Bartlet and Nathaniel Micklem) have willingly and to great effect shone like candles upon our endeavours, in lecturing, debate and by all other means.

It was approved 'without any sign of dissension'. The Principal reported that it had been 'a very proud moment'.[13]

In retrospect John Marsh wrote:

> The story of that important transition in the life of the College will never be properly told unless it be strongly affirmed that in making the application for its new status the Council of Mansfield was acting in the sure conviction that the change would enable Mansfield to fulfil in the circumstances of 1954 the aims of the founders who moved to Oxford in 1886—namely, that the training of ordinands should be conducted throughout in the full context of a University environment. Clearly in 1954 the ordinands at Mansfield were far more isolated in their training than the Founders ever intended; and to bring the University, as it were, inside the College, offered a sure and permanent remedy to that deficiency.[14]

In his letter to 'the Brethren of the Dispersion' in July 1955, the Principal wrote to reassure them that 'we have not surrendered one iota of our freedom'; the College would continue to hold on to 'the great ideals of our founders', but 'in the quite different social and educational set-up of this mid-century'. It would continue to be administered according to its constitution of 1899, rather than on the normal Oxford model of a college governed by Fellows.[15] There would be financial gains, but other gains too; already, the Board of the Faculty of Theology had placed Cadman, Routley, and Marsh on the list of Faculty Lecturers, 'which is the only list from which nominations to a stipendiary lectureship in the University can be made'.[16] His hope was to see a Mansfield Lecturer appointed to such a position.

The College now seeks the rank and standing of Private Hall and Hebdomadal Council has resolved to accept this request. Moreover Council has decided that the name "Mansfield College", well known for so long, should, by the passing of a Decree, be retained. Furthermore it is proposed that John Marsh, Master of Arts, Principal of this same College, should today become Master of the new Hall.

Most distinguished Vice-Chancellor, I wish to propose this Decree.'
(I am indebted to Dr Donald Sykes for this translation.)

[13] *MCM* 147 (July 1955), 273.   [14] *MCM* 188 (1985–6), 53.

[15] The existing College constitution guaranteed representation to the Congregational Union and the subscribers.

[16] *MCM* 147 (July 1955), 274. In the same issue (258–9) the death of Thomas Henry Martin (Mansfield 1888–91) was reported. He had entered the College before the building was completed, and had lived to see it become part of the University.

One curious discovery in the wake of the change of status was that the College was not entitled to use the coat of arms it had adopted in 1886. Now that Mansfield was entitled to have an entry, including its coat of arms, in the *Oxford University Calendar*, the University printers requested the date of the arms. The Principal wrote to the College of Arms for this information, only to be told that the arms had been confirmed to Lancelot Manfeld of Skirpenbek, Yorkshire in 1563, and could not be transferred.[17] Extensive attempts to discover a connection between Lancelot Manfeld and the Mansfields of Derby and Spring Hill failed.[18] After extensive correspondence with the College of Arms, and the payment of a fee, a new patent of arms was finally agreed (pl. 12). In good Reformed tradition, John Marsh chose the book (a bible) instead of Richmond Herald's suggestion of three springs; the fountain was inserted as a reminder of the College's original site.[19]

In keeping with Oxford college tradition, Mansfield had already (in 1953) adopted a Latin grace.[20] It was originally composed in Welsh for the University College of North Wales, Bangor, by Sir Ifor Williams, but translated into Latin to satisfy English students. It may be spoken in Latin or Welsh, but not in English, in College Hall.

The need to make the College financially viable had two immediate practical implications. The first was that among the larger number of students who would have to be accepted, some would be studying subjects other than theology. This was realistic in that, while the number of ordinands studying theology was not increasing, the number of students overall in Britain was increasing dramatically.[21] In the context of growing student numbers, and easier access to student funding, it was reasonable for Mansfield to expect to attract able non-theological students. Exactly how the balance was to be worked out, and the way in which this would affect the whole ethos and structure of the College, was a difficult issue which took some years to resolve. The second implication was that more accommodation

---

[17] Letter from Richmond Herald to John Marsh, 6 June 1955, MCA.

[18] Correspondence relating to this issue, MCA.

[19] Correspondence with the College of Heralds 1955–6, MCA.

[20] 'Omnipotens Deus Clementissime Pater omnis boni fons: in donis tuis gaudentes nomen tuum magnificamus: per Jesum Christum Dominum nostrum: Amen.' 'Almighty God Father of Mercies and fount of every good: in the enjoyment of thy gifts we bless thy name: through Jesus Christ our Lord: Amen.'

[21] The number of undergraduates in England and Wales almost doubled between 1939 and 1960.

MANSFIELD COLLEGE

On a Wreath Or and Gules
a Unicorn Sejant Gules
Armed Crined and Unguled Or
Gorged with a Celestial Crown Gold
Resting the Dexter Fore-hoof on a Fountain

———•———

Gules
An Open Book Proper
inscribed

Deus Locutus est
Nobis in Filio

in Letters Sable
Bound Argent
Edged and Clasped Or
between
Three Crossed Crosslets Gold

12. College Arms 1955

would have to be provided. The University's rule was that a PPH must not have more than five people 'in statu pupillari' (i.e. undergraduates or Bachelors of Arts receiving tuition) living out of college, though in 1956 Hebdomadal Council waived the rule in Mansfield's case for the next five years because it was understood that new building plans were in hand. The issue could not, however, be permanently shelved.

One possible solution was to develop formally into what Fairbairn had always hoped Mansfield would be: a Free Church theological college. Mansfield had trained Baptist students from the beginning until Regent's Park moved in 1938 into its new buildings in Oxford, which Mansfield had then shared during the war. The joint Department of Church History, with Horton Davies at its head, had raised many hopes for collaboration; but it was dealt a blow when Horton Davies moved to Princeton to become Professor of Ecclesiastical History in the new graduate school of theology at the end of 1955.[22] The arrangement did not survive much longer. It was a disappointment to Mansfield that Regent's Park was committed to a new building scheme and was not prepared to enter into any other closer collaboration. Behind this lay a more serious issue. The Congregational Union was already launched on the discussions with the Presbyterian Church of England which ultimately led to the formation of the United Reformed Church; this complicated any move towards collaboration with the Baptists.

These considerations highlighted the problem of the differing and sometimes conflicting loyalties of a Nonconformist college—to its denomination, to its university, and to other Christian churches and institutions. John Marsh had already demonstrated his commitment to all these spheres, as well as to British society more widely. But as a loyal Congregationalist and staunch defender of Congregational churchmanship, he welcomed the appointment of a Congregational Union Commission on the future of the theological colleges in September 1955, and served on its committee, together with the Chairman of the Mansfield Council (W. G. Moore), until its report

---

[22] While Horton Davies was at Mansfield, his book *Christian Deviations* (London, 1954) was published. In a review in *MCM* (146 (Jan. 1955), 241) H. Cunliffe Jones wrote: 'No one except the author of this book has ever written for me examination papers which were a sheer joy to read for their content, presentation, and legibility.' See Horton Davies, *A Church Historian's Odyssey* (Grand Rapids, Mich., 1993) for an account of his later career.

was published in 1958.[23] Its brief was to consider the recruitment and training of candidates for the ministry, which included an appraisal of the institutions in which they were trained. Not for the first time, it was recommended that the resources for theological training should be brought together in fewer institutions; colleges should be amalgamated. In Mansfield's case, negotiation with Cheshunt College, Cambridge was advised.[24] In October 1956 the Mansfield Council appointed six of its number to meet with representatives of Cheshunt's governing body; but Cheshunt's Governors were deeply divided on the issues, and the negotiations soon reached a stalemate. In the event, only one amalgamation took place at this time—that of the Yorkshire United Independent College and the Lancashire Independent College to form the Northern Congregational College in Manchester. For Mansfield, there was satisfaction in that, with reference to the training of future theological teachers, the Commission 'recommends that Mansfield should be regarded as the College at which this special work is done'.[25]

Almost simultaneously with the beginning of the Cheshunt negotiations another approach was made to the College, by the Lutheran Council of Great Britain. During and just after the 1939–45 war, Lutherans from Germany, Estonia, Latvia, Lithuania, and Poland had settled in Britain and formed their own communities and worship centres.[26] By the early 1950s, it was estimated that there were about 35,000 Lutherans in Britain, including 30 ministers. There was a further influx of Hungarian Lutherans in 1956. The Lutheran Council of Great Britain had been formed in 1948. It now believed the time had come to consider the training of new ministers in the country in which they would expect to serve. The Council leaders, advised by the theological department of the Lutheran World Federation, approached Oxford University, assuming in the first place that they would collaborate with Anglicans. But their first approach was unproductive, as was their approach to other universities; when Mansfield sent a positive response, they immediately opened negotiations.[27]

[23] Congregational Union, *Report of the Commission on the Colleges* (London, 1958).

[24] John Marsh had already made an informal approach to the College of which Fairbairn had also been Principal (Yorkshire United Independent College) for some form of amalgamation, but this had been rejected. See *MCM* 188 (1985–6), 52.

[25] Ibid. 20.

[26] There had been German and Scandinavian Lutheran congregations in England since the 17th cent.

[27] See W. E. Hulme, 'Luther Returns to England', *Christian Century*, 8 June 1960.

It was agreed that the Lutheran World Federation would finance a Lutheran teacher, appointed by the Federation in consultation with the Principal of Mansfield, to be called initially Dean of Lutheran students,[28] and that places would be found in Mansfield for a few Lutheran students, who would share in much of the normal college theological course. In Michaelmas 1957 the first Dean, Dr R. H. Fischer, Professor of Historical Theology at Chicago Lutheran Theological Seminary, joined the College staff for a year; he was the first of many (the term of office was usually short, and the early holders of the post were on sabbatical leave) who have continued to teach at Mansfield ever since.[29] At the same time two Latvian and one Estonian students were admitted.[30] By 1961 the Federation had cemented its relationship with the College by promising to continue to fund the lecturership even if there were no Lutheran students in the college; in addition, a Lutheran representative was elected to serve on the College Council.

Although the number of Lutheran ordinands has declined, the Lutheran Lecturers have made a notable contribution to College, University, and British Lutheran life, as tutors to non-Lutheran ordinands, chaplains to Lutheran students in the University, members of the University Theology Faculty, theological advisers to Lutheran congregations, and representatives of the Lutheran viewpoint in ecumenical conversations. For the Lutherans the post has been of special significance, in giving 'international Lutheranism something which might be difficult to arrange if attempted *de novo*: the chance to have a contributor and observer at a main intellectual centre of the English churches'.[31]

---

[28] In 1967 the title was changed to 'Lutheran World Federation Lecturer in Theology'.

[29] Although the Lutheran Lecturer could theoretically be appointed from any Lutheran Church in the world, in practice the post has always been held by Americans. Dr Fischer was succeeded by Professor W. E. Hulme, Professor of Pastoral Theology and Pastoral Counselling at the Wartburg Theological Seminary in Dubuque, Iowa, who was on sabbatical (1958–9), Dr H. H. Ditmanson, Lecturer at St Olaf College, Northfield, Minnesota, on leave for two years (1959–61), Dr F. E. Sherman (1961–6 and 1970–1), who left to become Associate Professor of Christian Ethics at the Lutheran School of Theology, Chicago, Dr R. W. Jenson (1966–8 and 1972–3), who moved to the Lutheran Theological Seminary at Gettysburg, Pennsylvania, and Dr Gerhard Forde (1968–70), of the Lutheran Theological Seminary, St Paul, Minnesota.

[30] Mansfield's first Latvian Lutheran student was Juris Jurgis, 1955–8. He was the first of nine Lutheran students trained at Mansfield who entered the Lutheran ministry in Britain. See Juris Jurgis, 'Latvia Revisited', *MCM* 193 (1990–1), 23–5.

[31] *The Lutheran Council of Great Britain* (London, 1975), 116.

John Marsh told the Annual Meeting of 1957 that he saw this as a first step towards an ecumenical theological college, for this was the first time that two denominations had agreed formally to train their ordinands at one institution in England:

> I think that by inviting them to come, the Council is fulfilling the aims which our founders had so much in mind; for we shall be helping a great sister Church of the Reformation; we shall be doing a service to the University; we shall be advancing the standards of theological education, both by bringing distinguished scholars to teach here, and by providing a more ecumenical setting for theological study; and finally, we shall be adding more amenities to this College, pledged to sound learning and true religion.[32]

This was in tune with John Marsh's own work on the world ecumenical stage. He had attended the second Assembly of the World Council of Churches at Evanston at the end of his first year at Mansfield, and on the return journey (by ship) wrote a short book on *The Significance of Evanston* (London, 1954). He expressed the hope that British churches would now begin to care more about 'the reunion of our fragmented British Church Life':

> In particular, that Congregationalists, who, in my view, can rightly be proud of a very 'ecumenical' churchmanship, will cease from shrinking into sectarians each time some Church union is planned; and that they will have the candour and honesty to admit to the present-day Church of England that bishops do not necessarily, and do not by any means always in fact, prevent Christ from ruling in his Church; that they will be honest enough to admit that in many Churches we are as 'clericalized' as Rome, that they will be ready enough to repent, and repent with their fellow Christians, and enter soon into a new and manifest unity with them all. I believe that no single thing would be of more service to the Ecumenical Movement than a restoration of the unity of the Church in Great Britain.[33]

He was a member of the World Council of Churches Commission on Faith and Order and of its Executive Committee, and Secretary

---

[32] *MCM* 148 (Jan. 1956), 13.
[33] John Marsh, *The Significance of Evanston* (London, 1954), 70.

of the Commission on Unity.[34] In 1961 he represented the Congregational Union again at the World Council of Churches Conference in New Delhi. Nearer home, he was Chairman of the Faith and Order Department of the British Council of Churches. These responsibilities took him all over the world, but most of all to the United States, where he was much sought after as a lecturer until and after his retirement.

In March 1962 he gave a personal confession of his commitment to the search for unity in a lecture in Oxford as part of a conference on the theme 'The Dialogue of East and West in Christendom', published under that title in 1963.[35] After confessing some of the things he had learned through his ecumenical experience, he highlighted two distinctive qualities of Congregational life: the gathering of the Church round two things which belong together—the preaching of the Word and the administration of the Sacraments, and the life in community as members of God's Covenant people. But he also stressed that Congregationalists 'need the Ecumenical encounter to know what it is that God has done with us in the past and we certainly need it to know what He wants to do with us in the future'.[36]

As a Nonconformist he was still not entirely *persona grata* in the religious life of the University. It was not until 1960 that a Nonconformist (Nathaniel Micklem) was appointed to the list of Select Preachers to the University, and not until the following year that he was himself appointed a Select Preacher.[37]

In addition to all these activities, John Marsh taught theology within the college. In 1954 he persuaded the Council to allow him to appoint a Research Scholar for two years—Roger Tomes, who for the following two years combined work on a research project with some teaching. But the two on whom the main burden of teaching fell until 1959 were W. H. Cadman, who was responsible for biblical studies, and Erik Routley, church historian, Librarian, musician, Chaplain—it was almost impossible to keep up with all his activities.

---

[34] In that capacity he was joint editor, with D. M. Baillie, of a WCC report on *Intercommunion* (London, 1952), to which he contributed a paper on 'Intercommunion: A Congregationalist Comment', 269–80.

[35] *The Dialogue of East and West and Christendom: Lectures Delivered at a Conference Arranged by the Fellowship of St Alban and St Sergius in Oxford 10 March 1962* (London, 1963).

[36] Ibid. 26.

[37] He first preached in that capacity on 15 Oct. 1961 at the University Church of St Mary's.

As a PPH, the College could no longer call its teachers 'professors': they were now, and for some time to come, 'tutors'. Cadman was Senior Tutor and Dean of Degrees.

William Healey Cadman had been associated with the College since 1917, when he came as a young theological student from New College, London. After a short pastorate at Tavistock and a two-year period as research student in Strasbourg, he came back to Mansfield in 1923 to assist Dodd in teaching New Testament, and to carry on his own research. He had just published *The Last Journey to Jerusalem: Its Purpose in the Light of the Synoptic Gospels* (London, 1923); for the rest of his life he worked on John's Gospel, constantly revising and reflecting on a book which never quite took shape; he never finally decided whether it was to be a commentary or a work of historical criticism. It was eventually prepared for publication by his former pupil George Caird, and appeared as *The Open Heaven: The Revelation of God in the Johannine Sayings of Jesus* (Oxford) in 1969. Despite so little in print in his lifetime, those who were his pupils recognized a teacher who could take them to the frontiers of scholarship, and who enabled generations of Mansfield men to understand something of the mystery of the Fourth Gospel. He had worked patiently and unobtrusively as Research Fellow for most of the years of Micklem's Principalship. Then in 1947 he was appointed Yates Professor of the New Testament, exchanging it for the title of Senior Tutor in 1955. It was during those last years of teaching that others realized his quality and worth most clearly: 'During the College's leanest days, those dreadful and exciting days when everybody was pontificating about the College's glorious past, the college owed more to Cadman for its academic survival than to anybody else.'[38] It gave both him and the College great satisfaction when the University of Aberdeen conferred an honorary DD on him in 1957.

Erik Routley[39] came up to Oxford from Lancing College in 1936. At the time, his minister, an old Mansfield man, wrote of him to C. J. Cadoux, 'he is really brilliant—almost, if not quite, a genius'. His friends and admirers would have said that his subsequent career bore this out. As a Mansfield student 1939–43 he made his mark not only as a theologian but also as a musician, and had the distinction of having one of his compositions performed at a Balliol Concert.

---

[38] Erik Routley, *MCM* 167 (Oct. 1965), 243.

[39] Erik Reginald Routley (1917–82). See R. A. Leaver and J. H. Litton (eds.), *Duty and Delight: Routley Remembered* (Norwich, 1985).

After leaving Mansfield, he worked in the pastoral ministry at Wed-nesbury and at Dartford before returning to Mansfield in 1948 as Lecturer in Church History and Librarian. He had so many interests that it was not easy to decide where his greatest gifts or his deepest interests lay. He once told a member of his congregation: 'People think of me as primarily a musician, but my deepest interest is in interpreting the Bible.' This might be borne out by one of the most original of his thirty-seven books, *Into a Far Country* (London, 1962). But music, its practice, composition, theology, was part of his life from beginning to end. His BD thesis was published in 1950 as *The Church and Music: An Enquiry into the History, the Nature and Scope of Christian Judgement on Music* (London); his D.Phil. thesis in revised form in 1957 as *The Music of Christian Hymnody: A Study of the Develop-ment of the Hymn Tune since the Reformation, with Special Reference to English Protestantism* (London).

From an early age he had collected a folder of hymns—words and tunes—which he considered worthy of worship, and this was the basis of his contribution to the production of the new Congregational hymn book in 1951, *Congregational Praise*.[40] He was organist in the College Chapel, and leader of a choir. While he was following in the tradition of Romilly Micklem, another minister-musician, it was during his time that the musical tradition of the College was fully established, and it was he who developed a theology to integrate music into the life of the College. Through his lectures, his books, his work as secretary of the editorial committee which produced *Congregational Praise* and author of the notes on music for *A Com-panion to Congregational Praise*,[41] and as Founder-President of the Congregational Organists' Guild, it was to flow into the life of the churches of which Mansfield men were ministers, and thence into the whole life of the denomination and beyond. His official college teaching was in church history, of which he was a lively exponent; this is borne out by a small book in the SCM Religious Book Club series, *The Wisdom of the Fathers* (London, 1957), and by the books which came out just before the 1662 Tercentenary commemoration, *English Religious Dissent* (Cambridge, 1960) and *The Story of Congre-gationalism* (London, 1961). Added to this were his library duties, and his role as Chaplain to the Congregational Society, through which

---

[40] Other Mansfield men were on the committee responsible for producing the new hymn book.

[41] K. L. Parry (ed.), *A Companion to Congregational Praise* (London, 1953).

he had a lifelong influence on many Congregational students, ordinands and non-ordinands alike.[42]

At the end of Trinity Term 1959 Will Cadman retired, and Erik Routley moved to Edinburgh to become minister of Augustine-Bristo Church. The only full-time academic member of staff remaining was the Principal. But some further continuity was provided by David Goodall (Mansfield 1948–51), who since 1956 had combined the pastorate of the Congregational church at Brill with part-time work as Bursar at Mansfield. In 1957 he relinquished his ministry at Brill, and his post was made full-time with the addition of responsibilities as Chaplain to Congregational students, and as College organist.[43] Another former Mansfield student, one of the last of 'Fairbairn's men', was Basil Yeaxlee,[44] who came to help the College in the years of his retirement; his career had been in education and in psychology (he was Oxford University Reader in Educational Psychology 1935–49). Here was a reversal of roles, for John Marsh had been the most junior member of staff at Westhill Training College when Yeaxlee was Principal in 1928; now he came with what John Marsh called 'his characteristic grace and humility' to take what could be viewed as the most junior post at Mansfield, that of Librarian (at first in a voluntary capacity).[45] In addition, he used his wide experience in helping with lectures on the psychology of religion.

The two full-time academic staff who now joined the College staff were both not only former Mansfield students but also future Principals: George Caird and Donald Sykes. Both were from a Scottish background. George Caird took the theological course and then a D.Phil. (on 'The New Testament Conception of Doxa') at Mansfield

---

[42] See Ruth Micklem, 'Music and the Pastoral Ministry: A Personal View', in Leaver and Litton, *Duty and Delight*. Erik Routley's later career took him to Edinburgh, Newcastle upon Tyne, and finally to the USA, where he was Professor of Church Music, Westminster Choir College, Princeton. Among many distinctions, he was appointed the first non-Anglican member of the Council of the Royal School of Church Music. He was President of the Congregational Church of England and Wales in 1970. See *MCM* 186 (1983–4), 42–5 for George Caird's address at the Thanksgiving Service for Routley's life in Westminster Abbey, 8 Feb. 1983.

[43] As the son of Dr Norman Goodall, illustrious ecumenical statesman and Chairman of Mansfield's Board of Education, he was well integrated into the Mansfield tradition. He was Organ Scholar at Balliol 1941–2 and 1945–7.

[44] Basil Yeaxlee CBE (1883–1967) was a student at Mansfield from 1906 until 1909. See *CYB 1968–69*, 443 and *MCM* 170 (Apr. 1968), 305–6.

[45] The day-to-day administration of the Library was in the hands of Miss Dorothy Pope—'the infallible Miss Pope'.

1939–43, after a brilliant career at Cambridge.[46] When Nathaniel Micklem was asked at the end of the war by some of his former Canadian colleagues to recommend a young scholar to teach biblical studies, he recommended Caird, then minister of Highgate Congregational Church. The Canadian authorities were taken aback to discover that they had appointed a New Testament scholar to a Chair in Old Testament Studies, and sent a telegram to Mansfield: 'Can Caird teach Hebrew?' Micklem assured them that he could—'and Persian too, with three weeks' notice'. And so the scholar who was to lead Oxford's teaching of the New Testament in the 1960s and 1970s began his academic teaching career in Canada as Professor of Old Testament Language at St Stephen's College, Edmonton, Alberta.[47] From Edmonton, he moved to Montreal as first Professor of New Testament Language and Literature in the new Faculty of Divinity at McGill University (for the last four years in conjunction with the Principalship of the United Theological College, Montreal). By the time he left Canada his scholarly reputation was such that he had been awarded DD degrees by both the universities in which he had taught.[48]

It might not have seemed promotion for this well-respected New Testament scholar, professor, and theological college principal to move to the position of Senior Tutor and Lecturer at an Oxford PPH, without as yet the prospect of University lecturership, and a salary lower than he could have received elsewhere. But he and his family wanted to return to Britain, and both he and his wife Mollie[49] had a deep affection for Mansfield and aspirations for its future. He was a man who accepted the honours which eventually came his way (and they were many), who did not waste energy on bemoaning the inevitable frustrations of academic life, but who rather concentrated on the fields of study and teaching which were open to him. It was

---

[46] He gained a First Class in both parts of the Classical Tripos, with distinction in Greek and Latin verse.

[47] The work for his doctoral thesis had involved detailed study of the Septuagint and the Hebrew Scriptures.

[48] While in Canada he had published three books: *The Truth of the Gospel* (London, 1950), *The Apostolic Age* (London, 1955), and *Principalities and Powers: A Study in Pauline Theology* (Oxford, 1956).

[49] George Caird married Viola Mary ('Mollie') Newport in 1945. She was a graduate of St Hugh's College. They had met as fellow members of the Congregational Society at Mansfield, and shared a deep love of language and poetry. Mollie Caird was twice awarded the Oxford University prize for a poem on a sacred subject. Her brother J. E. Newport (Mansfield 1944–9) was President of Cheshunt College, Cambridge from 1965 until 1976.

not long before all the brightest Oxford theological students, under-graduates and ordinands, were flocking to Mansfield to hear this profound scholar who lectured so fluently and wittily; his only aide a Greek New Testament.

Unlike many previous generations of Mansfield New Testament scholars, Caird had never studied in Germany; he had an antipathy to German scholarship, especially that of Bultmann. He 'repeatedly cited the Bultmannian positions as evidence of how far biblical scholarship could go wrong and had gone wrong'.[50] 'A gospel means news about historical events, attested by reliable witnesses, and having at their centre an historical person,' once wrote Caird.[51] It was to the study of the evidence for those historical events that he dedicated his scholarship; the excitement, the commitment, and the technical equipment he had acquired for that study were what brought so many students to his lectures. His integration of academic rigour, sense of beauty, and deep faith made those lectures an experience well out of the ordinary.[52] One of his students once wrote that 'If he had ever seen St Paul approaching him in the High Street, he wouldn't have treated him with exaggerated deference, nor would he have crossed the street to avoid him. He would probably have invited him to read a paper to his Postgraduate Seminar, and would have felt no em-barrassment at taking him into the Senior Common Room for tea beforehand.'[53]

It was not long before his appointment as Grinfield Lecturer in the Septuagint 1961–5 signified the University's formal recognition of his scholarship; and before he was invited to join the New English Bible Panel responsible for the Apocrypha. Mansfield could feel a certain pride when the New English Bible (New Testament) was published in 1961, for the Chairman of the New Testament panel (and Director of the whole project) was C. H. Dodd, former student and College Professor. Dodd was made a Companion of Honour in 1961 for his contribution.[54]

---

[50] James Barr, 'George Caird', *Proceedings of the British Academy*, 71 (1985; Oxford, 1986), 493–521.

[51] *Our Dialogue with Rome* (Oxford, 1967), 49.

[52] He brought these gifts also to the writing of hymns, three of which are included in *Rejoice and Sing* (Oxford, 1991).

[53] Quoted in Barr, 'George Caird', 509.

[54] 'he must have been one of the very few men entitled to wear his initials behind as well as in front of his name'; so wrote George Caird in his memoir of Dodd in *Proceedings of the British Academy*, 60 (1974), 508.

Donald Sykes, who also joined the Mansfield teaching staff in 1959, was a younger scholar who was just beginning his teaching career. A Classics graduate from St Andrews, and the son of a Congregational minister in Scotland, he decided soon after entering Mansfield in 1955 that he would make his career in teaching theology rather than in the pastoral ministry, and so was never ordained. After achieving the College's first 'First' as a PPH, he took a Diploma in Education in Glasgow and taught at Glasgow High School for a year before being invited back to Mansfield to teach church history in 1959. His special field was and remains patristics; he is as much at home in the fourth as in the twentieth century.

Until 1960, the College had no non-theological members of staff, though the Principal had tried to follow up the original suggestion of Sir Douglas Veale to offer Common Room membership to a few University lecturers without Fellowships. Undergraduates were sent out to tutors in other colleges, or sometimes to freelance tutors, of whom Oxford had a good supply. By 1960 there was a sufficient number of students reading English to warrant the appointment of two part-time tutors in English: Malcolm Parkes and Stephen Wall.[55] These appointments were made directly by the Principal, and then reported to the Council afterwards; it was to be some time before there was an established procedure for new appointments. The two new tutors organized a weekly discussion society called 'The Levellers', which attracted lively debate.

As life generally became more democratic, the 'College servants' played a more noticeable part in collegiate life. One of the most devoted, as well as one of the most acute critics of sermons, was Frank Macaulay Murray, who died in John Marsh's first term, aged 82, after serving the College for twenty-nine years. He had acted as gardener, verger, scout, and in any other required capacity, a friend and witty observer of everyone, an assiduous and entertaining correspondent to students and former students. When he rang the bell for morning prayers, he always ended with three single notes—'to let them at Manchester College down the road know that we believe in the Trinity'. When his work at Mansfield was over for the day, he would walk, wearing his bowler hat (it was said that he had worn out thirty-three bowler hats), to his other job as 'theologian in

---

[55] Both taught in other colleges as well, and both were eventually elected Fellows of Keble College.

Ordinary to the Lamb and Flag, and more recently to the King's Arms', as the Principal put it in a memorial address. As Murray was taken from the scene, so Walter (Wally) Buckingham, once scout to William Beveridge at University College) moved into a central position in the College as Head Scout, then Steward, and general supporter to the Principal. He and his family had first met John Marsh twenty-five years earlier when Marsh was student assistant at Marston Congregational Church, and he was very ready to move from Queen's at Marsh's invitation. With Harry King the gardener, and the rest of the scouts, an efficient and friendly team was formed.[56]

Life in the Junior Common Room was changing, especially after the admission of non-theological undergraduates and the increase in numbers. The first non-ministerial student had been admitted to read geography in 1956.[57] At first the student community perceived itself and was perceived by others as a group of ordinands with a few non-theologians at the periphery.[58] But this gradually changed; between 1953 and 1958 the numbers of students doubled, with theologians reduced to about half the JCR members (though most of the early non-theological students still came from Congregational backgrounds). This led to much debate; eventually, a new JCR constitution, formally adopted in October 1962, opened all JCR offices to non-theologians; in the event of the JCR President being a non-theologian, the ordinands would appoint their own representative to deal with any problems relating specifically to that group.

With larger numbers, Mansfield sport acquired a more significant profile. In any case, Mansfield men could no longer play with and for St Catherine's as many had done in earlier decades. In 1956 the College rented the last available sports ground in the University Parks for football and hockey. The 1956–7 season was described by the Principal as 'something of an *annus mirabilis*' in sport, with a half-blue for ice hockey, and distinguished performances in running, rowing, and cricket. For lighter diversion, there was the college punt (*Sarah Glover*), and the croquet set and billiards table given by Nathaniel

---

[56] Walter Buckingham and his family lived in the Lodge ('Buckingham Palace') for a time, then the Kings moved there until it was demolished. The Kings returned to live in the new Lodge until Harry King's retirement.

[57] David Allan was the son of a minister, and had an impeccable Congregational background.

[58] Reflected perhaps in the reference to 'guilt-edged [*sic*] securities' in the JCR Minutes, 21 Jan. 1960.

Micklem. In 1962 an Amalgamated Club Fund for Sports was formed, to cover all College sporting activities.

Mansfield students had normally not been allowed to marry during their course, though the occasional mature student had arrived already married. There was now pressure from the ordinands to be allowed to marry before the end of their three years. In April 1959 the Board of Education agreed that in 'special cases' the ordinands were to be allowed to marry during the long vacation before the last year of their course. The JCR Notes in the next issue of the *College Magazine* referred to 'a current rush of engagements'; 'the appellation "Romancefield", given by a perceptive nine year old girl, is fully merited.'[59] A regular College Dance replaced 'Terpsichore'—'a term which had been coined to veil the fact that the College held a dance'.[60]

The position of the occasional woman student was rather less happy after Mansfield became a PPH; as a part of the University, which as yet had no coeducational colleges, Mansfield had to observe University practice. Helen Wade, therefore, a student 1955–8, officially had fewer privileges than Constance Todd had enjoyed in 1913. She was not formally a member of the JCR, and was only allowed to use the Common Room until lunch-time, except with the President's special permission.

It was essential for the College's survival in the long term that more accommodation for both graduates and undergraduates be provided. At a meeting on 15 June 1956 the Council agreed to ask the architect Thomas Rayson to draw up plans for a new building on the south side of the College site. A few days later, the Principal again raised with the Registrar the possibility of Mansfield's receiving money from the University Grants Committee for new building. In his reply the Registrar advised him not to give up hope, 'though the omens for you are a little less propitious than they were when we talked about your desire to expand'.[61] He invited the Principal to prepare a detailed formal application for submission to the University Grants Committee (UGC), adding that the University would offer its support.[62] After consultation with the College Council and again with

---

[59] *MCM* 155 (July 1959), 446.
[60] JCR Minute Book 1957–71, entry for 23 Jan. 1963.
[61] Letter from Sir Douglas Veale to John Marsh, 6 July 1956, File MANF-1, Oxford University Offices.
[62] Sir Douglas Veale's memo, 14 Sept. 1956, File MANF-1, Oxford University Offices.

the Registrar, this document was finally presented in August 1957; it laid out plans for seventy-six student rooms, a lecture hall, common room, tower, Fellow's house, and kitchen extension.

The response from the UGC indicated that they wished to know how Mansfield's scheme fitted in with general University policy. The University's quinquennial grant from the UGC for 1959–64 would at that time have been under consideration. After further discussion with the Registrar, John Marsh then prepared a revised application; this was put before Hebdomadal Council on 1 November 1957, in order that Mansfield's claim might be considered in any general University application to the UGC. Hebdomadal Council referred the matter to its Committee on Financial Questions; acting on that body's advice, it resolved on 18 November that for the present no assistance could be offered to Mansfield.[63] The University's priority for new residential accommodation was St Catherine's, to be changed from Society into College in 1961, whose elegant new building on Holywell Great Meadow was now being planned.

John Marsh did not yet quite lose hope. In June 1958, seven months later, the Council heard from the Principal that

> the present position was that the University was now inviting applications from all Colleges for such assistance, that no such assistance would be available before 1960, and that it was dependent, first, on the UGC being willing (as now seemed possible) to make grants of such a kind, and second, on the success with which Mansfield could compete with other Colleges for assistance out of the total sum thus available to the University.[64]

But four months later, the Principal reported that he had been told that no UGC help could be made available before 1965.[65] This rejection led, rightly or wrongly, to a feeling of betrayal within the College community, who believed that Mansfield's undoubted contribution and potential had been ignored in discussions about the University's future shape.

[63] The correspondence relating to this issue is preserved in File MANF-1 in the Oxford University Offices.

[64] Minute Book of the Mansfield College Council and Board of Education 1953–71, entry for 23 June 1958, MCA.

[65] Mansfield Council Minutes, 10 Oct. 1958. A University Committee on a Possible Approach to the UGC for Financial Help for College Accommodation had suggested a scheme which excluded PPHs (Memo, 7 June 1963, in File MAN-F1, University Offices). In the event Hebdomadal Council did not proceed with the idea.

The continued life of the College now hung in the balance, though most members of the College were unaware of this. When the Council met on 17 April 1959 a decision was taken to build accommodation for a further thirty or forty students, a more modest scheme than originally envisaged, but even so a bold venture without the funds. At the following meeting on 22 June, the Council committed itself to an Appeal for £150,000—half of this was to finance the new building, and the other half was to increase the tutorial endowment fund. 'It is either this or the extinction of Mansfield', the Principal told the subscribers in June 1959.[66]

Two weeks later, on 6 July (during the Royal Agricultural Show at Kidlington), a quaint little ceremony was performed alongside the proposed site of Mansfield's new building. The Princess Royal came to plant a black mulberry tree in the Principal's garden, the site of 'Pinfold's Pasture', where the first Royal Show had been held 120 years earlier. Her spade now hangs in the Library, and the tree still flourishes in the Principal's garden.

The College Appeal was formally launched at a dinner in the House of Lords on 25 April 1960, presided over by Lord Macdonald,[67] at which Pastor William Schaeffer, who represented the Lutheran World Federation in Britain, presented a cheque for £8,000 on behalf of the Lutheran World Federation. When the Fund stood at £16,600 in the following summer, the Principal told the subscribers at their annual meeting that the College's situation reminded him of walking with the Congregational Society in the Lakes: 'To slip to right or to left was to fall to certain injury and possible death. So is the College poised now, as she walks this forward and upward path into the future. . . . it seems important that we should not look down or behind, but keep our eyes on what lies ahead.'[68] The Appeal progressed slowly, with contributions from former students, from Congregational churches, from friends of the College, and from charitable trusts. The only really large donation came from the Lutherans, who added a further £13,700 to their initial donation.

The previous day the Council had accepted the tender of Knowles and Sons to build the new block, and work began immediately. On

---

[66] *Mansfield College Calendar 1958–59*, 16.

[67] Gordon Macdonald, Baron Macdonald of Gwaenysgor (1888–1966), MP for Ince Division 1929–42, Governor of Newfoundland 1946–9, Paymaster-General 1949–51. See *Who Was Who 1961–70*.

[68] *Mansfield College Calendar 1959–60*, 13.

17 December (1960) the foundation stone was laid by Howard S. Stanley, Secretary of the Congregational Union, and Sir Oliver Franks.[69] Franks represented not only the University (he was a former Provost of the Queen's College) and the academic work of the College (both in his own right,[70] and as the son of R. S. Franks), but also the link with the USA (to which he was British Ambassador 1948–52). As the new building rose, part of the old had to go: 'I have seen the old Lodge demolished—with a very real pang of the heart, for it was so full of character in its siting and design,' the Principal wrote in the *Magazine*.[71]

The new structure[72] was mainly of Guiting stone, with Clipsham stone for the lintels and doorway. It lay along the southern side of what became almost a quadrangle, with another wing to the south, facing Mansfield Road, which at first provided two tutors' houses. By the time it was finished, the College Appeal had raised just over £50,000, only a third of the target figure, insufficient even to pay the builder. The new building would generate more income, not only through student fees but increasingly through conference income. But it was several years before the Appeal reached its target (in 1968), and before the College accounts broke even.

Almost 1,000 visitors assembled at the formal opening (pl. 13) on 25 June 1962 (reminiscent of the opening ceremony in 1889). They included not only the Vice-Chancellor, many heads of houses, and most of the Theology Faculty, together with representatives of the Congregational churches which had supported the Appeal, but also the Lord-Lieutenant of the county, the sheriffs, the mayor and other city officers, for the guest of honour was the Queen Mother. She arrived by car from Windsor, and before leaving by helicopter one and a half hours later, she had formally opened the new building and unveiled a plaque, made a charming speech, and met many of the guests. After the event, the Principal Emeritus (Nathaniel Micklem) wrote to John Marsh that he 'had never thought to see a Royal Ensign flying from the flagstaff of Mansfield College'. The Principal's speech to the Queen Mother was confident: Mansfield had, he said, sent

---

[69] Later Lord Franks.

[70] He was Fellow in Philosophy at the Queen's College 1927–37, and Professor of Moral Philosophy at the University of Glasgow 1937–45.

[71] *MCM* 158 (Jan. 1961), 63.

[72] It was not formally named until 1993, when most appropriately it became the John Marsh Building.

13. Opening of the new building 1962: the Queen Mother on the left, with the Principal, John Marsh, delivering his speech

many to Chairs and Lectureships in Theology, to movements of Christian social thought and action, as well as hundreds of men (and a few women) to the pastoral ministry, and had provided leaders of missionary societies and of ecumenical bodies all over the world. Now the College was to admit more non-theologians, and so try to bridge 'the immense gap between the Church and a large body of the nation', which was 'one of the great tragedies of our time'. The weather matched the happy atmosphere. But an underlying financial anxiety meant the prevailing feeling was hope rather than optimism.

The Caird family and Donald and Marta Sykes[73] now moved into the two new houses. These two families contributed much to the life and atmosphere of the College over the succeeding years. For Mollie Caird, moving into the new house before the builders had finished clearing the gardens meant hanging her washing on 'royalist ramparts':

> I hang my washing on King Charles' bank,
> And yet I often wonder what he'd think
> To see a non-conformist of low rank
> On such an errand from her kitchen sink.[74]

The new stage in the College's history which was now inaugurated owed more to John Marsh than to anyone else—to his vision, his ability, and his energy. But there was to be no lapsing into comfortable routine. During the 1960s educational institutions were moving into an era in which all members, whether staff or pupils, were asking for a share in decision-making, and this was not an easy transition for those holding positions of authority. A hint of what was to come can be noted in the report of the President of the JCR[75] in the *Magazine* for January 1963:

We have arrived at a watering-place rather than an immediate destination, and now refreshed we return to our senses and we must ask, not whether we are still on the right road, but which road we are now going to take. This is not the JCR's decision, but we are obliged to draw attention to it. So often we feel decisions are being

---

[73] Donald Sykes married Marta Whitehouse, a teacher, daughter of his father's church organist in Glasgow in 1962.

[74] For the rest of the poem see *MCM* 195 (1992–3), 27.

[75] John Greenland, the first non-theologian to be elected JCR President.

compromised; so often we feel that fundamental questions of policy are being put off for their being difficult to resolve. We sincerely hope that during the remainder of the year the right direction will be found.[76]

[76] *MCM* 162 (Jan. 1963), 149.

XIII

1962–1970: An Ordinary Oxford College?

DURING the 1960s Mansfield experienced greater changes than at any time in its previous history in Oxford. There was more than one view within the College community about its future character and the road it should now take. Was it to continue as essentially a theological college, with an agreed complement of students reading other subjects? Or was it to become a college of the University offering a diversity of disciplines much like any other? How was it to find its place in the modern Oxford in which the University itself, and therefore University policy, was to be as powerful as the Colleges?[1]

The decade of the 1960s was a significant one for higher education in Britain. The Robbins Report, recommending a planned expansion of universities and colleges to twice the existing number of students, as well as a coherent national policy for higher education, was published in 1963. Oxford responded to this by appointing its own Commission under Lord Franks. Before the end of the decade, the University had undergone an extensive process of reappraisal and reform. Pressure came from 'below' too; university students all over Europe and North America were challenging the values and hierarchical structures of society in general and universities in particular. In 1970 the age of majority in Britain was reduced to 18, which meant that legally a university became a community of equals. Equality of another kind was being vigorously asserted: feminism, and feminist scholarship, challenged social and academic assumptions in ways that could no longer be ignored.

A new wind was blowing through the churches. The Second Vatican Council opened on 11 October 1962, the first of four annual, epoch-making sessions, to which non-Catholic observers were invited (one of whom was George Caird). Before the Council ended, the

---

[1] Until the 20th cent. the colleges were collectively more important than the University. The new situation had the potential to be more helpful to an institution with few endowments like Mansfield.

British Faith and Order Conference meeting at Nottingham in 1964 had called for a united church in Britain by 1980. The Anglican–Methodist negotiations and the Presbyterian–Congregational discussions then under way gave some substance to that hope. However, within the universities, the Student Christian Movement had almost disintegrated, and denominational societies gained strength.

It was not altogether surprising that John Marsh was taken ill within a few months of the opening of the new building in 1962. Although he lived by Selbie's dictum that 'hard work never killed anybody', the Principalship of Mansfield had brought him stress and anxiety as well as hard work. His doctors diagnosed 'a particularly nasty virus' and advised him to take several weeks' rest in the autumn; he and his wife retreated to Cumberland for the term and left George Caird in charge of College administration.

When he returned, it was to another round of seemingly ceaseless activity. His work for the broadcasting and television authorities—as a member of the BBC's Central Religious Advisory Committee and as religious adviser to the Independent Television Authority—was recognized in the New Year's Honours List for 1964 with the award of the CBE. He had been elected Chairman of the Congregational Union of England and Wales for 1963–4; and his year of office took him all over the country. In addition he found time during this decade to write a substantial commentary on *The Gospel of St John* (London, 1968) for the Pelican Gospel Commentaries series, and to act as one of the General Editors of the SCM Torch Bible Commentaries.[2] The strain of doing all this while trying to retain control of all the details of administration within the College contributed to the difficult relations which developed between him and the Bursar, who had borne the burden of trying to balance the books against a diminishing income. The lack of clearly defined areas of responsibility was a further problem. David Goodall left early in 1964 and moved to Sunderland as Registrar of its Technical College. During his seven years as Bursar he had made a significant creative contribution to the planning of the expansion of the College. His successor was James Whalley, the first non-ordained Bursar, an Oxford graduate with long experience in the Nigerian Civil Service.

This appointment, however, left both the position of organist

---

[2] He had written the commentary on *Amos and Micah* (London, 1959, reissued 1965) himself.

and the Chaplaincy to Congregational students vacant. Acting on a sudden inspiration, and without any formality, John Marsh appointed Charles Brock as part-time Chaplain to the Congregational Society and tutor in ethics. It was an appointment with more significance than anyone could have realized at the time. Charles Brock had first come to Mansfield as a visiting student at the College during the academic year 1962–3, then spent the succeeding months as student pastor at Wheatley Congregational Church, near Oxford, and teaching a few classes in ethics. An American Presbyterian, he first graduated in industrial management at Carnegie-Mellon University, and worked for a short period in industry. Then he went on to read Theology at Harvard Divinity School, where Paul Tillich and Reinhold Niebuhr were among his teachers. It was not until ten years after he was first appointed that he was made Fellow and College Chaplain, and not until 1978 that he was given overall responsibility for ministerial training. Throughout his time at Mansfield, he has continued as minister at Wheatley, believing that those responsible for ordination training should also be actively involved in pastoral work.

As Chaplain to Congregational, later United Reformed, students, he has had considerable influence over future leaders of the denomination, with his easy relationship with young people and his fertile, questing mind; during the years of student unrest, he effectively challenged many students to distinguish among the many objects of protest those which were legitimate. Within the College he has been a popular figure in the SCR, holding a fine balance between his gastronomic and liturgical interests. In his relations with the Congregational, then United Reformed, Church he has done much to retain and increase goodwill for the College.

With this appointment came also a new College organist. David Goodall's immediate successor was an undergraduate reading English, Paul Crossley,[3] who has subsequently followed a distinguished career as a concert pianist. When he went down in 1966, Charles's wife Carolyn, a graduate of both Oberlin Conservatory of Music, Ohio and New England Conservatory of Music in Boston, Massachusetts, was appointed organist. She already had experience as organist and choir director in large churches in the United States, and now found herself in a very different world as the first woman organist in a predominantly male Oxford college. Since that time she has

[3] In 1993 he was awarded the CBE for services to music.

been responsible for Chapel music at all formal services and termly musical performances (as well as being musical director of other Oxford choirs). She has managed consistently to evoke a high standard of performance from singers of very mixed ability—some of near professional standard, others with more enthusiasm than musical skill. Her playing of organ voluntaries is such that Chapel congregations do not talk or stir until the final note is played after the end of a service.

In the same year as Charles Brock's appointment, Stephen Mayor, a Congregational minister from Lancashire, was appointed Leverhulme Research Fellow in Ecumenical Theological History for five years—the result of John Marsh's application for a special grant from the Leverhulme Foundation. His main research interest was church relations in Britain from 1850, with particular reference to the ministry and its place in ecumenical discussion, which led in time to a number of articles, including some on the ministry of women. His main publication during these years was a version of his doctoral thesis, *The Churches and the Labour Movement* (London, 1967).

The College relied a great deal on Fellows of other colleges and CUF Lecturers, who agreed to accept responsibility for Mansfield undergraduates reading subjects other than theology.[4] History teaching was in the hands of Dr C. K. Francis Brown, a retired headmaster and church historian who had offered his services to the College in 1962; after five years as tutor, he was appointed Honorary Senior Research Fellow.[5]

One of the most significant appointments, in terms of the College's future, was that of John Creaser as the first full-time Fellow[6] in English in 1966; 'having him around was a breath of fresh air', wrote one of his colleagues in the SCR.[7] He had come to the College as an undergraduate in 1961, when the JCR was still dominated by theologians, after several years in journalism; three years later he had gained

---

[4] In 1964, for example, as well as Malcolm Parkes (English) and Stephen Wall (English), they included D. R. McLintock (Modern Languages), A. R. Peacocke (Chemistry), and D. C. M. Yardley (Law). Three years later Bruce Harbert was appointed English Lecturer. Of these, Arthur Peacocke stayed longest (until 1973, when he moved to Cambridge as newly ordained Dean of Clare College) and made a significant contribution to the SCR through his experience of college administration.

[5] Later he founded University Hall, Buckland. His books included *The Church's Part in Education* (London, 1942) and *A History of the English Clergy* (London, 1953).

[6] There was still a certain ambiguity about the titles of Mansfield tutors which was not resolved until 1970.

[7] Stephen Mayor in a letter to the author in May 1993.

the College's first non-theological First (a congratulatory one), and continued as a postgraduate student. He established a fine reputation as an English tutor, and many of his pupils achieved an outstanding record in Final Examinations. His publications have primarily been on the poetry and drama of the Renaissance period, where he has particular interests in the writings of John Milton and Ben Jonson. While principally a literary critic, he has edited texts by Jonson and other dramatists, and also written on iconography and aspects of editorial and literary theory. While at Mansfield he joined the Council of the Malone Society—a famous learned society which exists to publish rare texts of early English plays and related documents—and since 1990 he has been its Executive Secretary. He is also a Co-director of the Index of English Literary Manuscripts, which is producing an authoritative, multi-volume survey of the manuscripts of major English writers over several centuries.

Before the end of the decade, he was joined by two further full-time tutors, Michael Mahony (History, a graduate of the College) and Anthony Ogus (Law, an Oxford graduate who had been teaching at the University of Leicester). Michael Mahony's research field was in mid-seventeenth-century English history.[8] Anthony Ogus was the first academic member of staff to be appointed after public advertisement of the post; as one who had previously had no connection with Mansfield, he brought a useful critical outlook.[9]

The Senior Common Room was changing its character. In the first place, it was becoming larger, with several part-time tutors as well as the gradual addition of non-theological full-time tutors. Most of these tutors were familiar with the common Oxford collegiate system of governing bodies composed entirely of Fellows, who elected their own college head. The old style of administration at Mansfield, suitable for a small theological institution, was no longer appropriate for a larger college with several disciplines, and, in common with

---

[8] Michael Mahony's main interests included the politics of the English Civil War and Interregnum, the interrelationship of government and society in the 16th and 17th cents., and the insights into early modern social and political change offered by contemporary literature. His major articles include 'Presbyterianism in the City of London 1645–1647', *Historical Journal*, 22/1 (1979) and 'The Savile Affair and the Politics of the Long Parliament', *Parliamentary History*, 7/2 (1988).

[9] While at Mansfield Anthony Ogus specialized in the teaching of comparative law, but his main research areas were tort law and social welfare law. In 1973 he published *The Law of Damages* (London), and then began work on social security law; with Eric Berendt, he published *The Law of Social Security* (London) in 1978.

other contemporary educational institutions, there was pressure from both senior and junior members for more participation in decision-making. Regular SCR meetings, properly minuted, began in the early 1960s. Pressure for change and development in the College began to build up within the SCR, whose relations with the Council, the official decision-making body of the College, were still not clearly defined.

The unresolved question was the future pattern of the College's development. When the Franks Commission was appointed by Congregation in March 1964, John Marsh hoped it would be able to offer advice. Its terms of reference were: 'To inquire into and report upon the part which Oxford plays now and should play in the future in the system of higher education in the United Kingdom, having regard to its position as both a national and an international University.' Its Chairman, Lord Franks (then Provost of Worcester College), was a former Spring Hill Trustee, son of one of the College's most distinguished old students;[10] many hopes were pinned on his advice. Now the opportunity to integrate Mansfield into University development policy seemed to have arrived. Public hearings were to be held twice weekly in the Examination Schools to receive oral evidence, and written evidence was also invited from the heads of all colleges and PPHs, partly in answer to questionnaires, partly in a form chosen by the college or PPH.

Mansfield, or more precisely the Principal of Mansfield with the advice of the College Council, made two written submissions to the Commission, one in response to questions relating to teaching and research, the other to questions relating to the organization of the University.[11] Mansfield's submission was much longer than that of any other PPH, reflecting the fact that it was experiencing a period of transition; it was on the nature of the goal of that process of transition that the College sought 'the fullest advice from the University':

> As is indicated in the body of the replies to the Commission's questions, the college is at the moment a mixed society of almost equal numbers of graduates and undergraduates. In contemplating further developments it will be true to say the future is, in spite

---

[10] R. S. Franks had died two months before the appointment of the Commission, on 19 Jan. 1964, aged 92.

[11] These are available in *Franks Commission: Written Evidence*, part vii, 167–73 and part xiii, 83–6 (Oxford, 1965).

of this, completely open. It would not be impossible to turn the college into a wholly graduate society in a relatively short time. It would be equally possible to increase the numbers of undergraduates considerably, if the college were to curtail the numbers of postgraduate theological students. It would be equally possible, and the college's own disposition is towards this, to continue to foster a society in which undergraduates and graduates are present in approximately equal numbers.

In view of the discussions that are being undertaken about mixed societies in the University, it is worth saying that Mansfield has envisaged already the desirability of erecting a block of buildings for married graduate students on the site. This has let the college reflect that it would be possible also for it to develop an undergraduate society in which there were equal numbers of men and women. This would involve additional buildings, and without aid the college cannot, of course, guarantee when this could be undertaken, but the possibility of such developments ought to be kept in mind in any attempt to formulate a long term policy for the college. In general then, the college offers its comments on the questionnaire in the hope that the Commission will see the problems of the college against the needs and policies of the University, and offer some guidance to the Governing Body, in order that it may act responsibly to the University and to the best interests of the University as well as the college.[12]

In addition, the Principals of PPHs were invited to give oral evidence before the Commission on 4 February 1965, in answer to specific questions from the Commissioners.[13]

Throughout the evidence, Mansfield repeated its desire to maintain and develop its association with the University. Before the Commission's report was published, John Marsh told the Council that Mansfield might have to consider seeking the status of a full college, though he referred to the difficulties that would be presented by the College constitution.[14] It was frustrating to the College to find that there was no mention of PPHs when the Commission's report was published in March 1966, in spite of the fact that the Commission

---

[12] *Franks Commission: Written Evidence*, part vii, 168.

[13] See *Franks Commission: Oral Evidence*, O.55, 1–19.

[14] Minute Book of the Mansfield College Council and Board of Education 1953–71, entry for 19 June 1965, MCA.

had consulted Hebdomadal Council about University policy towards PPHs (Mansfield and Regent's Park in particular). During that process of consultation, it had been made clear that no objection would be made to the expansion of either college, nor to an increase in the number of graduates and a reduction in the number of undergraduates, provided that any expansion in terms of building was at the colleges' own expense.[15]

After the disappointment over the Franks Report, the Council asked the Principal to discuss with the SCR 'the issues that were raised in our minds by the questions put by the Franks Commission, and report back with a view to formulating Mansfield's future on the basis of discussions with the University'.[16] The resulting SCR memo was presented to Council on 7 October 1966. Their first proposal was that 'the College should seek to become itself an incorporate legal entity'. This would enable it to relate more effectively both to the University (which was in process of defining its structure and the relationships within it more precisely) and to the Congregational denomination (which had just been transformed from the federal Congregational Union into the covenanting Congregational Church); in addition, it would enable the College to own property. Even more significantly, it was a necessary step towards full collegiate status. The second, practical proposal was that further student accommodation, financed by a capital loan, should be built in order to expand by another thirty to forty students, thus providing the means to appoint three more tutors, and so widening the range of teaching within the College. In response, the Council authorized the Principal and academic staff to investigate with both the Vice-Chancellor and Lord Franks the possibility of becoming a full college of the University; and to consult the architect about a further new building.[17]

The following month the Principal and Bursar met the Vice-Chancellor (Kenneth Turpin) and the Registrar (Sir Folliott Sandford, who had succeeded Sir Douglas Veale in 1958), in order to raise the question of incorporation (which would need the University's approval). The response from the University side was discouraging,[18]

---

[15] *Oxford University Hebdomadal Council Papers*, 252: 177–89, 8 Oct. 1965.

[16] *Mansfield College Annual Report 1965–66*, 14.

[17] Minute Book of the Mansfield College Council and Board of Education 1953–72, entry for 7 Oct. 1966, MCA.

[18] Memo, 21 Nov. 1966, File MANF-1, University Offices. The University was anxious to keep a strict control over any increase in undergraduate numbers.

and the Principal had to report to the next meeting of Council that 'there was no present possibility of the College changing its status in the University'.

For the SCR particularly, this was a great blow, since Mansfield's status and consequent absence from the scholarship groups of the admissions system meant that it could not attract the better candidates by offering scholarships;[19] in many cases it had to rely on offering places to candidates who had been turned down by other colleges (some of whom went on to achieve 'Firsts'). The University Handbook listed colleges in alphabetical order, then added PPHs at the end; this was not a particular disadvantage to PPHs offering specific ordination training, but for those who offered a wider range of courses, it proved a disadvantage in attracting good candidates, for applicants were asked to indicate their choice of colleges, and the Handbook was one of their major sources of information.

While Mansfield's relations with the University were under discussion, the College also had to manage a relationship with a denomination which was undergoing many changes. The Congregational Union (Congregational Church after 1966) was suffering a further decline in numbers, a decline common to almost all churches in the 1960s; during that decade alone, the number of members of Congregational churches fell by 20 per cent.[20] An inevitable consequence was a decline in the number of ordinands. A Commission of Theological Colleges had been charged with reducing the number of Congregational colleges to four. Negotiations between Mansfield and Cheshunt had failed in the 1950s; Cheshunt had now amalgamated with Westminster College in Cambridge. In 1965 the Commission suggested a union with Western College, Bristol, on the Mansfield site. This led to a series of discussions between representatives of the two colleges, but these too came to nothing.[21]

A greater change was likely to result from the positive negotiations

---

[19] If a college which was part of a group offered a scholarship to a candidate who had put another college as his or her first choice, the candidate was obliged to accept the scholarship. By this means the ablest candidates were shared among the colleges of each group. Mansfield's request to be assigned to a scholarship group was turned down in Feb. 1966 by a meeting of college representatives. File MANF-1, University Offices.

[20] The figures were 211,329 in 1960, 166,683 in 1970. See *CYB 1961*, 312 and *CYB 1971–72*, 328.

[21] Western College was closed in 1970 and merged with Northern College in Manchester.

now taking place between the Presbyterians and the Congregationalists in England and Wales. This impending union owed a great deal
to the influence of Mansfield theologians. John Marsh, 'never satisfied
with the theological definitions he had himself propounded at the
last meeting',[22] was closely involved as co-chairman of the 'Joint
Conversations Committee'. It was he who introduced 'A Statement
of Convictions on which a United Church, Both Catholic and Reformed, Might be Built' to the Congregational Union Assembly in
May 1965, and who two years later presented 'A Proposed Basis of
Union' between the two churches, a prelude to the formation of the
new United Reformed Church in 1972. In the intervening year, 1966,
most of the churches of the Congregational Union had covenanted
together as the Congregational Church, an action understood as a
necessary step towards union with the Presbyterian Church of England. A 'Declaration of Faith'[23] adopted in 1967, which found general
acceptance but was not intended as a binding document, revealed
further the influence of Mansfield, and of Nathaniel Micklem in
particular, for most members of the committee which formulated it
over a period of several years were former students of Micklem at
Mansfield.[24] John Huxtable, the Secretary of the Congregational Union
and then Minister-Secretary of the Congregational Church, who had
the prime responsibility for steering through all these changes, was
a Mansfield man. The formation of the United Reformed Church
underlined the fact that Mansfield now represented more fully 'the
traditions of the Reformation' (George Caird's words; Mansfield has
subsequently defined its purpose as representing 'the traditions of
the Continental Reformation and English Dissent').

John Marsh was looking to a still wider horizon within the ecumenical sphere. In 1964 the Nottingham Faith and Order Conference had expressed the hope that an ecumenical theological college
would be established in Britain. Three years later, when John Marsh
received a letter from David Anderson, Principal of Wycliffe Hall,

---

[22] A. Macarthur, 'The Background to the Formation of the United Reformed Church
(Presbyterian and Congregational) in England and Wales in 1972', *JURCHS* 4/1 (Oct.
1987), 15.

[23] Congregational Church in England and Wales, *A Declaration of Faith* (London,
1967). The provisional draft was published in 1964.

[24] In 1970 twelve of Nathaniel Micklem's former pupils produced a series of essays
in honour of his eightieth birthday entitled *Christian Confidence: Essays on 'A Declaration
of Faith of the Congregational Church in England and Wales'* (London, 1970).

one of the four Anglican theological colleges in Oxford,[25] suggesting some collaboration with Mansfield on a federal basis, he responded warmly and eagerly.[26] A month later, the Council also responded 'with extreme interest' and encouraged the Principal to explore the matter thoroughly. As the matter was regarded as 'extremely confidential', the SCR was not yet informed. Had they been so at this stage, it is almost certain that the majority of the tutors would have opposed the scheme, for they were looking towards a multi-disciplinary college in which ministerial training would play an important, but not a dominating, role.

John Marsh had long hoped for an ecumenical venture such as was now being proposed, for it was entirely consonant with Mansfield's theological tradition and original aims. The Principal of Wycliffe Hall, David Anderson, had had experience of a successful joint Anglican–Methodist college in Nigeria. Both wanted the idea to become a reality. For almost two years, Mansfield–Wycliffe College seemed a realizable goal. Wycliffe Hall's building would be sold in order to finance new buildings on the Mansfield site; an amalgamated staff would be able to offer more specialized teaching; the merged institution would assume Mansfield's existing role as a PPH,[27] and would continue to take both graduates and undergraduates studying non-theological subjects; and separate teaching to satisfy the requirements of the two churches whose ordinands were being trained would be included in the academic programme. The two Principals hoped that in a climate in which theology was so much questioned, 'The emergence of a strong inter-confessional theological college would be a factor of considerable weight in keeping the claims of theology in proportionate consideration of the whole University.'[28] In July 1968 a formal meeting was held between the representatives of the two colleges and the Vice-Chancellor and other representatives

---

[25] The others were Ripon Hall, Cuddesdon College, and St Stephen's House. Wycliffe Hall was founded in 1877 at the instigation of a committee of Evangelical clergy and laity, which was also responsible for the foundation of Ridley Hall, Cambridge in 1881. Under a Deed of Trust for 'Theological Halls at Oxford and Cambridge', four Trustees were responsible for both Halls and served on both Councils. See F. W. B. Bullock, *The History of Ridley Hall, Cambridge*, 2 vols. (Cambridge, 1941, 1953).

[26] The dates of the two letters were 6 Mar. and 8 Mar. 1967.

[27] Wycliffe Hall is an independent institution.

[28] Memo from John Marsh and David Anderson to the governing bodies of both Colleges, Feb. 1968, Wycliffe Hall–Mansfield College Correspondence, MCA.

of the University, at which it was agreed to put before Hebdomadal Council a proposal that the planned merged college could retain the status of a PPH and increase its total number of students.[29]

A complicating factor now appeared. An Anglican working party on ordination training was attempting to 'rationalize' the provision of theological colleges. The Church of England too was suffering a decline in the number of ordinands in training. In 1968 the working party recommended an amalgamation of Wycliffe Hall with Ridley Hall, Cambridge;[30] undeterred, the representatives of Wycliffe Hall still chose to press ahead with the Mansfield negotiations, and joint meetings between representatives of the two colleges continued. On 18 October 1968 one of these meetings sent to the Council of each college a resolution, 'That the Councils of Wycliffe Hall and Mansfield shall take all the steps necessary to create a joint college on the Mansfield site with the intention that the union be achieved and the new college begin by Michaelmas 1970.' This resolution was accepted unanimously by the Mansfield College Council.

Sensing the urgency of reaching a decision before other contrary pressures became too strong, John Marsh wrote a letter to the members of the Wycliffe Hall Council on Christmas Day (1968), appealing to them not to lose this unique opportunity to achieve

> for the first time, at any rate in Britain, a piece of genuinely ecumenical theological education. To have come within sight of this, and then to abandon it, at any rate before much more had been done to overcome the many real difficulties would, I believe, deprive the churches of Britain—and even of countries further away—of a very important factor for ecumenical growth.[31]

His hope that this appeal would influence the decision the Wycliffe Hall Council was to take in January was not realized. It was too late. On closer investigation, and after taking legal advice, the Wycliffe Hall authorities had discovered that according to their Trust Deed

---

[29] *Oxford University Hebdomadal Council Papers*, 260: 1047–52, 29 July 1968.

[30] *Theological Colleges for Tomorrow: Being the Report of a Working Party Appointed by the Archbishops of Canterbury and York to Consider the Problems of the Theological Colleges of the Church of England* (London, 1968), 76. The Report did favour ecumenical cooperation in ordination training, including the idea of a new ecumenical college.

[31] Minute Book of the Mansfield College Council and Board of Education 1953–71, entry for 17 Jan. 1969, MCA. In 1970 Queen's College, Birmingham became England's first ecumenical theological college.

(through which they were linked with Ridley Hall; see above), the proposed merger required the consent of a majority of the Council of Ridley Hall as well as of their own, at two votes taken at a year's distance from each other. At their January meeting, the Wycliffe Hall Council decided, with much regret, not to proceed any further with the negotiations.

It was a great disappointment to both Principals.[32] John Marsh was already 64, on the eve of retirement; had the merger been achieved in 1970, he would have stayed for a further two years to see the new institution launched, and would have rejoiced in the step towards Christian unity thus achieved. However, his courage and vision were such that, when plans for a common ordination training for all the Oxford theological colleges were put forward, he was able to tell the Annual Meeting in 1969 that the failure of the Wycliffe negotiations might ultimately be seen as 'a blessing in disguise', for the wider collaboration could (and in the event did) bring Mansfield a wider and even more ecumenical outlook.[33]

One member of the College who had experience of wider ecu-menism during the 1960s was George Caird, whose lectures were continuing to attract large audiences from all over the University and beyond.[34] As both a classicist and a theologian of exceptional ability, he was a natural choice when the International Congrega-tional Council was invited to send observers to the Second Vatican Council.[35] During the three long vacations 1964–6 he attended the Council in Rome, and returned as a great admirer, not only of Pope John XXIII, but also of Pope Paul VI. It was said that if any Roman Catholic criticized Pope Paul VI in a theological gathering in Ox-ford, it was George Caird who was the first to leap to his feet in the Pope's defence. He was invited to give the 'Congregational Lectures' in London in 1966, and chose as his theme 'Our Dialogue with

---

[32] David Anderson resigned in 1969 and became Senior Lecturer in Religious Educa-tion at Wall Hall College (now the Hertfordshire College of Higher Education).

[33] *Mansfield College Annual Report 1968–69*, 13. In retrospect one can see that if the amalgamation had gone ahead, a very different kind of college would have emerged, much more heavily weighted on the theological side, and out of tune with the expec-tations of most of the 'secular' members of the Mansfield SCR.

[34] 'if the College were to erect a toll-gate extracting from those attending Dr Caird's lectures the fee of threepence per person per trip, the College Appeal would be swiftly closed.' So John Marsh told the Trustees and subscribers at the Annual Meeting in 1965. In 1966 George Caird was awarded not only an Oxford DD, but another honorary DD by the University of Aberdeen.

[35] Many of the proceedings were in Latin.

Rome'.[36] The lectures, delivered in his customary elegant style, assumed that 'a genuine and worthwhile dialogue' with Rome was now possible 'without either side being compelled to relinquish any of their deepest convictions'.[37] The greater recognition of the guidance of the Spirit, the new emphasis on the centrality of Scripture, the declaration of religious liberty—all these he saw as hopeful signs for the future, while being sharply critical of both sides in the dialogue. In January 1966, during the Octave of Prayer for Christian Unity, a Roman Catholic (Monsignor Tomlinson, Administrator of Westminster Cathedral) preached in the College Chapel for the first time—an indication of a change of attitude from both the Catholic and the Protestant side.

It was during the 1960s that the links with the churches of the United States were strengthened by the institution of the North American Summer School (NASS). Founded by Walter Wagoner, a Congregational minister from Hartford, Connecticut, it became an annual event from 1963 onwards, and continued until 1992.[38] A large group of American ministers and their wives stayed in Mansfield for three weeks each July, attending lectures in the morning and evening, and sightseeing in the afternoon. Later, a shorter North American Winter School (NAWS) was also instituted, and continued until 1994. Through the links thus created, many generous financial donations came to Mansfield.

Ecumenical discussions and contacts, significant and absorbing though they were to the Principal, theological lecturers, and members of the Council, were still in danger of obscuring the growing significance of the non-theological staff and students within the College. The SCR, for example, was not told about the negotiations with Wycliffe Hall until they appeared to be almost a *fait accompli*.[39] While many members of the Council still thought of Mansfield as a theological college which took students studying other disciplines, for the non-theological tutors it was a Hall with a distinctive history in process of transformation into 'an ordinary Oxford college'.

---

[36] The lectures were published with the same title, *Our Dialogue with Rome* (Oxford, 1967).

[37] Ibid. 9.

[38] The subsequent organizers were Charles Havice, Jean and Dan Novotny, and Don Rudalevige.

[39] The first mention of them in the SCR Minutes appears in the record of the meeting on 17 June 1968, SCR Minute Book 1932–69, MCA.

Much of the pressure to recognize the plurality of culture within the College came from the Junior Common Room, which increased in size each year until 1966–7, when it reached ninety-three; the non-theologians now outnumbered the theologians (not all of whom were ordinands). They came from diverse backgrounds, and few had any Congregational affiliation. They were keen to participate in University activities—in drama, music, and every kind of sport—as well as to initiate new College societies and activities. The JCR President for 1966 wrote in the *Mansfield College Magazine*: 'Looking back over the year, I think that one of the most satisfactory things was the fact that the various undergraduate organizations in the University began to accept Mansfield as an ordinary college.'[40]

The Principal took great delight in the sporting achievements of the College. In 1964 he and the Steward, Wally Buckingham, formed the College Boat Club, and both worked as rowing coaches.[41] Over the next thirteen years, they and the whole College took pride in the fact that Mansfield's First Eight rose forty places, from 78th to 38th, in University ranking. This was more than a sport; it was 'a major expression of the College's corporate spirit' and a means of achieving prestige in the world outside.

In the later 1960s, pressure from students all over Europe and the United States against the values of the existing social institutions was beginning to build up. In May 1968 the situation exploded in Paris. The student unrest in Oxford was a pale shadow of what happened in Paris or even in some English universities, and Mansfield experienced less than some other Oxford colleges. The pressure for student representation on those University committees which made decisions relating directly to undergraduate life and work was resisted by the Franks Commission, but did not disappear. In the University it led eventually to the Hart Committee on Relations with Junior Members, whose report in 1969 resulted in new statutes on discipline in 1971. In Mansfield, from 1967 onwards, there was pressure for representation on the Finance Committee and on the Council; this was finally resolved at a Council meeting on 18 April 1970, when both the SCR and the JCR were given the right to nominate two

---

[40] *MCM* 168 (Nov. 1966), 278.
[41] Wally Buckingham had won a 'blue' for rowing for the Oxford College Servants Eight against the Cambridge College Servants. He was an active member of the United Oxford College Servants Sports Club. In his honour the Mansfield Rowing Club named its new boat the *Wally Buckingham*.

observers at each Council meeting (in addition to the two official SCR representatives).

There was a minor revolt against the wearing of gowns in Hall, which was defused with the help of the Steward, who tested the patience of the students beyond their endurance by painstakingly listing all their names while dinner remained unserved.[42] The SCR made a concession that gowns need no longer be worn on Saturdays and Sundays.[43] There was also pressure to change the College rules concerning visitors and visiting hours, especially after the reduction of the age of majority to 18 in January 1970. When this matter was brought to the Council,

> The Principal and other members of the SCR were asked to continue in conversation with the JCR, reporting to it on the Council's discussion and indicating to it the Council's willingness to accept the JCR as a real partner in the formulation and maintenance of an agreed and responsible way of community life, though pointing out that the change now under consideration must depend for its determination and implementation on administrative decisions in the University as well as in the College.[44]

The resolution of these problems was left for consideration by the new Principal.

In 1968 (2 December) the JCR had voted in favour of coeducation. The College Council had indicated its willingness to consider this in its submission to the Franks Commission, but no move of this kind, at least as far as undergraduates were concerned, could be made without University agreement.[45] The SCR's response (17 February 1969) was that it was prepared to consider becoming a mixed college if coeducation became University policy, and if the size of the College could be increased. Women were still being admitted to the ordination course, though officially their status was somewhat 'irregular'.

It was on 25 April 1969 that John Marsh told the Council of his wish to retire in June of the following year. A subcommittee

---

[42] Information supplied by Wally Buckingham.

[43] SCR Minute Book 1932–69, entry for 17 Feb. 1969, SCR Minute Book 1969–77, entry for 26 May 1969, MCA.

[44] Minute Book of the Mansfield College Council and Board of Education 1953–71, entry for 10 Jan. 1970, MCA.

[45] The Principals of at least three of the women's colleges had been unenthusiastic about the idea in their submissions to the Franks Commission, and it was not until 1974 that the first experiment in undergraduate coeducational colleges began.

considered several possible successors, but unanimously agreed to re-commend George Caird; his appointment was confirmed on 27 June. Judge Norman Carr, Chairman of the College Council since 1958, resigned because of ill health a few months later and died soon after. A deacon of Carrs Lane Congregational Church, Birmingham, he had proved a loyal supporter of and collaborator with the Principal in the years when Mansfield's future seemed uncertain. He was succeeded by Sir William Armstrong, Head of the Home Civil Service since 1968.[46]

By the time John Marsh reached the end of his term of office, the College was a community of eighty-six students and six full-time tutors (about to be renamed Fellows), together with several part-time lecturers. Although the range of subjects was being restricted to those in which the College could offer teaching by a full-time member of staff (and therefore subjects such as chemistry and modern languages soon had to be dropped), the College was building up a good reputation in its non-theological subjects. When a 'Letter from the Principal' replaced 'To the Brethren of the Dispersion' in the *College Magazine,* and the Old Men's Meeting was renamed the Mansfield College Association, there was a general recognition that the College was changing in character. The severe financial crisis of the beginning of John Marsh's Principalship had now been overcome; the books were balanced and the new building was paid for. This was due to the work of the College Treasurer, Kenneth Thorndyke,[47] and the Finance Committee, as well as that of the Principal and Bursar.

Mansfield owed a very great debt to John Marsh, who had given twenty-eight of the most vigorous years of his life in the service of the College. It is doubtful whether there was any other Congregationalist who could have done or would have been prepared to do what he did, not only to save the College from bankruptcy, but to guide it through the changes and challenges of the 1960s (while continuing to write on biblical subjects). As one brought up during and after the First World War, like others he found the student challenges of the late 1960s hard to understand; and his style of leadership was more authoritarian than many now wanted. But the farewell events of his last term demonstrated that the affection of Mansfield

[46] He was created Baron Armstrong of Sanderstead in 1975. He was at one time a member of Sanderstead Congregational Church.

[47] He became Treasurer of Mansfield on retiring as a Director of Boots and served for eleven and a half years.

staff and students for him was undiminished. As he told his last Annual Meeting, 'The story has turned out to be exciting to tell, as it was strenuous to live through.'[48] His final words at Commemoration looked not to the past but to the future: 'What I hope Mansfield can do is to work out what is the shape of a society where modern secular man, and the modern committed disciple of Jesus Christ, can live together in understanding, mutual respect and tolerance, without either giving the other grounds for annoyance or mistrust.'[49]

In retirement he continued to write and lecture on both sides of the Atlantic. Almost immediately he gave a series of lectures at Duke University, North Carolina which were eventually published as *Jesus in his Lifetime* (London, 1981). In his early retirement years he and his wife lived in Cumbria, where he continued to play an ecumenical role. His final home was back in Oxford, where he died in 1994.[50]

---

[48] *Mansfield College Annual Report 1969–70*, 15.
[49] Commemoration Sermon 1970, MCA.   [50] See *The Times*, 29 Jan. 1994.

XIV

The 1970s: Change and Aspiration

DURING the 1970s the implications of the changes of the 1950s and 1960s were being worked out in practice. At the beginning of the decade Mansfield was still a relatively small college of less than 100 members, governed under its now outdated constitution of 1899, struggling to gain a proper recognition of its contribution to the teaching, lecturing, and research of the University. The secularizing process began to accelerate towards the end of the decade. By 1980 its numbers had greatly increased, and it had become a fully co-educational college. Not without difficulty, it had achieved an accept-able balance between its traditional role of ministerial training and its more recent one of academic teaching and research in a wide range of subjects. Effective forms of consultation between junior and senior members had been developed. Above all its academic record was such that aspiration to full collegiate status had become a realizable goal. Though these years were very demanding for the staff, with few to share the increasing administrative tasks, and with all the pressures which change inevitably brings, the achievements were immensely rewarding.

George Caird (pl. 14) and his family moved into the Principal's Lodgings in the summer of 1970. The diverse artistic paths of the Caird children brought a host of people from outside to the Lodg-ings. During term members of the JCR were regularly invited there for games, refreshments, and conversation. Caird continued to give most of his energy to scholarship. He spent the majority of his time on biblical study—lecturing as before to capacity audiences, supervis-ing research students, writing, and sharing the ordination training with Charles Brock.[1]

The college over which George Caird presided in 1970 consisted

---

[1] Charles Brock now made it his responsibility to seek out and attract more minis-terial candidates—an effort which slowly brought results. The numbers were danger-ously low in the early 1970s.

14. George Caird, Principal 1970–77 (Photo: Ramsey and Muspratt)

of ninety-one junior members: thirty-four graduates (including eight ordinands) and fifty-seven undergraduates, reading between them nine different subjects—Chemistry, English, Geography, Jurisprudence, Mathematics, Modern History, Modern Languages, PPE,[2] and Theology.[3] This range of subjects was for a time reduced to five as it was recognized, first, that a tutorial group of fewer than fifteen was quite uneconomic, and secondly, that the criticism in the Franks Report of colleges who admitted undergraduates in subjects for which they had no Fellows had some justification. However, the actual number of students remained steady over the next seven years, before dramatically increasing at the end of the decade.

The ordinands now formed only a very small element in the College numerically, though the outstanding reputation of George Caird as a theologian meant that at the beginning of the decade Mansfield was still known primarily as a theological college. While the majority of the non-theological Fellows were young men who were just beginning to publish and establish scholarly reputations, George Caird's academic stature was assured.[4] Elegantly written articles flowed from his pen, none more so than his appreciation of C. H. Dodd in the *Proceedings of the British Academy* for 1974,[5] and beautifully constructed sermons, sadly rarely written down, were delivered but then lost to posterity except in individual memories. A third New Testament Commentary, on *Paul's Letters from Prison* (Oxford, 1976), came from his pen during his years as Principal.[6]

Like his predecessors at Mansfield, he had a strong sense of belonging to the whole Church, a sense sharpened and deepened by his experience at the Second Vatican Council. Like Micklem and Marsh before him, his ecumenism had a strong theological foundation. It was in accord with his ecumenical sympathies that he was appointed

---

[2] Philosophy, Politics, and Economics.
[3] There was now a steady flow of undergraduates reading Theology without thought of ordination.
[4] His election as Chairman of the Faculty of Theology in 1971 confirmed his standing in the University; as Moderator of the new United Reformed Church for 1975–6 the respect in which he was held within his own denomination; and as a Fellow of the British Academy in 1973 his position in the world of British scholarship. His appointment as co-editor (with Henry Chadwick) of the *Journal of Theological Studies* in 1977 was a recognition of his stature in the wider world of English-speaking New Testament studies.
[5] *Proceedings of the British Academy*, 60 (1974), 497–510.
[6] His other commentaries were on *The Gospel of St Luke* (London, 1963) and *The Revelation of St John the Divine* (London, 1966).

chairman of the committee of Oxford theological college teachers charged with drawing up the syllabus for a new Certificate in Theology, intended as an ecumenical preparation for ordination. It was flexible enough to offer a course for both graduates and non-graduates, and to be taken by members of Mansfield, Regent's Park, and the four Anglican colleges. In addition, it had the support, though not the participation, of the three Roman Catholic Halls (whose Principals were Caird's personal friends). Caird told the College Annual Meeting in 1971: 'We are all impatient of denominationalism, and we all feel ourselves to be proleptic members of that great, united church of the future, whose shape none of us would yet dare to forecast. But the repeated disappointments of the past have led us to put a very high value on the achievement of the possible.'[7] Mansfield ordinands, who were all graduates on their admission, continued for some years the general practice of taking Theology Schools at the end of their second year, but from now on used part of the Certificate course for the final year.

After the formation of the United Reformed Church (URC) in 1972, Mansfield became identified with the Presbyterian tradition as well as the Congregational. In anticipation of the URC, ex-Congregational and ex-Presbyterian students in the University already shared one society, the 1970 Society (later the Reformed Church Society), now based at St Columba's Church, Alfred Street,[8] the former Presbyterian church which was now part of the URC. The suggestion was now made and eventually accepted that the Sunday morning worship for URC (and other) undergraduates should take place at St Columba's; and in order to maintain the Mansfield link, the College Chaplain would preach at regular intervals.

The new URC almost immediately set up a Commission on Ministry, chaired by Professor W. R. Niblett, Professor of Higher Education in the University of London and a leading Congregational layman. In response to the Commission's interim report, George Caird wrote in justification of Mansfield's continuing role in the education of future theological teachers.[9] On 30 April 1974 the Commission paid

[7] *MCM* 174 (Dec. 1971), 2.

[8] Formed as a chaplaincy to Scottish Presbyterian students in 1915, sponsored jointly by the Church of Scotland, the United Free Church of Scotland, and the Presbyterian Church of England; it became a congregation of the Presbyterian Church of England in 1929.

[9] 'Response to the Interim Report on Ministry', Ministerial Training File 1968–85, MCA.

a visit to Mansfield and met members of the Senior Common Room. Immediately afterwards two College Fellows wrote to the Chairman of the Commission to express their unease at 'the emphasis in the Committee's questioning on Mansfield as actually or potentially an evangelical institution rather than a College dedicated to academic excellence'. Without 'aspiration towards academic excellence' Mansfield could not in their view serve the Church properly; and 'intellectual vitality can only be continued if the College continues to treat non-theological education as an end in itself of equivalent value'.[10] They reflected a feeling among many in the SCR that new developments at Mansfield had not been fully appreciated throughout the URC.

The hallmarks of the SCR during this decade, and beyond, were aspirations towards academic excellence, towards a more democratic self-governing status (while consonant with the college's continuing commitment to ministerial training within the Reformed tradition), and, ultimately, towards full collegiate status. The seven full-time senior members of the College who were in charge of departments were now all designated 'Fellows' rather than 'Tutors' (as from Michaelmas 1970), according to Oxford custom. A new salary scale was introduced, related to academic rather than ministerial salaries as previously. This was essential if the College was to attract new staff of the highest calibre. To the Fellows in Modern History (Michael Mahony), English (John Creaser), Jurisprudence (Anthony Ogus), and Theology[11] was now added a Fellow in Geography: Anthony Lemon, a research student at St Cross College, who was appointed Fellow in Geography in 1970 (after a year's non-stipendiary lectureship). Although his initial research was an investigation into the small towns of East Anglia, he has subsequently concentrated on, and made himself an authority on, Southern Africa.[12] In addition, James Whalley, the Bursar from 1964 until 1981, was now designated a Fellow. When Anthony Ogus moved to Wolfson College as Senior

---

[10] Letter from John Creaser and Anthony Ogus, 10 May 1974, MCA.

[11] Donald Sykes was now appointed Tutorial Fellow in Theology, rather than Tutor in Church History. In addition, there were several Lutheran World Federation Fellows during this decade, some of them serving for a second term: F. E. Sherman until 1971, Warren Quanbeck 1971–2, Robert Jenson 1972–3, James Burtness 1973–4, Paul Wee 1974–5, and Merlyn Satrom 1976–82.

[12] His publications in this field include *Apartheid: A Geography of Separation* (Farnborough, 1976), *Apartheid in Transition* (Aldershot, 1987), and *Homes Apart: South Africa's Segregated Cities* (London, 1991).

Research Fellow at the Centre for Socio-legal Studies in 1975, his place as Fellow in Jurisprudence was taken by Richard Buckley, from King's College, London, whose specialist field is in the law of torts.[13] It was on Richard Buckley that much of the work of preparation for a new constitution was to fall.[14]

The College was able to extend its range of subjects through the appointment of Michael Freeden as Fellow in Politics in 1978,[15] and Janet Dyson as Lecturer in Mathematics in 1977.[16] John Wilson, a philosopher of education at the Department of Educational Studies, was appointed a Supernumerary Fellow in 1979.[17] For three years J. D. H. Collinson was a member of the SCR as Leverhulme Senior Research Fellow in Social Ecology from 1974 until 1977. Part-time tutors, now designated 'Lecturers', continued to help with college teaching. And the SCR offered hospitality to a continuous flow of visiting scholars, most of them from the USA.

With the appointment of College Fellows, the opportunity was taken to appoint three Honorary Fellows: the two surviving retired Principals, Nathaniel Micklem and John Marsh, and Mansfield's most distinguished living biblical scholar, C. H. Dodd. After the death of Nathaniel Micklem another two were appointed: George Caird, when

---

[13] He has published *The Law of Nuisance* (London, 1981) and *The Modern Law of Negligence* (London, 1988, 1993) and edited, with R. F. V. Heuston, *Salmond and Heuston on the Law of Torts* (London, 19th edn. 1987, 20th edn. 1992).

[14] Three of these early Fellows of Mansfield have subsequently been appointed professors: John Creaser to the Hildred Carlile Chair of English Literature at Royal Holloway and Bedford New College, London; Anthony Ogus to Chairs in Law at the Universities of Newcastle upon Tyne and Manchester; and Richard Buckley to a Chair in Law at the University of Reading. See 'A Law Tutor Looks Back', *MCM* 195 (1992–3), 28–9.

[15] This was the first College appointment made in official collaboration with University Faculty representatives. Michael Freeden is a graduate of both the Hebrew University in Jerusalem and St Antony's College in Oxford. His special fields are British liberal political thought and Western political ideologies. Among his published works are *The New Liberalism: An Ideology of Social Reform* (Oxford, 1978), *Liberalism Divided: A Study in British Political Thought 1914–39* (Oxford, 1986), and *Rights* (Milton Keynes, 1991). Since his appointment he has built up Mansfield's PPE Department into one of the two largest in the College. He was elected to a British Academy Research Readership for the two academic years 1989–91.

[16] She has subsequently built up the College Mathematics Department. She was appointed Senior Research Fellow in 1987, and Tutorial Fellow and Special (non-CUF) Lecturer in 1993. Her special research field, in which she has collaborated with Professor Rosanna Villela-Bressan of the University of Padua, is the theory of non-linear evolution equations and how this theory applies to non-linear, non-autonomous functional differential equations.

[17] Among John Wilson's major contributions to the field are *A New Introduction to Moral Education* (London, 1990) and *Reflection and Practice* (Ontario, 1993).

he ceased to be Principal, and Norman Goodall (Mansfield 1919–22), retiring Chairman of the Board of Education, for many years Secretary of the International Missionary Council, and later Assistant General Secretary of the World Council of Churches.[18]

The teaching Fellows undertook their full share of University as well as College work: serving on faculty boards, examining, supervising research students, and lecturing, in addition to tutorial teaching and research. Through their own research and teaching, they were gradually building up the College's academic reputation in non-theological subjects, a reputation which was to gain increasing recognition in the next decade. When, in 1978, Mansfield gained 7 Firsts and 20 Seconds out of 31 candidates, John Creaser pointed out in a letter to *The Times* (22 August 1978) that these results placed Mansfield second to University College in its percentage of Firsts, and would have placed it fifth in the Norrington table[19] had it been a full college in the University. The record of Mansfield students of English in particular (many of whom had been rejected by other colleges during the admissions process) was outstanding.[20] This made it seem all the more unfair that the College should continue to be excluded from the official University admissions system; and all the more necessary for the Fellows to make strenuous efforts to seek out good candidates during the hectic weeks of interviewing in December and January each year.

Several approaches were made to the Colleges Admissions Committee, which eventually brought some improvement in the situation. In 1980 Mansfield was admitted to Group I of the Admissions Scheme, subject to a self-denying ordinance that it would not use entrance awards to 'poach' good candidates from other colleges. At least Mansfield was now brought more readily to the attention of potential applicants.

The role of the SCR was becoming more significant (while that of

---

[18] For Norman Goodall (1896–1985) see *MCM* 187 (1984–5), 48–51 and Norman Goodall, *Second Fiddle: Recollections and Reflections* (London, 1979) and *One Man's Testimony* (London, 1949, 1985; 2nd edn. with memoir by K. Slack).

[19] A table of Finals results suggested by Sir Arthur Norrington, President of Trinity 1954–70, and first published in 1964; in it, colleges were listed in order of the achievements of their students in degree examinations. The table was officially abandoned in 1991.

[20] Of the 53 Mansfield students who took the Final Examinations of the English School between 1977 and 1984, 12 gained Firsts, 38 (13 of whom were 'vivaed' for Firsts) gained Seconds, and three were awarded Thirds. Eight of these students gained University prizes.

the Board of Education was diminishing). They asked to be informed promptly of matters under discussion by the Council, to have the opportunity to make recommendations beforehand, and to be closely involved in discussion of their conditions of service. A signal of the Council's acceptance of their greater role in College management came when, after strong representation to the Chairman, three of the senior Fellows were appointed as members of the subcommittee of five appointed in 1976 to recommend the name of a new Principal.

The traditional idea of a PPH as vesting all administrative authority in the Principal was now in practice abandoned, and Fellows shared in the increasing tasks of administration. In 1970 Donald Sykes, returned from a year as Visiting Professor in Religion and Classics at St Olaf College, Northfield, Minnesota, was appointed not only Senior Tutor, with responsibility for the College Theology Faculty, but also Dean of Degrees and Tutor for Admissions. In 1977 there was a further devolution of responsibility when, at Donald Sykes's instigation, John Creaser was appointed Vice-Principal, Anthony Lemon Tutor for Admissions, and Michael Mahony Dean. These changes were welcomed by the SCR.

The College continued to enjoy the excellent services of its domestic staff, especially the Steward, Wally Buckingham. When he retired in 1977, the Principal said of him, 'he has contributed more to the discipline of the College than Principal and Fellows together, for he had the marvellous secret of speaking with swift and effective word of rebuke and forgetting both it and the offence a moment afterwards'.[21] Wally Buckingham has never really left the College, for not only did he continue to coach the First Eight for a time, but for many years continued to come in weekly to look after the cellar.[22]

Full collegiate status within the University was still Mansfield's ultimate objective. Without it, the College found it difficult to attract good first-choice applicants for most subjects, hard to raise money outside denominational sources and resources (which were progressively shrinking), and, because of statutory restrictions on PPHs, almost impossible to expand to an economic size. There was a 'catch-22' aspect to this problem, for the University was likely to lay down financial requirements for collegiate status, yet lack of that

---

[21] The Principal's report, *MCM* 179 (1977), 15.
[22] He was made an honorary member of the Mansfield Association. See 'Wally Talks', *MCM* 192 (1989–90), 25.

status was one of the major handicaps to raising the necessary money. Non-theological endowments were now badly needed, but elusive to obtain.

It was generally agreed that a new constitution was a prerequisite to collegiate status. The existing constitution, drawn up in 1899 as a revision of an earlier one, was now quite outdated (although it could be argued that the College was not actually doing anything specifically prohibited). The official purpose of the College was still 'the instruction in Theology of young men intended for the Christian ministry'; the designated curriculum was theological; and 'professors' were still theoretically required to make a declaration of faith (though the practice had long been abandoned). This outdated constitution proved a great handicap when the College appealed to trusts for contributions towards its endowment fund. The Council appointed a working party on the constitution in 1973; it was perhaps as well that the members did not know that fifteen years would elapse before their work would be completed.

A major difficulty in revising the constitution was the number of different authorities with which the College now had to negotiate: not only the Charity Commission and the University, but also the new United Reformed Church, the Congregational Federation, and the Evangelical Fellowship of Congregational Churches.[23] Mansfield representatives had to face tough, though courteous, questioning from the Charity Commissioners. The constitution in its various drafts was a recurring item of business on the agenda of both Council and SCR for the next fifteen years.

Relations between junior and senior members were good in the 1970s; the small size of the College encouraged this. A Joint Committee was set up in 1970 and met regularly each term to discuss 'matters of joint concern' (rather than 'discipline' as originally envisaged).[24] The most significant issue for discussion was that of charges for board and lodging. High inflation, and the fact that student grants were often increased by an amount lower than the inflation rate, simultaneously made both hardship for junior members, and

---

[23] These two Federations include most of the 26.4 % of Congregational churches (representing 17.3 % of the total number of members) which voted against joining the new URC in 1972. The percentages have been collated from *CYB 1972* and A. Macarthur, 'The Background to the Formation of the United Reformed Church (Presbyterian and Congregational) in England and Wales in 1972', *JURCHS* 4/1 (Oct. 1987).

[24] This Committee, now the Joint Consultative Committee, has continued to meet regularly ever since.

financial problems for the College. On 13 March 1973 George Caird addressed the JCR Annual Meeting and referred to the fact that more junior members would have to live out: 'He further emphasised his wish that the JCR should be taken fully into his confidence, and added that any question of College charges should be fully discussed.'[25] From then on, the two Common Rooms negotiated an agreed increase in charges with the Bursar (and occasionally an SCR representative), and dealt with problems relating to the College houses, which were bought in the late 1970s, in order to accommodate the increase in undergraduate numbers.[26] This additional accommodation enabled a larger number of junior members to be housed in College property, and therefore an increased number to be admitted, with benefit to the College finances, though adding further pressure on the Fellows. Thus the number of junior members increased greatly between 1976–7 (a poor year, in which the number had dropped from 90 to 84) and 1981–2, when the JCR numbered 144.

Such an increase meant a JCR whose procedures had to be more formalized in a new constitution drawn up in Trinity Term 1981 (revised Trinity 1984). Pressure for a properly designed and equipped JCR bar finally succeeded in 1979. In the University, the JCR was making its mark. In the first year of George Caird's Principalship, 1970–1, Mansfield students won between them nine blues or half-blues for sport (three for rugger, three cricket, one golf, one canoeing, and one polo). Though this number was not matched in succeeding years, there were always some blues to report at the end of each year. Mansfield students also made an impact on University drama, particularly in the middle of the decade, when the College provided the Presidents of both the Experimental Theatre Club (ETC) and the Oxford University Dramatic Society (OUDS).[27]

The question of a separate common room for graduates—a Middle Common Room—was raised in the JCR in 1974, and finally agreed after considerable debate. The MCR was instituted in Trinity Term 1975; MCR members remained members of the JCR, but their Common

[25] JCR Minute Book 1971–80, MCA.

[26] 212 Woodstock Road was bought in 1976, 20 Regent Street in 1978, and 2 Rectory Road in 1979 (the Rectory Road house was sold in 1993). For a time three flats in Leckford Road were also rented for student use.

[27] Bill Buffery was President of the ETC in 1975–6 and Philip Franks of OUDS in 1976. Both have subsequently had very successful careers as actors and directors.

Room was accorded separate representation on college committees. Its fortunes fluctuated as the numbers of graduate non-theologians varied from year to year. In 1978 the MCR President wrote in the *College Magazine* that, because of the predominance of ordinands and postgraduate theologians, 'the tendency has been for the old split between the College's theological past and its present secular reality to be magnified by the physical separation of the two Common Rooms'.[28]

The changes in the College had serious implications for the Library, built up since the Spring Hill days as essentially a theological library. The great majority of the College members were now reading other subjects, and it was necessary to provide for them. Gordon Trowell, the retired missionary who became Librarian in 1968 (assisted by Dorothy Pope), brought all his powers of organization to bear on reducing the theological stock (and finding suitable homes for the redundant books), building up the new sections, and finding space into which the library could expand. For several years theological periodicals had to share a room with the snooker table. When Gordon Trowell asked to reduce his hours in 1976, an assistant was appointed, Alma Bartholomew (now Jenner), who eventually succeeded him in 1984, and who has subsequently made the time to arrange and catalogue for the first time the valuable and extensive College Archive.[29]

The formation of college societies reflected the academic strengths being built up within Mansfield. The Norman Carr Society, whose principal meeting of the year is a dinner, sometimes followed by a moot, commemorated Judge Carr, Chairman of Council 1958–70. The 1887 Society was founded in 1970 to commemorate the appointment of Sir Halford Mackinder to the first Readership in Geography in the University in 1887 (which was also the first full year of existence of Mansfield College); meetings are both academic and social, and former Mansfield geographers often return to the annual dinner. A College literary society, 'Tristram', flourished for some years.

On 17 January 1976 George Caird told the Council that he had accepted the University's Dean Ireland Chair of Exegesis of Holy Scripture, in effect the main Chair in New Testament Studies, from Michaelmas 1977. Although he had been allowed to hold his honorary

---

[28] *MCM* 180 (1978), 19–20.
[29] See Alma Bartholomew, 'Shedding Light on the Library 1886–1945', *MCM* 189 (1986–7), 21–2, and 'Shedding Light on the Library 1945–88', *MCM* 190 (1987–8), 38–9.

University post as Reader as well as the Principalship of Mansfield, the University was not prepared to allow him to hold this more senior post jointly with Mansfield. It was at once a blow and an honour for the College. For Caird, it may have been a difficult decision; but his final choice indicates that the opportunity to spend the remaining years of his career as a scholar and teacher, rather than as an administrator-cum-teacher, was, to him, welcome.

The Cairds left Mansfield and moved to Letcombe Regis on the edge of the Berkshire Downs. The College did not altogether lose George Caird during the remaining seven years of his life, for though his base henceforward was at the Queen's College, he was still available to give advice and encouragement, to teach, and to lecture.[30] It was a great blow to the College and University when he died suddenly in April 1984, on the eve of his retirement.

After considering several names, and interviewing five other candidates, the nomination subcommittee recommended to the Council that Donald Sykes (pl. 15) should be appointed Principal, and the Council unanimously agreed. Donald Sykes was in line with Mansfield tradition in being a former student of the College, but broke new ground as the first lay (though theological) Principal.[31]

The new Principal, with his wife Marta and their two sons, moved from 6 Mansfield Road into the Principal's Lodgings in the summer of 1977, and their home continued to be a social centre of the College, as it had been since the early 1960s. Donald Sykes was fully committed to the new shape and character of the College, and it was during his Principalship that Mansfield's character as a college of many disciplines was generally recognized; unlike previous Principals, he had always known Mansfield as a multi-disciplinary college, and was positively committed to its development as such. He faced formidable challenges—'the goal of a royal charter, participation in the university admissions process, the expansion of student

---

[30] He used those years to bring to fruition in *The Language and Imagery of the Bible* (London, 1980) some of the ideas he had already explored in articles; and to work on a major book on *New Testament Theology* as well as on the revision of the New Testament section of the New English Bible (eventually published as the *Revised English Bible* in 1989). *New Testament Theology* was edited and completed by one of his former research students, L. D. Hurst, and published by the Oxford University Press in 1994. See that work for a complete bibliography of Caird's writings.

[31] He was an elder at St Columba's URC in central Oxford, having moved his membership from the Summertown Church (where for several years he was church secretary) after the formation of the URC.

15. Donald Sykes, Principal 1977–86 (Photo: B. J. Harris of Gillman and Soame)

numbers and academic subjects, and the securing of university fund-ing for college Fellows'[32]—and all this at a time of retrenchment in higher education in Oxford as elsewhere. As Principal, he continued to share fully in the work of the Theology Faculty, lecturing on patristics, teaching for Theology Schools and the Theology Certificate, leading seminars, and serving on the Faculty Board.[33] In the long vacation he organized and lectured for the North American Summer School. He shared with Charles Brock (who was still part-time minister at Wheatley United Reformed Church) the conviction that a director of ordination training should have current experience of pastoral ministry. Therefore he felt it right to put the overall responsibility for ordination training into the hands of Charles Brock. W. R. (Bill) Telford, a New Testament scholar from Glasgow, Cambridge, and New York, joined the College for two years as Research Fellow in Biblical Studies.

In 1974, five hitherto male Oxford colleges had for an experimental period of five years been allowed to admit women undergraduates: Brasenose, Hertford, Jesus, St Catherine's, and Wadham.[34] In 1977, as the time for review approached, it was agreed by Congregation that those colleges which now wished to become coeducational should be allowed to do so. Very few colleges rejected the opportunity. All Mansfield Common Rooms voted in favour of coeducation; and the Council readily agreed.[35] The ten women undergraduates who arrived at Mansfield in October 1979 were not the first female junior members of the college, for ever since 1913 Mansfield had admitted women to its theological courses, albeit in very small numbers. George Caird had been very supportive to women ministerial candidates.[36] When PPHs were given the right to graduate their own ordinands in 1971, he had encouraged Kate Chegwin (now Compston), who had matriculated through St Hugh's, to migrate to Mansfield for

---

[32] M. Mahony, 'Donald Sykes: An Appreciation', *MCM* 188 (1985–6), 21–2.

[33] He has been a regular contributor of articles and reviews to *Journal of Theological Studies*, *Studia Patristica*, and *Byzantinische Zeitschrift*, chiefly related to Gregory of Nazianzus. He has written the 'Introduction' and 'Commentary', and provided the translation, for *Gregory Nazianzen: 'Poemata Arcana'* (Oxford, forthcoming).

[34] Congregation was sensitive to the hesitation felt by the women's colleges, hence the limited nature of the experiment at first.

[35] After the passing of the Sex Discrimination Act of 1975 Mansfield could not actually have refused to take women undergraduates, since it already accepted women ordinands. But Mansfield's decision was a positive choice rather than a legal necessity.

[36] He wrote a significant article on 'Paul and Women's Liberty' in the *Bulletin of the John Rylands Library*, 54 (Manchester, 1972), 268–81.

graduation the following year. The ten pioneers of 1979 took an active part in College sport, music, and JCR life, and two of them were awarded Firsts; four of them married fellow students.[37] The College very soon settled into its new mode.

The first woman member of the SCR was Pamela Busby (now de Witt), Lecturer in English from 1971 until 1978.[38] By the time she left, Janet Dyson had already joined the SCR as Lecturer in Mathematics in 1977. The College broke new ground in 1980 by appointing Justine Wyatt (Mansfield 1977–80) as part-time Assistant Chaplain: the first Oxford woman college chaplain,[39] and the first woman member of staff in a URC theological college. Like the Chaplain, she combined her College responsibilities with a pastorate near Oxford (first at Abingdon, then at Cumnor). She taught church history, developed a course in spirituality, pioneered the new internship course for ordinands, and in a quiet way ensured that issues of feminist theology and inclusive language were put on the agenda.

The major problem facing the College was still financial; the Treasurer[40] felt the College lived a 'hand to mouth' existence. As well as the decline in Congregational and URC resources, other new factors made the balancing of the books even more difficult. In 1976 the Government had forced the universities to increase their charges, which in Oxford's case involved a rise of more than 300 per cent (£143 to £500) per annum. This did not affect students whose grants were paid by a Local Education Authority, but for those ordinands who were not eligible for further grants, the College bursary funds were stretched to the limit.[41] In addition, the College was having to meet a much higher proportion of its teaching costs than full colleges, since the salaries of Mansfield Fellows were not eligible for subsidy through the CUF scheme.[42] In this fragile situation, the role and

---

[37] See Helen Bower (née Fraser), *MCM* 191 (1988–9), 32–3.

[38] She is now the Bishop of Birmingham's adviser for lay adult education and training.

[39] Though, strictly speaking, Nuffield was the first 'full college' to appoint a woman chaplain.

[40] Emrys Evans, Senior Regional Director, Midland Bank for Wales, was College Treasurer from 1977 until 1988. His public work in many spheres was recognized with the award of the CBE in 1981.

[41] This situation was eased in 1976 when the URC began to assume more responsibility for its ministers in training.

[42] The Common University Fund (CUF) was established at the end of the 19th cent. Individual colleges subscribe according to their income, and the Fund is used to finance University lecturerships.

support of the Finance Committee (officially a subcommittee of the Council) was crucial.[43]

Donald Sykes had been assiduous since becoming Principal in meeting and corresponding with both the Registrar (A. J. Dorey) and the Vice-Chancellor (Sir Rex Richards) to plead Mansfield's case. A meeting in January 1978, between Donald Sykes and John Creaser on Mansfield's side, and the Registrar and Vice-Chancellor for the University, offered some encouragement for the possibility of Mansfield obtaining some kind of arrangement with the CUF, but no encouragement concerning any increase in student numbers. Many months later, in December 1979, the Principal learned that Hebdomadal Council was to set up a working party to consider CUF arrangements for the College.

In 1979 one of the world's largest film companies (United Artists) sought an Oxford college with some visual resemblance to Harvard. When they approached Mansfield for permission to use the College buildings as a setting for the opening scenes of *Heaven's Gate*, the proffered fee of thousands of pounds was too much to resist. When the scale of the operation became apparent, the College negotiated more than double the sum initially offered (it finally received £41,000, equivalent to two years' deficits on operating accounts). Passers-by along Mansfield Road in the following April were astonished to see not only a new wall along the entrance, but also a huge tree in the middle of the lawn (closer inspection would have revealed that its branches were held on with nuts and bolts). The enterprise produced the welcome revenues for the College, and even a little personal profit for those members of the College who enrolled as 'extras', though the disruption was more than had been expected.[44]

During the year 1979–80, as members of Council and SCR looked towards the coming Centenary of the College and viewed its still uncertain financial position, the decision was taken to launch another Appeal. That was to be a major preoccupation of the succeeding decade.

---

[43] The Finance Committee included representatives of both Council and Fellows, and the JCR and MCR Presidents.

[44] The film itself was a box-office failure.

XV

1980–1995: A New Constitution; New Developments

THE planning of a new Appeal involved further consideration of the way in which the College should continue to develop as the centenary (in 1986) approached. First thoughts were of 'survival'; but as money began to come in the emphasis changed from 'survival' to 'development'. And 'development' has been the hallmark of the College's life in the years 1980 to 1995.

After much discussion, it was decided that the target for the Appeal should be £1 million, and that its primary objects should be the renovation of the College building, and the endowment of the non-theological posts which were essential to the College's academic development. Plans for an additional building were postponed. In 1980 a legacy of £50,000—the largest single donation at that date in the history of the College—from Miss Beatrice Dale, granddaughter of R. W. Dale, gave a very encouraging start.[1] In 1982 another large donation in memory of Elfan Rees was earmarked for an overseas student scholarship. Elfan Rees (Mansfield 1925–9)[2] had worked for UNRRA, for the World Council of Churches as Adviser on Refugee Affairs, and then for twenty years as Secretary of the World Council of Churches Commission on International Affairs, in which capacity he frequently attended the Assemblies of the United Nations.

A College Principal could no longer be expected to bear the major load of running an appeal as well as administering a multi-disciplinary college in a rapidly changing university. It was therefore a most appropriate arrangement that Peter Spicer, who had just taken early retirement from the Oxford University Press, was appointed Appeal Director in 1981; it was his grandfather, Sir Albert Spicer, who

---

[1] Beatrice Dale's gift in shares was later valued at £60,000.

[2] Elfan Rees (1906–78) was the son of Thomas Rees (Mansfield 1896–9), for many years Principal of Bala-Bangor College. See 'Nearly Two Years with UNRRA', *MCM* 129 (July 1946), 174–8 and 'Refugees', *MCM* 134 (Jan. 1949), 205–8. In 1974 he delivered the Dale Lectures on 'Freedom'.

had helped Dale and Fairbairn to raise the money for the new building in 1889.[3] Donald Sykes put his full weight behind the Appeal,
and he and Peter Spicer toured the United States in search of funds
early in 1983.

Steady progress was made, and by June 1985 the fund had reached
£650,000; by 1988 it had passed its target of £1 million. The alumni,
particularly those of earlier decades, were remarkably generous. A
further witness to the kind of loyalty which the College had inspired
was the gift of the cost of re-turfing the ground in front of the College from Harry King, the former Barnardo's boy who served Mansfield for over twenty years, fifteen years after his resignation as lodge
porter.[4]

As the Centenary approached, 'Mansfield 2000' was launched. A new
Appeal Committee was set up under the chairmanship of Anthony
Lunch, a former Mansfield student now running his own company,
with a mandate to draw up a College Development Plan for 'Mansfield
2000', Howard Hull assumed the role of professional Appeal Adviser,
and Maggie Lyons was appointed Appeal Co-ordinator. From this there
grew the College Development Office, whose responsibility was not
only to raise money but also to work with the Council and SCR (later
the Trustees and Governing Body) in developing new projects and
emphases within the College.

In 1983 the Architects Design Partnership of Henley-on-Thames
was asked to produce a structural survey and feasibility study on the
College buildings. The stonework was badly worn, as little had been
done since 1889. At the same time an approach was made to the
Department of the Environment and the Historic Buildings Council
to see whether a government grant might be obtained. The Council's
architect, who visited the College in the autumn of 1983, reported
that he had 'rarely enjoyed a site visit so much as this during a great
many years' and described the College as 'truly a great design'. The
building was given a '2A' grading, and was awarded a maximum
grant (of 40 per cent) on the first £200,000 of expenditure (i.e.
£80,000; later a further £20,000 was awarded).[5] In April 1984 the

---

[3] Peter Spicer continued to serve the College as a member of Council and Trustee
after his work as Appeal Director was finished in 1985. He died in 1993. See Tony Tucker,
'Peter Spicer: An Appreciation', *MCM* 195 (1992–3), 53.

[4] For Harry King, see *MCM* 192 (1989–90), 7.

[5] See R. N. Burton, 'Repair and Renovation of College Buildings', *MCM* 186 (1983–4),
27–32; see also John Maddison, 'The Champneys Buildings', *MCM* 185 (1982–3), 28–32, an
article commissioned by the Victorian Society in support of the Appeal.

Council therefore felt sufficiently confident to authorize the first stage of the renovation programme: the external fabric of the Chapel (except the west entrance) and the main building. Joslins were the contractors; their recently installed computerized equipment for the cutting and moulding of stone enabled them to offer the most competitive tender.

For the next two years, as the first phase of the renovation programme was carried out, the noise of scaffolding being put up and taken down, builders' lorries moving in and out, pressure washers, chisels, and hammers became a part of College life. Seven men, four of them skilled stonemasons, worked on the Chapel and main building as far as the tower, washing down, identifying, and chiselling out decayed stone, and replacing it with carefully cut new stone from Clipsham quarries. Gargoyles, old and new, were sometimes to be seen lying about in the College quad. When the scaffolding finally came down in time for the Centenary celebrations, the full splendour of the Champneys buildings was revealed.[6] Inside the College, the SCR was refurbished and restored to its earlier elegance.

Improvements to Chapel and Library continued. In 1987 new and attractive lighting, provided by concealed lamps at the base of the windows, was installed in the Chapel in memory of Norman Goodall, the gift of Elizabeth Welford and Charles and Carolyn Brock. The new illumination revealed all too clearly the need to clean the woodwork, a task effectively undertaken by Robin McGarry, the Steward, during his holidays. Similar work was undertaken in the Library, in which extensive reorganization took place in the 1980s. The former Council Room was transformed into a library extension for theology and law, many books from the Spring Hill collection were repaired and cleaned (though not, sadly, the 200 stolen during the summer vacation of 1982 and never recovered), discreet but efficient lighting on both sides of each reading bay in the Main Library was provided, and extensive redecoration was undertaken. The lack of an adequate bookstack necessitated further sales of older periodicals and books.

The draining of College finances was in part relieved in 1981, when, after many approaches by Donald Sykes and others, to both individuals and committees, the University agreed to make three Special

---

[6] Phase II of the renovation programme was continued after the Centenary during 1986–8. A final phase, which was too expensive to complete in 1988, included the west door of the Chapel, and was eventually completed in 1989.

non-CUF Lecturerships available to PPHs. Individual faculty boards were then asked to address their teaching needs by nominating candidates from the staffs of PPHs, from whom the General Faculty Board would make a final choice. It was a source of pride and satisfaction to Mansfield that two of these three posts were awarded to Mansfield Fellows in October 1982: John Creaser (English) and Anthony Lemon (Geography).[7] Subsequently, when John Creaser moved to London, Michael Freeden (Politics) was awarded a Special non-CUF Lecturership. This development was not only a financial advantage to the College, but also enhanced its academic reputation within the University.

In 1985, the College was finally placed on an equal footing with all other colleges in the new Admissions Scheme established in the wake of the Dover Report.[8] Entrance awards were now abolished, and it was no longer a requirement that candidates had to make a choice between colleges; this meant that a share of those candidates who did not state a definite college preference would be allocated to Mansfield for interview. These changes, which many felt were the most important academic advances achieved by the College since 1955, not only raised the number of Mansfield's applicants, but strengthened the College's claim to full collegiate status.

Meanwhile the range of subjects was being expanded to include Engineering (though at first only students from outside the UK and the EEC could be admitted). John Harding, a Lecturer in the Department of Engineering Studies whose connection with the College went back to his undergraduate days as a member of the Congregational Society, was appointed a Supernumerary Fellow in 1982, and a Tutorial Fellow in Mechanical Engineering in 1986.[9] In 1987 John Sykes, University Lecturer in Metallurgy and Materials Science, was appointed a Supernumerary Fellow, later Tutorial Fellow, in Materials

---

[7] The third Special non-CUF Lecturership was awarded to Rex Mason of Regent's Park College, who also served as Lecturer in Old Testament Studies at Mansfield.

[8] A committee chaired by Sir Kenneth Dover, President of Corpus Christi College, with a remit to simplify the admissions system, and to remove perceived discrimination against state schools. Mansfield's inclusion was only agreed after the College had circularized every member of every college governing body, asking them to oppose the original proposal of the Dover Report that PPHs should be excluded from this reorganization.

[9] John Harding's special interests and publications are in the field of testing techniques and mechanical behaviour of material at impact rates of loading.

Engineering and Tutor for Graduates,[10] and Norman Booth, University Lecturer in Nuclear Physics, was appointed a Supernumerary Fellow in Physics.[11] When the College was offered a 'New Blood' appointment in 1982 (a government scheme to enable universities to improve their staffing), it welcomed Ian Sargent, University Lecturer in Obstetrics—but his specialty was not added to the College curriculum.

In 1985 John Creaser's quality as a teacher and scholar was recognized by his appointment as Hildred Carlile Professor of English Literature at Royal Holloway and New Bedford College, London. His successor was Kate Flint, the College's first woman Tutorial Fellow. Her specialist fields are Victorian and early twentieth-century literature and art history.[12] She also served as Senior Tutor and Tutor for Women, and played a major part in drawing up the College's Code on Harassment which was finally adopted in 1992.

Donald Sykes, sometimes accompanied by one or two College Fellows, was now in frequent consultation with the University Registrar concerning the limits to be placed on undergraduate and graduate numbers (as well as the possible use of part of Mansfield's land for a joint University and College scheme—an idea which finally bore fruit in the next decade). For a college which was so dependent on fee income, any cut in numbers could prove fatal, and nothing worried Principal and Treasurer more than this threat. This situation was fully shared with the SCR.

In 1982 a new University PPH Statute limited the number of undergraduates from Britain and the EEC who might be admitted to Mansfield to a level of ten below those already studying in the College. Therefore the only way to increase student numbers further was to seek them from overseas. In addition to taking overseas

[10] See John Sykes, 'Passive or Uninhibited?', *MCM* 194 (1991–2), 13. His special interests lie in corrosion science. His publications include work on metallic and organic coatings, adhesion, stress-corrosion cracking, passivity, and the corrosion of steel in concrete.

[11] See Norman Booth, 'Physics: What's It For?', *MCM* 195 (1992–3). His main interests are in neutrino physics and astrophysics, especially the detection of solar neutrinos, and in the field of non-equilibrium superconductivity and the development of superconducting particle detectors.

[12] Her publications include *Dickens* (Brighton, 1986) and *The Woman Reader 1837–1914* (Oxford, 1993), and she has edited *The Victorian Novel: Social Problems and Social Change* (London, 1987) and *Impressionists in England* (London, 1984). In 1992 she moved to a University Lectureship in Victorian and Modern English Literature in conjunction with a Fellowship at Linacre College.

undergraduates (especially engineers from South-East Asia and PPE students from the USA), Mansfield, along with some other colleges, developed special one-year courses for overseas students (mostly from the USA) for which they were awarded credits by their home institutions. Their numbers were subject to a quota decided by the University. From 1982 onwards, these Visiting Students became part of Mansfield life.

It was a matter of great regret that Donald Sykes had to take early retirement as Principal in the spring of 1986, after a considerable period of ill health; the stress of change and hard negotiation had taken its toll. However, it was a source of satisfaction that he was able to continue his association with the College as Senior Research Fellow. His eight and a half years as Principal, very difficult years for British higher education generally, had seen great progress towards the goal of collegiate status, a fine balancing of the different needs and interests within the College, the securing of entry into the full admissions system of the University, and the award of non-CUF lecturerships to two Mansfield Fellows. In his 'Appreciation' of Donald Sykes's contribution to the College, not only during his years as Principal, Michael Mahony wrote of

> his wholehearted commitment to the new direction given to the College by the vision of John Marsh, his loyal support and assistance as Senior Tutor to the much missed principal of the 1970's, George Caird, his selfless contribution to the easing of tensions unavoidable in a small Senior common Room, and his unstinting consideration for newcomers to the College.[13]

In succession to Donald Sykes, the Council appointed the Vice-Principal, Jan Womer (pl. 16), who had succeeded Merlyn Satrom as Lutheran World Federation Fellow in 1983, to be Principal 'until it was expedient to search for a new Principal under the intended new scheme of the Charity Commission'.[14] Jan Womer had studied at Pacific Lutheran Theological Seminary in Berkeley, California before coming to Jesus College, Oxford in 1965 to study for a D.Phil. on 'Caesarius of Arles and his Methods of Communicating the Christian Faith and Life' (during which time he also rowed for his college Eight). Before returning to Oxford in 1983 he had had experience of both

---

[13] M. Mahony, 'Donald Sykes: An Appreciation', *MCM* 188 (1985–6), 20.
[14] Council Minutes, 8 Feb. 1986.

16. Jan Womer, Principal 1986–88

pastoral and academic work:[15] pastoral work in Lutheran churches in California and academic work as Professor of Theology at Nommenson University, Sumatra, Indonesia from 1971 until 1975. His own research led to his editing and contributing to *Ecclesia-Leiturgia-Ministerium* (Helsinki, 1977) and to his editing *Morality and Ethics in Early Christianity* (Philadelphia, 1987). Throughout his time at Mansfield, he played an active part in Oxford's Theology Faculty.

As Principal, he followed Donald Sykes's example in entering into negotiations with the University Registrar and Vice-Chancellor about Mansfield's desire for full collegiate status; in this he was fully supported by the Council at their meeting on 17 May 1986. Together with the Bursar he met with various University committees to discuss the implications.

It was Jan Womer who presided as Principal over the Centenary celebrations of June and July 1986. Commemoration was celebrated on 21 June: the morning was taken up with the Chaplain's talk on 'A Hundred Years of Mansfield Ministerial Training' (assisted by others), and a second talk, on Mansfield House by its Warden, the Revd Geoffrey Hooper. Charles Brock pointed out that Mansfield was the only place in England where one could train for ministry alongside those studying other subjects in the same building. Geoffrey Hooper told of the recent changes at Mansfield House and of his hopes for renewed co-operation between College and Settlement. After a cricket match, in which the Present Students narrowly defeated the Alumni, many more alumni and alumnae gathered in Chapel for the Commemoration Service, at which John Marsh preached. Madrigals in the Principal's garden preceded a large Buffet Dinner.

Six hundred guests attended a Centenary Ball on 27 June. Some days later, on 2 July, a Centenary Luncheon was held for guests from the University. The main guest of honour was the Vice-Chancellor, Sir Patrick Neill, Warden of All Souls; the presence of the Master of Balliol, the Warden of Merton, and the Master of St Catherine's was recognition of the part their predecessors had played in Mansfield's earlier history.

A new Honorary Fellow was appointed at the time of the centenary: John Huxtable (Mansfield 1935–7), who retired as Chairman of

---

[15] He was ordained in Uppsala by Bishop Bengt Sundklar under a Call from the Lutheran Council of Great Britain in Jan. 1968.

the Board of Education. A great ecumenical statesman, he was one of the architects of the United Reformed Church and its first joint General Secretary; he ended his career as Executive Officer of the Churches' Unity Commission.[16]

There was now a growing professionalism in the administration of the College, as in British higher education generally. After a succession of short Bursarships since the departure of James Whalley—Peter le Sage Harris (1981–2),[17] Ronald Burton (1982–4),[18] and David Kinnersley (1985–6)[19]—it was recognized that the work required the full-time commitment of a person in mid-career. The College was fortunate in the appointment of Duncan Forbes in 1986; his previous experience as an administrator in the National Health Service has enabled him to develop the Bursar's role creatively as a pivotal one with the College and in negotiations with the University. In addition, his literary and theological gifts have enriched the worship in College Chapel. He has been ably supported by another migrant from hospital administration, Robin McGarry, who was appointed Domestic Manager (his title was later changed to Steward) in 1988.

The College had moved further towards a collegiate structure with the formation of an Academic Policy Committee, on which all College Lecturers and Tutorial Fellows served, whose formal meetings began in October 1986. From that time on, the Principal and Fellows met together in what was now called 'Governing Body' (though strictly this was not its formal title until two years later), and Principal, Fellows, and Lecturers constituted the Academic Policy Committee. In 1982 the post of Junior Dean was created.

The increase in numbers also contributed to the development of the negotiating function of the JCR. Government pressures on higher education meant that student grants were not keeping pace with inflation, and the tight control of university funding put pressure on colleges. In 1982, for example, the SCR were told that while College costs were due to increase by 12 per cent, grants were to be raised by only 4 per cent. In that situation, the SCR and JCR negotiating

---

[16] For John Huxtable (1914–90), see *As It Seemed to Me* (London, 1991) for his own reflections on his life and career. See also *MCM* 193 (1990–1), 41–2.

[17] Retired lieutenant-colonel, Royal Marines.

[18] Ronald Burton's background was in teaching and the Civil Service. He came to Mansfield from a Research Fellowship at Nuffield College.

[19] David Kinnersley, Research Fellow at Nuffield College 1983–4, had previously been Senior Economic Adviser to the National Water Council. He helped to launch Water Aid.

teams had a difficult task. However, their work was carried out with good humour and acceptable compromise each year until the late 1980s.

In 1987, for several autumn weeks, a rent strike by the JCR created a very unhappy atmosphere. The dispute was resolved by a combination of threat and persuasion. The threat was contained in a letter which was sent to all JCR members at the beginning of the Christmas vacation, warning that those who held out against payment would not be allowed to return. More importantly, many students were persuaded of the College case during a JCR telephone lobbying campaign, which enabled senior members to explain the necessity for the College's proposals. The essentially good relationships between the Common Rooms were fortunately soon restored, and there was a general realization that the fundamental problem lay at another level, in government policy towards higher education. A sign of the basic goodwill was the fact that the profits from the JCR Winter Event during the strike were set aside to pay for the floodlighting which now enhances the College buildings.

The College was keen to widen its intake, particularly by giving positive encouragement to potential candidates from comprehensive schools. This has proved a more difficult task for all Oxford colleges than was originally envisaged, but open days, school visits, and personal contact have reaped some success. Members of the JCR themselves have taken the initiative in contacting schools and showing potential students round the College.

The sporting reputation of the College reached the national and international headlines in 1987 when the mutiny of the American crew members of the Oxford boat, incensed by the exclusion of one of their compatriots, was a matter for daily press comment in the weeks preceding the Oxford and Cambridge University Boat Race. The President of the Boat Club was Donald MacDonald, a mature student reading English at Mansfield; two other Mansfield students, Chris Huntington and Jonathan Fish, were among the mutineers. Donald MacDonald showed great courage in standing firm, and, against many odds, his crew defeated Cambridge on 28 March without the support of the mutineers.[20] He himself paid tribute to the support he received from within the College: 'At Mansfield it was a

---

[20] The whole story is told in Daniel Topolski and Patrick Robinson, *True Blue* (London, 1989).

family crisis and for three months the College seemed to hold its breath;' and he was able to comment a year after the event that Mansfield rowing was 'a wonderful mixture of commitment and fun'.[21]

During the decade of the 1980s there were more changes in the ministerial course and in those entering it than in the previous ninety years, in common with many other churches and theological colleges. It was now rare for anyone to join the course straight from a first degree; the average age of new ordinands rose considerably after 1982.[22] From the mid-1970s more women came forward and were accepted for training for the ministry; for the first time URC churches were in practice beginning to consider women alongside men as candidates for vacant pastorates (though many obstacles remained). By the end of the 1980s the numbers of ordinands were more or less evenly balanced between men and women. In addition, the College, and the denomination, was now willing to consider the admission of non-graduate ordinands; the first arrived in 1981.

The focus of the training changed from a concentration on the academic to an integration of the academic and the practical. Students were encouraged to take the three-year certificate course, rather than a two-year degree course followed by the third year of the certificate.[23] As well as more emphasis on secular placements—work in hospitals, prisons, industrial missions—the recognition that Britain is now a multi-cultural society led to the introduction of an integrated course on 'Christianity and Other Faiths' in 1980. A greater emphasis was placed on spirituality.[24] From 1985, a fourth year of 'internship', during which an ordinand combines attachment to a church with College training one day a week, became a requirement for all URC candidates.

Ecumenical co-operation developed further. The days when protests could be made about Mansfield students being recommended

---

[21] 'Muted Mutiny', *MCM* 190 (1987–8), 42–3.

[22] This trend had increased when the URC introduced a Course III mode of training for candidates over the age of 30 at the end of the 1970s: part-time, home-based training followed by a final year in College. It became not uncommon for professional people to take early retirement in order to train for the ministry in later life, and for those in middle life to enter training as their children grew older.

[23] In 1992 the Certificate in Theology became the Bachelor of Theology (B. Theol.) degree.

[24] See Justine Wyatt, 'Spirituality and Ordination Training', in *MCM* 188 (1985–6), 1973–4.

to attend lectures by Roman Catholics were long past. Dominicans taught ethics, Jesuits advised on Ignatian exercises, and Anglo-Catholics were invited to give a perspective on the Reformation. Mansfield staff in turn were invited to teach courses at Anglican colleges.

For at least fifteen years, the new College constitution had been an item of business at most Council and SCR meetings. Lord Armstrong, Chairman of Council until his death in 1980, had steered the early deliberations. It then fell to Ian Bancroft (created Lord Bancroft in 1982),[25] who became Chairman in 1981, to oversee the later discussions. A balance had to be achieved between the desire on the one hand to be faithful to the original purpose of the College, yet on the other the need not only to abolish denominational restrictions on the appointment of new staff (apart from the Principal, who, it was finally agreed, should be 'a member of a Christian Church'—not necessarily of the URC), but also to recognize the equal status of non-theological subjects in the work of the College. In this process, Charles Brock played a key role, in that with his goodwill and strong liberal convictions he was able to carry the Congregational and URC Councils with him in support of these new developments. And his colleagues in the SCR supported the guarantee of a permanent place in the College for ministerial training in the Reformed tradition.

In 1983, when Donald Sykes was still Principal, the proposed Royal Charter scheme was submitted to the Charity Commissioners. They replied with the disconcerting view that the College was probably already operating *ultra vires* in respect of the 1899 Scheme. Michael Mahony remembered that this was 'an acutely uncomfortable revelation, which led to a hard-hitting session in London [on 9 January 1984] with a Senior Commissioner'. It required 'the collective persuasive skills' of Donald Sykes, Richard Buckley, Michael Mahony, and Ron Burton (then Bursar) to retrieve the situation and avoid losing all that had been gained since 1955.[26]

The Charity Commissioners were eventually persuaded that the original purposes of the College would be safeguarded by the appointment of a body of Trustees (including four appointed by the General Assembly of the URC, one appointed by the Congregational

---

[25] Lord Bancroft was Head of the Home Civil Service and Permanent Secretary to the Civil Service Department 1978–81.

[26] I am indebted to the late Michael Mahony for this information.

Federation, four Fellows appointed by the Governing Body, together with individually appointed co-optative Trustees) who were granted overall control, while the Governing Body of Fellows was to be responsible for the day-to-day administration. The Reformed tradition of the College was endorsed by the requirement that both the Chaplain and the Director of Ministerial Training (then one and the same person) should be ordained ministers of the URC, or of a Congregational Church, and a Ministerial Training Committee was to be responsible to the Trustees for the ordination course.[27] A Finance Committee was to act in an advisory capacity.

The constitution was finally agreed at the beginning of 1988, and the new scheme was publicized in the *Times Educational Supplement.* Jan Womer had departed at the end of Hilary Term, at short notice, to take up a senior post in the Lutheran Church in the USA, after just two years as Principal. He had been invited to lead the department of the newly formed Evangelical Lutheran Church in America responsible for worship and music; since his term of office as Lutheran World Federation Fellow was due to end in 1989, and as Mansfield's new constitution was about to take effect, he felt it right to accept the invitation and allow for the election of another Principal under the new arrangements.[28] It therefore fell to Michael Mahony, as newly appointed Acting Principal, to preside over the celebrations for the new constitution, sealed by the Charity Commission on 25 June 1988. The Council had accepted its own demise, and a smaller group of Trustees was now in office. Few realized at the time how soon they would again be discussing a constitution, this time for a full college of the University.

When the new Trustees met in July 1988, Lord Bancroft was elected Chairman. It was agreed that their first priorities were the acquisition of more money and the achievement of full college status. And the first priorities for spending were the funding of an Economics Fellowship and the construction of a new building to house students and provide extra teaching rooms. For all these objects a new Principal with appropriate experience was vital. A Search Committee of

[27] The former members of the Board of Education were invited to become members of the new Ministerial Training Committee, to serve for terms of six years. Bernard Thorogood, Chairman of the Board of Education since 1986, was elected Chairman of the new committee.

[28] Unfortunately the funding for his new post in the USA came to an end in 1991. Since 1991 Jan Womer has combined service as pastor to a Lutheran congregation near Los Angeles with an Adjunct Professorship at Claremont School of Theology.

four members was set up with a brief to bring names to the Trustees and Governing Body.

Until the appointment of a new Principal (which proved to be a period of eighteen months), the day-to-day administration of the College was placed in the hands of Michael Mahony with the assistance of the Senior Fellows. During this difficult period a great deal was achieved by a united team: the Associate Student programme was consolidated, the profile of the development programme was raised, and the interest and support of alumni was further stimulated by the holding of a special dinner in the House of Lords, at the invitation of Lord Bancroft.

The new Governing Body now regulated its procedure so that its agenda was divided into three parts: the JCR and MCR as well as the whole SCR were represented during the first agenda, the Fellows and a Lecturers' representative[29] alone stayed for the second, and the third was confined to Principal and Fellows. The College continued to depend on the commitment of a small number of Fellows, who bore a heavy administrative load in addition to their teaching.

On 3 June 1989 the Trustees appointed Dennis Trevelyan (pl. 17) as Principal, the first non-theological Principal in the College's history. His background was Anglican, but he has subsequently proved to be a loyal supporter of the religious traditions of the College. He and his wife Carol moved into the Principal's Lodgings in September of the same year. He was the first Principal with an administrative rather than an academic background, and the first whose time was to be entirely occupied with administration. His career had been spent in the Civil Service, after reading History as an Open Scholar at University College in the early post-war years. Work at the Home Office when Roy Jenkins was Home Secretary was a useful asset, as it turned out, for one who was to become an Oxford Head of House under Lord Jenkins's Chancellorship. His most senior appointments, among many wide-ranging responsibilities, were as Director-General of the Prison Service (probably less useful for his later career) and as First Civil Service Commissioner. Immediately after settling in

---

[29] This was a recognition of the significant contribution of the Stipendiary Lecturers to the work of the College. During these years, the College has benefited greatly from the teaching of Pamela Berry (Geography), Arthur Burns (History), George Carras (Theology), Nicholas Horsewood (Economics), David Leopold (Politics, also Junior Dean), Katherine Morris (Philosophy), Frank Romany (English), Lucinda Rumsey (English), Simon Skinner (History), and Kate Ward-Perkins (English).

17. Dennis Trevelyan, Principal 1989–

Oxford, Dennis Trevelyan proceeded with great energy to endeavour to put into effect, in collaboration with the Trustees and Governing Body, the plans already prepared.

In the autumn of 1988 Michael Mahony had discussed with the University Registrar again the possibility of a change in Mansfield's status in the University. Through his persistent and persuasive negotiations Hebdomadal Council agreed in principle, a year later, that Mansfield should become a full college, on certain conditions: the College was required to secure an endowment of £5.5 million, at July 1988 prices, before 31 July 1994 (though it was indicated that a slightly later date might be acceptable), and to accommodate at least two-thirds of its students in college-provided accommodation. Mansfield would then be eligible to bid for joint appointments with the University on the same basis as other colleges.

As a sign of Mansfield's greater recognition the new Principal was given individual representation at the Conference of Colleges (unlike the other PPHs who had one representative between them). The Principal's personal reputation, as well as the College's, was recognized in his appointment as Chairman of the Equal Opportunities Committee. Mansfield was becoming more ambitious. Was this the reason for the invitation to Mansfield's Principal to preach the University sermon on 'the sin of pride' in November 1990?

The acquisition of more than £5 million seemed an almost impossible task. However, it was necessary to look to the future, and Governing Body decided on the appointment of a new Development Officer, whose brief would be to look not only for new sources of funding, but also for new projects acceptable to the University which might attract funding. Adele Smith, who was appointed in November 1989, had a wide experience of fund-raising, and in just over four years was to help the College to find new areas of funding.

In 1991 the Principal announced in his report that the College had two new plans for the future, formulated after much discussion with those within and without the University. The first was for an environmental centre, in accord with the widespread and fast-growing 'green' movement: an Oxford Centre for the Environment, Ethics, and Society (OCEES). This was to be an interdisciplinary centre, concentrating on environmental ethics, law, and economics. The inclusion of ethics made the proposed centre unique in the UK, and also linked it with the College's theological tradition. The Centre owed much to the inspiration of Yvonne Workman, part-time Ethics Tutor for all too short a time from 1989 until her premature death in 1991. She had attended the Basel Conference of the World Council of Churches on the theme 'Justice, Peace and the Integrity of Creation' in 1989.[30] The Principal found considerable interest in such a project during a tour of the United States. Also interested was the World Wide Fund for Nature (UK), who contributed an initial sum to start the centre, and then agreed to formal collaboration. The Centre was launched formally at a ceremony at which 'Heads of Agreement' were signed on 22 May 1992.[31]

Since then, the Centre (with an Executive Committee chaired jointly by Michael Freeden and John Muddiman, representing the disciplines of Politics and Theology, and advised by James Meadowcroft of the University of Sheffield[32]) has organized seminars and conferences, and established its own offices at 64 Banbury Road, while awaiting a permanent building on the College site. The Centre's first Research Fellow, funded by Sun Life Assurance, the anthropologist Laura Rival, was appointed in 1993; the following year, Bhaskar Vira and Antonia Layard were appointed as additional Research Fellows. Not unrelated to this environmental concern, a year earlier Andrew Linzey was appointed to the IFAW Research Fellowship—the world's first academic post in ethics and animals—funded by the International Fund for Animal Welfare.[33]

The second plan is for an Oxford Institute for American Studies, a joint venture with the University. A new building spanning the boundary of Mansfield with Rhodes House is to house the Bodleian Library's American collection and provide teaching and conference facilities, and Mansfield will offer hospitality to some of its staff. Thus Mansfield's many suggestions for making a more profitable use of its land, in co-operation with others, have finally come to fruition. The Appeal for this centre was included in the official 'Campaign for Oxford', the University's fund-raising scheme. This too links with Mansfield's tradition, for its connections with the United States have

---

[30] A fund in her memory provides for an annual lecture and provides grants to help the College's staff and students with research in related areas.

[31] See the *University Gazette*, 28 May 1992.

[32] See James Meadowcroft, 'The Oxford Centre for the Environment, Ethics and Society', *MCM* 194 (1991–2), 37. In 1993 James Meadowcroft was made an Associate Fellow of the Centre.

[33] Andrew Linzey, who came to Mansfield from the University of Essex, is the author of numerous works on the moral status of animals, including *Animal Theology* (London, 1994). He is also Special Professor in Theology at the University of Nottingham.

always been strong. Charles Brock, himself an American, has been one of the most enthusiastic College supporters of the scheme, with his particular interest in the links between the British Puritan tradition and the 'American dream'.[34] Mansfield's representatives, Dennis Trevelyan and (until his death) Michael Mahony, have been involved in the task force charged with planning the project. In 1994 Dr Steven Gillon was appointed University Lecturer in the History of the USA and a Fellow of Mansfield.

New academic institutes required new buildings, for the College itself could not even provide separate offices for each of its academic staff. During the 1980s John Kempster of the Architects Design Partnership had prepared plans for a new building which would provide student accommodation and tutors' rooms, to be sited in the Principal's garden opposite the Lodgings; planning permission had already been obtained. It was now decided that this building should house the proposed environmental centre, for which outside finance would hopefully be obtained, and that a new accommodation block sited behind the John Marsh Building to provide forty student rooms should be built as soon as possible.[35] Brewer, Smith, and Brewer prepared a 'design-and-build package' for a self-financing building at a cost of £600,000; the income, from student rents and conference fees, would enable the necessary loan to be repaid. Work began in the summer of 1992, and was completed by the following May—a tribute to the efforts of the committee, Michael Mahony (chairman), Duncan Forbes, John Sykes, and Geoffrey Higham (Trustee), which supervised the design competition, the finances, and the building of the new block.

This new block (for which a name has yet to be chosen) was formally opened on a fine summer Saturday, 26 June 1993, by the Chancellor, Lord Jenkins, in the presence of 500 guests. He complimented the College on owning the finest Champneys buildings in Oxford. Among the guests were Gladys and John Marsh, whom the College now honoured by naming the block which he had been instrumental in building as the 'John Marsh Building'. Several generous individuals and small groups from amongst the alumni of the College

---

[34] His book, *Mosaics of the American Dream: America as New Israel—A Metaphor for Today* was published (Wheatley, Oxford) in 1994.

[35] After modifications required by the planning authorities and by tax regulations, the block has provided thirty-six students' rooms, a computer room, common room, and kitchens.

had donated money to furnish and equip rooms, and the Mansfield JCR M2000 Committee had raised £3,000, mainly through its Winter Event, to furnish and fit a specially adapted room for a disabled student.[36]

After rather a lean time for Mansfield's Theology Faculty as far as numbers of staff were concerned (especially after Justine Wyatt's appointment as Oxford and Reading Area Director for Christian Aid in 1991), the 1990s have seen a great strengthening of the College's Theology Department, which now provides eight members of the University Faculty.[37] Two new sources of funding have helped: a bequest of £248,000 (the largest, to date, the College has ever received) from Geoffrey Morley-Adlam[38] and a contribution of over £100,000 from the G. B. Caird Memorial Trust, launched by George Caird's children in 1990 to celebrate the life and scholarship of their father by endowing a permanent post in Biblical Studies attached to the Faculty of Theology and based at Mansfield.[39]

In 1990 John Muddiman, an Anglican scholar who had already served the College as a Lecturer a decade earlier, was appointed Fellow in New Testament Studies;[40] both through his earlier experience of teaching in an Anglican theological college, and through his wide experience of ecumenical dialogue, including membership of the Anglican–Roman Catholic International Commission (ARCIC) since 1992, he has brought a new dimension to the ecumenical involvement of the College. As Secretary of the Theology Faculty he contributes much to the University, and as Admissions Tutor and Co-Director of OCEES a great deal to the College.

The Lutheran World Federation, after much discussion and

---

[36] See 'Summer Celebrations', *MCM* 195 (1992–3), 28–9.

[37] A series of lectures on 'Radical Theologies' in Michaelmas Term 1993, planned and hosted by the College, attracted considerable interest.

[38] Geoffrey Morley-Adlam of Norwich was accepted for ordination training at Mansfield in 1919, and was then matriculated at the Non-collegiate (later St Catherine's) Society in order to take his first degree in Greats. He did not proceed to ministerial training, but developed a lifelong affection for Mansfield. In his will he left his estate to found a 'Katherine Emma Morley-Adlam Fellowship' for ministerial training in memory of his wife, whom he met in Oxford and married late in life.

[39] See *MCM* 193 (1990–1), 23–5. Through individual donations and the proceeds of concerts and other events the Fund had raised over £100,000 by the beginning of 1994, and has been able to contribute towards the cost of Mansfield's Fellowship in New Testament Studies.

[40] He is the author of *The Bible Fountain and Well of Truth* (Oxford, 1983) and several articles on New Testament subjects. With John Barton he is editor of the *Oxford Bible Commentary*.

consultation, decided to appoint a Lecturer to work jointly at Mansfield and the Anglican Ripon College at Cuddesdon. Scott Ickert, a Reformation scholar and church historian,[41] joined Mansfield in 1990 as Supernumerary Lutheran Fellow, and, through his work at Cuddesdon, has become the chief formal link between the Lutheran World Federation and the Church of England. Anthony Tucker, Lecturer in Pastoral Theology since 1989, was appointed Associate Director of Ministerial Training in 1993.[42] In 1994 the Revd Flora Winfield, a newly ordained Anglican priest, was appointed Associate Chaplain. The theological staff continue practical pastoral work alongside their academic commitments as a matter of principle.

The inter-faith interests of the College were extended in 1991 when Ron Nettler, a Fellow of the Oxford Centre for Postgraduate Hebrew Studies (now the Oxford Centre for Hebrew and Jewish Studies) and a Lecturer in the Oriental Studies Institute, was appointed to a Supernumerary Fellowship at Mansfield, in conjunction with the University. His teaches Islamic religious thought, theological and exegetical, medieval and modern.[43] He has been instrumental in forging a link between Mansfield and the Centre for Hebrew and Jewish Studies (of which Charles Brock is now an Associate Scholar, and Dennis Trevelyan a Governor). In 1993 Charles Brock was elected Co-chair (together with a representative of the Sikh community) of the Advisory Committee of the newly established Interfaith Centre in Oxford.

The College's international character was further enhanced with the appointment of Antoni Chawluk, of the Universities of Warsaw, London, and St Andrews, to a Fellowship in Economics and a University Lecturership in Soviet Economies and their Transformation, a post funded jointly with the University, in 1991.[44] Alex Boraine (Mansfield 1960–3), a Methodist minister in South Africa, who co-founded the Institute for a Democratic Alternative in South Africa

[41] Scott Ickert was previously a parish pastor in Virginia, USA. He has published several scholarly articles in the field of Reformation studies.

[42] Anthony (Tony) Tucker (Mansfield 1951–4) has had a long connection with the College as Council member, Trustee, and part-time Lecturer in Pastoral Theology. After three pastorates, he was for many years Head of Student Services at the Oxford Polytechnic (now Oxford Brookes University). His special interests include the development of the modern counselling movement.

[43] Ron Nettler's special interests include theological aspects of Islamic–Jewish relations, Islamic mystical thought (especially of Ibn al-Arabi), Islamic theological responses to modernity and the West.

[44] See A. Chawluk, 'New Capitalism in Central Europe', *MCM* 195 (1992–3), 32–3.

(IDASA—the first organization to bring together Afrikaners and the ANC), was elected to an Honorary Fellowship in 1990.[45]

International links were further developed through an Associate Student Programme (alongside the arrangements for Visiting Students), by which overseas students come for a year and undertake an academic programme which counts as part of their home degree course. In the late 1980s, the programme was arranged through the Washington International Studies Council, but from 1990 onwards the College has arranged its own programme directly with American colleges (in the United States principally with Holy Cross College, Massachusetts); there is also a separate scheme for Japanese students. These students are fully involved in the life of the College, and their prowess on the sports field has been particularly welcome. The Junior Research Fellow in Humanities (Ewan West 1987–92, a musicologist, and Margaret Kean from 1992, a specialist in the literature of the seventeenth century) has taken responsibility for both recruiting and arranging the programme.[46]

Apart from these Associate Students, the international dimension has increased among the 'ordinary' students. Twenty-four out of the eighty-four 'freshers' who entered the College in 1992 came directly from overseas (from the USA, Italy, Poland, Bulgaria, Germany, Singapore, Australia, India, South Africa, and Switzerland).

The concerns of the JCR during the years 1988–94 have included government policy on student finance (a concern shared by the SCR), green issues, women's issues, and widening the field of College admissions. The JCR has established a Schools Link Committee in order to try to broaden the range of applicants to Mansfield, and a JCR Women's Group has tried to encourage more women to apply to the College. Mansfield JCR members have continued to take an active part in University student life.

Such activity, achievement, and variety surely merited a proper recognition of Mansfield's contribution to the life of the University. In May 1992 Lord Bancroft and the Principal went to see the Vice-Chancellor to ask yet again for collegiate status, primarily on the grounds of student and staff contribution to University life. They pointed out the basic unfairness of withholding full collegiate status from Mansfield, which in all ways performed as a full college of the

---

[45] See Alex Boraine, 'The Struggle for Democracy', *MCM* 190 (1987–8), 41–2. Lord Beloff and Paul Crossley were also elected to Honorary Fellowships.

[46] See Ewan West, 'Associate Student Programme', *MCM* 193 (1990–1), 36.

University. The Vice-Chancellor (Sir Richard Southwood) was supportive, and set in train a series of discussions which culminated in a vote in Congregation on 26 January 1993 in favour of Mansfield being granted collegiate status without the prior acquisition of a £5.5 million endowment at 1989 prices.[47] In addition, the University agreed to make available finance for five additional special (non-CUF) posts at Mansfield; these were awarded to Michael Mahony, Janet Dyson, John Muddiman, Rosalind Ballaster (appointed Fellow in English in 1993),[48] and Roderick Bagshaw (appointed Law Fellow in 1994).[49]

It was a sad blow to the College when, just before Christmas 1994, Michael Mahony died suddenly at the age of 51. He had been a member of the College since 1963, as undergraduate, research student, tutor, Fellow, and, for a time, Acting Principal. For some years he and his family lived in a College house. He was in many respects the linchpin of the College, popular, generous, balancing wisdom with good humour, always ready to give time to the administrative tasks on which the College's efficiency and effectiveness depend. His whole professional life had been devoted to the College, and he will be sorely missed.

On 31 May 1995 the Queen gave her approval to a new Royal Charter for the College, granting it full collegiate status within the University. This was the culmination of a series of negotiations and petitions over the preceding two years. On 24 June a great gathering of over 850 people met in the College to celebrate the occasion. The new statutes dispense with Trustees, so that Governing Body now assumes full responsibility for the College. There is entrenched a statute which obliges the College to provide training for ministerial students of the URC and the Congregational Federation, to appoint a Director of Ministerial Training, and to set up a smaller Ministerial Training Committee to supervise it. And so Mansfield enters a new stage in its history, continuing its tradition in a manner appropriate for the end of the twentieth century.

---

[47] The College had to give a binding undertaking not to seek support from the Colleges Contributions Scheme until its endowment has reached the equivalent of £5.5m. at July 1989 prices.

[48] Rosalind Ballaster's main interests are in 17th- and 18th-cent. culture, women's writing, critical theory, and contemporary popular/mass culture. Her publications include *Women's Worlds: Ideology, Femininity and the Women's Magazine* (London, 1991) and *Seductive Forms: Women's Amatory Fiction 1640–1740* (Oxford, 1992).

[49] Roderick Bagshaw's special interests include public law, tort, contract, and evidence.

XVI

Conclusion

MANSFIELD was an exclusively theological college for the first seventy years of its life, pioneering the contribution of Nonconformists to the theological teaching and religious life of the University, and to ecumenical relations in the country at large, and mediating a wider culture to the Nonconformist denominations. But the words of Mark Johnson in *The Dissolution of Dissent* (298, 298–9) are a challenge to the historian who attempts to evaluate the early significance of Mansfield College. 'Mansfield's message was no more than the idea that there should be unconditional freedom in religious matters.' 'Ecumenism was the final phase in the dissolution of Dissent.'

Since the days when Fairbairn rallied the Congregational Union Assembly with his call to promote the 'New Puritanism', English Congregationalism, and later the United Reformed Church, have declined numerically and in influence. Religious practice in general has diminished, and the confidence with which Mansfield began its life was not subsequently justified. Mansfield, in common with other theological colleges, has known hard times. Since Mansfield was now a college in a national university of international standing, and in a sense representative of Nonconformity's bid to contribute to the mainstream of English religious and cultural life, its difficulties and their solutions had a wider significance.

It has been argued in previous chapters that while many of those who supported Mansfield's move to Oxford did not have a clear idea of the theological foundations of their distinctive role as Nonconformists, it was Mansfield which contributed most to the rediscovery of that role. The fact that the College had to struggle well into the twentieth century to achieve proper recognition for its contribution to Oxford scholarship proved a stimulus and rallying point. During its years as an exclusively theological college, it made a significant contribution to the revival and renewal of the Reformed tradition, of that strand of the Puritan inheritance which had during the nineteenth century been overbalanced by the separatist, more individualist thread. Principals Micklem and Marsh, particularly, through their broadcasting, journalism, preaching, and books, found inspiration in their seventeenth-century roots and reminded their fellow Congregationalists of their responsibilities as church members in covenant. They, together with members of staff such as Romilly Micklem, Erik Routley, and Charles Brock, revived the Genevan tradition of worship,[1] and they and others connected with the College have enriched the musical traditions of the Reformed churches. Mansfield's fine tradition of biblical scholarship, appropriate in a college which has emphasized the importance of both Word and Sacrament in worship, was established by scholars such as G. B. Gray, C. H. Dodd, and George Caird.

Through its international contacts, Mansfield has been able to mediate Reformed theology from Scotland, Germany, and the United States to Oxford in general. 'Paradoxically the nonconformist colleges [Manchester College and Regent's Park College, as well as Mansfield], seen at first as culturally provincial, became the most outward-looking and international of Oxford's religious institutions.' So has written the author of the chapter on 'Religion' in the twentieth-century volume of *The History of the University of Oxford.*[2]

The understanding of ministry, debated in Fairbairn's study at the turn of the century, and taught within a distinctive tradition at Mansfield, remains an important witness to those of other Christian traditions. It enabled Mansfield to pioneer, albeit for long hesitantly, the ordained ministry of women.

Mansfield members of staff (and many distinguished former students such as John Huxtable and Norman Goodall) have been pioneers in the ecumenical movement. Some have regarded this participation as witnessing the strength of what Congregationalists and members of the URC have been able to contribute. Others, especially some historians and sociologists,[3] have viewed the ecumenical movement itself as a response to the weakness and decline of the churches in

---

[1] For a discussion of this tradition, see Horton Davies, *The Worship of the English Puritans* (London, 1948).

[2] Frank Turner, 'Religion', in B. Harrison (ed.), *The History of the University of Oxford,* viii: *The Twentieth Century* (Oxford, 1994), 298.

[3] See especially R. Currie, *Methodism Divided* (London, 1968) and B. R. Wilson, *Religion in Secular Society: A Sociological Comment* (London, 1966), part iii.

a secularized society, leading to further decline and a failure to meet the intellectual challenges of the age. Motivation is difficult to evaluate. But the theologian as well as the sociologist has to be heard on this issue. David Thompson has reminded both that 'one of the questions posed by supporters of the ecumenical movement is whether a united or a divided church more properly represents the mind of Christ.... To assume that division is a sign of religious vigour is bound to lead to the conclusion that union is a sign of weakness.'[4] The leaders of the ecumenical movement, including all the ordained Principals of Mansfield and many of its staff, have acted out of the conviction that it is a united Church which 'represents the mind of Christ'; and their witness must be accounted part of the evidence.[5]

Before the year 1955, Mansfield had educated more than 400 students. Of the 421 who completed a course lasting at least two years, 214 spent their entire careers in pastoral ministry. Another 75 divided their careers between pastoral ministry and other related activities. A few former students moved to the Church of England, but the percentage (5 per cent) is not large. Seventy-three spent at least part of their careers in theological education, in most cases educating the Congregational ministers of the future. While the numbers applying to the College had not grown as many had hoped, those who took the College course did in most cases use their training for the purpose for which it was undertaken.[6]

Since 1955, the year in which Mansfield began to take students reading disciplines other than theology, the College has re-created its tradition in a form appropriate to the late twentieth century. Its students have made a full contribution to University life, and have gone on to careers of distinction in law, the media, the arts, and academic life; its Fellows and Lecturers have established fine academic reputations, and some have been appointed to Chairs in other universities. As a multi-disciplinary college Mansfield is heir to the

---

[4] David Thompson, 'Theological and Sociological Approaches to the Motivation of the Ecumenical Movement', in D. Baker (ed.), *Religious Motivation: Biographical and Sociological Problems for the Church Historian*, Studies in Church History 15 (Oxford, 1978), 475.

[5] See Robert Towler, *Homo Religiosus: Sociological Problems in the Study of Religion* (London, 1974), 165.

[6] See the chart in App. II for further figures. It gives a more positive picture than that presented by Mark Johnson in *The Dissolution of Dissent 1850–1918* (New York, 1987), 229.

traditions of the Dissenting Academies as well as the universities; in training ministers alongside students of different cultural and religious traditions, it is responding to the needs of contemporary society; and in initiating and participating in two interdisciplinary institutes it is in the forefront of academic development. It has achieved these changes through a democratic process involving the Trustees of the original Spring Hill Endowment, the churches for whose ministry it was originally founded, its subscribers, and its teachers. Whereas in its earlier years the College was shaped primarily by its Principal (occasionally in tension with the Council), its present policy is worked out collaboratively. It has now achieved recognition as a full collegiate member of the University of Oxford.

The words of Fairbairn in 1889 have a contemporary ring: 'We believe that there are greater things before us than lie between us and our fathers, and greater things are now possible than were ever possible before.'[7]

---

[7] A. M. Fairbairn, 'Theology in the Modern University', in *Mansfield College, Oxford: Its Origin and Opening* (London, 1890), 134.

APPENDIX I

Mansfield Students and their Later Careers

The following tables provide information about the denominational affiliation on entry, and the later careers, of all students who entered Mansfield between 1886 and 1954 (i.e. when it was an exclusively theological college), and who completed a course of at least two years.

(a) DENOMINATIONAL AFFILIATION

	1886–1918	1919–54	Total
Congregationalists	180	178	358
Baptists	24	17	41
Methodists	4	7	11
Welsh Independents	2	2	4
Welsh Presbyterians	2	2	4
Lutherans	—	3	3
TOTAL	212	209	421

(b) CAREER ON LEAVING

	1886–1918	1919–54	Total
Pastoral ministry in UK, USA, or Empire/Commonwealth	105	109	214
Pastoral ministry +			
Education	5	5	10
Social work	4	2	6
Church administration	2	3	5
Missionary service	9	9	18
Media work	1	2	3
Theological teaching	17	16	33
Theological teaching	20	20	40
Other university teaching	3	3	6
Missionary service	15	4	19
Social work	3	2	5
Other	11	8	19
Unknown	15	20	35
TOTAL	212	209	421

Sources: *Mansfield College Magazines*; *Congregational Year Books*; Charles E. Surman, 'Directory of Dissenting Ministers', at Dr Williams's Library, London; *Baptist Handbooks*; W. Leary, *Directory of Primitive Methodist Ministers and their Circuits* (Loughborough, 1990); *Crockford's Clerical Directories*; individual biographies and personal knowledge.

APPENDIX II

Admissions since 1955, at Five-Yearly Intervals

	1960	1965	1970	1975	1980	1985	1990
Chemistry		3					
Education (PGCE)	1	4		1		5	
Engineering Science and Metallurgy					1	3	6
English	1	2	5	8	6	8	5
Geography		1	6	6	6	6	8
Human Sciences						1	
Law	1		4	6	6	6	5
Mathematics, and Mathematics and Philosophy		1			4	4	3
Modern History		3	7	6	6	6	6
Modern Languages		3					
PPE and Social Studies	2	1			8	8	10
Physics		2					
Theology (including ordinands and graduate students with percentage of total in brackets)	10 (67%)	19 (54%)	9 (26%)	5 (16%)	10 (21%)	10 (16%)	9 (13%)
Visiting Students						10	13
TOTAL	15	35	35	31	48	62	70

APPENDIX III

College Officers

APPENDIX IV

Presidents of the Junior Common Room

1887–8	Norman Smith
1888–9	W. B. Selbie
1889–90	H. T. Andrews
1890–1	G. B. Gray
1891–2	Griffiths Thatcher
1892–3	T. Dixon Rutherford
1893–4	Andrew Hamilton
1894–5	D. S. Chrichton
1895–6	J. F. Shepherd
1896–7	R. S. Franks
1897–8	H. Wheeler Robinson
1898–9	R. J. Evans
1899–1900	Frank Lenwood
1900–1	H. C. Carter
1901–2	R. L. Franks
1902–3	Malcolm Spencer
1903–4	Thomas Watt
1904–5	Thomas Rook
1905–6	R. K. Evans
1906–7	Joseph Jones
1907–8	Leonard Brooks
1908–9	Gordon Matthews
1909–10	Allan Gaunt
1910–11	C. H. Dodd
1911–12	Wilfred Bradley
1912–13	D. W. Langridge
1913–14	B. I. Macalpine
1914–15	G. W. Haydock
1915–16	C. M. Coltman
1916–17	Alan Knott
1917–18	O. J. Francis

Presidents of the JCR

1918–19	O. J. Francis
1919–20	Romilly Micklem
1920–1	N. A. Turner-Smith
1921–2	W. N. H. Tarrant
1922–3	J. B. Middlebrook
1923–4	Norman Castles
1924–5	Norman Snaith
1925–6	W. T. Bowie
1926–7	Geoffrey Edmonds
1927–8	J. R. Theobald
1928–9	R. L. Franks
1929–30	Arthur Halfpenny
1930–1	John Marsh
1931–2	L. A. Simpson
1932–3	John Wilding
1933–4	L. M. Wheeler
1934–5	R. R. Osborn
1935–6	R. G. Wilkinson
1936–7	J. E. Farrar
1937–8	H. B. Hutchinson
1938–9	W. A. Whitehouse
1939–40	W. A. Whitehouse
1940–1	Arthur Kirkby
1941–2	Philip Lee-Woolf
1942–3	W. T. Pennar Davies
1943–4	Thomas Hawthorn
1944–5	Donald James
1945–6	Geoffrey Beck
1946–7	R. Tudur Jones
1947–8	Norman Spoor
1948–9	Laurence Binder
1949–50	John Bennett
1950–1	David Goodall
1951–2	John Bradshaw
1952–3	William Brown
1953–4	Roger Tomes
1954–5	Raymond Moody
1955–6	John Marsden
1956–7	Brian Nuttall
1957–8	Barry Jones

1958–9	Noel Shepherd
1959–60	Joseph Pratt
1960–1	Kenneth Lintern
1961–2	A. J. Groom
1962–3	John Greenland
1963–4	D. J. Kingston
1964–5	Geoffrey Roper
1965–6	Robert Smith
1966–7	John Ballantyne
1967–8	David Parry
1968–9	Sidney Blankenship
1969–70	Mike Culver
1970–1	Viktor Anderson
1971–2	Charles Long
1972–3	Robert Jope
1973–4	Richard Talbot
1974–5	Graeme Longmuir
1975–6	Andrew Eastgate
1976–7	Andrew Allen
1977–8	John Gambles
1978–9	Tim Shortis
1979–80	Philip Jones
1980–1	Henry Kopel
1981–2	John Willis
1982–3	Jeremy James
1983–4	Richard Klein
1984–5	Ian Blatchford
1985–6	Jonathan Hopkins
1986–7	Gale Macleod
1987–8	T. J. Storrie
1988–9	Nick Chism
1989–90	Nigel Hall
1990–1	Edward K. Cox
1991–2	Jason Edwards
1992–3	Gill Kirk
1993–4	Alastair Smith

Select Bibliography

MANUSCRIPT SOURCES

In the Spring Hill and Mansfield College Archive:

Minute Books of the Spring Hill College Committee of Management.
Minute Books of the Spring Hill College JCR.
Minute Books of the Mansfield College Council.
Minute Books of the Mansfield College Board of Education.
Minute Books of the Mansfield College SCR.
Minute Books of the Mansfield College JCR.
Minute Book of the Oxford University Nonconformists' Union.
JCR Conference Minute Books.
Minute Book of the 'Minor Prophets'.
Book of Building Fund Circulars.
News Cuttings Books.
A. Thomas, 'Notes of Selbie's Lectures on Preaching'.
Architectural plans, Mansfield College.
Correspondence with the College of Heralds 1955–6.

George Street Congregational Church Minute Book I (Oxfordshire County Record Office).
Mansfield Files (Oxford University Offices).
Cadoux Papers (Bodleian Library).
Sanday Papers (Bodleian Library).
Souter Papers (Bodleian Library).
Minute Book of the Executive Committee of Mansfield House (Stratford Library, London).

TAPE RECORDINGS

(deposited in Mansfield College Library)

Interviews with:
Walter Buckingham.
John Marsh.
Eric Shave.
John Whale.

Select Bibliography

PRINTED WORKS

IN MANSFIELD COLLEGE ARCHIVE

Reports of the Committee of Management of Spring Hill College (Birmingham).
Mansfield College Annual Reports and Calendars.
Mansfield College Magazines.
Mansfield House Magazines.
Information for Intending Candidates 1896.
Abstract of the Trusts Contained in the Spring Hill College Deed.
FAIRBAIRN, A. M., *Our First Term and its Moral* (1886).

PERIODICAL PUBLICATIONS

Architect.
British Congregationalist.
British Monthly.
British Quarterly Review.
Builder.
Builders' Journal.
Bulletin of the John Rylands Library.
Christian Century.
Christian Commonwealth.
Christian World.
Church Quarterly Review.
Church Times.
Congregationalist.
Congregational Quarterly.
Congregational Review.
Congregational Year Book.
Contemporary Review.
Derby Mercury.
Journal of the United Reformed Church History Society.
Liverpool Mercury.
Methodist Times.
New Blackfriars.
Nineteenth Century.
Nonconformist.
Nonconformist and Independent.
Oxford Chronicle and Berks and Bucks Gazette.
Oxford Magazine.
Oxford University Gazette.
Oxford University Hebdomadal Council Papers.
Presbyter.
Queen's Quarterly (Kingston, Ontario).

Select Bibliography

Review of the Churches.
RIBA Journal.
The Times.
Transactions of the Congregational Historical Society.

OTHER PRINTED WORKS AND THESES

(The place of publication is London unless otherwise stated)

ABBOTT, E., and CAMPBELL, L., *The Life and Letters of B. Jowett*, ii (1987).

An Appeal to All Christian People (1920).

ARNOLD, M., *Culture and Anarchy*, ed. R. H. Super (Ann Arbor, 1965).

BARNETT, S., *Settlements of University Men in Great Towns* (Oxford, 1884).

BARTLETT, J. V., *Church Life and Church Order during the First Four Centuries*, ed. C. J. Cadoux (Oxford, 1943).

BEBBINGTON, D. W., 'The Dissenting Idea of a University: Oxford and Cambridge in Nonconformist Thought in the Nineteenth Century', Hulsean Prize Essay, University of Cambridge, 1973.

BELL, G. K. A. (ed.), *Documents on Christian Unity 1920–24* (1924).

—— and DEISSMANN, A. (eds.) *Mysterium Christi* (1930).

BINFIELD, J. C. G., *So Down to Prayers: Studies in English Nonconformity* (1977).

—— 'Chapels in Crisis: Men and Issues in Victorian Eastern England', *Transactions of the Congregational Historical Society*, 20/8 (Oct. 1968).

—— 'We Claim our Part in the Great Inheritance: The Message of Four Congregational Buildings', in K. Robbins (ed.), *Protestant Evangelicalism: Britain, Ireland, Germany and America* (Oxford, 1990).

Blackheath Group, *A Re-statement of Christian Thought* (1934).

BRADLEY, W. L., *P. T. Forsyth: The Man and his Work* (1952).

British Academy, *Proceedings*.

BROWN, E. B. *In Memoriam James Baldwin Brown* (1884).

BROWN, J., 'Reminiscences', in F. J. Powicke, *David Worthington Simon* (1912).

BROWN, K. D., *A Social History of the Nonconformist Ministry in England and Wales 1880–1930* (Oxford, 1988).

BRYAN, F. C. (ed.), *For his Friends: Letters of Second Lieutenant P. G. Simmonds* (Oxford, 1918).

BRYCE, J., *Studies in Contemporary Biography* (1903).

—— 'Nonconformity in the Universities', *British Quarterly Review*, 79 (Apr. 1884).

BULLOCK, F. W. B., *The History of Ridley Hall, Cambridge*, 2 vols. (Cambridge, 1941, 1953).

BYRNE, M. St C., and MANSFIELD, C. H., *Somerville College 1879–1921* (Oxford, 1922).

Select Bibliography

CADOUX, C. J., *The Case for Evangelical Modernism: A Study of the Relation between Christian Faith and Traditional Theology* (1941).
—— *The Congregational Way* (Oxford, 1945).
—— *The Early Christian Attitude to War: A Contribution to the History of Christian Ethics* (1919).
CAIRD, G. B., *The Language and Imagery of the Bible* (1980).
—— *New Testament Theology*, ed. L. D. Hurst (Oxford, 1994).
—— *Our Dialogue with Rome* (Oxford, 1967).
CAMPBELL, R. J., *The New Theology* (1907).
—— *A Spiritual Pilgrimage* (1916).
CARLYLE, A. J., *et al.* (eds.), *Towards Reunion: Being Contributions to Mutual Understanding by Church of England and Free Church Writers* (1919).
CARROLL, L., *Works*, ed. R. L. Green (1965).
CHAMPNEYS, B., 'The Planning of Collegiate Buildings', *RIBA Journal*, 3rd ser. 10/8 (Feb. 1903).
CHEYNE, T. K., 'Reform in the Teaching of the Old Testament', *CR* 56 (Aug. 1889).
Church Relations in England: Being the Report of Conversations between Representatives of the Archbishop of Canterbury and Representatives of the Evangelical Free Churches in England (1950).
CLEMENTS, K. W., *Lovers of Discord: Twentieth Century Theological Controversies in England* (1988).
Congregational Church in England and Wales, *A Declaration of Faith* (1967).
Congregational Union of England and Wales, *Report of the Commission on the Colleges* (1958).
Congregational Year Books.
COOK, C., and STEVENSON, J., *The Longman Handbook of Modern British History* (Harlow, 1988).
COOPER, R. E., *From Stepney to St Giles: The Story of Regent's Park College 1810–1960* (1960).
COX, J., *The English Churches in a Secular Society* (Oxford, 1982).
CUNNINGHAM, C., and WATERHOUSE, P., *Alfred Waterhouse 1830–1903: The Biography of a Practice* (Oxford, 1992).
CURRIE, R., *Methodism Divided* (1968).
—— GILBERT, A., and HORSLEY, L., *Churches and Churchgoers: Patterns of Church Growth in the British Isles since 1700* (Oxford, 1977).
CURTIS, M. H., *Oxford and Cambridge in Transition* (Oxford, 1959).
CURTIS, S. J. *History of Education in Great Britain* (1953).
DALE, A. W. W., *The Life of R. W. Dale of Birmingham* (1899).
DALE, R. W., *The Atonement* (1875).
—— *Manual of Congregational Principles* (1884).
—— 'George Dawson: Politician, Lecturer, and Preacher', *Nineteenth Century*, 2 (1877).

Select Bibliography

DAVIES, H., *A Church Historian's Odyssey* (Grand Rapids, Mich., 1993).
—— *The Worship of the English Puritans* (1948).
—— *Worship and Theology in England: The Ecumenical Century* (1965).
DAVIES, W. T. P., *Mansfield College: Its History, Aims and Achievements* (Oxford, 1947).
DAVIS, V. D., *A History of Manchester College* (1932).
Derbyshire Parish Registers.
The Dialogue of East and West and Christendom: Lectures Delivered at a Conference Arranged by the Fellowship of St Alban and St Sergius in Oxford 10 March 1962 (1963).
Dictionary of National Biography (2nd edn. 1908–9).
Dictionary of National Biography: Second Supplement 1901–11 (1912).
Dictionary of National Biography 1912–21 (1927).
Dictionary of National Biography: Missing Persons (Oxford, 1993).
DILLISTONE, F. W., *C. H. Dodd: Interpreter of the New Testament* (1977).
DODD, C. H., *Apostolic Preaching and its Development* (1936).
—— *The Meaning of Paul for Today* (1920).
—— *Parables of the Kingdom* (1935).
DRIVER, S. R., *A Treatise on the Use of the Tenses in Hebrew* (1874).
ENGEL, A. J., *From Clergyman to Oxford Don* (Oxford, 1983).
ESCOTT, H., *A History of Scottish Congregationalism* (Glasgow, 1960).
FAIRBAIRN, A. M., *Catholicism: Roman and Anglican* (1899).
—— *The Christian Ministry and its Preparatory Discipline* (1877).
—— *Letter to the Regius Professor of Divinity on the School of Theology— 8 March 1898* (Oxford, 1898).
—— *The Philosophy of the Christian Religion* (1902).
—— *The Place of Christ in Modern Theology* (1893).
—— *Religion in History and in the Life of Today* (1884).
—— *Studies in Religion and Theology* (1910).
—— *Studies in the Philosophy of Religion and History* (1876).
—— 'Experience in Theology: A Chapter of Autobiography', *CR* 91 (Apr. 1907).
FARNELL, L. R., *An Oxonian Looks Back* (1934).
FIELD-BIBB, J., 'Women and Ministry: The Presbyterian Church of England', *Heythrop Journal*, 31 (1990).
FLETCHER, C. R. L., *Gladstone at Oxford 1890* (Oxford, 1908).
FLETCHER, S., *Maude Royden* (Oxford, 1989).
FLEW, R. N. (ed.), *The Nature of the Church: Papers Presented to the Theological Commission Appointed by the Continuation Committee of the World Conference on Faith and Order* (Oxford, 1952).
FORSYTH, P. T., *The Charter of the Church* (1896).
—— *Lectures on the Church and the Sacraments* (1917).
—— 'Unity and Theology', in A. J. Carlyle *et al.* (eds.), *Towards Reunion* (1919).

FRANKS, R. S., 'The Theology of A. M. Fairbairn', *Transactions of the Congregational Historical Society*, 13 (1937–9).

Franks Commission: Written Evidence, vii and xiii (Oxford, 1965).

Franks Commission: Oral Evidence (Oxford, 1965).

Free Church Fellowship, *The Free Church Fellowship 1911–65: An Ecumenical Pioneer* (Royston, 1967).

FREMANTLE, W. H., *Recollections of Dean Fremantle* (1921).

—— *The World as the Subject of Redemption* (1885).

GARRETT, J., and FARR, L. W., *Camden College: A Centenary History* (Sydney, 1964).

GARVIE, A. E., *Memories and Meanings of my Life* (1938).

GILLEY, S., *Newman and his Age* (1990).

GLADSTONE, W. E., *Diaries*, vi, vii, ed. H. C. G. Matthew (Oxford, 1978, 1982).

GLOVER, W. B., *Evangelical Nonconformists and Higher Criticism in the Nineteenth Century* (1954).

GOODALL, N., *A History of the London Missionary Society 1895–1945* (Oxford, 1954).

—— *Second Fiddle: Recollections and Reflections* (1979).

—— 'Nathaniel Micklem CH 1888–1976', *JURCHS* 1/10 (Oct. 1977).

GORE, C. (ed.), *Lux Mundi: A Series of Studies in the Religion of the Incarnation* (1889).

GRANT, J. W., *Free Churchmanship in England 1870–1940* (n.d. [1955]).

GRAY, G. B., *Sacrifice in the Old Testament: Its Theory and Practice* (1925).

HALL, N., *Autobiography* (1898).

HAMPSON, D., 'The British Response to the German Church Struggle' (Oxford D.Phil. thesis, 1973).

HARRIS, J., *Unemployment and Politics: A Study in English Social Policy 1886–1914* (Oxford, 1972).

HARRISON, B. (ed.), *The History of the University of Oxford*, viii: *The Twentieth Century* (Oxford, 1994).

HASTINGS, A., *A History of English Christianity 1920–85* (1985).

HATCH, S. C. (ed.), *Memorials of Edwin Hatch MA* (1890).

HEADLAM, A. C., *The Study of Theology* (Oxford, 1918).

—— 'Degrees in Divinity', *Church Quarterly Review*, 76 (July 1913).

Helmstedter, R., 'The Nonconformist Conscience', in P. Marsh (ed.), *The Conscience of the Victorian State* (Hassocks, 1979).

HINCHLIFF, P. B., *God and History: Aspects of British Theology 1875–1914* (Oxford, 1992).

—— *Benjamin Jowett and the Christian Religion* (Oxford, 1987).

HOPKINS, M., 'Baptists, Congregationalists and Theological Change: Some Later Nineteenth Century Leaders and Controversies' (Oxford D.Phil. thesis, 1988).

HORTON, R. F., *An Autobiography* (1917).

—— *The Courage of Conviction: An Address Delivered before the Oxford University Nonconformists' Union, 26 November 1882* (Oxford, 1882).

—— 'Free Churchmen and the Modern Churchmen', *CQ* (1926).

—— *Inspiration and the Bible* (1888).

HUXTABLE, J., *As It Seemed to Me* (1991).

—— MARSH, J., MICKLEM, E. R., and TODD, J., *A Book of Public Worship: Compiled for the Use of Congregationalists* (1948).

INGLIS, K. S., *Churches and the Working Classes in Victorian England* (1963).

International Congregational Council, *Authorised Record of Proceedings* (1891).

JASPER, R., *A. C. Headlam: Life and Letters of a Bishop* (1960).

JOHNSON, D. A., 'The End of the Evidences: A Study in Nonconformist Theological Transition', *JURCHS* 2/3 (Apr. 1979).

—— 'Pastoral Vacancy and Rising Expectations: The George Street Church, Oxford 1879–86', *JURCHS* 3/4 (Oct. 1984).

JOHNSON, M. *The Dissolution of Dissent 1850–1918* (New York, 1987).

JONES, P. d'A., *The Christian Socialist Revival 1877–1914* (Princeton, 1968).

JONES, R. T., *Congregationalism in England 1662–1962* (1962).

JORDAN, E. K. H., *Free Church Unity: History of the Free Church Council Movement 1896–1941* (1956).

KAYE, E., *C. J. Cadoux: Theologian, Scholar and Pacifist* (Edinburgh, 1988).

—— 'Constance Coltman: A Forgotten Pioneer', *JURCHS* 4/2 (May 1988).

Der Kirchenkampf: The Gutteridge–Micklem Collection at the Bodleian Library, Oxford (1988).

KNOX, R. B., *Westminster College Cambridge: Its Background and History* (Cambridge, n.d. [1979]).

The Lambeth Joint Report on Church Unity (1923).

LEAVER, R. A., and LITTON, J. H. (eds.), *Duty and Delight: Routley Remembered* (Norwich, 1985).

LEGGE, H. E., *James Legge* (1905).

LENWOOD, F., *Jesus: Lord or Leader?* (1930).

LLOYD, J. E., and JENKINS, R. T. (eds.), *Dictionary of Welsh Biography* (1959).

LOACH, J., 'Reformation Controversies', in J. McConica (ed.), *The History of the University of Oxford*, iii: *The Collegiate University* (Oxford, 1986).

Lutheran Council of Great Britain, *The Lutheran Council of Great Britain* (1975).

MACAN, R. W., *Religious Changes in Oxford during the Last Fifty Years* (Oxford, 1917).

MACARTHUR, A., 'The Background to the Formation of the United Reformed Church (Presbyterian and Congregational) in England and Wales in 1972', *JURCHS* 4/1 (Oct. 1987).

McCLELLAND, V. A., *English Roman Catholics and Higher Education 1830–1903* (Oxford, 1973).

MACDONAGH, G., *A Good German: Adam von Trott zu Solz* (1989).

MACFADYEN, D., *Alexander Mackennal* (1905).

MACHIN, G. I. T., 'Gladstone and Nonconformity in the 1860s: The Formation of an Alliance', *Historical Journal*, 17/2 (1974).

MACKENNAL, A., *Sketches in the Evolution of English Congregationalism* (1901).

MACKINTOSH, W. H., *Disestablishment and Liberation: The Movement for the Separation of the Anglican Church from State Control* (1972).

MCLACHLAN, H., *English Education under the Test Acts: Being the History of the Nonconformist Academies 1662–1820* (Manchester, 1931).

MALLET, C. E. *A History of the University of Oxford*, iii (1927).

MANNING, B. L. *Essays in Orthodox Dissent* (1939).

—— *This Latter House: Emmanuel Church, Cambridge 1874–1924* (Cambridge, 1924).

Mansfield College Essays (1909).

Mansfield College, Oxford: Its Origin and Opening (1890).

MANSON, T. W., *The Teaching of Jesus* (Cambridge, 1931).

MARSH, J., *Congregationalism Today* (1943).

—— *The Gospel of St John* (1968).

—— *Jesus in his Lifetime* (1981).

—— *The Significance of Evanston* (1954).

—— *Intercommunion* (with D. M. Baillie) (1952).

MARTY, M., and PERMAN, D. G. (eds.), *A Handbook of Christian Theologians* (Cambridge, 1984).

MATHESON, P. E., *Life of Hastings Rashdall DD* (Oxford, 1928).

MATTHEWS, A. G., *Calamy Revised* (Oxford, 1934).

—— *The Congregational Churches of Staffordshire* (1924).

MEARNS, A. (attributed), *The Bitter Cry of Outcast London* (1883).

Memorials of the Founders of Spring Hill College (Birmingham, 1854).

MICKLEM, E. R., *Miracles and the New Psychology: A Study in the Healing Miracles of the New Testament* (1922).

MICKLEM, N., *A Book of Personal Religion* (1938).

—— *The Box and the Puppets* (1957).

—— *The Church Catholic: Addresses to the Friends of Reunion* (1935).

—— *Congregationalism and the Church Catholic* (1943).

—— *Congregationalism and Episcopacy* (1951).

—— *Congregationalism Today* (1937).

—— *The Doctrine of our Redemption* (1943).

—— *Europe's Own Book* (1944).

—— *Law and the Laws* (Edinburgh, 1951).

—— *May God Defend the Right!* (1939).

—— *National Socialism and the Roman Catholic Church* (1939).

—— *Officia Brevia* (Oxford, 1939).

—— *Prayers and Praises* (1941).

—— *A Religion for Agnostics* (1965).

—— *The Religion of a Sceptic* (1976).

—— *The Theology of Politics* (Oxford, 1941).

—— *Ultimate Questions* (1955).

—— *What is the Faith?* (1936).

—— 'A Modern Approach to Christology', in G. K. A. Bell and A. Deissman (eds.), *Mysterium Christi* (1930).

—— 'The Theological Watershed', *Queen's Quarterly*, 41 (1934).

—— (ed.), *Christian Worship: Studies in its History and Meaning* (1936).

MICKLEM, R., 'Music and the Pastoral Ministry: A Personal View', in R. A. Leaver and J. H. Litton, *Duty and Delight: Routley Remembered* (Norwich, 1985).

MILNER, A., *Arnold Toynbee: A Memoir* (1895).

Minutes of the Proceedings of a Conference of Delegates from the Committees of Various Theological Colleges Connected with the Independent Churches of England and Wales (1845).

MOFFATT, J., *Introduction to the Literature of the New Testament* (Edinburgh, 1911).

MÜLLER, F. L., *The History of German Lutheran Congregations in England 1900–50* (Frankfurt, 1987).

MUNSON, J., *The Nonconformists: In Search of a Lost Culture* (1991).

NETTLESHIP, L. E., 'William Fremantle, Samuel Barnett and the Broad Church Origins of Toynbee Hall', *Journal of Ecclesiastical History*, 33 (1982).

NEWLAND, F. W., *Newland of Claremont and Canning Town* (1932).

NORWOOD, D. W., 'The Case for Democracy in Church Government: A Study in the Reformed Tradition with Special Reference to the Congregationalism of Robert William Dale, Peter Taylor Forsyth, Albert Peel and Nathaniel Micklem' (London Ph. D. thesis, 1983).

NUTTALL, G. F., *Richard Baxter* (1965).

—— *The Holy Spirit in Puritan Faith and Experience* (Oxford, 1946).

—— *Visible Saints: The Congregational Way 1640–60* (Oxford, 1957).

ORCHARD, W. E., *From Faith to Faith* (1933).

Oxford Society of Historical Theology, *Abstracts of Proceedings* (Oxford).

PAGET, S., *Henry Scott Holland* (1921).

PARKER, I., *Dissenting Academies in England* (Cambridge, 1914).

PARRY, K. L. (ed.), *A Companion to Congregational Praise* (1953).

PATON, J. L., *John Brown Paton* (1914).

PAYNE, E. A., *Henry Wheeler Robinson: Scholar, Teacher, Principal: A Memoir* (1946).

PEAKE, L. S., *Arthur Samuel Peake* (1930).

PEEL, A., *The Congregational Two Hundred 1530–1948* (1948).

—— *Inevitable Congregationalism* (1937).

—— *These Hundred Years: A History of the Congregational Union of England and Wales 1831–1931* (1931).

—— (ed.), *Essays Congregational and Catholic* (1931).

PEEL, A., and MARRIOTT, J. A. R., *Robert Forman Horton* (1937).

PINN, T. W., 'Reminiscences', in F. J. Powicke, *David Worthington Simon* (1912).

PLATT, D. C. M., *The Most Obliging Man in Europe: The Life and Times of the Oxford Scout* (1986).

POWICKE, F. J., *David Worthington Simon* (1912).

—— 'Frederick Denison Maurice: A Personal Reminiscence', *CQ* 8 (1930).

PRESTIGE, G. L., *The Life of Charles Gore* (1935).

RAMSAY, W. M., *The Cities of St Paul: Their Influence on his Life and Thought* (1907).

REASON, W. (ed.), *University and Social Settlements* (1898).

RICHARDS, E. R., *Private View of a Public Man* (1950).

RICHTER, M., *The Politics of Conscience: T. H. Green and his Age* (1964).

ROBBINS, K., *History, Religion and Identity in Modern Britain* (1993).

—— (ed.), *Protestant Evangelicalism: Britain, Ireland, Germany and America* (Oxford, 1990).

ROBINSON, H. W., *The Christian Experience of the Holy Spirit* (1928).

ROGERS, H., *The Eclipse of Faith* (1852).

—— *Essays on Some Theological Controversies of the Time* (1874).

ROUTLEY, E. R., *English Religious Dissent* (Cambridge, 1960).

—— *Into a Far Country* (1962).

—— *The Music of Christian Hymnody: A Study of the Development of the Hymn Tune since the Reformation, with Special Reference to English Protestantism* (1957).

SANDAY, W., 'The Future of English Theology', *CR* 56 (July 1889).

—— (ed.), *Different Conceptions of Priesthood and Sacrifice* (1900).

SCHWEITZER, A., *Civilization and Ethics*, trans. C. T. Campion (1929).

—— *The Decay and the Restoration of Civilization*, trans. C. T. Campion (1923).

SELBIE, W. B., *Charles Silvester Horne* (1920).

—— *Congregationalism* (1927).

—— *The Freedom of the Free Churches* (1928).

—— *The Life of Andrew Martin Fairbairn* (1914).

—— *The Psychology of Religion* (Oxford, 1924).

—— *The War and Theology* (Oxford, 1915).

—— 'Some Very Minor Prophets', *CQ* (1943).

—— (ed.), *Evangelical Christianity: Its History and Witness* (1911).

SELL, A. P. F., 'Presbyterianism in Eighteenth Century England: The Doctrinal Dimension', *JURCHS* 4/6 (May 1990).

—— 'A Little Friendly Light: The Candour of Bourn, Taylor and Towgood', *JURCHS* 4/9 (Dec. 1991) and 4/10 (May 1992).

—— 'Henry Rogers and *The Eclipse of Faith*', *JURCHS* 2/5 (May 1980).

SELWYN, E. G., *Essays Catholic and Critical* (1926).

SMEATON, O., *Principal James Morison: The Man and his Work* (Edinburgh, 1902).

SMITH, B. (ed.), *Truth, Liberty, Religion: Essays Celebrating Two Hundred Years of Manchester College* (Oxford, 1986).

SMITH, G. A., *The Book of Isaiah*, 2 vols. (1888–90).

—— *Modern Criticism and the Preaching of the Old Testament* (1901).

SMITH, L. A., *George Adam Smith* (1943).

SPICER, [?], *Albert Spicer 1847–1934* (1938).

STACPOOLE, A., 'The Return of the Roman Catholics to Oxford', *New Blackfriars*, 67 (May 1986).

STANNARD, J. T., *The Divine Humanity* (Glasgow, 1892).

SUTHERLAND, L. S., 'The Curriculum', in L. S. Sutherland and L. G. Mitchell (eds.), *The History of the University of Oxford*, v: *The Eighteenth Century* (Oxford, 1986).

SYKES, C., *Troubled Loyalty: A Biography of Adam von Trott zu Solz* (1968).

TATLOW, T., *The Story of the Student Christian Movement* (1933).

—— *Martyn Trafford: A Sketch of his Life and his Work for the SCM* (1910).

Theological Colleges for Tomorrow: Being the Report of a Working Party Appointed by the Archbishops of Canterbury and York to Consider the Problems of the Theological Colleges of the Church of England (1968).

THOMAS, G. L., *The Moral Philosophy of T. H. Green* (Oxford, 1987).

THOMPSON, D. M., 'Theological and Sociological Approaches to the Motivation of the Ecumenical Movement', in D. Baker (ed.), *Religious Motivation: Biographical and Sociological Problems for the Church Historian*, Studies in Church History 15 (Oxford, 1978).

TOMES, R. (ed.), *Christian Confidence: Essays on 'A Declaration of Faith of the Congregational Church in England and Wales'* (1970).

TOON, P., *God's Statesman: The Life and Work of John Owen* (Exeter, 1971).

TOPOLSKI, D., and ROBINSON, P., *True Blue* (1989).

TOWLER, R., *Homo Religiosus: Sociological Problems in the Study of Religion* (1974).

TROTMAN, H. R. and GARRETT, E. J. K., *The Non-collegiate Students and St Catherine's Society* (Oxford, 1962).

TURNER, F., 'Religion', in B. Harrison (ed.), *The History of the University of Oxford*, viii: *The Twentieth Century* (Oxford, 1994).

TURRELL, H. J., *Letters 1887–96* (Bodleian Library).

Twenty-One Years at Mansfield House 1890–1911 (1918).

WALLIS, J., *Valiant for Peace: A History of the Fellowship of Reconciliation 1914 to 1989* (1991).

WARD, W. R., *Victorian Oxford* (1965).

WATSON, C. E., *Rodborough Bede Book* (1943).

WATTS, M., *The Dissenters: From the Reformation to the French Revolution* (Oxford, 1978).

WATTS, R., *Professor Drummond's 'Ascent of Man' and Principal Fairbairn's 'Place of Christ in Modern Theology' Examined in the Light of Science and Revelation* (Edinburgh, 1894).

WHITEHOUSE, A. (ed.), *Christendom on Trial: Documents of the German Church Struggle* (Friends of Europe, 1938).

Who Was Who 1961–70.

WILKINSON, J. T., *Arthur Samuel Peake: A Biography* (1971).

WILSON, R. C., *Frank Lenwood* (1936).

Index